ECONOMICS

Edited by
David Burningham

David Burningham, Paul Bennett,
Martin Cave and David Higham

TEACH YOURSELF BOOKS

Hodder and Stoughton

First published (as Understanding Economics*) 1978*
Second edition 1984
Third edition 1991

British Library Cataloguing in Publication Data
Economics.
1. Economics
I. Burningham, David
330

ISBN 0-340-52708-0

Printed and bound in Great Britain for
Hodder and Stoughton Educational,
a division of Hodder and Stoughton Ltd,
Mill Road, Dunton Green, Sevenoaks, Kent
by Clays Ltd, St Ives plc.
Photoset by Rowland Phototypesetting Ltd,
Bury St Edmunds, Suffolk.

ECONOMICS

Edited by
David Burningham

David Burningham is Senior Lecturer in Economics at Brunel University, has worked as a consultant in central and local government and was Economic and Marketing Adviser to the Industrial and Commercial Finance Corporation. **Paul Bennett** is Lecturer in Economics at Brunel University and also lectures at the Civil Service College and to several private companies. He is Chief Examiner in Economics to the International Baccalaureate, Geneva. **Martin Cave** is Professor of Economics and Dean of the Faculty of Social Sciences at Brunel University. His principal research is in industrial economics and the economies of Eastern Europe. **David Higham** was formerly Head of the Economics Policy Section of the Economics Directorate at the Confederation of British Industries and has lectured at Brunel University.

TEACH YOURSELF BOOKS

Contents

Preface ix

1 Introducing Economics 1
What economics is about. Is economics a science?
Model-building and economics. Summary.

PART ONE *Markets and Prices* 17

2 Economic Systems 19
Introduction. Different systems. Some weaknesses
of the market. The government and market systems. Summary.

3 How Markets Work 34
Introduction. Demand and supply. Market equilibrium. The consequences of price fixing. Summary.

4 The Firm 46
Introduction. The firm's decisions. Company
finance, ownership and management. Summary.

5 Production and Costs 64
Introduction. Production – inputs and outputs.
Costs – the firm's choice of how to produce. How
costs vary with output – total cost, average cost,
marginal cost. Increasing and decreasing returns to
scale. The long run and the short run. The multi-
product firm. Summary.

6 Consumer Behaviour 86
Introduction. A first look at consumer behaviour. How the consumer chooses – the individual demand curve. The total demand curve. Price and income elasticities of demand. The measurement of price and income elasticities. Shifts in the demand curve – substitutable and complementary goods. How free is the consumer's choice? Advertising and information. Summary.

7 Determination of Price: Perfect Competition and Monopoly 107
Introduction. The firm and the industry. Profit maximisation and its implications. Perfect competition – the short run. Perfect competition – the long run. The pricing and output decision of a monopolist. Monopoly with price discrimination. Monopolistic competition. Summary.

8 Oligopoly 130
Introduction. Measuring market structures. Competition among the few. Interdependence. Game theory. Kinked demand. Price leadership. Collusive pricing. Entry-limit pricing. Barriers to entry. Cost-plus pricing. Two case studies. Oligopoly and other market structures. Structure – Conduct – Performance. Summary.

9 Markets and Efficiency 155
Introduction. Prices and efficiency. Market failure. Competition and efficiency. Market structure and market performance – the evidence. Contestable markets. Summary.

10 Markets and Government Policy 173
Introduction. Structural policies. Nationalisation, privatisation and regulation. Externalities and the price system. Summary.

11 Factor Markets and the Distribution of Income 191
Introduction. Factor shares and the distribution of income. The firm's demand for factors of production. The pricing of factors of production. The supply curve of a factor and economic rent. How satisfactory are micro-economic explanations of factor payments? – the case of trade unions. Summary.

PART TWO   *The Economy as a Whole*   211

12   The National Income   221
National income accounting. Comparisons over
time. Comparisons between countries. Economic
growth and its costs. Summary.

13   The Level of Output and Employment   240
Introduction. The causes of involuntary unemployment. Disturbances to the circular flow of national
income. Savings and investment. Exports and imports. Government expenditure and taxation. The
determination of equilibrium output – the 'Keynesian Cross'. The effect of changes in injections and
withdrawals. The size of income changes – the
multiplier. Full employment and the inflationary
and deflationary gap. Summary.

14   The Components of Demand   258
Introduction. Consumption. Investment. Government. Summary.

15   Money and Banking   282
Introduction. What is money? Characteristics of
money. Money in practice. The modern development of money. The banking system and the
creation of money. The UK monetary system.
Summary.

16   The Control of the Monetary System   303
Introduction. The quantity theory of money. The
Monetarist–Keynesian controversy. Summary.

17   International Trade   319
Introduction. Comparative advantage. Terms of
trade. Protection. Free trade and developing countries. Economic integration. Summary.

18   The Balance of Payments, Exchange Rates and the   336
International Monetary System
Introduction. The Balance of Payments. The ex-
change rate. Have floating exchange rates been a
success? The international monetary system.
Summary.

19   Managing the Economy: The Problems of Macro-   356
economic Policy
Introduction. The similarities between 'Keynesian'

and 'Monetarist' theories of inflation. Cost-push theories of inflation. The 'expectations-added' Phillips curve. Aggregate demand and supply. Reducing inflationary expectations. The balance of payments and economic growth targets. 'Supply side' economics. Economic management in the developing countries. Growth policy in the developing countries. Summary.

Plan for Further Study   382

Index   387

Preface

The aim of this book is to introduce the reader who is new to the subject to the principles of modern economics and to demonstrate their application in the study of some of the major problems in contemporary society. It will be valuable both for those with a keen interest in current affairs who simply wish to penetrate the meaning behind the media headlines, and for the student, with more formal requirements, preparing for an examination.

The text is in two parts: *Part One* examines the role of markets (the arrangements whereby goods and services are exchanged for money), the interaction of buyers and sellers, how the price of a good is determined and the way in which firms and households make their economic decisions. *Part Two* considers operations on a larger scale. Instead of single markets it looks at the factors influencing national and international levels of economic activity – for example, national income, the general level of prices, total employment.

Although there are cross references, each part is fairly self-contained. Thus the reader whose interests largely concern problems such as inflation and unemployment can turn directly to Part Two. Those more concerned with industry and the operations of firms and markets will find most of what they need in Part One. The first two chapters are introductory and should be studied by all readers.

The book covers topics necessary for those studying for the professional examinations of the Chartered Institute of Bankers, the Institute of Chartered Secretaries and Administrators and professional accounting examinations, as well as the GCE A-Level and BTEC certificates and diplomas. A selection of questions from past examination papers is appended to each chapter. The book may also be useful for those reading economics as a subsidiary to other main courses in a first-year undergraduate degree. Clearly in a book of this nature we cannot hope to cover the range of material offered in the introductory heavyweight texts, used by students for whom economics is the main course. To attempt to do so would be unwise. There is danger of providing 'instant economics' catering for what Professor F. R. Leavis has described as the ' "never at a loss for a subject man", who knows "something about everything and nothing about anything" '. To avoid this, the treatment of some aspects is deliberately restricted to give prominence to what we regard, in the context of this book, as the key issues.

Despite the limitations imposed by size, we believe that this text will not only provide an adequate introduction to economics, but also a bridge for those wishing to cross over to more serious studies of the subject. For such readers, a categorised 'Plan for Further Study' is given at the back of this book.

David Burningham
Brunel University

Preface to the Third Edition

Within the compass of a small introductory book we have tried to discuss some of the more significant of the many changes that have occurred in the world economy since our Second Edition in 1984. The preoccupation then was with the problems of unemployment and world recession. Their possible reappearance remains a major concern, but more recently attention has focused on economic liberalism. Governments in many countries, not only the communist ones, are turning to market solution for activities that have long been regarded as the province of state planning and regulation. Environmental issues have also become high on the agenda, although the relevance of market solutions to these problems is proving much more controversial. As far as space permits, we have touched upon these issues and changes in such areas as banking and international trade. We have also covered some of the changes in economic theory and applied economics, which are beginning to be reflected in questions set by the examination boards, who once again have kindly given us permission to include a selection from past papers.

David Burningham
Brunel University

Acknowledgements

The authors and publishers are grateful to the following for permission to reproduce questions from examination papers: Associated Examining Board; Chartered Institute of Public Finance and Acountancy; Chartered Institute of Bankers; Institute of Chartered Accountants in England and Wales; Institute of Chartered Secretaries and Administrators; Chartered Institute of Management Accountants; Joint Matriculation Board; Joint Oxford and Cambridge Schools Examination Board; Langley College of Further Education; Oxford Delegacy of Local Examinations; Royal Society of Arts Examinations Board; Society of Company and Commercial Accountants; Southern Universities' Joint Board; University of London University Entrance and School Examinations Council; Welsh Joint Education Committee.

The contributors thank Angela Gendron for the index and those who patiently deciphered handwriting, collated and typed the drafts of this book: Christine Newnham, Barbara Aldridge, Jo Hichens, Natalie Zafrani-Smith. Others to whom acknowledgement is due, for permission to quote statistical information, are the Controller of Her Majesty's Stationery Office; the Department of Applied Economics, Cambridge, and the Cambridge University Press; the Statistical office of the European Communities.

1

Introducing Economics

Economics is the study of the arrangements that societies make for the use and development of their scarce resources. It uses the same techniques as other sciences – the collection of facts with which to test theories. Because economics is concerned with the study of human organisations and communities, the problems of measurement and forecasting are more difficult than in the natural sciences. Economists cannot study their subjects in a laboratory. In the absence of controlled experiments, model-building is used by economists to help understand and predict the working of an economy. A model is a replica or imitation of the economic activities in a market, region or country. The connections between the activities are usually expressed in diagrammatic, verbal or mathematical form. Simplification is an important part of the model builder's art.

What economics is about

Among the many difficulties which face the world today, three sets of problems are pre-eminent:

1 Problems associated with stability

Nearly all governments, whatever their ideology, are committed to programmes designed to promote the growth of living standards and a more even distribution of wealth both nationally and globally. Can we achieve these objectives without serious conflict between and within the nations? Certain problems, such as the recent world recession, with falling output and rising unemployment, have threatened the achievement of both these objectives.

Some economies can be likened to rather unstable and temperamental machines that overheat or occasionally break down. Inflation – prices have more than doubled in most countries in the last twenty years – is also regarded by many as a major problem confronting us today. History shows quite clearly that the political and social consequences of inflation are most powerful. It has caused the downfall of many governments and the rise of many others. Economic breakdown, a collapse of demand with consequent unemployment, has equally serious political and social repercussions.

Further instability and conflict can arise from the systems which different countries have adopted in pursuit of growth and wealth redistribution. For example, private-enterprise market economies versus state controlled systems found in various communist countries. Because the economic performance of the tightly controlled communist systems has been so disappointing, most of them are now changing to decentralised liberal market economies. This is a radical and painful transformation. In the Soviet Union, this involves the reforms of *Perestroika* (economic restructuring), *Glasnost* (openness) and *Demokratizatsiya* (democratisation). In the short run the changes may produce rising prices and unemployment. Can such radical reforms be achieved without unleashing forces of discontentment and dissension which may defeat the purposes for which the changes were launched? Will the aspirations of different nationalities and national groups create divisions which undermine the transformation?

2 Problems associated with growth
Can we increase the output of goods and services to match rising demand? This demand comes not only from rising world population, which is currently estimated to be nearly four and a half thousand million and which may reach over five and a half thousand million by the end of the century, but also from rising expectations of higher living standards. Worldwide we see this challenge to traditional values – the expectation that people should be better off and better educated than their grandparents or parents. The dream of life in the affluent suburbs is becoming an almost universal pattern. It applies as much to the young Sicilian peasant moving with his family to Milan as to the Birmingham factory worker.

The extent to which population growth could, or should, be controlled is a fiercely controversial issue but it is most unlikely that the rising tide of consumer expectations can be halted. As the economic historian, Rostow, has commented: 'experience of higher living standards, like the loss of innocence, is apparently an irreversible change'. Against the undoubted benefits that growth brings must be set the 'costs' of the stress of congested urban life, the destruction of forests and countryside and the pollution of the earth's rivers, oceans and atmosphere. Such costs are not inevitable but may arise where growth is too rapid or unplanned.

3 Problems associated with distribution

The startlingly unequal distribution of world wealth is a well-known fact. It is calculated, for example, that the people of the advanced industrialised countries, who account for only 34% of world population, consume approximately 87% of the world's output whereas underdeveloped countries with 66% of world population consume only 13% of world output. Evidence suggests that the gap between rich and poor countries is tending to get wider. That is to say, the rate of growth in the output of goods and services per head of the population is greater in the industrially advanced countries. Is this gap between rich and poor countries inevitable? Can it be halted or reversed?

This uneven distribution is partly a problem of population pressure as the poor countries are frequently confronted with the largest increases in population. But it is also a matter of the arrangements we make for the transfer of resources – technology and equipment – from one country to another. The distribution of wealth is also uneven within countries. In the United Kingdom, for example, a recent study showed that 5% of the population owned 56% of the nation's assets. In some other countries, the distribution of assets and income is yet more uneven. This again raises the question at a national level of the causes and desirability of such a situation.

The groups of problems which we have sketched here all have one feature in common: they concern the *arrangements that societies make for the use and development of their scarce resources*. This is what economics is about. Note the word 'scarce'. By this we mean 'the demand for goods and services by a community exceeding the available supplies'. Most goods and services are scarce because at any given time the supplies of raw materials, land, equipment, as well as the human skill and energies needed to create them, are also scarce. Thus, whatever its political or social organisation, every society must decide how best to allocate its productive resources and how the limited supplies are shared among the community.

Scarcity forces upon communities and individuals the necessity of making choices. The question which a mother puts to her child in the toy or sweet shop 'which one do you want?' is the first basic lesson in economics common to all societies and all individuals.

If all productive resources are fully employed, an increase in the output of one commodity or service can only be produced by having less of another – more refrigerators may mean less steel for cars; more land for factories and roads may mean less for agriculture, and so on. The sacrifice of alternatives implicit in producing a commodity or service is known as *opportunity cost*, a concept first outlined by the Austrian economist Wieser. For example, the 'opportunity cost' of building fifty houses is the factory, school, shops or offices that might have been built in their stead.

The answer to the question 'should agricultural land be built over?' requires a comparison of the opportunity costs of various alternatives for society. If there were a superabundance of resources of all kinds the question 'which one?' would not arise. Economists would be redundant. However, it is unlikely that even the richest societies or individuals will ever completely escape from scarcity. Even the oil-rich millionaire who, according to the apocryphal story, gets rid of the Cadillacs when the ashtrays are full, is confronted with the problem of a limited life-span, a shortage of time. Like the child in the sweet shop, even he must choose which of his yachts or villas he wishes to sit in, or which part of his industrial empire he will visit.

Economists thus distinguish between 'free goods' such as sunshine, air and water, which are normally available in such abundance that they don't have to be shared and are free, and 'economic goods' which are so scarce in relation to demand that they have to be allocated by some scheme of sharing or by price. The definition of scarcity is not simply 'goods which are few in number'. A unique but obsolete machine tool which is not required even by museums or scrap merchants is not a scarce good in the economic sense. Scarcity can only be assessed in relation to demand or need.

Is economics a science?

Although the problems of the preceding section are fundamentally concerned with the development and allocation of scarce resources, they are clearly not exclusively the domain of the economist. They also raise issues of social organisation, of politics and of ethics. This being so, it is natural to ask what sort of contribution the economist expects to make to the understanding and solution of those problems. Are the skills of the economist comparable with those of the scientist or technologist, or are they more like those of the politician or even philosopher?

The 'economist' in ancient Greece – a title derived from the words *Oikos* (house) and *Nemo* (manage) – was really a steward or estate manager. Not surprisingly the first treatises on economics were really manuals about farming.[1] There was a natural but very slow development of this subject from 'estate management' for noblemen to 'state management' for kings and princes. *Economica* (300 B.C.), which might be regarded as an early economics text-book, dealt with what is still one of the central issues of state craft – raising revenue through various forms of taxation. Also included were some practical and what might be called Machiavel-lian hints, such as taking the money for hostages after they had been executed. *Political Economy*, a title given to economics in the eighteenth century, reflected a view of the subject as simply a body of matter-of-fact advice for the use of statesmen rather than as a science.

By contrast, the modern use of the term *economics*, with its scientific-sounding 'ics' suffix which makes it seem on a par with electronics or physics, does reflect a change in the discipline. There has been an enormous growth in the availability of economic statistics – i.e. on production, employment, income and expendi-ture – which, coupled with the development of *econometrics* (the art of formulating economic theories into mathematical form and subjecting them to quantitative empirical testing), has transformed the subject into a complex and highly numerate discipline. The question is whether all this measurement and testing really make economics as scientific as physics or electronics?

The economist uses exactly the same techniques as the scientist; he carefully measures the phenomenon he is studying, using the data to test hypotheses which attempt to explain what is happening. From this he develops statements about general tendencies. These can be used for prediction. To this extent the economist is a scientist. The fact that the economist's measuring and testing does not take place in a laboratory does not in itself make it any less scientific than other 'non-laboratory' subjects such as astronomy. However, there are important differences between economics and other sciences. These are associated with measurement and fore-casting. They make it more difficult for the economist to come up with definite answers in the same way as a physicist or an electronics engineer:

1 The problem of measurement in economics
In the natural sciences, in contrast to the human and social sciences, the dependence of one measurable quality on another can be expressed in exact terms – volume, mass or temperature. In econo-mics this is more difficult. Some ideas such as 'population growth'

can be expressed in unambiguous numerical terms. Other equally important concepts cannot be expressed in this way. Take for example the idea of 'competition'. This is central to the economist's analysis of industries and to the sort of recommendations that he might make to governments on policy. There is no clear-cut definition of this important idea which can be put in numbers. Whether a three-firm industry is more or less competitive than a thirty-firm industry is a very tricky question which cannot be answered with reference to a formula or numerical table.

Even where numerical measurements are possible in economics, they often lack the precision we expect when speaking of such things as temperature or weight. This is because economic measurements often involve a notion of value or usefulness which it is difficult to calculate. Take for example the important question of the 'standard of living'. If we are comparing money incomes and we are trying to find out whether people are better or worse off at different points in time or between countries, we must obviously take into account prices (i.e. what the money will actually buy in terms of goods and services).

This can be done with a technique known as a Price Index. However, the resulting calculation, although it may be illuminating and significant, can never be more than a fairly crude measure. This is because the type and quality of goods consumed may alter through time – how can one compare in numerical terms a television set with an old-fashioned pianola? Equally important is the question of how we make allowance for factors such as the conditions of work, educational facilities and opportunities for leisure. These contribute significantly to the standard of living and cannot be expressed in a single index number.

2   The problem of forecasting

(a) *Time-lags and people*. A further difficulty arises when economists try to establish the type of relationship which exists between the phenomena or variables which they are studying. These relationships can be divided into two main groups, the *technological* and *behavioural*. The first are concerned with such things as how much equipment, labour and land, etc. (factors of production) is needed to produce a particular commodity or output; how technical progress affects the ratio of inputs to outputs or of labour to capital. These relationships or functions depend upon the techniques of production and can be fairly precisely defined and measured. In the short run, at least, they are fairly stable and predictable.

The behavioural group of relationships is more difficult. It is concerned with such things as the effect of prices on how much people will buy; how businessmen might react to a rise or fall in profits. Although these behavioural relationships may be expressed numerically – in terms of the quantity that people may be expected to buy at a given price – they are much more tricky to handle than the technological ones; they depend upon human evaluation of past experience as well as human expectations about the future.

Because we are dealing with the reactions of human beings and not machines, there may be a considerable and variable time-lag between the stimulus and the response, for example, to a change in price. These lags may occur at three stages: (i) recognition of the problem; (ii) deciding what to do; (iii) implementing the decision. It may take even a housewife some time to adjust to the increase of the price of some foodstuff and to make changes in her shopping list by finding cheaper substitutes or even altering the family diet.

Consider how much more complicated would be the time-lags involved in the reaction of an organisation, such as a firm, to a rise in the price of one of its components or raw materials. The information, if the organisation is a large one, may pass through a hierarchy of committees and meetings for consideration before a decision is finally reached. These time-lags, whether they occur in households, firms or government organisations, are difficult for the economist to predict. Yet they are important in determining the behaviour of either the market for a commodity or the whole economy. The extent of the time-lags may make all the difference between the steady flow of output and prices or violent fluctuations – a point discussed in more detail in Chapter 9.

(*b*) *Experiments in economics.* Economics attempts, like other sciences, to make forecasts of what is likely to happen. Even the observations of astronomers are analysed with the aid of concepts derived from laboratory work in astrophysics and chemistry; one of the problems confronting the economist in attempting to make forecasts is that he is rarely able to make such experiments. Instead he must rely on looking at the record of events as they have actually occurred. By looking at statistics for temperature and for ice-cream sales, for example, we can measure – using a statistical technique known as *correlation* – the extent to which temperature affects ice-cream sales. This information can then be used to help forecast the level of demand in hot weather.

Cause and effect are quite obvious here. However, for many of the things the economist is interested in studying, the connections are more complex. For example, the connection between the supply of money and the general price level (see Chapter 16). This is far more complicated than the connection between temperature and ice-cream sales and is the subject of strong controversy among economists. A statistical correlation does not establish the exact origin of the cause. The concurrence of events can lead researchers into all sorts of spurious correlations. Economists should always remember Ogden Nash's comment that 'the wind is caused by the trees waving their branches' – the problem of disentangling cause and effect is never easy for the economist. For many of the events the economist wishes to study, not one but many things are happening at the same time. Reverting to our ice-cream example, if at the same time as temperatures rose, incomes and the price of soft drinks also rose, then isolating the impact of hot weather would be more difficult – something which could not be dealt with by laboratory experiment.

The economist is often concerned with phenomena which involve a whole community or, on an international scale, many countries. The experience of a single factory or small community may be a misleading guide as to what will happen for a whole country.

Just because economic changes do affect whole communities, it is often undesirable or impossible for the economist or policy-maker to adopt a 'see what happens' experimental approach. With issues such as state ownership of industry or a customs union such as the Common Market, this could be politically and socially disastrous. Once made, these changes would be enormously expensive or irreversible. We are dealing with people whose habits and attitudes may be profoundly altered by the change. Thus, we cannot wipe the slate clean and begin with a fresh experiment if the first does not work out as we had predicted.

(*c*) *The 'Oedipus Effect'*. Not only does the economist have to struggle with the difficulty of relying largely upon historical data to support his predictions; he also has to contend with the fact that the predictions may themselves change the very event which he is attempting to predict. This does not happen in meteorology or astronomy. It is unique to the social sciences and has been named the *Oedipus Effect* by Karl Popper, the philosopher. The prophecy that Oedipus would one day kill his father, which led to Oedipus's abandonment and to the event as forecast, is an example of a self-fulfilling prophecy very much like the prediction that share prices or foreign exchange rates will fall. As a result of either of the latter predictions, panic selling results, creating the very losses that people are seeking to avoid. While economic forecasts are unlikely to create new trends, they may powerfully reinforce existing ones.

Popper has suggested that when speaking of predictions, a distinction should be drawn between a straightforward prophecy such as 'there will be a hurricane' and what might be called an engineering forecast, e.g. 'if your house is constructed in this way with these materials, it will not blow down'. Forecasts that economists make are usually of the latter kind. They are not predictions of events as certainties, such as the eclipse of the sun. The economist's forecasts must nearly always be conditional. Furthermore, because of the nature of the subject-matter, they are sometimes much more tentative than the conditional forecast of the engineer in the above example.[2]

3 Positive and normative economics

Despite the difficulties of measurement and forecasting that we have just discussed, it is clear that economics is in its method scientific. It is concerned with the careful testing of explanations and theories against the facts. The influential position of modern economics and of economists as advisers to governments and industries owes much to this approach. The role of the economist may legitimately be compared with that of the scientist or technologist. Does this mean that the economist is always a neutral figure, whose politics and personal values have as little to do with his professional judgement as would be the case for a doctor diagnosing and treating a patient?

If we regard the economist as the 'doctor' and the economy as the 'patient', suffering for example from inflation (see Chapter 19), then three types of question arise: (1) Diagnosis: *what is taking place* – the identification of the nature of the ailment. For example, what is the type and cause of the inflation the country is suffering. (2) Prognosis: *what may take place* – the probable course of the inflation; whether it will intensify or slacken. (3) Treatment: *what ought to take place* – the specific remedies that the government should adopt to improve the situation, making the patient better.

As far as a doctor is concerned, diagnosis, prognosis and treatment are nearly always questions of professional judgement – not of politics or personal values. This is not so for the economist as only the first two questions are purely professional matters of economic fact and theory, which can be assessed objectively. This is the concern of *positive economics*.

In the third case, treatment by the economist must entail personal judgements of an ethical or political nature. This is because the 'patient' is the community. Certain courses of 'treatment' may make some sections of the community better off and others worse off. Take, for example, a government policy to deal with inflation by control on prices and personal incomes. This may make a powerful group of employees or employers, whose bargaining position is normally strong, feel at a disadvantage. Less powerful groups, such as old-age pensioners and employees without trade unions, may welcome the change.

Do the disadvantages accruing to certain groups balance or outweigh the advantages to others? There is no way of measuring this objectively, as a doctor might take a temperature. It is a question of subjective judgement. The control of inflation might be regarded as the ultimate test, but the benefits of inflationary control may be unevenly distributed. Some groups may be worse off than before, relative to others.

Economic policy thus raises questions of 'what ought to be' and 'how much better off will the community be, as a result of this course of action'. These questions, unless they are purely technical, may involve ideas of value or moral judgement and thus constitute what is known as *normative economics*. Some claim that economists should stick to positive economics and that questions of treatment should be left to the policy-makers and the politicians. Others argue that on matters of policy advice, economists must inevitably and rightly reflect in their judgements a personal view of what society ought to be like.

Model-building and economics

The principal method used by economists to understand and predict the working of an economy is known as *model-building* – a technique employed because they are unable, for the reasons previously explained, to conduct controlled experiments. Model-building is a rather impressive sounding and currently fashionable phrase – every social scientist is expected to have a model in his research and, to clear up any misconceptions, we shall describe very simply what is involved.

1 Machines and maps
A model can be a large or small-scale physical replica or imitation of the system or thing being studied – a typical example being the model ship or aircraft which designers use. From a study of the performance in a wind tunnel or water tank, designers can predict what is likely to happen in reality. In engineering, especially civil

engineering, physical replicas of systems are common. The American economist Fisher made a model of a market price-system using large water tanks with floats; A. W. Phillips invented a machine which pumped coloured water through a complex network of pipes and valves to represent the flow of income and expenditure in the whole economy – unfortunately, it leaked!

Clearly, the majority of models in economics are concerned with the analysis of phenomena too complicated to be described in terms of physical replicas. Instead, the models are theoretical constructions in which the interrelationships are expressed in diagrammatic, verbal or mathematical terms. At the simplest level, a model may be little more than a sort of map or a table of numbers describing the structure of the object of study. The model might, for example, be a series of balance sheets showing the assets and liabilities of the banks comprising the banking system, and their relationship with the Central Bank.

Such a model is a *description* and may be compared with *anatomy* in medicine; a static picture of the anatomy which can be grasped from dissection. By contrast the system in motion, the flow and interrelationship between the parts, would require a different sort of model showing what may be described as the *physiology* of the system. We must remember, however, that even a simple 'anatomical' description can lay the foundation for more elaborate models.

2   The art of simplification

In model-building we are attempting to imitate a real-life situation. We are not trying to duplicate it in every particular way, as to do so could make a model hopelessly complicated and unmanageable. It would also include some highly irrevelant things; factors whose influence is small enough to ignore. A model aircraft for a wind tunnel, for example, need not include a miniature hostess with a tray of drinks unless it was reasonably thought that this would affect the stability of the aircraft. The skill of the model-builder is to select and simplify; to isolate for study the features in which one is interested but not to oversimplify.

The physicist Eddington used to illustrate the importance of selection and of simplification in model-building with the following problem. An elephant is sitting on a hillside. How long does it take to slide thirty yards down a hill? Draw a diagram. To the layman, possibly an arts graduate untrained in model-building, the diagram might look like the one on page 12:

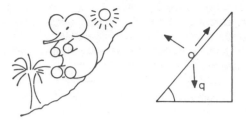

The engineer or mathematician would of course recognise this as a problem in dynamics. He would extract only the relevant features – the elephant becomes a point mass and he would consider the main forces acting on the elephant such as gravity and the angle of the slope. The topographical features drawn by the art student may have some bearing on the problem but probably only a very slight one and for the purposes of simplification in the model, can be ignored.

3   A junior economist's model kit
We shall illustrate some of these points with a very simple model. Suppose we are trying to predict the level at which the price of a product in a market will eventually settle and what quantities will be supplied. Let us suppose that we have a substantial amount of information on all aspects of the market – its history, a record of quantities purchased and supplied at various prices. Where should we begin? A model that tries to include everything: the workers' disposition to strike, the weather, the government, the leading personalities in the industry and so on, would be so complicated that it might predict that almost anything could happen – an untestable or non-operational model.

We must simplify and select from the mass of facts available only the most relevant. Facts are as dead as mutton unless they are ordered in a specific way and this is the task of theory. An important part of economics is concerned with the theory of markets and Chapters 7 and 8 deal with this in detail. Here we give only a summary. This theory stresses the role of price, which plays a major part in influencing the decisions of buyers and sellers. In its simplest form, the theory suggests that suppliers may be more willing to supply more of a product the higher the price, and vice versa. Buyers, on the other hand, will tend to buy less at a higher price and more at a lower price. When the quantity of goods that sellers wish to sell is equal to the quantity that consumers wish to buy, there will be no tendency for unsold goods to pile up in shops and warehouses. Nor will there be queues of dissatisfied customers unable to buy as much as they want at the prevailing price. When the market is in this state, it is said to be in *equilibrium*. The market is *cleared* and the price will be steady, neither rising nor falling.

How shall we build our model? We could construct a physical model using pipes and tanks like Irving Fisher but this is not advisable unless you are good at plumbing. We could draw diagrams, but instead, we shall use some simple mathematics. If you think you are not very good at maths or have forgotten what you did learn, don't worry. Remember the *ideas* which are behind the maths and you will find that it is not nearly as difficult as it looks.

We now have the theoretical components from which to build our model. We have three propositions:

1 The *quantity of units supplied in a month* (Xs) depends on the price (p) in £s per unit. This is called a *function* (f) and in mathematical shorthand we write it:

$$Xs = f(p)$$

2 The *quantity demanded in a month* (Xd) depends on the price (p); another function:

$$Xd = f(p)$$

3 Finally, the *equilibrium condition*:

$$Xs = Xd$$

a situation in which the quantity suppliers wish to supply (Xs) equals the quantity buyers wish to buy (Xd).

From an examination of the statistics on the quantities supplied at different prices, let us suppose we find that supply responds to price in the following way:

$$Xs = 10P - 1$$

that is to say, as price (P) rises, so does the supply (X); the *constants* or parameters are 10 and -1 and they show for this particular commodity by exactly how much the supply will increase. If, for example, the price is 2, then

$$Xs = (10 \times 2) - 1 = 19$$

If the price rises to 3, the monthly supply increases to 29 and so on.

From our statistics relating to the quantities people wish to buy at various prices, suppose we find

$$Xd = 120 - P$$

that is to say, as the price falls, more is demanded.

If in equilibrium the quantity demanded equals the quantity supplied then

$$Xs = Xd$$

From our equations above, showing the parameters for Xs and Xd we get

$$10P - 1 = 120 - P$$

Then, moving the $-P$ to the left of the equation and the -1 to the right

$$11P = 121$$
$$P = £11$$

By substituting this value of P into the supply or demand functions, we can predict what the monthly sale would be:

$$Xd = 120 - P = 120 - 11 = 109$$

Thus our model predicts that the market will settle down to an equilibrium price of £11 with monthly sales at that price of 109 units. What this means is simply that, at the price of £11, the quantity which suppliers wish to sell is exactly equal to the quantity which buyers wish to buy at that price. If this seems difficult, don't worry. It is explained again, with diagrams, in Chapter 3.

4   Different types of models
It could be that our prediction is wrong. Remember that our statistics are a record of what has happened in the *past*. If the habits and tastes of buyers change, or the conditions of supply alter because of, for example, new technology or a change in costs, then the statistics become misleading. The parameters change: possibly, but not in this case, the theory is wrong. However, the advantage of model-building is that it forces the model-builder to put his cards on the table – to state his assumptions and the way in which the facts are interpreted. These can then be challenged by anyone who disagrees. The predictions can also be tested against events.

A limitation is that our model is an *equilibrium model*, which ignores the difficulty of tracing the way in which the equilibrium level of price and output is eventually reached. This is an important practical question. Price and output may oscillate for a long time before settling down, especially where there are time-lags in adjusting to changes in price on the part of suppliers or consumers. A *process model* may be used instead to trace out such paths of adjustment, indicating the conditions under which steady movements or swings are expected.

Our model may be further classified as of the *micro-economic* type, that is dealing with a few closely related variables; in this case, price and output in a particular market. It is not concerned with interrelationships with all parts of industry and the rest of the economy as a whole. By contrast, a *macro-economic model* would deal with such interrelationships because the theories and models on which it is based are concerned with the forces working to determine the total level of demand, production, consumption, prices and employment.

Macro-economic models have been extensively developed from the construction of total or national income accounts (see Chapters 12–13). Macro models are extensively used by governments to help explain and predict the reactions of the economy as a whole to, for example, changes in the level of employment and inflation. The technology of high-speed computers has enormously aided the model-builders' task but the art is in its infancy and much of the crudity of pioneering effort is still evident.

Because macro-economic models deal with the big issues of total employment and output that affect everyone in the community, it is sometimes thought that micro-economic models and theories are less important. This is not so. The former relate to large groups, the latter to small groups of individuals and firms but the two branches of economics are complementary rather than rivals. However, there is an important distinction: what is a sound course of action for an individual is not necessarily so for all individuals; what may be calamitous for an individual may be advantageous for a group. The 'paradox of thrift' is a good example: attempts by individuals to spend less and save more, while desirable from an individual standpoint, may actually, in a period of unemployment and falling output, make the situation worse by reducing the demand for goods and services thus creating more unemployment.

Summary

Three major sets of problems facing the world are associated with scarce resources – growth, distribution and the stability of arrangements to deal with these tasks. Choice concerning the use of resources involves consideration of *opportunity cost* – the alternatives forgone in producing a commodity. The study of these problems raises issues of *positive economics* – the collection of economic facts and testing of theories, as well as *normative economics* – concerned with prescription and policy questions of 'what ought to be done'. It is in the area of prescription that the economist may touch upon political issues involving value judgements. The models economists use may be micro-economic, concerned with the working of part of the economic system, such as a market, or they may examine inter-connections in the economy as a whole and total levels of economic activity, i.e. macro-economic models.

Questions

1   Which of the following is a normative statement?
   (a)   the fight against inflation should be the most important economic policy objective of the UK government,
   (b)   Entrepreneurs would maximise profits if output was fixed at the level at which marginal costs equal marginal revenue,
   (c)   normally a reduction in the standard rate of tax should lead to an increase in consumption,
   (d)   to help increase employment, the government could increase public expenditure,
   (e)   the rate of the UK economic growth may be increased by a higher level of net investment.
   (Joint Matriculation Board, A-Level)
2   If astronomers can predict an eclipse of the sun, why can't economists predict a business recession?
3   Comment on the following:
   'Economics has nothing to do with politics.'
   'Economics is nothing but politics disguised as science.'
4   Why is model-building necessary in economics?
5   Compare the problems of measurement confronting the economist with those confronting the engineer.

Notes

1   Schumpeter, J. A., 'Graeco-Roman Economics' in *History of Economics Analysis* (Oxford University Press, London, 1954).
2   Popper, K., *The Poverty of Historicism* (Routledge & Kegan Paul, London, 1970).

PART ONE

Markets and Prices

2

Economic Systems

Introduction

Scarcity forces upon most communities the necessity of making choices – what to produce, how to produce and to whom the goods and services are to be distributed. It is useful to isolate for analysis the institutions of a community whose decisions determine these questions – what is known as the *economic system*. Such systems can be classified according to where these decisions are taken. In almost any economy the government will inevitably play an important role. However, some systems are characterised by predominantly government-controlled methods of resource allocation – a *command economy* – while in others resources are determined largely by market prices – a market economy. This book concentrates on the economic systems that are predominantly of the latter type, sometimes called *mixed economies*.

In mixed economies there is usually a substantial public sector with the government playing an important role, but in all other respects they are market systems. The analysis of these systems has three elements: (i) the *theory of supply* (Chapters 4 and 5), (ii) the *theory of demand* (Chapter 6), leading to (iii) the *theory of price* (Chapters 3, 7 and 8).

Apart from a review in this chapter, we do not attempt elsewhere in this book to compare the market economy with other types of system; nor do we defend or justify its existence. Chapters 9 and 10 examine the sources of weakness in competitive markets and the ways in which governments may try to remedy them. The impact of the price-system on incomes, sometimes known as the 'Theory of Distribution', is examined in Chapter 11.

Different systems

We now apply the principle of simplification in model-building to help us get a broad view of the arrangements that different societies make for the use of their resources. This will be a useful background for an understanding of the operation of the mixed market type of economy which is the theme of the remainder of this textbook.

All communities are confronted with three questions concerning the use of their resources: (1) What to produce? (2) How to produce – the choice of inputs and technology? (3) For whom to produce – how the goods and services produced are to be allocated among the members of the community? These questions arise because resources are scarce in relation to needs. Although these questions are common to all communities, the methods used for dealing with them will naturally vary enormously – ranging from the tribal potlatch of primitive subsistence economy to the complex market mechanisms of an industrialised society. They reflect nothing less than the whole range of values, beliefs, symbols, goals, traditions and ways of looking at the world that the society in question embraces.

To try to explain how all these influences determine the use of resources would be an incredibly complicated task. The art of the economist, as we have shown, is to simplify. The economist focuses his attention on the institutions of a community – laws, established ways of behaviour and organisation – which together have a direct bearing on decisions to allocate resources. He might look at, for example, the laws relating to property, and such things as trade-union organisations, and the profit motive. All these institutions constitute what is known as an *economic system*. However, we do not intend to imply by the use of the word 'system' a consciously planned set of institutions. In some economies this may be the case; in others, most institutions have evolved over many years without conscious planning.

Is the idea of an economic system a useful way of studying the problem? Some textbooks, when explaining systems, give as an example Robinson Crusoe marooned on his desert island – a simple one-man economy. His problem is presented as one in political economy – in the management of the little state which consists of himself so as to maximise his economic welfare. He is pictured as trying to work out how best to allocate his time in searching for coconuts, fishing, building a boat with which to escape. On arrival, it is highly likely that he did nothing of the sort. The first thing he probably did was to get down on his knees and thank the Almighty that he was alive. He then may have wondered whether there were any women on the island, and only then turned his attention to the question of resource allocation. Clearly economic man, or woman, does not exist in a compartment, which is entirely separate from social, religious or political life.

For this reason the concept of 'homo economicus' is a matter of some derision among critics who claim that economists do not understand the complexity of human nature and make naïve simplifications. Although economists may sometimes be guilty of this, the idea of an economic system is a useful abstraction. By removing one social mechanism – the economy – from the matrix of other systems, we are able to isolate certain features in a way that enables us to understand their workings more clearly.

In any community a wide variety of individuals and organisations can, in different ways, influence the use of scarce resources – farmers, factory managers, housewives, shopkeepers, civil servants, etc. However, to make our analysis manageable it is convenient to think of these groups, whether they are acting as individuals on their own behalf or as part of an organisation, as falling within three categories of decision-making units – households, producers and the state. The latter includes any central planning and decision-making body, whether it be an elected government or a dictatorship. Clearly individuals will have more than one role. Householders, for example, are not just consumers but are also involved in production as suppliers of labour and, if they are shareholders, as suppliers of capital,

In so far as the central authority is democratically elected, or responsive to representation from consumers and producers, then these other groups can be said to be involved in the decisions of the state. Nevertheless the distinction between these different groups is a useful one and is used in the three simple models in Fig. 2.1 which attempt to classify economic systems in terms of where decisions are made about the use of resources. These are purely hypothetical economies. They do not attempt to present actual systems but simply to highlight some of the features that will be found in real-life economies. They are primarily 'descriptive' in the sense explained in the previous chapter. That is to say, they are 'maps', showing the anatomy of the systems – where decisions are made – but do not, except on one or two points, explain the physiology of the systems in motion.

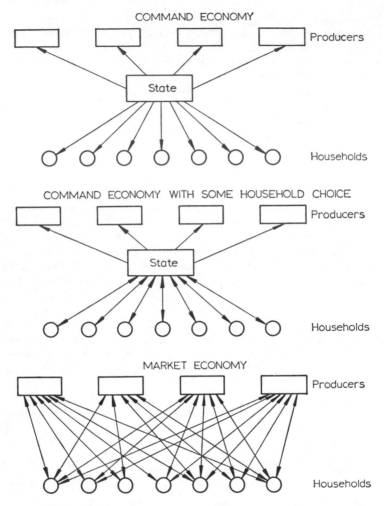

Fig. 2.1 Simple models of three types of economic system.

1 Command economy with planners' sovereignty

As the arrowed lines on the diagram indicate, this is a community in which all decisions about what, how and for whom are made by a dictatorship or central planning authority that issues a series of directives or commands to all producers and households. These specify what is to be produced and how goods are to be distributed.

A complete command economy involves the direction of labour and possibly some system of rationing, in preference to allowing people to buy as much as they want of any particular good. If people were free to decide the type and location of jobs they undertook, as well as the way in which they disposed of income, it would be difficult for the state planners to exercise complete control over the use of resources. Productive capacity may be diverted to the manufacture of commodities which do not accord with the state plan. Similarly, people may seek employment in industries in numbers that do not match the priorities of the central authority.

The state planners in a command system will have to tackle a formidable array of problems when deciding how resources are to be used. Take, for example, the apparently straightforward decision concerning whether plastics could be used instead of steel for the manufacture of certain parts of motor-vehicle bodies. There is firstly the technical question of the feasibility of substituting plastic for steel. However, the issue may not be resolved by technical experts. There are technical arguments for and against the use of steel and plastics in motor vehicles. Since the experts from the steel and plastics industries will naturally have a vested interest in promoting the widest use of their products, they will tend to stress the advantages and minimise the disadvantages.

The state planners will have to look beyond the technical issues and consider the possible repercussions of substituting steel for plastic on other parts of the economy. If plastic is to be used, where is it to come from? Can the output of the plastics industry be increased? If not, should the plastic needed for cars be diverted for other uses? If less plastic is available for other industrial and domestic products, can alternative materials such as wood or metal be substituted? If not, then for which plastic-made industrial and domestic products should output be reduced? By how much should it be reduced? What effect would this have on exports? These are only a few of the questions to consider.

2 Command economy with some household choice

In this type of economic system some of the decisions about *what? how?* and *for whom?* are made by householders in their role as consumers and suppliers of labour. The central planning authority may take some household preferences as a starting-point for making decisions, but then modify them in line with the central priorities. The productive units of the economy – such as factories and farms – then receive orders in line with the targets of the master plan.

It is because a complete command economy with planners'

sovereignty imposes what for many people would seem to be an unacceptable restriction of individual liberty that such systems do not usually last very long. They are tolerated only in times of national emergency – famine, war or revolution – when such restrictions are regarded by the community as an equitable solution to urgent problems. Thus most command economies in the real world admit some measure of household choice.

3   Market economy with consumers' and firms' choice

In this sort of system, households and producers – subject to restrictions in the interest of, for example, public health and safety – are free to decide between themselves what to produce, how and for whom. They do so with reference to prices determined by the interplay of supply and demand in free markets – hence the title 'market economy'. Its most enthusiastic advocates claim that the miracle of a properly working price system is that it will answer all the questions of the type confronting the state planners in the previous example simultaneously, taking into account all relevant considerations. It can do this without any centralised bureaucracy or elaborate planning apparatus. However, critics would argue that the answers the market economy provides are far from perfect. Its weaknesses are examined elsewhere in this book, but even the sternest critics would acknowledge some of its merits.

The operation of a market economy can be understood with reference to the question posed above concerning the supply of plastics. In any kind of economic system it is essential to ensure that the supply of any commodity is matched with its demand. Failure to do this will result in extreme waste and inefficiency – unwanted surpluses of some goods and acute shortages of others. In the latter case, if they are essential commodities, this may bring the economy to a standstill. Taking the example of plastics, one way of dealing with this in a command system would be for the planners to ask for a list of the demands for all goods containing plastics likely to be used in factories, offices, hotels, schools, hospitals and private houses and so on. Clearly the compilation of such a list would be a substantial undertaking. It is also possible that the supplies of plastics of various kinds may not match the demands and if the supplies cannot be increased this leaves the planners with the problem of deciding how demands should be reduced.

Naturally each organisation will be able to advance powerful arguments showing why its supply of plastic goods should not be cut. The state planners will need some order of priorities if they are to sort out competing demands on limited supplies. They might decide that plastics for use in the electrical engineering industry (as insulation for cables and wires, for instance), should have priority over what are regarded as less essential uses such as for leisure goods. This priority list may be backed by a system of quantitative controls. The central planners may hand out licences to the firms converting the raw materials into plastic goods, entitling them to purchase only a limited amount of materials. These licences may be conditional on materials being converted into specified types of product. Provided the planners have done their calculations correctly, the balance they desire between demand and supply will have been achieved. However, in a situation where demand considerably exceeds available supplies, licences to purchase various materials may be very valuable. The officials handing out the licences may be subject to all sorts of pressures and the process may become a breeding-ground for bribery and corruption. Other distortions may creep in as some firms take over others in order to obtain extra licences. These things need not necessarily happen but it is very likely that they will.

With the price system the balance of supply and demand is achieved in a different way. The essence of this system is that buyers and sellers are free to enter into contracts at whatever prices and quantities they choose. If the demand exceeds the supply, this means that some manufacturers will get less than they want. Rather than go without they may be prepared to pay extra to ensure the supplies they need. If this is widespread in the market then the price of plastics will tend to rise which will have two effects: firstly, it may stimulate an increase in the supply of plastic materials because the rising price and higher profits likely to be associated with this are an encouraging signal for producers; secondly, the high price will force buyers of plastics to consider their demands very carefully, stimulating the search for substitutes and the avoidance of waste or improved designs incorporating less material. Thus the responses invoked by the high price – stimulating supply and choking off excess demand – will tend to correct the imbalance.

Prices can be regarded as signals helping to guide and coordinate the activities of producers and consumers. The price acts as an automatic rationing system in allocating resources, which does not require central administration. The advantages of this are that the strengths of competing claims on scarce resources can be evaluated on comparable terms in an objective manner. If, for example, there is a tremendous demand for products of the electrical industry, then it will be worthwhile for the manufacturers to pay a high price for plastics for insulating material. This high price that they are willing to pay reflects what is known as a *derived demand* for the electrical products containing plastic insulation. An administrative priority list is unnecessary with a market mechanism. The test is simply the ability to pay. Firms with the highest derived demand will get highest priority because they will be willing to pay the higher price and will have to cut back least in their demand.

The planners may have been right to assign a low priority to plastics for domestic leisure-goods or they may have been mistaken in their calculations. The market place would provide an automatic test for this. If derived demand is really low, then the manufacturers of leisure-goods containing plastic materials will not be able to pay the higher prices and may be forced to cut back their demand.

The price mechanism not only helps to achieve a balance of supply and demand in particular markets but also guides the selection of occupations and the distribution of productive resources between different industries. Sharp increases in demand for the products of particular industries will tend to push up prices and consequently the rewards of productive resources in those industries. The desired expansion will take place as labour and capital are attracted into those industries by higher profits, salaries and wages. They will probably be drawn away from industries whose products face declining demand and where the factor rewards are poorer.

The key features of the market system are thus: (i) freedom of enterprise; (ii) freedom of choice by consumers; (iii) the existence of private property. This implies that consumers are free to spend their income as they choose, while the owners of the factors of production – labour, capital and land, may offer these services in any market for the highest price they can get. At the same time the organisers of production, the factory and farm managers, are free to hire whatever resources they require to produce whatever quantities of commodities they choose.

In short, through the price system, competitive markets provide an effective way of supplying information and powerful incentives to act on the information so that resources are used efficiently. This contrasts with the command economy. In theory the command planners should be able to match supply and demand and also take account of consumer preferences. As the experience of communist countries has shown, in practice this has proved to be an almost impossible task. The command systems have been cumbersome, expensive and inefficient. Surpluses of unwanted goods and acute shortages of needed goods abound. A Polish survey, for example, showed that the average time spent queuing per household rose from 63 minutes a day to 98 minutes a day between 1966 and 1976, while in Bulgaria in 1984 the waiting time for delivery for a car was

20 years.[1] India and other countries, particularly in the developing world, once considered the Soviet Union as a model for economic modernisation. Now they are also dismantling many of their state controls and turning towards market solutions. It should not be inferred, however, that markets are without their problems – a point explored in the remainder of this chapter.

Some weaknesses of the market

Some commentators argue that the bedrock of the market economy is the institution of private property, the use of which is guided by the 'sticks and carrots' of the profit and loss system. Since it is the owners of productive capital – farms and factories – who hire labour and are responsible for the organisation of production, the effectiveness of their operations is critical. Incentives and deterrents are provided through prices generated in free markets. Profits might be regarded as a reward for reading the market signals correctly, and as recompense for enterprise, risk taking and successfully coping with the uncertainties of changing market conditions.

Firms that misjudge the market, delivering the wrong goods at the wrong time, or those that are simply inefficient, high cost producers, will incur losses. If these losses persist such firms will be driven out of the market. It is said in some textbooks that in all this, 'the consumer is king'. That is to say, it is the preferences of consumers, as shown by the ways in which they spend their money, that determine what should be produced. Success or failure in business depends upon responding to these preferences.

This view of the market economy has been criticised by some economists. It is said that profits may not be a reward for being enterprising but simply for being large and powerful. In markets which are dominated by a handful of large firms, much of the initiative in determining what is produced may rest with the suppliers, who may be slow to respond to consumer preferences, because they are large bureaucratic organisations and are not greatly worried by smaller competitors. It has been suggested that because these large firms have to plan years ahead when introducing a new product, and as they have such a substantial commitment to special-purpose equipment even before they start production, they must sell what they produce. This can be achieved by massive advertising which moulds the consumers' preferences to conform with the wishes of suppliers. It is what the American economist Galbraith has called the 'revised sequence', to indicate that it is no longer the consumer that is sovereign but the firm.

The fact that this theory is something of an exaggeration, can be judged from the spectacular product failures of some large firms, despite extremely heavy advertising. It must be recognised that although there is consumer choice, it would be unrealistic to say that the consumer is king. The balance lies somewhere between producers and consumers, which is why we have labelled the market system as one with producers' and consumers' choice. In short decision making is much more diffused in a market economy than in a command economy and it would be unrealistic to think of any one group as sovereign. We might also add another dimension to this picture which is the existence of organised labour in the form of trade unions, who exercise an important influence on resource allocation.

In practice, economic systems rarely operate purely in any one of the forms discussed above. Most systems are mixed with the command and market systems operating in different sectors of the same economy. It is possible to see that some economies correspond to some variant of the command system, such as that of the Soviet Union, while others, such as the United Kingdom are substantially market systems. Even in what are generally regarded as market economies the autonomous decision-making role of households and firms is limited by the activities of the government. In the United States, commonly quoted as an example of a market economy, approximately one-fifth of the national product is spent by government authorities and is not subject to the forces of the market system.

The government and market systems

Governments play such an important role, even in market economies, for two reasons:

1 Because of the inability of the market mechanism to deliver certain types of goods.
2 Because of weakness in the market system.

The first reason concerns what are known as *public goods*. It is a characteristic of such goods that once they are provided, their benefits extend to all members of the community, whether or not an individual has contributed towards the cost of the goods. No one can be excluded. The maintenance of law and order through the police force and the judiciary and national defence through the armed services are good examples.

If the supply of these goods was left to the market mechanism – perhaps with people purchasing vouchers entitling them to defence or police protection – the result would be an inadequate organisation for these services. This is because the provision of defence or the maintenance of law and order cannot be confined to an individual or even a section of a community. Arrest of a criminal in one area will benefit people in other areas. Similarly defence of national boundaries would be of benefit to the whole community and not just to selected individuals. Since, for each individual, the benefit from public goods appears to be unconnected with the amount of his contribution, there will be strong incentive to pay as little as possible. Thus voluntary contributions on an individual basis are unlikely to produce an adequate supply of public goods. Collective arrangements for their finance and possibly for their provision will be necessary.

It may be more efficient for the government to concentrate only on finance, leaving the production of the goods involved to private firms, as with defence equipment; or the government may both provide finance and organise a service, as is the case with military operations. The need for some form of collective arrangement for the finance and/or supply of goods, which cannot be efficiently provided by a market system of individual purchases 'over the counter', is also apparent with road networks. It is possible to finance some major roads through toll booths, but this system could not be used for all roads.

The other reason why governments may intervene – weaknesses in the market mechanism – is much more complex and raises many controversial issues. Since the market system operates through prices, it is argued that this is unjust to those with low incomes. Hence the government may intervene to subsidise, or even provide free, essentials such as food, housing, medical care and education. Assisting people with low incomes is not the only motive for a government to reduce market prices in this way. It may also wish to actively encourage the consumption of what are known as *merit goods*. These are goods regarded by the State as having some special merit, not fully appreciated or understood by consumers, who would not purchase 'adequate' quantities. It is claimed, for example, that education and medical care would be undervalued if left to the voluntary choice of many individuals, even when they can afford to pay for these services. The problems this creates may extend beyond the individual to the rest of the community and even to future generations. Thus, in the case of education, most governments are so anxious to ensure its consumption that it is not only free to users but also compulsory, with the option of fee paying private education for those who do not want to use State schools.

The opposite of merit goods are *merit bads* – commodities such as drugs and pornography – judged by some to have harmful effects, underestimated by consumers, whose consumption of these products should be discouraged by the government. It is said that with merit goods and merit bads, consumer sovereignty does not result in the most desirable outputs in the long run, either for individuals or the community. On the other hand, it is argued by many that the paternalism of 'the government knows best' can become oppressive.

Weaknesses in market structure, such as the existence of powerful monopolies who may restrict output and create artificially high prices – or what are regarded as the excesses of wasteful competition – may also cause governments to attempt to modify the unfettered workings of the price system. Governments may do this in a variety of ways, ranging from legislation prohibiting certain actions to direct control through public ownership. See Chapter 10.

Finally a competitive market economy, if left unregulated, may be subject to slumps and booms because of the periodic lack of balance between total supply of goods and services and total demand. It may require some form of government action to help correct the situation – a point examined in Chapter 19.

The important role played by the state in any type of modern economic system is regarded by most experts as inevitable. However, the extent of government action and its method of intervention are a matter of fierce dispute, not only among politicians and social reformers but also among economists. At opposite ends of the spectrum are the influential views of Adam Smith (1723–90) and Karl Marx (1818–83). In his book, *The Wealth of Nations*[2], Smith, regarded by some as a prophet of the Industrial Revolution and modern capitalism, argued strongly in favour of the competitive market mechanism, whose 'invisible hand' coordinated the activities of producers and consumers, ensuring that the right quantities were produced at the right market price, without the need for an elaborate government bureaucracy to run the economy. Smith and others, known as the 'classical economists', writing between 1750 and 1850, laid the foundations for the analytical understanding of the operation of the market type of economy.

A common impression gained from the writings of the classical economists is that they believed in maximum individual economic freedom and the minimum government regulation. This is something of an over-simplification. They were basically reformers, aiming to highlight and remedy outmoded and restrictive state policies, which had lingered on from the sixteenth and seventeenth centuries. They did acknowledge that where it is not possible to achieve efficiently operating markets through institutions and laws, then the government should intervene. Adam Smith favoured government assistance for infant industries until they were sufficiently developed to be able to compete on equal terms with established ones. The object of state intervention, favoured by clasical economists and subsequent advocates of the market economy, was to support and strengthen the market mechanism, not replace it completely.

The opposing view was vigorously presented by Karl Marx in a series of books and pamphlets published between 1848 and 1882. He argued that the profit-motivated market system, backed by private property, had inherent weaknesses which would lead to its eventual downfall. Unlike the efficiency to which Smith drew attention, Marx stressed the conflicts and crises of the system. All capitalist institutions would finally be replaced by a one-party dictatorship of the proletariat, based on the state ownership of all means of production, distribution and exchange.[3] These concepts inspired the 1917 Bolshevik Revolution and subsequently formed, until recently, the basis of Russian political thinking and action. However, Marx has been subjected to many different interpretations. China, Yugoslavia and Cuba have all built systems very different from that of the USSR – many of which are now being reformed. Most of the left-wing parties of western Europe are far less radical; they accept a multi-party system and aim only at state ownership of key or basic industries, combined with government planning and social security schemes.

Much of the debate on the merits of the various types of economic systems has centred on the question of their performance. When comparing the performance of different systems, the economist can use a number of measurements: the distribution of income, growth in output, technological advance, stability, output per head and so on. However, such a comparison is unlikely to produce a conclusive or acceptable answer about the superiority of any one system, because, when making these comparisons, we are likely to be concerned with economic welfare and the standard of living in the community.

This is a complex question which cannot be easily determined by statistical measures. There are many important qualitative aspects of welfare, such as the conditions of work, job satisfaction, opportunities for education and recreation. These are difficult to define and measure satisfactorily. The comparison of living standards in different countries extends to consideration of the quality of life in general, which raises not only a difficult problem of definition and measurement but also questions of value judgement. What can we say about communities that allocate their resources differently? How, for example, can we compare an economy that directs its resources to technology and defence with one which spends more on education or welfare services? Whether or not military power and technological advance, rather than education and welfare services, are more relevant measures of the efficiency of a particular economic system is not a question that can be resolved by economists. It concerns an ordering of priorities reflecting personal values and beliefs, and political and religious convictions.

The economist may merely confine his studies to setting the stage for the debate on the merits of different systems by presenting comparative facts and analyses of how they operate. This is the positive economics explained in the last chapter. Alternatively he might go beyond this and plunge into the argument as an advocate for the advantages of a particular system. Unless the arguments are restricted to fairly narrow technical issues, such advocacy will inevitably take economists into the area of value judgements and politics. Thus Adam Smith and Karl Marx were not only positive economists in their presentation of facts and analysis but also ardent reformers – Smith favouring the strengthening of competitive capitalism and Marx supporting its replacement by state ownership and planning.

Summary

In a command economy the key questions concerning the use of scarce resources will be settled by a central planning authority. In order to avoid unwanted surpluses or shortages, the planners must devise ways of matching demand and supplies for various goods and services. In a command economy it is likely that most factories, farms, etc., will be owned and operated by the state on behalf of the community. The enterprises will receive directives or commands from the state planners instructing them what to produce. The market system is usually characterised by the institution of free enterprise and private property. In a market economy the balance between supply and demand and the questions of resource allocation are achieved through the operation of prices determined by the interaction of buyers and sellers in free markets. Many systems are 'mixed' with command and market sectors existing side by side. Public goods, of which defence and justice are good examples, cannot be effectively produced through the market place. In any system these will have to be financed and supplied by the state. Governments may also intervene in the market economy to remedy weaknesses in the market system; such actions may range from subsidies and price controls to complete public ownership of certain industries. The extent of the state's role in the economy is a controversial issue among economists as well as among social reformers and policy-makers. Some economists favour state activities being limited to the provision of public goods and, where necessary, improving the operation of the market system. Others support a more radical approach believing that the market system based on private property has such serious defects that it must be replaced by state planning and control of productive resources. Economists who favour one system rather than another are often acting on the basis of their own value judgements.

Questions

1   Ruritania is a country which has abolished money. It is reported that there are no wages and no private property, and that decisions are taken by committees. What decisions must the Ruritanian government take which in Western countries are left largely to market prices? (The Institute of Bankers, Banking Diploma Examination)
2   What are the particular economic problems of a centrally planned economy? (Associated Examining Board, A-Level Economics)
3   What are public goods? Comment on the proposition that these have to be provided by the State. (Chartered Institute of Public Finance and Accountancy)
4   Compare and contrast the principal economic characteristics of a free market with those of a planned economy. (University of London, A-Level Economics)
5   Discuss the role of the price mechanism in the allocation of economic resources. (The Society of Company and Chartered Accountants, Economics of Industry and Trades Examination)

Notes

1   Winicki, J., *The Distorted World of Soviet-type Economies* (Routledge, 1988).
2   Smith, A., *An Inquiry into the Nature and Causes of the Wealth of Nations (1776)* (Methuen, London, 1961).
3   Marx, K., *The Communist Manifesto (1848)* (Penguin, London, 1967).

3

How Markets Work

Introduction

In the previous chapter a market system was described as a way of allocating resources on the basis of voluntary decisions to buy or sell made in response to price signals. Markets are commonly thought of as specific places where buyers and sellers meet: shops, street markets or specialised markets, like Stock Exchanges for shares, or Commodity Markets for goods such as grain, coffee and metals. However, a market is not necessarily confined to a particular place. On the Commodity and Stock Markets, for example, the buyers are not usually buying for themselves, but are middlemen acting on behalf of clients scattered throughout the world, with whom they are in close contact by telephone and telex. A market may therefore be defined as any area over which buyers and sellers are in contact, directly or through dealers, and where prices obtainable in one part of the area can influence prices in another part.

Using a broad classification, four principal groups of markets can be identified (see opposite).

Each of these markets has its own special features, called *market structure* by economists – the characteristics of the buying and selling side and the type of product – which will determine the behaviour of prices. For example, where goods are perishable, such as cut flowers and fruit, prices are more variable than for storable goods. In the latter case, temporary fluctuations in demand can be met by allowing a rise or fall in stocks, which acts as a kind of 'shock absorber', insulating the system from erratic price variations. The prices of shares and foreign exchange rates may also be volatile for

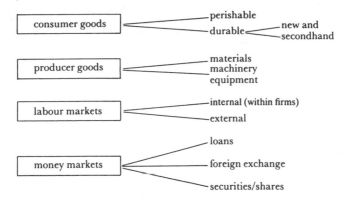

quite different reasons, reflecting frequently revised expectations about future events.

This chapter concentrates on the general principles underlying the working of all markets. Using the concepts of simplification and model-building outlined in Chapter 1, we shall analyse markets with simple graphs. For the reader not used to this, it may at first appear to be an unrealistically abstract way of studying such a complex institution as a market. It is worth persisting with this chapter because it provides a key to understanding the detailed operations of the markets listed above which are discussed elsewhere in the book.

Demand and supply

As we have just shown, the function of the market is to provide a medium for transactions between buyers and sellers, or between the *demand side* and the *supply side*. In the case of most markets for goods and services, the supply side is made up of firms and the demand side of households (in the case of consumption goods), or of other firms (in the case of intermediate or producer goods). In the labour market, it is households which make up the supply side – offering their labour for sale – while production units make up the demand side. The same basic principles are at work in each case, so for simplicity we shall take the market for a particular type of consumption good as an illustration.

The amount of that good which households will want to buy depends on a broad range of factors. However, one factor which is likely to influence demand strongly is the product price. Generally speaking – and this issue is analysed in more detail in Chapter 6 – the cheaper a product is, the more of it households will wish to buy. This assumption is recorded graphically in Fig. 3.1A. Since we shall be using this sort of diagram extensively, it is useful to take this opportunity to explain how it is drawn.

Diagrams in economics are used to represent or summarise relationships between two or more variables. In the case of Fig. 3.1A, the information represented covers the quantities of the good purchased by all households at various prices. The basic data underlying Fig. 3.1A are as given in Table 3.1.

Table 3.1 The data underlying the demand curve D_1D_1 in Fig. 3.1A

Price per unit (£)	Quantity purchased per week (millions)
1	25
2	20
3	15
4	10
5	5
6	0

To represent this information graphically, we simply mark on the diagram, against each price, the quantity purchased. Thus at a price of £4 per unit, the quantity purchased is 10 million per week. At a price of £2 per unit, the quantity demanded would be 20 million per week. By drawing a line between the points indicated in the table, we are able to show how many units would be purchased at any price of between £1 and £6 per unit. This line D_1D_1, which we shall call the *demand curve*, indicates that as the price falls, the quantity demanded increases. (Thus demand is greater at a price of £2 per unit than at a price of £4 per unit. Alternatively the curve D_1D_1 is described as downward sloping.) Often in economics we are concerned with the general nature of a relationship rather than its precise numerical value. In such cases (Fig. 3.1B for example), we only draw in the general shape of the graph, rather than derive it from a numerical table such as Table 3.1.

A demand curve such as D_1D_1 in Fig. 3.1A only captures the responsiveness of demand to price. It is drawn on the assumption that all other factors affecting household choice are constant and that only the price is allowed to vary. What other factors might affect demand? Clearly consumer tastes have some influence. If

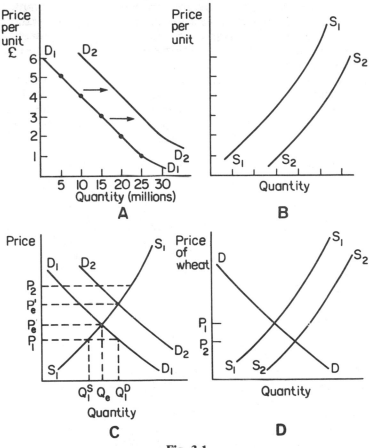

Fig. 3.1

consumers generally develop a stronger preference for a particular
item, they are likely to demand more of it at each price, and the
demand curve will shift to the right. For example, suppose that
demand increases by 10 million units per year at each of the prices
given in Table 3.1, so that demand at a price of £2 per unit shifts to
30 million units, and so on. The result will be a new demand curve
D_2D_2 (see Fig. 3.1A). Equally, if households' incomes rise, the
effect may be to increase demand to a new curve such as D_2D_2. Any
one of a large number of other factors – from a change in the
weather to a change in the price of other goods – may generate a
similar shift.

We now consider the factors affecting firms' supply of the product. Again, price is a major factor. Generally speaking – and this issue is analysed in detail in Chapter 5 – a higher price will evoke a higher level of supply. This general assumption is recorded in Fig. 3.1B, where the line S_1S_1 indicates that as the price rises, the quantity supplied rises too, i.e. S_1S_1 has an upward slope.

As in the case of demand, the supply of goods is affected by factors other than price. How much firms produce at any price depends on the costs of production, and a technological change which reduces costs will shift the supply curve to S_2S_2. Equally, how much is supplied at any price will be affected by the costs of inputs – labour, materials, etc. – and by the price firms can get for other goods which they might produce. An appropriate change in either of these factors (or in one of several others) would shift the supply curve to S_2S_2.

The obvious next step is to combine the demand and supply curves in a single diagram as we do in Fig. 3.1C. Holding all other factors at a particular level, D_1D_1 shows how the quantity demanded depends on price. S_1S_1 shows how quantity supplied depends on price, assuming that all other factors relating to supply are held constant. The price of the good is thus a factor influencing both supply and demand.

Market equilibrium

Let us now suppose that the price is P_1. At P_1, as we can see from the demand curve (in Fig. 3.1C), the quantity demanded is Q_1^D. From the supply curve, we can see that firms wish to supply Q_1^S, a lesser amount. Some customers will not have their demands satisfied at P_1; in other words, there is excess demand at P_1. Conversely, if the market price were P_2, demand would be less than supply and some firms would be unable to sell all the output they want to produce; there would be excess supply. Clearly there is just one price, P_e, at which there is a balance between supply and demand. We call this the *equilibrium* price, or the *market-clearing* price, because at that price buyers wish to buy the very amount which suppliers wish to sell; i.e. the market is in equilibrium or balance. The equilibrium quantity is represented by Q_e.

Naturally, if either the demand curve or the supply curve shifts, a new equilibrium price is normally created. Suppose, for example, that a change in tastes shifts the demand curve to D_2D_2. This will generate a new equilibrium price P_e' and a new equilibrium quantity. A shift in the supply curve will have a similar effect.

Notice that we have *not* stated that markets are always in equilibrium. There may be some institutional reason why the equilibrium price is not achieved (an illustration of this is provided below). More generally, adjustment to equilibrium may take some time. For example, suppose that the market represented in Fig. 3.1C is initially in equilibrium at P_e with demand curve D_1D_1 and supply curve S_1S_1. Now let the demand curve shift to D_2D_2. The price may initially remain at P_e, with demand exceeding supply. The new equilibrium price P_e' may be achieved only when customers who would otherwise have their demand unsatisfied seek to bid prices up, or when suppliers realise that they could sell the output they want to produce even if they charged a higher price for it.

Such instances of permanent or temporary disequilibrium are quite common in any actual economy, and, as noted in Chapter 2, they are important to any assessment of market forms of allocation. However, they do not undermine our general argument that in most markets there is an equilibrium between supply and demand which could potentially be found. Thus the market system is one possible means of coordinating transactions in the economy.

A good example of a market in which an equilibrium price is generally found is the wheat market in the United States. The demand curve for wheat – based on a demand for human and animal foodstuffs – is fairly constant from one year to the next – DD in Fig. 3.1D. The supply curve, however, is affected by the weather in the growing and harvest periods, and shifts markedly from year to year. Thus in a poor year, the supply curve may be S_1S_1 (in Fig. 3.1D), yielding an equilibrium price of P_1. In a bumper year, the supply curve may shift to S_2S_2 with an equilibrium price of P_2. Although we do not discuss this issue here, the evidence suggests that the equilibrium price is quickly found in the wheat market, and this explains why farmers do not always benefit financially from a bumper crop; the price may fall so low that they do not even cover their costs.

Not all markets find their equilibrium so easily. The forces shaping supply and demand – tastes, technology, income, etc. – may all be on the move. The curves in our diagrams, and so the equilibrium point, will be constantly shifting. Despite this, the tendency towards equilibrium is a strong one and helps us to interpret many price movements. Speaking of this the economist Boulding used the following analogy: 'We need the rabbit to explain the behaviour of the dog even if the dog does not always succeed in catching the rabbit'. The following section examines the effects of institutional arrangements blocking market forces.

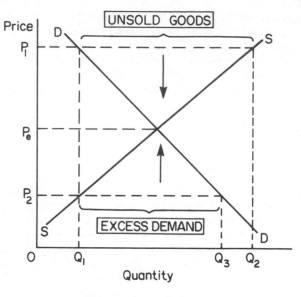

Fig. 3.2　Price fixing

The consequences of price fixing

We have seen how market forces, if left to themselves, tend to produce a market-clearing or equilibrium price, at which there are neither unsold stocks of goods nor queues of unsatisfied customers. This clearing price occurs through the interaction of many buyers and sellers without the necessity for intervention by any external authority. What will happen if, for example, the Government or an association of producers tries to fix a maximum or minimum price? As Fig. 3.2 shows, this depends critically on where the maximum or minimum price is in relation to the market-clearing price – P_e. Suppose the aim is to prevent the price falling below a *minimum* P_1. At this price, the quantity supplied exceeds demand by Q_1Q_2. The resulting surplus will put a downward pressure on price, as distributors cut their prices in order to clear unsold stocks, also reducing orders to manufacturers, who in turn will lower their output. At the same time as supply is diminished, the lower prices will stimulate increased demand and further reduce the excess supply until the equilibrium price P_e is reached. Unless something can be done about the unsold stocks, the price fixers will be defeated in their objective of establishing a minimum price. On the other hand, if P_1

is regarded as a *maximum* price, nothing could be easier, as market forces will ensure, without any action by the price fixers, that price will settle at P_e.

By contrast, attempts to establish a *maximum* price P_2 *below* P_e will encounter severe difficulties. Suppliers will supply quantity OQ_1, but the amount which buyers wish to buy at price P_2 exceeds this by Q_1Q_3. This will create an upward pressure on price. Some buyers, rather than go without, will pay a higher price than P_2 to get what they need. If the maximum price is not vigorously enforced, sellers will be tempted to meet this demand by selling above the declared maximum price and an unofficial or 'black' market will flourish. If unchecked, the price will continue to rise until the clearing price, P_e, is reached. No difficulties will arise if P_2 is set as a *minimum* price, and this would be unnecessary, since market forces alone will pull the price above this. To summarise: fixing a minimum price *above* or a maximum price *below* the market-clearing level will not work unless steps are taken to deal with the consequent excess of supply or demand.

Rent controls in the UK housing market demonstrate the effects of the Government fixing *maximum* prices – in this case for the hire of living accommodation – below the market level. Rent Acts, restricting the amount of rent a landlord can charge, were first introduced in 1915, during World War I, to protect tenants from the hardship of high rents caused by what was regarded as a temporary housing shortage. Rent controls of various kinds remained in force for nearly 70 years until the market was substantially deregulated, subject to protection of certain classes of tenants, by the Housing Acts of 1984 and 1988.

As a short-term emergency measure to relieve hardship, rent controls have undoubtedly helped; over a longer period they have made the accommodation problem worse by creating an artificial shortage. This can be understood with reference to Fig. 3.2. The controlled rents, represented at level P_2, are generally below the market level P_e, so there is an excess of demand over supply, Q_1Q_3. At this lower price P_2, both the quality and quantity of rentable accommodation is reduced, because the financial incentive to private developers to build new houses and flats solely for renting is weakened, and fixed rents make it impossible for landlords to maintain property in good condition. The shortage has been exacerbated as many home owners who might otherwise have let flats or rooms were unwilling to supply accommodation, because of the Rent Acts.

Statistical evidence supports this analysis: when rent control was originally introduced there were 7.5 million rented dwellings – approximately 90% of the total housing stock. By 1983 the total rented accommodation was under 3 million and represented only 12% of total stock.[1] Although part of this decline has clearly been due to increased home ownership as living standards rise, rent controls have been an important contributory factor. The lack of incentives to invest in rented accommodation was reflected in the fact that over 20% of these properties were classified as unfit and in need of repair.

Some consequences of *minimum* price fixing can be seen with the European Community's Common Agricultural Policy (CAP). Nearly 70% of its farm output is covered by price fixing arrangements. The intention is to rectify some of the instability of farm incomes created by the uncertainities of weather and erratic markets and to encourage investment in modern farming methods. When the market price for a particular farm product starts to fall below a specified intervention level, the CAP authorities respond by purchasing whatever quantities come onto the market at that price. This maintains the price level and relieves the market of the pressure of unsold stocks, which are stored with the intention of selling them later when the market price is more buoyant. The effect of intervention prices is buttressed by import levies, which reduce the competitive impact of cheap foreign imports, and by export subsidies, which make it easier for EC farmers to sell in world markets.

In terms of Fig. 3.2, there is for some products a persistent excess of supply Q_1Q_2, as farmers continue to produce more than the market can absorb at intervention prices set at P^1. In 1987, for example, there was a butter 'mountain' of 1.3 million tonnes and in 1985 a 750 million litre 'lake' of wine.[2] The resulting surpluses are purchased by the CAP authorities – shifting DD to the right. The surpluses are expensive to store, and difficult to dispose of abroad, because food producers in other countries object to the dumping of subsidised surpluses, which reduce food prices and producers' earnings. Eventually the excess of production can only be dealt with by reducing prices and output. Although this is now being implemented by CAP administrators, it is nevertheless a solution which market forces would also have produced eventually.

Thus a necessary condition for an efficient price stabilisation scheme is a price range which reflects the interests of consumers as well as producers, but is also consistent with a long-run balance of supply and demand. This may be difficult to achieve for technical reasons associated with estimating the shape and movement of the supply and demand curves, and hence equilibrium prices. A further complication is likely to be the existence of pressure groups representing various consumer and producer interests. The farm lobby is politically important in the European Community. The principles outlined here also apply to international arrangements for commodity price stabilisation, such as the International Grains Agreement and the International Coffee Agreement, although the detailed operations and objectives differ from those of the CAP.

The difficulty of excess production has also frequently troubled the Organisation of Petroleum Exporting Countries (OPEC), comprising some of the major oil exporters and controlling 60% of the world's known oil reserves. It is a cartel operating a formal agreement among its members to fix the price of OPEC oil sold in world markets. The OPEC problem can also be appreciated with reference to Fig. 3.2. Assume P_1 is the price set for a particular grade of oil, above the market clearing price, P_e. A system of output quotas among members is supposed to restrict output to OQ_1, preventing an excess of supply, $Q_1 Q_2$, from depressing the price. In practice, when prices do rise, some OPEC producers cannot resist the temptation to sell more oil than their quotas permit. Consequently the price gets depressed towards the market level P_e.

Evidently OPEC has difficulty in getting all its members to stick to their quotas. This is not surprising because the members of the cartel vary greatly in terms of the size of their oil reserves, national income and pressure of population. Agreement about cartel objectives and quota arrangements is hard to reach. For example, countries such as Iraq which need foreign exchange are interested in high prices, while small Sheikhdoms with big reserves of oil prefer a lower price and larger market share. Despite conflicts in the Gulf and the failure of OPEC to regulate its output it seems likely, according to recent expert forecasts, that rising world oil demand will in any case absorb excess production and help to maintain prices. If correct, this would mean, in terms of Fig. 3.2, a shift in DD to the right so that surplus production $Q_1 Q_2$ is sold and the OPEC price maintained at P_1.

It is evident from these cases that attempts to regulate markets by price fixing frequently result in over or under production and other wasteful distortions. The supporters of competitive markets claim that this is a powerful reason for deregulation.

Summary

In a market system, prices provide signals coordinating the activities of producers and consumers. There is usually a strong tendency towards the establishment of equilibrium or market-clearing prices. Institutional arrangements to fix prices at other than the clearing levels are likely to break down unless steps are taken to deal with the resulting excesses of supply or demand.

Questions

1   'The price mechanism in a free market does not always lead to prices that are acceptable to either consumers or producers.' Briefly discuss this statement and
   (a)   examine the possible economic effects of fixing minimum prices,
   (b)   examine the possible economic effects of fixing maximum prices,
   (c)   give examples to show where the fixing of maximum and minimum prices has resulted in serious economic problems.
   (Institute of Chartered Accountants in England and Wales, Foundation Exam)

2   Explain why official market intervention to stabilise agricultural prices can lead to excessive stocks of certain commodities. (University of London, A-Level Economics)

3   'Price controls are an inefficient method of helping poor people because they always lead to shortages'. Discuss. (Associated Examining Board, A-Level Economics)

4   Other things being equal, if the government fixed a maximum price on a good in order to protect consumers, but this price was above the level prevailing in a free market,
   (a)   suppliers would increase their prices,
   (b)   the demand for the good would fall,
   (c)   the demand for the good would increase in anticipation of higher market prices,
   (d)   output would increase because of the higher maximum price,
   (e)   none of the above.
   (University of London, A-Level Economics, Paper 2)

5   (a)   Why do governments sometimes fix maximum or minimum prices for certain markets?

(*b*) What are the economic effects of such price fixing?
(Institute of Chartered Accountants in England and Wales,
Foundation Examination)

Notes
1 Parker, J. and Mirrlees, C., *British Social Trends since 1900*, ed.
   Halsey, A. H. (MacMillan 1988).
2 *EEC Yearbooks of Agricultural Statistics*.

4

The Firm

Introduction

As we have seen in Chapters 2 and 3, in a mixed or predominantly market economy, many of the important questions for resource allocation – *what? how?* and *for whom?* – are determined by the impact of prices generated through the interaction of buyers and sellers in free markets. To understand the working of this market price mechanism we need an explanation or theory of supply, and also a theory of demand. This chapter provides an introduction to the former which is explored in some detail in subsequent sections of the book. It is significant that in most economics textbooks the theory of supply is discussed in terms of the firm. In some books the theory of supply becomes the theory of the firm. By contrast, the buying side of a market is not usually discussed with reference to such detailed study of individual buyers or groups of buyers. For example, to understand the operation of the market for bread or beer, it may be necessary on the supply side to know something about the size and internal organisation of the firms involved but on the buying side, the size and internal organisation of households is less important. There is no theory of the household exactly comparable with the theory of the firm. Although the way in which consumers and households make their buying decisions is a starting-point for an understanding of the demand side of a market (see Chapter 6), it is the impact of these decisions in total rather than individual consumer units which is the focus of attention.

The firm's decisions

As a supplier of goods or services what sort of decisions does a firm have to take and how does it make them? The key questions facing a firm may be:

1 What is the best way of producing the goods?
2 What is the best level of output?
3 What price should the firm charge? Should its prices be the same at all times and for all classes of customer, or can it 'price discriminate', charging different prices at peak times or in different markets?
4 What is the most effective way of selling the product? – i.e. should the firm concentrate on TV and press advertising, or attractive packaging, or some combination of these? Will minor variations in the design of the product – standard and deluxe models – help to sell more?
5 Should expansion be financed from the firm's own funds, from bank loans or from the issue of shares to the public?

Possible answers to these questions are considered elsewhere in this and other chapters in the book. At this point it will be helpful to consider in general terms the way in which decisions are made by any individual or organisation and for this we need to turn to the Theory of Decision Taking. Every rational decision involves the following:

1 Consideration of the various alternatives open to the decision-taker
2 A knowledge of the objectives that it is wished to achieve. It is this standard of values – sometimes known as an objective function – that provides the criteria to judge the various alternatives
3 Information on the results from the choice of a particular alternative.

In real life, particularly in business, where the results of alternative actions may be very uncertain, a range of outcomes may be considered in the light of the probability of their occurrence. Thus the businessman, when considering whether to install cost-saving but expensive machinery, will have to balance the probable gains in profits against the risk that losses may occur if sales revenue is not high enough to cover the cost of the equipment. Decision-taking involves more than choosing between alternatives. It also requires an information system to ensure that decisions are carried out to achieve the desired results – information for control. The data on costs and revenues supplied to a firm's top management by its engineers, accountants, salesmen and market researchers constitutes its information system, which is used to assist in the interrelated tasks of control and evaluation.

These three elements in decision making – the range of alternatives, the firm's objectives and its information system – will be influenced by the way in which the firm is organised and controlled, as well as by the markets in which it operates. As we shall explain in Chapter 7, the question of what price a firm should charge simply does not arise in a highly competitive market where there are a large number of firms selling identical products. In such a situation, the firm would be a 'price-taker' and not a 'price-fixer'. It would have to accept the price prevailing in the market. Its scale of output being only a tiny proportion of the total it would have no influence on that price. Because in such a perfectly competitive market its product is identical with that of its rivals, there would be little scope for price discrimination and little point in persuasive advertising of the 'brand X is the best' variety. By contrast, a large firm selling a product which is similar but not identical with that of rivals, for example, refrigerators or record players, will have to make imporant decisions about pricing, advertising and the style of its products, knowing that because it is large its actions will have some impact on the market, particularly in the reaction of its rivals. The nature of the market may have a similar influence on the objectives which a firm pursues. Decisions on points 1 to 3 in our list of questions may be taken with reference to the single objective of maximising profits – the difference between costs and revenues.

In the long run, in a highly competitive market, prices will be driven down to a level where only normal profits can be earned. That is to say profits will be just sufficient to keep firms in that particular line of business and recompense them for risks and trouble involved. If they earn less than a normal profit they will eventually be forced to leave the industry. Profit maximisation is necessary for survival and it is really the only objective open to the firm. The firm's decisions on the points listed will be guided by this criterion. However, a larger firm in a less competitive industry, which perhaps because of the high cost of entry due, for example, to the substantial investment needed, is protected from rivalry of newcomers and may be able to earn above normal profits over a longer period. In this situation there is more room for the firm to manoeuvre. It is not obliged to maximise profits in order to survive.

Various studies suggest that firms in many industries may pursue a variety of objectives including profit: in particular, maximising turnover (sales revenue), output or growth. These objectives may or may not be compatible. Increases in sales revenue and the scale of output may enhance profits. Nevertheless there may be circumstances in which there is a conflict between them. Beyond a certain point costs may rise faster than increases in revenue or output and profits may decline. The extent to which one objective may be pursued at the expense of others will depend upon the way in which the sometimes conflicting interests of different groups involved with the firm are resolved. Theories of modern corporations recognise that the firm is, in fact, a coalition of participants with disparate demands.[1] The policies that emerge and the targets that firms set for themselves are a compromise between these interests. Thus within the firm the objectives of employees, managers and shareholders may sometimes overlap and sometimes diverge. They all have common interests in the survival of the firm and in so far as profits are necessary for this then the profit objective will be a shared one. However, the appropriate level of profit needed to achieve this may be a matter of fierce debate within the boardroom and elsewhere.

The interest of economists in what goes on within a company is in marked contrast to earlier traditional theories of the firm which were not concerned with boardroom battles. This is because, in perfectly competitive markets of the kind examined in Chapter 7, the competitive struggle ensures that in the long run profit maximisation is the sole objective. This is determined in the market place and not the boardroom. The internal workings of the firm are therefore less relevant to the economist. In other types of market, particularly those characterised by very large firms, profits, although still of major importance, may not be the only objective of the firms concerned. The internal operations of such companies then become more interesting to the economist.

Thus we see that the three elements of a firm's decision-making process are interconnected, each influencing the other. The range of alternatives open to a firm will be restricted by the objectives which it sets itself. For example, the answer to point 5 in our list of questions concerning sources of finance for expansion will be determined partly by the firm's objectives concerning control of the company. If it is a family business reluctant to allow control to pass to outsiders, then it will be obliged to rely upon sources of finance other than the issue of shares. This may restrict its growth. The connection between forms of finance, company management and ownership which is important in modern theories of the firm is discussed in more detail in the following section.

In a similar way a company's pursuit of its objectives may also be restricted by weaknesses in its information system which reflects the way in which it is organised. Studies by the American economist Williamson[2] indicate that firms with a large number of products will tend to lose control of their operations if the manufacturing, selling and research functions for each product are controlled from a single company headquarters. This structure, known as unitary organisation, tends to reduce the effectiveness of the transmission of information between headquarters and subordinate departments. This is because it usually involves a long chain of command. The interpretation and summarising of information as it passes upwards in the power hierarchy may lead to distortions, especially if information is withheld or suppressed when it is felt that it could be threatening to the status of the communicator. In addition, the single company headquarters may be so overburdened with decisions on all aspects of its products that it is unable to give them adequate attention. This lack of control from the centre may be exploited in the subordinate divisions which build up local empires in research, sales and manufacturing without regard to the overall objectives of the corporation. The costs may rise and profits decline. This apparently was the experience of some large American companies such as Du Pont and General Motors. A decline in their fortunes prompted them to reorganise and adopt what is now known as the multi-division form of organisation. In this, each product has a separate company or division with its own sales, manufacturing and research functions and is entirely responsible to the group headquarters for its performance. In this way control is improved and inefficiency can be more readily detected. The profit objective is likely to be more obtainable with the multi-division arrangement than with the unitary form of organisation where the information system would probably be weaker.

Company finance, ownership and management

Companies raise the money they need for their operations both from internal and external sources. Profits are the major source of internal finance; they may also be an important condition for raising external finance from borrowing of various kinds. External funds consist mainly of bank borrowing and raising loans from other sources, in both the short and long term. These will carry a fixed rate of interest which the company is legally obliged to pay, together with a return of capital at some stage. Another source of external funds is from the issue of ordinary shares, often called *equity* (known as common stock in the United States); these shares do not carry a fixed rate of interest but instead receive a dividend from company profits. The dividend is usually determined after all other expenses and claims by creditors have been met. It will vary with the fortunes of the company and may be a great deal, or nothing if business is bad. Ordinary shareholders are therefore the true suppliers of risk capital. Their rights and obligations will vary with the type of ordinary share issued but generally they are entitled to appoint or remove from office directors responsible for running the company. Ordinary shareholders are in effect the owners of the business. In a small company they may themselves be directors – owner/managers.

The way in which a company finances itself from the sources discussed above, sometimes known as *capital structure*, will have a profound effect upon the ownership and style of management of the company. This is best understood by tracing the path of an imaginary firm through its various stages of growth. Picture a small-scale manufacturer of toys, mainly hand-made and using the minimum amount of equipment, perhaps manufactured in a simple workshop or garage. The toys would probably only be sold locally through market stalls or small shops. There would be little or no advertising and other selling and distribution expenses would be slight. Such a business may well be run by only one man – a sole trader – who finances the business entirely from his own savings and profits. If the toys are particularly good and the business prospers, he may require extra finance. This may be needed for *working capital* – additional stocks of raw materials and components or additional labour to help with finishing and packaging to meet rising demand. Alternatively additional funds may be needed for *fixed capital* – extra equipment or an extension to the workshop.

At this point the extra finance may be beyond the internal resources of our one-man firm. Short-term funds such as a bank advance or overdraft may be sought. These are short-term in the sense that they may be repaid at notice from the bank or over a short period. Although it is unlikely the bank will insist on complete repayment at any given moment, conditions of abnormal credit supply (see Chapter 15) may force the bank to cut down on credit at a time which restricts the company's expansion. This may be when credit is most needed; in the case of our example seasonal toy trade around Christmas time. A further source of short-term finance might be trade credit. Practically every firm both gives and receives a certain amount of finance in the form of trade debts, for every purchase and sale which is not immediately settled in cash creates a temporary debt. This form of finance may be rather expensive, for many suppliers give a discount to trade buyers on accounts paid immediately, which is forfeited if the bill is allowed to run over a month. Moreover, the obligation to repay a large amount of quickly maturing trade debts in a short period may be financially embarrassing for the firm if it in turn is waiting for repayment from its buyers. Although short-term finance is fairly flexible and not too difficult to arrange, it has clear disadvantages.

In addition to the problem of finding a more stable source of finance than short-term loans, the owner may find that he has other difficulties such as, for example, the need to provide for additional managerial skills to cope with the increased workloads as the business expands. Extra managerial skill might be needed on the buying or selling side of the business which becomes more important as trade grows. One way of solving both these problems is to form a partnership. In this case a common arrangement would be for the partner or partners to contribute money and managerial skills to the business, drawing a salary and participating in the profits according to their share of the capital. The legal form of Sole Trader and Partnerships varies between countries but they frequently have *unlimited liability*. The owners are liable without limit to the full extent of their personal fortunes for any debts contracted by the business, even if it means selling their homes and family possessions to meet these obligations. If one or more of the partners cannot pay their part of the debt then the others will be liable.

This arrangement is both a source of strength and of weakness. It ensures that the owners pay the closest possible attention to the running of the business. On the other hand, because the mistakes of one partner may involve the others in limitless liabilities, there may be a great reluctance to enter such a business unless each of the participants is absolutely confident about the business judgement of his colleagues. So long as each of the partners knows his colleagues well and understands what is going on in all parts of the firm this need not be a problem, which explains why partnerships are usually restricted to small-scale personal enterprises. Nevertheless the firm in our example may have reached the point where the Partnership form of enterprise is no longer viable. Additional finance may be needed on such a scale that it would require so many partners that the business would be difficult to manage – an unattractive proposition to both newcomers and existing partners. Some countries set a legal limit on the number of partners. In the UK the maximum, with certain exceptions, is twenty.

Limited liability

At this stage the owners may decide to turn their enterprise into a Private Limited Company. This embraces two important legal principles: it is a *corporation*; in other words it is, in the eyes of the law, a person, just as Mr Smith is a person and can own property, have a bank account in his name, sue and be sued. It is quite distinct from the persons who are its members at any given moment, unlike a partnership which is simply the aggregation of individual partners. Secondly, it involves the principle of *limited liability*, which means that the liability of shareholders is restricted to the amount of money they have invested in the company, even if it fails and large losses are made. Throughout the world all mixed economies have adopted, with variations, these principles of incorporation and limited liability. In the United Kingdom the legal history of the modern corporation began just before the middle of the last century, when in 1844, the first Companies Act set up the Registrar of Joint-Stock companies. Before this date, obtaining legal permission to become a corporation was a cumbersome and uncertain process, involving royal favour or petitioning Parliament for a Charter. Further legislation in 1855 and 1856 introduced the right to conduct business with the safeguard of limited liability. Many Victorians at the time had serious misgivings about this on the grounds that it would enable unscrupulous traders to practise all sorts of dishonesty yet remain within the law. These suspicions were largely unfounded. Although company law has deficiencies, it has over the years been amended and strengthened so as to make malpractices extremely difficult.

Despite this, the belief that 'gentlemen do not limit their liabilities' still lingers, especially in the professions – lawyers, doctors, accountants and so on – where unlimited liability is usual. One historian has described the device of limited liability as being as 'important for the Industrial Revolution as the invention of the steam engine'. Without it the finance necessary for the exploitation of large-scale modern technology would not have been forthcoming, nor would it have been possible to recruit all the managerial skills necessary for running such complex enterprises. It tapped a huge reservoir of savings from individuals who had neither the time nor skill to become directly involved in firms in which they were investing, but were nevertheless willing to supply capital with the safeguard of limited liability. No longer, as in the case of the partnership, was it necessary to participate in the business to safeguard one's interests. The running of the company could be entrusted to professional managers. As one lawyer has observed it was 'a device for marrying brains with bank balances'.

Although the toy manufacturing business in our example has grown greatly since the time when it was a *Sole Trader*, it is probably still a comparatively small-scale enterprise. Like many private companies, the ownership is likely to be confined to a fairly close-knit group of investors, probably relatives and friends of the original founders. However, as the business continues to grow the need for further capital may necessitate widening the circle of investors, so that the firm can no longer remain a family business. This is a dilemma which commonly faces small- and medium-sized firms that need long-term capital for growth and yet wish to retain family control. Up to a point the problem can be avoided by raising the long-term funds through the issue of securities called *debentures*. They carry a fixed rate of interest and are really a kind of mortgage because if the interest is not forthcoming, the debenture holders can legally apply for the sale of the company and repay themselves from the proceeds of the sale. Alternatively the company could issue *preference shares* that give their holders prior claim to payment at a fixed rate before any dividend is paid on ordinary shares, but after the interest has been paid to debenture holders. Since the latter do not have votes, and those of preference shareholders are restricted or non-existent, the company may in this way be able to retain control within the original group of ordinary shareholders. There are limits to this. If what is known as the company's *gearing* – the ratio of the annual amount payable on debentures and preference shares to the expected distributable profit – is high, then in a poor year there may be little or nothing left over for ordinary shareholders. Thus, if a company's income is liable to fluctuate, high gearing is unlikely to be popular with them. The gearing ratio is sometimes defined as the ratio of debt finance (money invested by those who are not owners) to the total of debt plus equity. The implications are the same.

For the founder members, their relatives and associates who wish to retain close control of the business they own, the legal status of the *private limited company* has many advantages, which have been strengthened by the Companies Acts of 1980 and 1981 – later consolidated in the Companies Act of 1985. Control is unlikely to pass easily to 'outsiders' since it is a criminal offence for a private company to offer its shares to the general public. Moreover, elderly members can remain on the Board clinging to power as there is no statutory age limit on the directors.

Nevertheless, when a private company has reached a stage in its growth where it needs more funds and cannot safely raise its gearing or obtain further money from its immediate circle of investors, it may apply for re-registration as a *public limited company*. It can then advertise its activities by issuing a prospectus, and can sell its shares or debentures directly to the public. Alternatively, it is more likely to raise funds by an 'offer for sale' – selling its shares to an Issuing House who will in turn sell to the public. A third possibility is to raise capital 'by placing'. This can be done through the company's financial advisors placing the shares privately with various financial institutions such as insurance companies and investment trusts. They may also be clients of the company's advisor and, therefore, willing to listen to his recommendations about the company's growth prospects.

The change in status from private to public involves greater disclosure of information about the company's activities, as well as scrutiny and comment in the financial press. This publicity may come as something of a surprise to those used to the comparative privacy of a business owned and run by family and close associates. However, it is the increase in information about progress and prospects, together with the lack of restrictions on the transfer of shares from one person to another, which makes the public company a more attractive investment for a member of the general public lacking an insider's knowledge of the business.

The Stock Exchange
It must be remembered that when an individual sells a share he owns to someone else, his stake in the ownership of the company, represented by the share, is transferred to the purchaser. The price paid for the share reflects the purchaser's view about the company's prospects, and hence the profit the share might earn. The sale brings no money to the company. This only happens when the company makes a *new issue* of shares, thus enlarging its capital.

If the company continues to prosper and the scale of operation further increases, it may obtain a *quotation* on a Stock Exchange (the latter is simply a market place where securities are bought and sold). To obtain a quotation a company must be large enough to have sufficient shares changing hands to establish a market price. In addition it must meet the requirements of the controllers of the exchange – in London the Stock Exchange Council or in America the Securities and Exchange Commission – drawn up to protect the shareholders against misleading information on the standing and prospects of the company. The advantages of a market for shares are threefold. For the company, regular dealings in its shares on an established Stock Exchange make it easier for the company to obtain additional long-term capital. For the investor, the existence of the Stock Exchange makes quoted investments more attractive by insuring that they can be exchanged for cash if necessary. For the economy, a quoted price for shares, since it is not fixed but determined by the supply and demand, provides a measure of the value of shares which reflects future expectations of profitability based on past performance. This is important in the comparison of efficiency between companies and will affect the cost of capital to a firm. This is a key function of the Exchange. It is not only a market for the sale of existing shares but also for raising a new issue of share and loan capital. The existing shares of a company whose record is good and about whose prospects investors are optimistic, will command a high price. Such a company will find it cheaper to raise money through the issue of new shares on the Stock Exchange than one with a poor record and low share prices.

Over the last ten years, an important feature of the Stock Market has been the growing size and influence of institutional investors – pension funds, insurance companies and unit trusts who are invest-ing money on behalf of their subscribers. These institutions are now more important than individual shareholders and over half of the ordinary shares of UK companies quoted on the Stock Ex-change. Some observers believe that their impact weakens the efficiency of the Stock Market. Because they are responsible for other people's savings, it is said they are very cautious, preferring to invest in well-established quoted companies, exhibiting rather sheep-like behaviour as they do so, all tending to buy and sell the same shares at the same time and basing their decisions on advice from the same influential stockbrokers or investment analysts who think alike. Consequently, it is argued, fluctuations in share prices are much more violent; finance for risky but worthwhile ventures such as new technology is not forthcoming, and smaller unquoted companies are starved of finance. The Royal Commission on the Functioning of Financial Institutions (in *The Wilson Report*) found that although these were points for concern, the evidence to support the assertions was inconclusive.

The separation of ownership and management
As a quoted public company, our toy manufacturer is now probably typical of the larger scale modern corporation. Unlike the days when his company was a sole trader, it will now be a fairly complex organisation, possibly with separate divisions or subsidiary com-

panies, some of which may be established overseas for selling and manufacturing. The ownership is likely to be scattered among a large number of shareholders. In some large corporations shareholders are actually more numerous than the employees. Although the original founders of the company may still be important, they will no longer dominate the business. Control of the company will be entrusted to a number of career director/managers, who will probably be specialists in various aspects of the company's operations such as finance and marketing. They will not necessarily have shares in the company. Thus the owners of the firm – the hundreds or thousands of shareholders – are no longer the managers.

So far we have considered only the advantages of the corporate form of enterprise. At this point it will be relevant to examine what some commentators feel are the disadvantages. These arise not from fraud and dishonesty, as the Victorians had feared, but from the consequences of the separation of ownership and management referred to above. J. Burnham was one of the first to draw attention to this in his book *The Managerial Revolution*,[3] although the change was in reality a gradual one, stretching back to the reforms in company law in the mid-nineteenth century, from which date the older form of owner/manager enterprise slowly yielded to larger corporations with many hundreds of shareholders, who delegated their authority to directors and professional salaried managers. Does this make any difference? In law ordinary shareholders are entitled to elect directors answerable to them to run the company on their behalf. These directors may be removed from office if the shareholders have reasonable grounds for believing that the conduct of company affairs has been negligent. This being so, it might be argued that directors will do exactly what shareholders want them to do and that the separation of ownership and management makes little or no difference to the efficient running of the firm. It could be further argued that as shareholders have no career in the business and do not see it as a way of life but are only interested in the dividends on their shares, then the large-scale corporate enterprise is just as likely, or even more likely than the smaller family business, to give top priority to maximising profits as an objective.

This line of reasoning rests on two propositions:

1 The mechanism by which directors are made accountable to shareholders is completely effective.
2 The ambitions and interests of directors coincide with those of the shareholders.

The first proposition is questionable. The information on which company performance and hence the stewardship of directors can be judged, is specified by law. Among the disclosure requirements are Directors' Reports, Company Accounts and Balance Sheets. Nevertheless, the facts contained in the latter may be interpreted in various ways. Naturally the directors will wish to present their actions in their report in the most favourable light. Considerable expertise may be necessary to judge the performance of a complex modern company, requiring skills and time beyond the capacity of most shareholders. Even for the expert, additional information, beyond that required by company law, may be necessary – for example, comparison with the balance sheets of competitors. It is at the *Annual General Meeting* (*AGM*) that shareholders can, in theory, question their directors, express their views and give effect to the latter by vote. However, in practice the AGM is not a particularly effective instrument for shareholder control. Shareholders may have insufficient information to ask challenging questions. Because voting power is likely to be dispersed among a large number of shareholders, it will be difficult to get a consensus in order to express a majority vote of 'no confidence' or remove directors from office. Some observers take the view that in many large companies the Board of Directors, once elected, tends to be self-perpetuating, unless the company runs into serious difficulties. The presence among the shareholders of institutional investors such as Pension Funds and Insurance companies may modify this picture. Such institutions are likely to have more expertise in assessing company performance than the small private investor and may be able to ask awkward questions behind the scenes. However, even this may not be an adequate safeguard because institutional investors are likely to hold a portfolio of shares and securities in a wide number of companies in different industries. They may not therefore have the time or inclination to enquire too closely into the running of one company, representing only a small part of their total investment.

Even if the mechanisms through which directors are accountable to shareholders are sometimes weak, this may not matter so long as the second proposition concerning the identity of shareholders' and directors' interests is valid. Several economic and sociological studies have shown that among the factors determining objectives set by directors/top management are: (*a*) the way in which the 'best interests' of the company are perceived, and (*b*) the standards of professional managerial competence.

It is difficult to be precise about the responsibility of directors.

Neither Company Law nor the interpretation of it by the courts provides an unambiguous definition. It has variously been interpreted as that of 'trustee, agent and MP' – three very different roles.

Although in some respects, the responsibilities of directors to shareholders are similar to those of trustees, the comparison is imprecise, because trustees are not normally elected or dismissed by their beneficiaries. The comparison with MPs is also inexact. Directors, like MPs, once elected are only normally called to account through re-election, but there is nothing comparable to the 'opposition': likewise with agents, who can be appointed at any time and whose dismissal is a matter of the contract. Nor is it absolutely clear what is meant by 'the company' in whose interests directors are supposed to act. If this is narrowly defined as being synonymous with shareholders, does it mean present or future?

Thus it is clear that the directors of a modern corporation have substantial discretion in the way in which they interpret their duties. From the studies referred to, it is apparent that directors see shareholders as simply one of the groups to whom they are responsible, with responsibility also to customers and employees of the company.

Limits to the power of the directors
Successful growth is an important way in which managerial competence is demonstrated to the business community because growth presents the testing challenges of developing new organisations, opening up new markets and launching new products. It will probably bring with it the prestige and higher salaries that go with larger organisations. As noted previously in this chapter, there is a substantial overlap in all these objectives. Evidence shows that there is usually a close relationship between growth and profitability, which favours not only top management and shareholders but also employees because it may provide employment opportunities. Nevertheless, growth may be pushed to the point where it is at the expense of profits, at least in the short run. Costs may rise faster than revenues due to the expense of establishing new organisations, launching new products, etc. It must be remembered that potentially the directors have substantial discretion in pursuing growth as an objective because of their control over company dividend policies. Although the entire profit of a company belongs to the owners, it is the directors who decide what part of this shall be retained to finance the business and how much shall be paid as a dividend to shareholders. In recent years in the UK, these retained profits have

financed three-quarters of the investment and working capital of industrial and commercial companies. As we have seen, it may be difficult for shareholders to challenge dividend policies at the AGM.

A number of financial specialists and some economists, notably Marris,[4] have pointed out that there are important alternatives to the AGM which may set limits to growth policies. Good relations with the financial world – merchant banks, brokers and financial press – are regarded as important by top management. The possibility of adverse comment on a company's growth performance and future plans may induce shareholders to sell their shares, thus depressing market prices, triggering off a further wave of adverse comment. Moreover the high level of retained profits necessary for expansion will restrict or reduce dividends paid to shareholders and may also have a depressing effect on share prices. Instead of voting at the AGM, shareholders are 'voting with their feet' by disposing of their shares through the Stock Exchange.

This deterrent effect may be reinforced by the possibility of a takeover bid. The low price of the company's shares on the Stock Exchange may make it an attractive bargain for a bidder – perhaps a competitor or company wishing to diversify – who believes that with different management policies the company would be worth more. A takeover bid is an offer for shares in order to gain a controlling interest in the company – all or the majority of voting shares. This distinguishes the bidder from an ordinary investor. To succeed in a bid, the price must be well above the Stock Exchange price. To justify this the bidder must be convinced that the prevailing price is too low and that dividends could be increased. The bidder would probably propose to do one or more of the following:

1   To distribute more of the available profits to shareholders.
2   To increase the amount of profits earned by the running of the company more efficiently – perhaps less ambitious growth plans.
3   To maintain company profits by using some of the company's assets in other ways – perhaps disposing of some corporate white elephants acquired during an over-zealous expansion phase.

If the bidder is successful and past experience is any guide, it is likely that the directors and some of the top management may be removed from office because the policies on which they ran the company are contrary to those of the new owners. The advice given by the medieval diplomat Machiavelli in his book *The Prince*[5] on the subject of conquered territories is appropriate, 'men ought either to be well treated or crushed because they can avenge themselves of lighter injuries, of the more serious ones they cannot'. In the modern corporate state this might be translated as: 'senior men in taken-over firms should be warmly welcomed and encouraged or sacked: because if they are sacked they are powerless, whereas if they are downgraded they will remain united and resentful and determined to get their own back'. Some see the Stock Exchange as a kind of corporate policeman, deterring over-ambitious management from reckless growth. While there is some doubt about the effectiveness with which the Stock Exchange can perform this task, as rumour and speculation may obscure the proper valuation of a company's performance, it is clear that for a full understanding of the operations of a modern corporation consideration must be given not only to accountability through the AGM but also to the network of relationships shown in the accompanying diagram (Fig. 4.1).

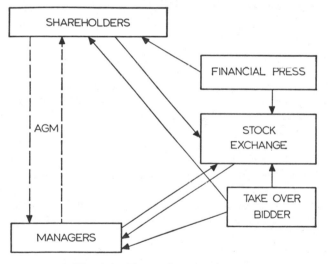

Fig. 4.1 The modern corporation

Summary

The issues on which a firm may have to decide include pricing policy, its selling methods and production techniques as well as the way its growth is financed. The firm's decisions will depend upon:

1 The range of alternatives confronting it.

2   Its objectives.
3   Its information systems.

These three elements in decision-making will in turn be influenced by the kind of market in which the firm operates, as well as the way it is managed. A company's *capital structure* – the sources and form of its finance – can also have an important impact upon the way in which it is owned and managed.

In the course of its growth a company may develop from being a one-man enterprise (Sole Trader), passing through the stages of a Partnership, and a Private Limited Company, finally emerging as a Public Limited Company with a Stock Exchange quotation. This is the characteristic form of enterprise for the large-scale modern corporation. The device of limited liability has facilitated the raising of large sums of money necessary for the exploitation of modern industrial technology. The consequent separation of management and ownership has given the managers of the modern corporation wide discretion in the use of company assets.

Questions
1   Why might a company wish to expand? (Institute of Cost and Management Accountants)
2   Consider the argument that in many joint stock companies ownership is divorced from control. (Welsh Joint Education Committee A-Level Economics)
3   (a)   What do you understand by the concept of corporate status?
    (b)   What are the characteristics of public and private companies? (BTEC National Certificate/Diploma (Langley College))
4   Discuss the role of the Stock Exchange in the allocation of investment capital. How has the growth of larger institutional investors increased market imperfections? (University of London, A-Level Economics)
5   Explain the term 'gearing' in relation to the capital structure of a limited company. (Institute of Cost and Management Accountants)

Notes
1   Cohen and Cyert, *Theory of the Firm*, Chs 17–18 (Prentice Hall, New York, 1975).
2   Williamson, O. E., *Markets and Hierarchies* (Free Press, New York, 1975).

3   Burnham, J., *The Managerial Revolution* (Indiana University Press, 1941).
4   Marris, R., A Model of Managerial Enterprise, *Quarterly Journal of Economics* (May 1963).
5   Machiavelli, N., *The Prince*, Translated by G. Bull (Penguin, London, 1970).

5

Production and Costs

Introduction

Production is the process whereby the various factors concerned (land, labour, capital equipment) are brought together and transformed, using available technology, into an *output*. The output can take various forms. It can be a good or a service. In the former case it is a physical commodity, in the latter it is a function provided for the customer (for example, the output of a dry-cleaning shop is the service of cleaning clothes). It can be a good produced for direct use by the consumer, like a pair of shoes or an article of household furniture, or the output can be used to produce further goods or services; this is the case with items of machinery for use in industry, or with materials like steel which are produced for use in other processes, like car-making.

Each production process has its own special character, and scientists or engineers are usually needed to develop particular technologies of production, or ways of turning inputs into outputs. Economists have tried to explain the general direction of changes in these technologies, which make up technical advance, but they cannot contribute to technological development themselves. What we shall do in this chapter is to look at economic aspects which are common to all production processes: how firms choose which method of production to use; how the size of output affects costs; and how costs of production can be broken down into various components.

1 Production – inputs and outputs

It is fairly easy to identify the output of a particular production process, for it is usually a readily identifiable single commodity, such as an estate car, a packet of biscuits, petrol of a particular octane or a machine tool of a certain kind. All the products of a single production process need not be identical. For example, the motor cars need not be of the same colour, and some may have extra refinements. But by and large it is relatively easy to identify and count outputs of the production process.

On the input side, the situation is a great deal more complicated, as the inputs have little of the fundamental similarity of outputs. Let us consider the example of car manufacturing again. A partial list of the inputs in this process would include the following:

1   *the labour force*, consisting of thousands of individuals, performing hundreds of different functions classified according to various skill grades;
2   *the capital equipment* used in production: this will consist of machinery of various types, performing the whole range of functions required to make cars, and also the factory buildings which house the production unit;
3   *the land* on which the factory is sited which is essential for the operation of the process;
4   *enterprise or entrepreneurship*; in other words, the willingness of the owners of the factory to take the risk of producing goods for sale, and the ability of the owners or managers to organise production.

This is a list of the four basic inputs into the production process, the basic factors of production. Of these four we shall concentrate particularly on the first two – labour and capital. Land is of secondary importance – except, of course, in agriculture – and enterprise, the willingness of the owners to take the risk of organising production is essential for all production, and has little relevance to the question with which we are concerned here, which is how a particular technique of production is chosen.

The first thing to note is that the two categories, labour and capital, are composed not of identical units, but of a whole variety of distinct and different entities. This is clearly true of capital: machinery can take virtually any shape or form, and buildings, which are also an item of capital equipment, can do likewise. But it is also true of labour. Even within a given skill grade, some workers may work harder than others or be more efficient, so that to treat them as identical is misleading.

This brings us back to the problem of model-building in economics, which was referred to in the first chapter. It was stated there that the art of model-building was to isolate those special features of a situation which are of particular importance, and ignore the rest. This leaves us with a simplified model of reality, which can then be used as a basis for argument and conclusions.

In this case the special feature which we isolate is the distinction between capital equipment as a whole on one hand, and labour on the other. The features of reality we ignore are the differences between items of capital equipment and between different members of the labour force. Whether this simplification is valid depends on the way in which we apply the conclusions of our simple model to the real world. It must be said at once that economists are deeply divided over one aspect of the simplification we make here, the way in which we treat all capital as if it were the same and work out the total capital used in production by adding together the *values* of all the separate items of capital equipment. But let us see how the model works.

Suppose a firm wants to achieve a particular level of output (we shall see later in the chapter how that level can be determined). There will be a number of possible techniques of production which could be used, some using more capital and less labour, others less capital and more labour. We can imagine the firm possessing a book of blueprints, supplied by engineers, each showing how the output level can be achieved by different combinations of labour and capital. Let us take the case of a firm wanting to produce one thousand units of some commodity per week. One possible technique of production may be to employ 100 workers and use £100000 worth of capital equipment. This combination of inputs can be represented by point A on Fig. 5.1, which shows quantities of labour on the horizontal axis, and quantities of capital on the vertical axis. Another possible technique may be to employ 75 workers using £150000 worth of capital equipment. This technique is represented by point B on Fig. 5.1. It is clear from the diagram that as less labour is used, more capital equipment must be brought into service, to produce the same output. A third technique, represented by point C on Fig. 5.1, uses 50 workers and £250000 of capital equipment.

So far only three techniques have been recorded on the diagram, but there will usually be a range of other techniques using quantities of labour and capital midway between the points already recorded. This may be true even in cases where the number of basic variants of production is very small, as is the case in steel-making, for example. Even when the basic process involved in production of a commodity can only be performed by a single combination of capital and labour there will still be a variety of ancillary activities in the factory which can be performed using more or less capital equipment. For exam-

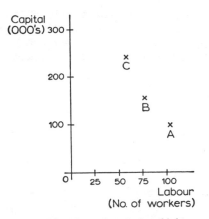

Fig. 5.1 Alternative combination of capital and labour capable of achieving the same output level

ple, transport in the factory can be done by one man and a fork-lift
truck or by several men using carts. If we record all these other
possible variants of production on our diagram we shall get a
situation such as that shown in Fig. 5.2, where all the points on the
curve show combinations of capital and labour capable of producing
1000 units per week of the product. Fig. 5.2 also shows the curve
DE, which illustrates the possible combinations of labour and
capital equipment capable of producing 2000 units of the product
per week. Naturally, more inputs are required for this. These curves

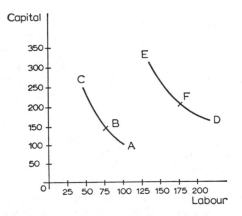

Fig. 5.2 Isoquants corresponding to different output levels

are sometimes called *isoquants*, from the Greek and Latin words for
'equal quantity'.

The curves are shown bulging inwards towards the origin of Fig.
5.2 (point O). The reason underlying this is an aspect of production
which can be illustrated by comparing the points A, B and C on Fig.
5.2. The difference between A and B is that in moving from A to B,
twenty-five workers are withdrawn, and replaced by £50000 of
capital equipment. Between B and C, another twenty-five are
withdrawn from the production process, but they have to be replaced by £100000 of capital equipment. As successive batches of
workers are withdrawn, the quantity of capital equipment needed to
replace them grows progressively.

But this pattern is one which followed from the numerical illustration given above. Is it actually borne out in practice? The evidence
from industry does support it. Isoquants estimated either for individual industries or for an economy as a whole, generally do exhibit
the shape given in Fig. 5.2, and the same conclusion is derived from
more detailed research involving factors of production other than
capital and labour. For example, an American economist has
looked at different ways of transporting oil in a pipeline.[1] The two
key variables, or 'factors of production', are the size of the pipeline,
and the size of the motor driving the oil along it. In other words, the
same quantity of oil can be shifted either in a large pipe using a weak
motor, or in a small pipe using a powerful motor. Actual tests
showed that the shape of the curves showing combinations of
horsepower and pipe diameter capable of shifting a given quantity
of oil tended to correspond to our assumptions about the general
shape of isoquants.

We shall be making a further and closely related assumption
about the technological nature of production, or the conversion of
inputs into outputs. This assumption relates to a situation in which
the levels of use of all inputs except one are held constant, while the
quantity of a single factor of production is allowed to vary. The
assumption is known as the *Law of Diminishing Returns*. It states
that: *As more and more units of a single factor of production are
added, while the input of other factors of production remains the
same, the rate of increase of output falls*. We can illustrate this with
an example taken from agriculture. Suppose there is a fixed amount
of land, to be cultivated by labour only. In one year, two men are
working on the field, and they achieve an output of 50 tons of wheat
(i.e. 25 tons each). The next year three men are working, and output
rises to 70 tons – weather and all other conditions are the same. The
work of the third man has increased output by 20 tons; this increase

can be called the marginal return. In the third year four men are employed; output rises to 80 tons. The extra output from using four men instead of three is only 10 tons (see Fig. 5.3). This is an example of diminishing marginal returns to a factor. As more labour is used, output rises by successively smaller amounts. It is quite distinct from the case in which the amounts of *all* factors of production are allowed to change by the same amount. In this case the increase in output depends upon the presence of increasing or decreasing returns to scale; it is discussed below.

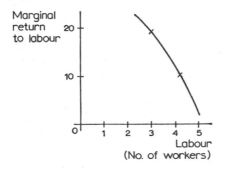

Fig. 5.3   The Law of Diminishing Returns

2   Costs – the firm's choice of how to produce

The organisation responsible for production is the firm, and the firm's choice of which particular technique of production to apply will be determined by the firm's objectives. To achieve a given level of output, the firm will be interested above all in achieving the lowest possible costs. We assume the firm is starting up production of the product and can make a free choice of all the available techniques, unencumbered by the results of any decisions made in the past. Which technique of production will the firm choose?

In general terms, the choice will depend upon the price of the factors of production, labour and capital. If the price of labour is low, in a low-wage economy, firms will want to employ a larger quantity of labour and less capital equipment than they will in a high-wage economy. We can show this precisely using the techniques already illustrated in Fig. 5.1. Suppose the price of labour (the wage) is £2000 per man per year, and that the cost of capital is 20%, so that for each £100000 of capital equipment £20000 must be set aside to cover interest charges, depreciation and *normal profit*. [Normal profit is the profit required to keep firms operating in an industry. It depends upon the degree of risk involved and may vary from industry to industry.] For simplicity we assume the firm has to choose between techniques A, B and C. We can work out the cost of each of these techniques in the following table:

Table 5.1

Technique	A	B	C
No. of workers	100	75	50
Cost of labour	£200 000	£150 000	£100 000
Quantity of capital	£1 000 000	£1 500 000	£2 500 000
Cost of capital	£200 000	£300 000	£500 000
Total costs	£400 000	£450 000	£600 000

The firm will choose technique A, which uses more labour and less capital equipment than either of techniques B and C. But suppose the wage rate were £6000 per year instead of £2000. The cost table would then be as follows:

Table 5.2

Technique	A	B	C
No. of workers	100	75	50
Cost of labour	£600 000	£450 000	£300 000
Quantity of capital	£1 000 000	£1 500 000	£2 500 000
Cost of capital	£200 000	£300 000	£500 000
Total costs	£800 000	£750 000	£800 000

Technique B is now the cheapest, and will be chosen by a firm minimising its costs. If the wage rate were even higher, then technique C, which uses most capital and least labour, would become the favoured technique.

3   How costs vary with output – total cost, average cost, marginal cost

The previous section has shown how the firm's choice of production technique depends upon the prices of the factors of production which the firm uses to produce its output. We now assume that the prices of the factors of production – the wage rate and the price the firm has to pay for the use of its capital equipment – are constant and we see how the total costs of production change as the level of output increases. For each output level the firm uses the technique of production which minimises its costs at that output level. We have already seen how the firm makes its choice in order to achieve the output level of 1000 units per week. This gives us the minimum cost of producing one thousand units of the product. To discover the minimum cost of producing 2000 units, we repeat the procedure in the previous section and discover which point on curve DE in Fig. 5.2 is associated with the lowest total costs. With a wage rate of £2000 per annum and a charge for the use of capital of 20%, this may be the combination of capital and labour represented by F in Fig. 5.2; 180 workers and £2 000 000 of capital equipment. Thus the lowest possible costs of producing output levels of 1000 and 2000 units can be presented in the following table:

Table 5.3

Output level	Quantity of labour	Cost of labour	Quantity of capital	Cost of capital	Total cost
1000	100		£1 000 000		
		£200 000		£200 000	£400 000
2000	180		£2 000 000		
		£360 000		£400 000	£760 000

These data can be represented on a graph, as in Fig. 5.4. The horizontal axis shows the level of output, and the vertical axis shows the lowest cost of producing it. We could calculate the lowest cost of producing other levels of output as in Table 5.4, and represent those costs on Fig. 5.4. This will give us the total cost curve, as shown in Fig. 5.4.

Two features of this deserve special attention. The first is that doubling the size of output does not necessarily mean that the costs of production are doubled. In this particular case, doubling the level of output from 1000 to 2000 units has led to an increase in costs of slightly less than double, from £400 000 to £760 000. The reasons for this are discussed below. Secondly, when the level of output is increased, it may no longer be desirable to combine the factors of production (capital and labour) in the same proportion as before. In this case, the higher output level of 2000 units is produced (see Table 5.3) with twice as much capital as the lower output level of 1000, but the size of the labour force has less than doubled, from 100 to 180 workers. At a higher output level it may be cheaper to use the factors of production in a different combination than at a lower output level. Typically the change will be towards using relatively more capital.

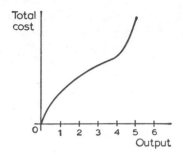

Fig. 5.4   A total cost curve

Fig. 5.4 shows the total costs of producing various levels of output. From this information the average cost of production, or the cost of producing a single unit, can readily be calculated. The data on which Fig. 5.4 is based are shown in the following table. (Note that average costs are usually calculated including an allowance for normal profit.)

Table 5.4

Output level	Total costs £	Average costs (Total costs ÷ output level)
1000	400 000	400
2000	760 000	380
3000	1 110 000	370
4000	1 460 000	365
5000	1 850 000	370
6000	2 280 000	380

Average costs per unit of output can then be shown in Fig. 5.5. We see from Fig. 5.5 and from Table 5.4 that average costs per unit first fall, as output increases from 1000 to 4000 units. Then as output expands beyond 4000 units, average costs start to rise. Fig. 5.5 illustrates the so-called U-shaped cost curve, with a single point at which average cost reaches a minimum.

We have now seen how to calculate total costs and average costs, and how to represent them in Figs 5.4 and 5.5. But a table such as Table 5.4 can furnish one other piece of information, the marginal cost of production. Marginal cost is defined as the extra cost incurred in producing a single extra unit of the product in question. Let us consider the following simple example. Suppose the total

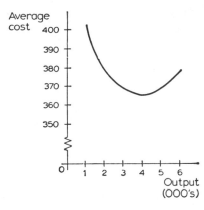

Fig. 5.5 An average cost curve

costs of producing various quantities of a commodity are as shown in the second column of the following table:

Table 5.5

No. produced	Total cost	Average cost	Marginal cost
1	11	11	11
2	19	9½	8
3	25	8⅓	6
4	30	7½	5
5	37½	7½	7½
6	48	8	10½

The average cost can be calculated as before, by dividing the total cost by the number produced. This is done in column 3. But we can also calculate the marginal cost of producing each item. For example, the cost of producing three units is 25; to produce four units costs 30. The extra cost incurred is therefore 30 minus 25, or 5. This is shown in column 4, which gives marginal costs.

We can now plot the marginal and average costs of our table on the same diagram. This is done in Fig. 5.6, which shows the relation between the average and marginal cost curves. When the average cost curve is falling the marginal cost curve lies below it. This is true in the figure for all output levels less than five units. Since the marginal cost of producing the fourth unit (say) which is 5, is less than the average cost of producing the first three units (8⅓), the average cost of producing four units is lower than for producing

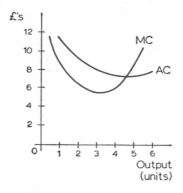

Fig. 5.6 Average cost (AC) and Marginal cost (MC) curves

three. Where the average cost curve in the figure levels out at a production level between four and five, it is because the marginal or extra cost of producing the fifth unit is equal to the average cost of producing the first four units. When the marginal cost curve lies above the average cost curve, at production levels of five or more, the average cost curve begins to rise. These are numerical relationships of great importance, as will become clear in later chapters, and they apply to all average and marginal cost curves. To recapitulate:

1 when the average cost curve is falling, the marginal cost curve lies below it;
2 when the average cost curve rises, the marginal cost curve lies above it;
3 when the average cost curve is flat, the marginal cost curve passes through it.

4   Increasing and decreasing returns to scale

Why should the average cost curve be of the shape illustrated in Fig. 5.5? The explanation is to be found in the character of the production process, which transforms inputs into outputs. It is not necessary that, in order to increase output by a given factor, all inputs be increased by the same factor. In the first place, some operations which are necessary for production need be done only once, whatever the level of production required. For example, the preparation of design drawings and building of prototypes must be done either for a single example of most engineering products, or for an immense series of them; successive units do not require the duplication of the design work. Instances where part of the costs of production is independent of the scale of output are called *indivisibilities*, as they may not be lessened (or divided) if output is reduced. Most development and design costs come into this category.

A second reason for declining average costs is that for physical reasons it may be cheaper to work on a large scale. The classic example of this is to be seen in the use of tankers and other containers of ever-increasing scale. The capacity of a tank is its cubic capacity; as the dimensions of the tank are expanded the capacity increases faster than does the area of the walls of the tank. Unless the walls have to be drastically thickened the capacity increases at a faster rate than the costs of production, so that the unit costs are lowered. The existence of these savings from increased dimensions accounts for the enormous expansion in the size of oil tankers. Once the technical problems of building and manoeuvring large vessels were overcome, it became possible to lower the unit costs of transporting oil by using super-tankers.

In addition to these two sources of *economies of scale*, there may be a tendency for average costs to fall from the use of better or more specialised techniques at a higher output level, or from the *learning effect* of higher production levels. The learning effect occurs when the work-force masters the operations it has repeatedly to perform in the production process, and can therefore carry them out faster. This lowers the costs per unit of output. A famous instance of this was observed at aircraft factories in the United States. It was noticed that as each aircraft was produced, the labour time necessary to produce it declined. By learning the operations required of them, the work-force continually reduced the time needed to produce each plane.

These factors explain the fall in average costs illustrated in Fig. 5.5 as output levels increase from 0 to 4000 units. However, after 4000 units the average costs as shown in Fig. 5.5 begin to rise, and beyond 4000 units there are diseconomies of scale. Why should this be so? The reason is that, as well as the forces mentioned above which tend to lower unit costs, there are other forces which tend to raise them. The actual shape of the average cost curves depends upon the joint impact of the forces pulling in opposite directions. In Fig. 5.5 the factors leading to a reduction in average costs predominate up to an output level of 4000 units. Thereafter the opposite factors are more powerful and average cost rises. The factors leading to diseconomies of scale are as various as those tending to economies of scale. In some processes, for technical reasons, a higher output leads to higher average costs. Management of a larger organisation may be more complex and relatively more costly. And labour relations may be worse in a large factory or organisation. All of these reasons may cause average costs to rise as output expands beyond a certain point.

A substantial amount of research has been done into the question of whether economies of scale exist, and how large they are. For example, an economist at Cambridge University, C. F. Pratten, has examined twenty-five industries in the United Kingdom in order to establish the level of output needed to exploit economies of scale and achieve lowest average production cost. He called this the *minimum efficient scale of production*. He then estimated the increase in average costs of manufacture which would arise if a plant of capacity equal to one-half of the minimum efficient scale were used; for example, in oil refining, the minimum efficient scale of a new general-purpose refinery is 10 million tons per annum, but in a refinery of half that capacity, refining costs per unit would increase by 27%. His results for selected industries are shown in the following table.[2]

Table 5.6

Activity or product	Minimum efficient scale of output	Percentage increase in unit costs at factory of half minimum efficient scale
General-purpose oil refinery	10 million tons p.a.	27
Production of sulphuric acid (new plant)	1 million tons p.a.	19
Manufacture of polymer	80 000 tons p.a.	23
Beer (new brewery)	1 million barrels p.a.	55
Bread (new bakery)	30 sacks per hour	30
Detergent (new plant)	70 000 tons p.a.	20
Cement plant	2 million tons p.a.	17

The results show increases in average costs from halving the level of output in a plant which are always significant and in some cases (beer, for example), very substantial indeed.

The reader may have noticed an implication of these findings on economies of scale which seems to contradict ordinary observations about business conditions: if the minimum efficient scale for producing a particular product is very high – as it is, for example, for the production of bread in a new bakery – then how can a small bakery survive, when its average costs will be higher? More generally, if there is a single scale of output for a firm at which average costs are lowest, as our Fig. 5.5 suggests, what accounts for the survival of firms of different sizes? Some writers have drawn from the existence of firms of different sizes in an industry the conclusion that the average costs of all these firms must be the same, and that economies of scale are not a significant factor. However, this assumes that competitive conditions are such that no firm can survive unless its average costs are at the minimum level possible. But in many cases, as we shall see later in Chapter 8, this is not true. When markets are not competitive, firms may be producing with different levels of average costs, earning different rates of profit.

5 The long run and the short run

In the previous sections it was assumed that the firm was able when minimising its costs to choose quite freely the quantities of the factors of production it would use to achieve the desired level of output, and to combine them in any possible way. But is this always realistic? When a firm is building a new plant, it has a free choice. For any desired output level it can select the technique of production and quantities of labour and capital which will keep total costs as low as possible. But when the firm has decided for what scale of output to build and incurred other costs such as the installation of machinery, then the firm is, to a degree, the prisoner of its early decisions. Many of the costs will still be the same whatever the actual level of output, whether it is lower or higher than the output level originally expected.

The distinction being made is between the firm's area of freedom in the *long run* and in the *short run*. In the long run, the firm can adjust the amounts of all the factors of production it uses. It can install or scrap capital equipment, it can extend or rebuild the whole factory. The long run is defined in this way; its actual length varies with the nature of the industry. In industries where plant and equipment take a long time to order and install, the long run will be longer than in industries where inputs of all factors of production can be varied more easily. So the actual duration of the long run for a particular industry cannot be assessed with great precision. It can be ten years or more in the case of such industries as electricity generation.

The short run, by contrast, is the period within which the use of some factors of production cannot be varied: it is fixed by earlier decisions. Thus, in the short run the firm's costs fall into two categories, *fixed* and *variable*. (In the long run all costs are variable.) Most capital costs are fixed in the short run. If a firm has capital equipment installed in a factory, it has to incur most of the costs of that capital whether it is actually in use or not. The only cost saved is on actual wear and tear of machinery. The costs of borrowing the money to buy the equipment, and the loss of value from obsolescence, are incurred in any case. The costs of labour, on the other hand, are usually counted among variable costs. If output declines, a firm can adjust the size of its labour force by declaring workers redundant, rehiring them if orders improve. But even labour cannot be discarded or engaged at will. Extensive redundancies may involve heavy redundancy payments or may lead to industrial disruption which imposes a cost on the firm involved. Workers may acquire special skills at their place of work; if the firm dismisses them and subsequently replaces them with other workers who have to be taught the special skills, the firm will again incur extra costs. As is so often the case in economics the distinction between two categories, in this case fixed and variable costs, is quite straightforward in principle, but more difficult to use in specific cases.

The existence of costs which are fixed in the short run means that firms are not always able to use the combination of factors of production which they would have chosen if they had expected the level of output which actually materialises. They may have either more or less of the fixed factors than they would like. So in the short run their total costs may be higher than they would be in the long run, when the input of all factors is adjustable. There will be two cost curves: the long-run total cost curve, which we have already encountered, and the short-run total cost curve which is shown, together with the long-run total cost curve in Fig. 5.7.

The shape of the short-run total cost curve can be explained as follows. Some costs are fixed, whatever the output level. Even if the output level is zero, those costs will be incurred. (On the long-run cost curve, if output is zero then all factors of production are dispensed with and no costs are incurred.) The short-run total cost curve has a single point in common with the long-run total cost curve – point A in Fig. 5.7. If the firm has correctly predicted the output level and uses the quantities of factors of production appropriate to that output level, then the short-run total costs will be exactly equal to the long-run total costs. To the right of A, the quantities of fixed factors are too low for the output level. The technique of production being used is not the best one, and short-

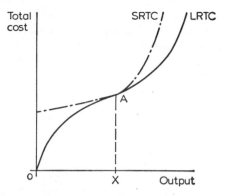

Fig. 5.7 Long-run (LRTC) and short-run (SRTC) total cost curves

run total costs are higher than long-run total costs. This may arise where a firm underestimates the level of output it will want to maintain and installs too little capital equipment. To produce the higher output the equipment must be used too intensively, and average costs are higher than they would have been if more capital equipment were available. With the supply of capital fixed, extra labour used in production runs into diminishing returns: each successive unit of labour added yields a progressively smaller increase in output. This causes total costs to rise more and more steeply.

Corresponding to the short-run total cost curve, there is a short-run average cost curve, obtained by dividing short-run total costs by the level of output. This is illustrated in Fig. 5.8, together with the long-run average cost curve, which we have met in Fig. 5.5. Since

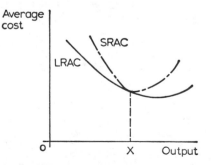

Fig. 5.8 Long-run (LRAC) and short-run (SRAC) average cost curves

short-run total costs are greater than long-run total costs for any level of output except one (that is the output level OX in Fig. 5.7), the same is true of average costs. In Fig. 5.8, the short-run and long-run cost curves have only one point in common, at the output level OX.

Now the short-run total cost curve in Fig. 5.8 is drawn on the basis of a fixed and given input level of at least one factor of production. Had the firm chosen a different input level for that factor of production, then the short-run total cost and average cost curves would be different. Had the firm installed more fixed capital, its average costs for higher levels of output would have been lower than those already shown, while for lower output levels costs would be higher. This case is shown in Fig. 5.9, in the short-run average cost curve SRAC II. Conversely, if less capital equipment were instal- led, average costs would be lower for low levels of output, but at higher levels costs would rise very sharply, as capital equipment is overused. This is shown by SRAC III in Fig. 5.9. Corresponding to each level of fixed factors there is a short-run cost curve; and each short-run average cost curve has a single point in common with the long-run average cost curve.

Similarly the short-run marginal costs of production can be calculated. These show the extra costs of producing one more unit of output, assuming that at least one factor of production is used in a fixed amount. The relation between short-run average and short- run marginal costs is the same as that between long-run average and marginal costs (see pages 72–4 above). It is illustrated in Fig. 5.10.

The distinction between the long run and the short run is an important one. It captures the idea that a firm is to a certain extent

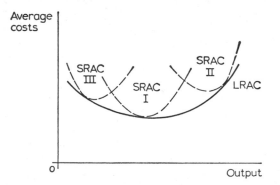

Fig. 5.9   Three short-run average cost curves corresponding to different levels of fixed factors

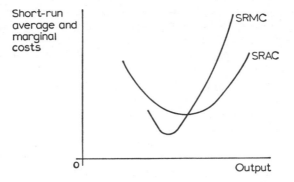

Fig. 5.10 Short-run average cost (SRAC) and marginal cost (SRMC) curves

limited in its freedom of action by the decisions it has taken in the past. Only over an extended period of time can a firm escape from these limitations, and dispense with or acquire more of the factors of production which are fixed in the short run. This has implications for a firm's business policy. Suppose that the price of the product the firm makes falls, so that the total costs of producing any level of output exceeds the revenue the firm will get from selling it. The firm will operate at a loss. At first sight it may seem to be in the firm's interest to cease production forthwith. But remember that the firm is employing some factors of production which it must pay for whatever the level of output; for example, it will still have to pay for the capital which it cannot dispose of. This means that it will still incur some expenditure even if it does shut down, and these losses may be greater than those it would incur by producing and selling some output. In fact in the short run, the firm should carry on producing providing that it covers the variable costs – the payments to factors of production it can dispense with at will. The fixed costs will have to be paid in any case.

This argument applies to the short run. In the long run, over the time period in which capital equipment wears out or can be sold, the firm will cease production. No firm will install new capital when it expects to make a loss on production over an extended period.

6   The multi-product firm

In seeking to explain the size of firms, it is useful to distinguish between economies of scale, economies of scope and economies of expansion. As noted above, an economy of scale arises when the average cost of production falls as a firm produces more of a good.

Economies of scope arise when it is cheaper for one firm to produce specified quantities of each of two or more goods than for a separate firm to make that amount of each good. Economies of scope promote multi-product not single-product firms.

One obvious scource of economies of scope is the case of joint outputs. It is cheaper to produce calves and milk together than separately. Other situations arise when a single piece of capital equipment is used to provide two or more services, for example local telephone calls and long distance or trunk calls. There may be economies in management costs available from producing multiple outputs.

The third form of economy is economy of expansion. The economist, Edith Penrose, in her illuminating book, *Theory of the Growth of the Firm*,[3] has stressed that there may be economies which relate to the dynamic process of expansion itself, quite apart from economies associated with the state of being bigger (economies of size or scale). Economics has traditionally stressed economies of size – bigger oil refineries and motor assembly plants – but the advantages arising from growth are also important.

. It must be remembered that many firms are multi-product, producing a range of goods and services, each of which may be quite different. Such firms are described as *diversified*. The cigarette manufacturers are a very good example. Without exception all the producers of leading brands have diversified into other products - drinks, snacks, cereals, packing for industrial, food and domestic use, labelling. The products of such diversified firms are often made in different factories by separate divisions or subsidiary companies, each with its own management. Thus although the economies of scale discussed earlier in this chapter may help us to understand what determines the size of a factory or plant manufacturing only one of the items just listed, it does not explain why a firm manufactures all these things. To understand the size of firms we also need some explanation of diversification.

This is found in the concept of *economies of expansion*. These arise from the process of expansion itself and do not refer to economies connected with any particular size of operations. An oil refinery or a motor-vehicle assembly line, once built, will continue to yield its economies of scale. They will last as long as the plant. However, the economies of expansion are not enduring. The advantages arise simply from getting started but once the expansion is completed, the firm will not enjoy any special advantages over competitors of equivalent size. For example, a motor-vehicle manufacturer may decide to diversify into the manufacture of refrigerators. This decision may be taken since it already has a substantial knowledge of mass production and marketing methods relevant to refrigerators, derived from its experience in motor vehicles. A firm without such knowledge would take longer to get started and face greater risks. Even if it hired the best experts as managers and consultants to help, it would be difficult to evaluate the quality of advice it received. The recruiting of advisers could be a slow and cautious process. By contrast the motor-vehicle manufacturer would be well placed to act quickly if the opportunity arose – for example the chance to take over a refrigerator firm. The advantages of expansion in this sense are strategic rather than technological.

Once established, the refrigerator division of the motor manufacturer may be no different in operating costs from other comparable refrigerator manufacturers. It may even be possible to detach the refrigerator division from the motor manufacturer and operate it as an independent company without any increase in costs. This assumes, of course, that there are no significant economies achieved by sharing certain facilities such as research staff or sales offices, etc. Thus the 'Frigidaire' refrigerator division of one of the largest vehicle manufacturers in the U.S., General Motors, does not produce the cheapest refrigerators in America, but ones that are comparable in price and quality with those of its major competitors. The decision to diversify into refrigerators can be explained not in terms of economies of size but economies of expansion.

It may therefore be possible, by diversification, for firms to overcome the limitations to their growth imposed by the markets in which they traditionally operate. It was this for example that prompted much of the diversification in the tobacco industry. The choice of products reflected existing contacts and skills in the industry. For example, food and drink, which included everything from cake mix and cat meat to scotch and soda water, could be marketed in much the same way as cigarettes. 'A marketing machine', is how the Chairman of the American cigarette firm Philip Morris described its operations. If the limits of a particular market can be overcome by diversification, it is relevant to ask in the first place why firms do not expand at an unlimited rate and diversify into all products and, secondly, how the continuing existence of small firms can be explained.

There are two aspects of the firm which set limits to the extent and rate of diversification – (*a*) the firm as an administrative and planning unit and (*b*) the firm as a collection of resources. Limits arise from demands on (*a*) above, created by the training and planning necessitated by expansion, which may overburden existing staff. So much time may be absorbed by the tasks of diversification that current operations may be neglected. The hiring of extra staff to relieve the problem is itself restricted by the organisation's existing capacity for recruitment and training.

The firm's 'collection of resources' includes not only equipment and personnel but also patents, trade secrets, access to markets, contacts with both suppliers and customers and the goodwill associated with existing products. Although these resources may be redeployed in ingenious ways to help the firm diversify the direction of diversification may be restricted by the specific qualities of the resources available. Thus the cigarette manufacturers in our example may be able to diversify without undue strain into lines such as foodstuffs and packaging but find it more difficult to break into the construction of nuclear power plant. A firm that diversifies into a product about which it knows nothing in terms of technology or marketing and has neither contacts, nor favourable access to information in the field, may encounter severe difficulties. It may make some expensive mistakes, even if diversification in very unlikely directions is feasible. It may be very costly in terms of the time and resources required to collect and evaluate information. This suggests there are limits to the extent of diversification. These arise not so much from the diseconomies associated with size itself but with the rate of growth. The internal factors discussed here, as well as competition from other large firms, may limit a firm's capacity to diversify. Particularly in an expanding economy, this always leaves gaps in the market which can be filled by small firms. Even if there are economies associated with larger productive units, small firms may still be able to compete by offering specialist or 'one-off' goods which cannot be mass produced.

Summary

The techniques of production a firm chooses will be largely determined by the relative prices of the factors of production it uses: the firm will normally choose that technology which minimises cost of achieving a given level of output. As a firm's output level changes, the minimum cost of production will vary. This variation is reflected in the long-run total cost curve, from which long-run average and marginal cost curves can be derived. The shape of the long-run average cost curves reflects the presence of increasing or decreasing returns to scale in production, and empirical evidence points to the existence of significant increasing returns to scale. While in the long run a firm can vary its inputs of all factors of production, in the short run only some of these can be varied. Thus a firm will have short-run total, average and marginal cost curves corresponding to any given level of inputs of factors of production fixed in the short run. These concepts are used in the next chapter to show how levels of output and prices are determined in the market.

As a firm can grow by diversification, an understanding of the economies of expansion is essential. The limits to this process arise from, (*a*) the firm as an administrative and planning unit, and (*b*) the firm as a collection of resources. The capacities inherent in both these aspects will determine for any given firm the profitable limits to the rate and direction of diversification.

Questions
1 Define and describe the sources of internal economies of large scale production. In view of such economies, how do you account for the continued existence of small firms? (Associated Examining Board, A-Level Economics)
2 How do the factors determining the average cost of production differ in the short run from the long run? (Southern Universities Joint Board, A-Level Economics)
3 Large plants tend to have more strikes, higher absenteeism and a larger proportion of indirect or non-productive staff. If this statement is true does it mean that there are only diseconomies of scale and no economies of scale? (Institute of Chartered Secretaries and Administrators, Economic Policies and Problems)
4 How do firms decide what combinations of factors of production to use? (Oxford Local Examinations, A-Level Economics)
5 When describing the technological relationship between inputs and outputs, economists use two terms: (i) the law of diminishing returns, and (ii) returns to scale. Distinguish, giving examples where possible, between these two concepts. (Institute of Chartered Accountants of England and Wales, Foundation Examination)

Notes
1 L. Cookenboo, Jr., in Townsend, H. (ed.), p. 200, *Price Theory* (Penguin, London, 1971).
2 Taken from Pratten, C. F., *Economies of Scale in Manufacturing Industry*, pp. 269–77 (Cambridge University Press, London, 1971).
3 Penrose, E., *Theory of the Growth of the Firm* (Wiley, New York, 1959).

6

Consumer Behaviour

Introduction

A chief aim of economic activity is consumption. Hence the study of consumer behaviour is a major preoccupation not only of firms and corporations which offer commodities for sale to consumers but also of the government which is concerned with the standard of living, or levels of consumption, of the population. In this chapter we will look at a breakdown of consumption of various commodities and analyse how consumption decisions are made. To do so we will first of all discuss consumer behaviour at the level of the individual, and then turn our attention to the combined effects of the behaviour of all the consumers in the economy.

We shall try to answer questions such as these: How does a consumer decide how to allocate his income? What factors influence his choice of consumer goods? How is the demand for a commodity affected: (*a*) by its price; (*b*) by the price of other products; (*c*) by the income level of consumers? What effect does a government decision to alter the rate of taxation on goods have on the demand for them? What effect does advertising have on the behaviour of consumers? Is advertising in the consumer's interest, or does it benefit only producers?

1   A first look at consumer behaviour

Currently, about 60% of the United Kingdom's *Gross Domestic Product* goes on consumers' expenditure. (The UK Gross Domestic Product in any one year is the total value of goods and services produced in that year. It is discussed further in Chapter 12.) The way in which the total is broken down into major categories of consumption has changed substantially in the post-war period. Discounting the effects of inflation, consumers' expenditure on food has increased only slightly, while expenditure on alcohol and tobacco, durable household goods, and cars and motor-cycles has increased dramatically. The proportion of *retail sales* (i.e. sales from shops) in total consumer expenditure has consistently declined in the post-war period, as the pattern of spending has altered.

This information is taken from data on total expenditure, as reported by returns from organisations selling to consumers. Another source of information on consumer behaviour is the Family Expenditure Survey, through which the government collects detailed figures on the expenditure of a sample of households of various types. For example, the Family Expenditure Survey for 1987 shows that a family with two children with a household income of £250–£375 per week allocated its consumption expenditure as in Table 6.1:[1]

Table 6.1

Commodity or Service	£	Percentage of Expenditure
Housing	37.32	16.5
Fuel, light and power	11.28	5.0
Food	47.52	21.0
Alcoholic drink	8.90	3.9
Tobacco	4.35	1.9
Clothing and footwear	18.04	8.0
Household goods	17.40	7.7
Household services	9.08	4.0
Personal goods and services	8.54	3.8
Motoring expenditure	29.52	13.0
Fares and other travel costs	4.53	2.0
Leisure goods	13.75	6.1
Leisure services	14.32	6.3
Miscellaneous	2.20	1.0
	226.73	100.2

These facts on aggregate expenditure on consumption in the United Kingdom or on the average pattern of spending of households of a particular type derive ultimately from millions of decisions taken by individuals. How can we get behind statistical evidence of this kind and penetrate the decision process of the individuals concerned? Clearly, no two individuals or households will make identical spending decisions, however similar their circumstances. These decisions reflect the tastes and preferences of a particular person, and tastes vary in ways which cannot be explained by an economist. This may seem to lead us to a dead end. If a consumer's decisions are determined by his tastes and if we cannot explain his tastes, then it may seem that we can say nothing about consumer behaviour. There is, however, a way round this impasse. We can assume that an individual has given tastes, and then analyse how he is likely to behave in response to changes in the circumstances in which he has to exercise choice. The basic assumption we make is that consumers behave rationally, and make their decisions consistently on the basis of their preferences. To some even this assumption may seem unrealistic but a partial answer can be made to these doubts. If consumers do not, every time they make a purchase, go through an elaborate process of rational choice, then in many cases this may be because much spending is of a routine or repeated character, and the original decision may have been based on a careful evaluation of alternatives.

2   How the consumer chooses – the individual demand curve

The basic consumption unit in the economy is the household. A household may be a single individual or a group, usually a family, which pools its resources and makes its consumption decisions as a unit. We shall refer to the decision unit simply as 'the consumer', although it will often be a household of two or more people.

Consumers are limited in what they are able to buy by their incomes. Each consumer is subject to a 'budget constraint' – a limit set on possible purchases by the financial resources of the consumer. There is some flexibility in the budget constraint because the consumer can borrow, but such loans must be repaid, and we shall assume that the budget constraint is fixed in any particular period.

The budget constraint only puts an overall limit upon what the consumer can buy. It still leaves a substantial margin of choice as there are many combinations of goods which satisfy the budget constraints. Consumers choose from amongst these alternatives in accordance with their tastes. Consumers tend to maximise the satisfaction they get from their purchases. It has become customary in economics to refer to this satisfaction as *utility*. This word has rather unfortunate overtones of practicality, even of ugliness, but we shall follow the usual practice and use it here.

No one can measure a consumer's utility directly – not even the consumer can do so. You can say that one bundle of goods gives you more satisfaction or utility than another, but it is impossible to assign a definite numerical value to the utility gained in each case. There is no agreed base point or scale for the measurements of utility as there is, for example, for the measurement of temperature. Utility is an entirely subjective concept as it reflects only the tastes and preferences of the individual consumer.

Logically, if a consumer is maximising his utility, he will arrange his purchases in such a way that the utility provided by the last pound of expenditure on each good which he buys is the same. If this were not so, the consumer could increase his utility by rearranging his purchases. For example, suppose that a consumer was in a position where the last pound of his expenditure on food yielded less utility than his last pound of expenditure on housing. Then obviously he would be better off by reducing his expenditure on food and increasing it on housing, and then continuing to switch expenditure in this way until the utility gained from his last pound of expenditure was the same for both goods.

This important result is known as the principle of *equi-marginal utility*. It can be set out in the form of the following relationship. At a consumer's utility maximum,

$$\frac{\text{The marginal utility of X}}{\text{Price of X}} = \frac{\text{The marginal utility of Y}}{\text{Price of Y}}$$

(Here, the marginal utility of a good is the utility provided by the last unit consumer.)

By rearrangement, this relationship can equally well be expressed as

$$\frac{\text{The marginal utility of X}}{\text{The marginal utility of Y}} = \frac{\text{the Price of X}}{\text{the Price of Y}}$$

This principle is a logical consequence of utility maximisation whatever the tastes of the consumer. It implies nothing about the particular goods which a consumer will buy.

There is, however, another aspect. The prices at which a consumer buys goods are observable quantities, as is the income of the consumer, which sets a limit to what he can buy. We can analyse the way in which a consumer with given tastes is likely to behave in the face of changes in prices or the income he can dispose of. This is the core of the economic analysis of consumer behaviour.

The influence of these factors is shown in the demand curve, which relates the quantity of a good which a consumer will buy to the price at which the good is sold. The consumer is assumed to be buying goods in proportions and quantities which miximise his utility subject to a constraint on the income he can spend.

The demand curve D_1D_1 in Fig. 6.1 shows a negative relationship between price and quantity demanded. When the price is high, demand is low; when the price falls, demand increases. This corresponds to the facts of casual observation about our own and other people's behaviour in the face of price changes when income remains constant, but we shall see in a moment that an upward-sloping demand curve indicating that more is bought as the price rises is in fact a theoretical possibility.

The demand curve in Fig. 6.1 is drawn on the basis that the consumer's income and tastes and the prices of all the other goods which he buys are held constant, while only the price of the good in question varies. How would the demand curve be affected if the consumer's income changed? The demand curve would shift from D_1 D_1 in Fig. 6.1 to a new curve such as D_2D_2. This new curve lies outside D_1D_1, and therefore indicates that at any given price level the quantity demanded is greater at the new income level than at the old. This outward shift of the demand curve is one that is normally associated with an increase in income, as a consumer will want to buy more of a good when his income goes up if all his other circumstances are unchanged. However, this need not be the case. For some commodities it is a *reduction* in income which pushes a demand curve outwards from D_1D_1 to D_2D_2. Consumers buy more of these commodities when their incomes fall.

The explanation of this apparently odd situation is that there are some commodities which people buy at low levels of income, but

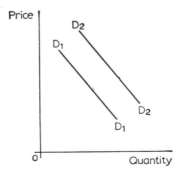

Fig. 6.1 Two demand curves corresponding to different income levels

which they abandon in favour of a more expensive substitute when their incomes rise. Conversely, if incomes fall, they revert to their original position, in which they buy more of the cheaper product. Cheaper cuts of meat may be an example of this kind. If a family's income falls it may consume more cheaper cuts rather than less, as it is using them in place of more expensive substitutes. Thus a fall in income shifts the demand curve outwards. Another example is remould tyres. Goods having the property that as incomes fall consumers buy more of them are called *inferior* goods as they are inferior substitutes for a more expensive alternative which consumers buy when they can afford to.

We have seen how a change in income may shift the whole demand curve from a curve such as D_1D_1 to another such as D_2D_2. This gives us a basis for expanding the explanation of the shape of any demand curve drawn on the basis of a constant level of income with only the price allowed to vary. Both the curves in Fig. 6.1 arc downward sloping, which is the normal case: when the price falls, the quantity consumed increases. This is the result of two factors. When the price of a product falls people switch to consuming more of it, and away from the now relatively more expensive alternatives. This substitution effect increases consumption. But there is another effect as well. If the price of a commodity falls, it is as though the income of any person consuming it had risen. The consumer can buy all that he did before, and still have some money left over for additional spending. This extra income, or its equivalent in increased purchasing power, gives rise to an income effect, as the consumer adjusts his consumption levels of all commodities to that appropriate to a higher income level. If the commodity is not an inferior one, the income effect of a price rise will cause a consumer to buy more of a product whose price has fallen, and this will reinforce the substitution effect which, as we have seen, always causes the quantity demanded to go up as price falls. The two effects operate in the same direction and together ensure that the demand curve is downward sloping.

However, we have seen that in the case of an inferior good the income effect will operate in the reverse direction: if a consumer's income rises he will demand less of that commodity. In this case the impact of a price fall on quantity demanded is no longer so certain. The substitution effect alone, as before, will induce the consumer to demand more of the good. But the fall in price has raised the consumer's income, and since the good is an inferior one the income effect causes him to demand less. The overall effect of a price change is the result of these two opposing forces. It is theoretically possible for the demand curve to slope upwards, as it does in Fig. 6.2, if the income effect is dominant; that is, if the good is sufficiently inferior for the income effect to outweigh the substitution effect. Goods of this kind which are so strongly inferior that they have an upward-sloping demand curve are called Giffen goods after Sir Robert Giffen, a nineteenth-century economist who claimed to have noticed this effect in Ireland in connection with the demand for potatoes. As the price of potatoes fell, the demand for them also fell, according to Giffen's observations. This was because the fall in the potato price raised incomes, in equivalent terms, to a point where the population could afford meat. Conversely a rise in the potato price caused incomes to fall (in equivalent terms) and forced consumers to switch from meat to potatoes. Giffen's observations have been questioned, and few convincing examples of Giffen goods can be cited. So although an upward-sloping demand curve is a theoretical possibility we are justified in ignoring this case for practical purposes and working with the conventional downward-sloping curves of Fig. 6.1.

Fig. 6.2   The upward-sloping demand curve of a Giffen good

In this section we have isolated three basic factors on which the individual's demand for a commodity depends. It depends upon his tastes, which we were not able to analyse; it depends upon the price at which the product can be bought, and this dependence is expressed by the demand curve D_1D_1 in Fig. 6.1; it depends upon the consumer's income, and a change in income will cause a shift in the demand curve from the original curve D_1D_1 to a new curve such as D_2D_2. In the following sections we shall consider ways of measuring the effect on demand of income and price changes and analyse the effect of other factors on demand.

3 The total demand curve

A manufacturer will not be able to concern himself with the demand curve of each of the millions of consumers who buy his product. He will be concerned with the overall or total demand curve, which shows how the total quantity demanded by all consumers collectively responds to a change in price. The relationship between the individual demand curves and the total demand curve can be presented fairly simply.

Let us take the case of two consumers, A and B. Each will have given tastes, which will almost certainly be different. Each has to choose a combination of purchases of X and Y, which satisfies his budget constraint: he cannot spend more than his income. If we take the price of Y as given, and vary the price of X, then we can draw an individual demand curve for each of them, as we did in Fig. 6.1. Fig. 6.3A shows A's demand curve, Fig. 6.3B shows B's demand curve. Figs 6.3A and B show, for example, that if the price of X is £2 per unit, A will buy 15 units of X and B will buy 20 units of X. Thus between them they will demand a total of 35 units. This information can be entered on Fig. 6.3C which shows that, at a price of £2 per unit, total demand is 35 units. From Figs 6.3A and B we also see that, at a price of £1 per unit, A will demand 20 units of X and B 30 units – a total demand of 50 units. This information can also be shown on Fig. 6.3C. By repeating this exercise we can work out the total quantity of X demanded at any price and establish any point on the total demand curve shown in Fig. 6.3C.

However large the number of consumers, we can always add up their individual demand curves in this way to find the total demand curve. The resulting total demand curve will then demonstrate how the change in price affects demand for the product, when all other factors are held constant. It is important to grasp the distinction between a movement along a given demand curve and a shift in the demand curve. A movement along a demand curve occurs when all other factors (principally consumers' tastes and incomes) are held constant, and only the price of the good in question varies. But if these other factors are changed, there will be a shift in the demand curve. For example, if households' incomes generally rise, then the demand curve will normally shift outwards, unless the good in question is an inferior good. Equally, a redistribution of income amongst consumers would probably have the effect of shifting the demand curve in some way. Finally, if the price of another good changes, it may have the effect of shifting the demand curve illustrated in Figure 6C, outwards or inwards, as people would readjust their purchases in the light of the new relative prices.

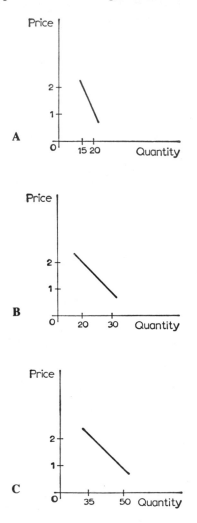

Fig. 6.3 The construction of a market demand curve (C) from two individual demand curves (A and B)

4 Price and income elasticities of demand

One very important property of the total demand curve is its steepness, for this indicates how responsive the quantity demanded is to a change in price. This will be of great significance to a manufacturer, for example, who will want to know how much extra demand there will be for his product if he lowers his price, or how much less he will be able to sell if he raises it. Again let us take two examples. In Fig. 6.4A we see that the total demand curve is such that if the manufacturer drops his price from £10 to £9 per unit his sales increase from 1 000 000 units to 2 000 000 units. In Fig. 6.4B, by contrast, a similar reduction in price raises sales by only 50 000 to 1 050 000.

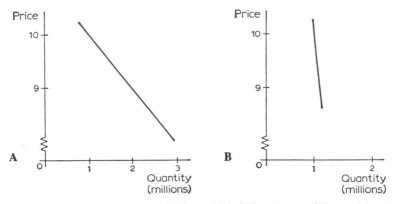

Fig. 6.4 Demand curves exhibiting a high (A) and a low (B) elasticity of demand

The usual way of measuring how responsive demand is to price is by calculating the so-called *price elasticity* of demand. The price elasticity of demand is the proportionate change in quantity demanded divided by the proportionate change in price. For example, in our first case, illustrated in Fig. 6.4A, we have the following figures:

$$\text{Percentage change in quantity} = \frac{2-1}{1} \times 100$$

$$= 100\%$$

$$\text{Percentage change in price} = \frac{10-9}{10} \times 100$$

$$= 10\%$$

$$\text{Price elasticity of demand} = \frac{\text{Percentage change in quantity}}{\text{Percentage change in price}}$$

$$= \frac{100}{10} = 10.$$

For the case illustrated in Fig. 6.4B we have the following figures:

$$\text{Percentage change in quantity} = \frac{1\,050\,000 - 1\,000\,000}{1\,000\,000} \times 100$$

$$= 5\%$$

$$\text{Percentage change in price} = \frac{10 - 9}{10} \times 100 = 10\%$$

$$\text{Price elasticity of demand} = \frac{\text{Percentage change in quantity}}{\text{Percentage change in price}}$$

$$= \frac{5}{10} = \frac{1}{2}.$$

Contrary to what one may expect, a straight-line demand curve does not exhibit the same price elasticity of demand along its whole length. This can be demonstrated from Fig. 6.4A. Suppose that price falls again, from 9 to 8 per unit, and quantity rises again by the same amount as before, from 2 000 000 to 3 000 000 units. We now have the following figures:

$$\text{Percentage change in quantity} = \frac{3 - 2}{2} \times 100\% = 50\%$$

$$\text{Percentage change in price} = \frac{9 - 8}{9} \times 100\% = 11\%$$

$$\text{Price elasticity of demand} = \frac{50}{11} = 4\frac{1}{2}.$$

It is always true that, as in this case, the price elasticity of demand falls as we move down a straight line demand curve. Moreover, exactly half way down the straight line demand curve, the price elasticity of demand exactly equals 1. At this point, any proportionate increase in price is exactly compensated for by an equal proportionate decrease in quantity demanded, maintaining total revenue constant. Above that mid-point, the price elasticity of demand exceeds 1, and an increase in price will lower revenue.

Below that mid-point, the price elasticity of demand is less than 1, and an increase in price will increase revenue.

When a given percentage increase in price causes a high percentage increase in quantity demanded, as in Fig. 6.4A, we say that elasticity of demand is high or demand is elastic. When the quantity response to a price change is low, the demand is said to be inelastic. One would expect different goods to have varying price elasticities of demand. Let us take the case of a fairly staple food such as bread. There are no very close substitutes for bread, and one therefore expects that if the price of bread is raised then the quantity bought would remain roughly the same. Some wastage may be eliminated, and some families may substitute other foods for bread, but demand would remain substantially unaffected. In other words, demand for bread is fairly price inelastic. For other commodities we would expect demand to respond more to a price change. If the prices set by a single car manufacturer rise by 10%, while those of his competitors remain constant, then customers will switch to a rival product and demand will fall substantially. If it fell by 50%, the price elasticity of demand would be 50/10 or 5. This explains why a government may seek to impose a special tax or tariff on imported cars. They become more expensive, while prices of domestically produced cars are unchanged. Consumers may then switch in large numbers from buying imports.

Some estimates of the price elasticity of demand are presented in a later section. First we will introduce the concept of the *income elasticity* of demand.

Price elasticity of demand is calculated by holding everything else – income and other prices – constant, and varying the price of the commodity in question. Similarly we can hold all prices constant, varying income alone, and examine how demand responds to an income change. Again we use the elasticity measure: we calculate the percentage change in demand in response to a given percentage change in income. For example, suppose that levels of income rise by 10% and the proportionate change in demand for a particular commodity, bread say, rises by 5%. The income elasticity of demand for bread is then calculated:

$$\text{Income elasticity of bread} = \frac{\text{Percentage change in demand}}{\text{Percentage change in income}}$$

$$= \frac{5}{10} = \frac{1}{2}.$$

In other words, using the figures in our example, when income rises by a given proportion, expenditure on bread will rise, but it will rise by proportionately less, so that consumers will spend a smaller fraction of their income on bread. This is because bread is a necessity for which consumption needs are limited. When income rises consumers will be able to divert more of their incomes to other items of expenditure. Research has shown that as incomes rise people spend a smaller proportion of them on food as a whole. In other words, the income elasticity of demand for food is less than one. This is known as Engel's Law after Ernest Engel, one of the pioneers of social statistics. The law is supported by British post-war experience. Expenditure on food has grown much more slowly than consumers' incomes.

An extreme case occurs where the income elasticity of demand is negative. This is a property of inferior goods, which, as the reader will recall from Section 2, were defined as goods with the property that, as income rises, the consumer buys less of them. Take the following hypothetical example. Suppose income rises by 10% and demand falls by 2%.

$$\text{Income elasticity of demand} = \frac{\text{Percentage change in demand}}{\text{Percentage change in income}}$$
$$= \frac{-2}{10}$$
$$= -1/5.$$

At the opposite end of the spectrum are commodities with an income elasticity of demand greater than one. For example, for a consumer durable such as a television set or washing machine we may find the following figures:

$$\text{Income elasticity of demand} = \frac{\text{Percentage change in demand}}{\text{Percentage change in income}}$$
$$= \frac{20}{10}$$
$$= 2.$$

Commodities with income elasticities of more than one are sometimes called *luxuries*, as they are purchases to which consumers devote a higher proportion of their incomes as they become better off.

5 The measurement of price and income elasticities

There is clearly much scope for economists to measure the price and income elasticities of demand for various commodities. But before presenting these results a number of qualifications must be mentioned. There are two basic ways of estimating the value of variables in economics. By one method, data covering the same variable are collected at different time periods and the variations are analysed. This is called the *time-series* method. To measure a price elasticity by this method we would collect information on the quantities of a commodity sold on two different dates, at which different prices have prevailed, and the difference in quantity sold would be explained at least partly in terms of the price change. By the second method we collect information for a number of different groups or individuals at the same time. For example, to measure an income elasticity we would collect information on the amount of a commodity bought by families at different income levels, and again the variation in quantities bought would be explained at least partly in terms of different incomes. This is known as the *cross-section* approach.

Now the problem arises that the price elasticity of a good should be calculated in a situation in which only the price of that commodity is changed, with consumers' levels of income and all other factors which influence demand held constant. If, using the time-series method, we collect data for market demand at two different periods, between which the price of the commodity has changed, then it is very probable that some of these other factors, which should be constant, will also have changed. For example; income levels will have changed, tastes may have changed, and the prices of other commodities may also have changed. So the change in quantity demanded will be the result of all these factors and not of the price change of the commodity alone. Similarly, if, when calculating income elasticities of demand, we use the cross-section method and collect information on the quantities consumed by various families at different income levels, we face the problem that there may be other differences between the families than simply the income level. For example, their tastes may be different, or the prices at which they buy the good may not be the same. The quantities purchased will be the result of all these factors, and not of income levels alone.

Economists and statisticians have devised means of dealing with this problem, but they are by no means perfect, and the results which they yield can only be considered as estimates, and not exact calculations. The real problem is that in economics it is impossible to set up a laboratory experiment to work out conclusive answers to questions which depend ultimately on human behaviour.

A very thorough recent analysis of consumer behaviour has been undertaken by Angus Deaton of Princeton University.[2] He analysed the demand for thirty-seven categories of expenditure, excluding consumer durables, using UK data from 1954 to 1970. A large number of price and income elasticities were calculated, using different techniques. For example, the results show that in 1963 the income elasticities of demand range from −2.33, for domestic service, to +3.88 for electricity. Of the thirty-seven goods, nine were inferior, with negative income elasticities, and eleven were necessities with an income elasticity of demand of between 0 and 1; this group included seven categories of foods. The remaining seventeen were luxuries with an income elasticity of demand in excess of 1; these included recreational goods, wines and spirits and expenditure abroad. The analysis revealed substantial variation in price elasticities. For example, the price elasticity of demand for cigarettes and tobacco was shown to be 0.149. In other words, a 10% increase in price would reduce demand by about 1.5%. This figure is of some significance from the point of view of taxation. Indirect taxes on alcohol and tobacco are an important source of government revenue. If the government raises the tax on cigarettes, say, it will want to know how much the increase in price will affect the quantity of cigarettes sold, and therefore the revenue accruing to the government. Thus the government suffers from a conflict of interest. On one hand it wishes to raise revenue through taxation, and has an interest in buoyant sales of cigarettes, which yield substantial revenue. On the other hand, it wants to protect its citizens from the harmful personal and social effects of smoking, and therefore wants to restrict consumption. This issue, of course, raises the question whether consumers should be allowed to or are able to make their own decisions about what they will consume, uninfluenced by outside bodies. We return to this point at the end of the chapter.

6 Shifts in the demand curve – substitutable and complementary goods

When price elasticity of demand is calculated, all other factors influencing consumer choices are assumed to be constant, and only the price of the commodity in question is varied. It is now time to look at some of these other factors. One of them, income levels, has already been considered, and the concept of income elasticity of demand introduced. A change in income causes not a movement down the demand curve, but a shift in the demand curve for a commodity. Even when the price of that commodity is unchanged, demand may increase or decrease if the income of consumers changes. The whole demand curve shifts either to the right or to the left, as in Fig. 6.5. But such a shift can be brought about by other factors.

Among these other factors influencing consumer behaviour, one of the most important is the price of other commodities. Let us consider, for example, the effect of a change in the price of butter on demand for margarine. Clearly, butter and margarine are alternatives or substitutes. Buying more of one will usually mean buying less of the other. If the price of butter falls, then, even if the price of margarine is constant, demand for margarine will contract. The demand curve will shift to the left from D_1D_1 to D_3D_3 in Fig. 6.5. This is a characteristic of goods which are substitutes: a decrease in the price of one good will cause a decrease in demand for another. Other examples of substitutes are travel by car and travel by rail; holidays at home and holidays abroad; the purchase of a washing machine and the use of a launderette.

But not all commodities are substitutes. Some goods are usually consumed in conjunction with others, so that if the price of one good of the pair falls, the result will be not a fall but a rise in the demand for the other good. For example, if the price of cameras decreases, the demand for film will rise even if its price remains constant. The whole demand curve for film will shift to the right from D_1D_1 to D_2D_2 in Fig. 6.5. Such combinations of goods are called *complementary*: the effect of an increase in the price of one of them is to

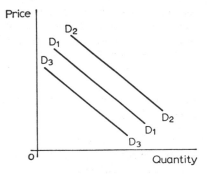

Fig. 6.5 Shifts in the demand curve

decrease demand for the other, and vice versa. Other examples of such pairs of goods can be cited: cars and petrol; whisky and soda; cigarettes and matches; television sets and television licences. All these are examples of complementary goods.

As we have seen, the possibility of shifts in, rather than movements along, the demand curve complicates the problem of measuring price elasticities of demand. The existence of substitutable and complementary relations between commodities is one cause of such shifts. Another possible cause is a change in the tastes of consumers. This aspect is of particular significance since one of the sources of a change in consumers' tastes is the deliberate activity of manufacturers to alter tastes and preferences through such methods as advertising.

7   How free is the consumer's choice? Advertising and information

Another source of a shift in the demand curve for a product is the manufacturer's deliberate decision to make it better known or more attractive to the customer, through advertising. *Advertising* can be defined as *mass paid communication, intended to influence consumers to the benefit of the advertiser*. Usually it is designed to sell goods and services, but it may also be designed to influence opinion in other ways, through political advertising, for example. The amount of resources given to advertising in advanced capitalist countries is surprisingly large – in the UK in the 1980s about 1.4% of national income was spent on advertising. The figure for the United States is slightly higher (about 1.5%). Heavy expenditure on advertising is a result of the economic system adopted as well as the level of economic development. The formerly socialist countries of eastern Europe devote only a fraction of the proportion of national income to advertising that the advanced capitalist countries do. But even among those countries there are marked differences, with those with a more rigidly centralised system, like the USSR, spending less on advertising than those like Hungary which have always given more independence to firms and production units.

In general terms, the intention of the advertiser can be stated quite simply. It is to influence consumers to buy more of the product at the prevailing price, or to shift the demand curve to the right, from D_1D_1 to D_2D_2 in Fig. 6.5. This will enable the producer to make a larger profit and at the same time to be re-imbursed for the cost of the advertising campaign. From the producer's point of view, advertising is a strategic weapon in the struggle he wages against competitors in the market. The way this weapon is used is discussed in Chapter 8, which considers the market situation from the point of view of the producer. In this chapter we are concerned with the consumer, and the way advertising affects his decisions.

At the beginning of this chapter we assumed that the consumer chose rationally which goods to buy in order to maximise his utility. In making this supposition we assumed he had adequate knowledge of the properties of each of the commodities he was offered. Now, to the extent that advertising imparts information about products, it helps the consumer to make a better and more soundly based choice. But not all advertising is merely informative; some of it may be designed to influence choice on irrational grounds, without imparting new information.

The supporters of this distinction between informative and persuasive advertising argue that some forms of advertising, for example classified advertisements in newspapers or announcements of new products in trade newspapers, merely inform potential consumers of the availability of products and of their properties, while persuasive advertising furnishes no useful information for making a rational choice but tries to influence consumers to buy products by, for example, associating the product with other desirable properties, such as wealth, a happy family life, or good looks. Other economists have denied the distinction between informative and persuasive advertising, arguing that even information is specially selected to make a persuasive point, and that to describe the information contained in allegedly persuasive advertisements as not useful is to make an unjustifiable value judgement. Our view is that a distinction exists and can readily be made in extreme cases, but that a clear dividing-line between the two categories cannot be drawn in intermediate cases. The reader should form his own opinion after examining a number of advertisements on television and in newspapers.

In theory, the existence of persuasive advertising makes no difference to our analysis of consumer behaviour. We assumed tastes to be fixed, but did not stipulate that they must be fixed independently of the skills of advertising agencies. A new advertising campaign may change tastes, and is of course intended to do so, and thereby bring about a shift in the demand curve. But, as we have seen, it is only one of many factors which may shift the demand curve. A change in income levels, a change in the price of substitutes or complements, or a change in tastes not due to advertising will also shift the demand curve.

However, there is a cost to the consumer in advertising, inasmuch as expenditure on advertising is another cost to be recouped in the selling price of the product. If the advertising serves no useful purpose for the consumer and is designed merely to shift demand from a product made by one firm to an indistinguishable one made by another, then the consumer's welfare suffers. Moreover, since competitors retaliate, a firm does not gain by raising advertising expenditure. When the Monopolies Commission investigated the British market in household detergents in 1965, their report took the view that expenditure on advertising and promotion in the industry, amounting to between a fifth and a quarter of manufacturers' costs, was too high, and they recommended a reduction in the price of the goods accompanied by a reduction in advertising costs. This is an exceptional case, but in other industries as well it can be argued that promotional expenditure is wasteful and acts to the detriment of the consumer.

There is a second and wider argument about the effects of advertising. Although, formally speaking, advertising makes no difference to the analysis of consumer choice, it does raise the important question of how free the consumer's choice really is. If the consumer works out his preferences and makes his choices independently of any outside influence, then we can say that the consumer is sovereign. Consumers collectively determine what is produced. This property of consumer sovereignty is claimed for market economies, in contrast to centrally planned economies where output levels are fixed by the state. But if the consumer has his tastes managed and manipulated by the producer, through advertising, then the pattern of production does not correspond to the independent preferences of consumers, but to the requirements of profit-seeking producers. In this case the producer is sovereign, not the consumer.

Many economists now argue that in affluent capitalist societies producer sovereignty is important. At low levels of income, the possibilities for manipulating consumer tastes are small. No advertising campaign will persuade a starving man to buy an expensive consumer durable. But once basic wants are satisfied the scope for persuasion increases. Critics of the power of large corporations contrast the weakness, isolation and limited knowledge of the individual household with the power and strength of the large corporation which seeks to influence the consumer's tastes. This is a vital question in the assessment of different and competing economic systems, capitalist and socialist.

Summary

Consumption decisions are made by individuals or households with the aim of achieving the highest possible level of satisfaction, or utility, for the consumer. The level of utility achieved is not measurable, nor can the economist explain the tastes of an individual consumer. However, the consumer's decisions as to what to buy are effected through a market, and are constrained by observable quantities such as the prices of commodities and available income. The influence of these factors on quantities purchased can be analysed and measured.

A basic tool for this analysis is the *individual demand curve*, which shows the quantities purchased by an individual at different prices. Individual demand curves can be added together to show the quantities purchased by all consumers taken together corresponding to different prices. This is the *market demand curve*. Commodities can be classified according to the degree of responsiveness of quantity purchased to price changes, using the price elasticity of demand as an index. When responsiveness is large products are said to show a high price elasticity of demand; when the effect of a price change is minimal, the product is said to be price inelastic.

If consumers' incomes rise, there will be a change in quantities purchased, even if prices are unaltered. Again, commodities can be classified according to the direction and extent of the change in demand in response to a change in income. The index of responsiveness is called the income elasticity of demand. If consumers buy more of a product as their incomes rise, the income elasticity is positive. If consumers buy less as their incomes rise the income elasticity is negative and the good is called inferior.

Thus, a change in incomes is one of the factors which may cause a shift in the market demand curve. The demand curve for a product may also shift in response to a variation in the price of another product which is consumed either as a substitute for or as a complement to the product in question. Another factor which may alter the demand for a product without an alteration in its price is advertising by the product's manufacturer. The advantages and disadvantages of advertising are a hotly debated subject on which economists often disagree. For some, advertising is an information service provided to the consumer, to assist him in making his spending decisions. According to others, advertising raises the cost to the consumer and enables the producer to manipulate consumer preferences.

Questions

1 'The demand for a commodity will usually be greater the lower
the price, other things unchanged'. Explain why this is so and
discuss the significance of 'other things unchanged'. (Associated
Examination Board, A-Level Economics)

2 (*a*) What do you understand by the concept of elasticity of
demand?

   (*b*) Describe the factors which may affect the elasticity of
demand.

   (*c*) Using diagrams explain what is meant by the terms: (i)
elastic demand, (ii) inelastic demand, and (iii) unit elasticity of demand.

   (*d*) What use might a supermarket manager make of the
concept of elasticity of demand?

   (Institute of Chartered Accountants in England and Wales,
Foundation Examination)

3 Explain what is meant in the theory of consumer behaviour by
the terms 'normal', 'inferior' and 'Giffen' goods. Are Giffen
goods likely to be observed in practice? (Welsh Joint Education
Committee, A-Level Economics)

4 What determines market demand? Illustrate with a diagram.
(Institute of Cost and Management Accountants, Foundation
Stage)

5 'Expenditure on advertising is a waste of scarce resources.'
Discuss. (University of London, A-Level Economics)

Notes

1 *Family Expenditure Survey for 1987*, Table 11 (HMSO, London 1989).
2 Deaton, A., *Models and Projections of Demand in Post-War Britain*
(Chapman and Hall, London 1975).

7

Determination of Price: Perfect Competition and Monopoly

Introduction

Our discussion of how markets work in Chapter 3 simply assumed the existence of supply curves and demand curves and identified the questions we need to ask about a market equilibrium on that assumption. Later, in Chapters 5 and 6, we examined the supply side and demand side more fully, by analysing firm and household behaviour. We are now in a position to bring together the results of these two chapters and study the equilibrium prices and quantities which will emerge in different types of markets.

Naturally to do this we have to make further assumptions about what objectives firms have and how they behave. Moreover, the way in which price and output levels are determined depends crucially upon the nature of the market, particularly the number of firms supplying it. In this chapter we restrict our attention to two extreme cases of market structure, and examine only markets in which there is either a very large number of firms operating or a single firm. In addition we examine a third case which combines elements of competition and monopoly in a special way. These cases, as well as being interesting in their own right, lay the groundwork for the examination of other cases, which is done in the following chapter.

1 The firm and the industry

An *industry* is defined as *the set of firms producing a particular product*. This definition is relatively straightforward in principle, but it raises a number of serious difficulties in practice, as it is not always clear exactly how similar products must be for the firms producing them to be counted as being in the same industry. Let us take an example, the production of motor cars. It is usual to refer to the companies producing cars as the 'motor industry', but it is clear that not all the firms in the industry are producing the same product: Rolls-Royces, for example, are not the same product as inexpensive family saloons.

Government agencies concerned with collecting data on the levels of output of different sectors of the economy have developed classification systems for identifying particular industries. The best known of these, which is used in a modified form by the United Nations and other international organisations, is the *Standard Industrial Classification* (*SIC*). This system breaks down production into twenty-seven categories or orders which are then further subdivided into 181 *Minimum List Headings*. For example, mining and quarrying form one item in the initial breakdown, but in the further subdivisions particular branches of mining and quarrying, such as coal-mining and stone and slate quarrying, are distinguished.

This kind of classification goes some way towards defining the industry, but it does not really answer our purpose. The Standard Industrial Classification puts commodities in the same group on the basis of their similarities in production, while we are in fact more interested in the extent to which commodities serve the same purpose to the consumer. These two different principles of classification yield completely different results. For example, in the Standard Industrial Classification, carpets appear in the textile order, while other floor coverings are placed in another order. Yet from a consumer's point of view these two products are alternatives.

We need to define an industry from this point of view, because we are vitally concerned with the concept of competition in an industry or more generally with the exercise of power in a market. By a *market*, we mean *an arrangement whereby goods or services are exchanged for money*. The term originates from, and includes, a traditional street-market but is used more widely here to include *any* arrangement for the sale and purchase of goods. Thus the market is the link between the producers and distributors of the good on one side, and the consumers or users of the good on the other. When we speak of an individual or firm having *market power*, we mean that he can influence or control the terms and conditions at which goods are bought and sold. Market power can be exercised on either side of the market, by producer or consumer. In spite of the growth of organised consumer groups, in most cases markets are controlled, if they are controlled at all, by the selling side of the market, and it is the market power of firms we shall be concerned with in this chapter.

Market power has many dimensions, and the extent to which any individual firm can exercise it depends on many factors. But one crucial element is the number of firms in the industry. A firm which is the sole supplier of a product will clearly be in a better position to exercise market power than a single firm in an industry made up of an enormous number of small firms. In this chapter we shall examine the implications for price and output levels of different kinds of market structure. Firstly, we shall look at the way in which price and output levels are fixed in *perfectly competitive markets*: that is, markets in which the number of firms is very large indeed, so that no single firm can influence price and all firms take the price as given. Then we shall look at the opposite extreme, when only one firm supplies the market. This is the case of *monopoly*, a word made up from the two Greek words for 'single seller'. These two extreme cases form the limits between which any actual markets must fall, but in practice most industries are made up not of an enormous number of firms, or a single firm, but of some intermediate number. This case, to be considered in the next chapter, is that of *oligopoly* (from the Greek words for 'few sellers'). This is the most realistic case, and perhaps for that reason, the most difficult to analyse. In doing so, however, we can use elements of the analysis of the extreme cases of perfect competition and monopoly contained in this chapter.

2 Profit maximisation and its implications

Firstly, we must give some thought to the objectives of the firm and its managers. In the previous chapter we considered chiefly technical matters – the choice of techniques, the relation between average cost and output levels. In this chapter we are examining the behaviour of the firm in the market, and we must therefore make some assumption about the goals and objectives of the firm.

Throughout this chapter we assume as a first approximation that the firm has as its objective the maximisation of profit, the difference between the costs of and the revenue from production. Now this is an assumption which can be attacked on a number of grounds. In the first place it is, in practice, ambiguous. Does it mean that the firm maximises its profits over a quarter (three months), or over a year or over the firm's whole lifetime? We should be specific on this point, as there may be a conflict between maximising short-run profits and maximising profits over a longer period. Secondly, a large modern corporation may have several objectives rather than the single one of profit maximisation. A large organisation may contain several important groups each of which has a separate objective. For example, the financial controller may want to maximise profits and the sales department to maximise sales. In this case the objective of the organisation as a whole will be a mixture of the goals of the component parts. Both of these objections are powerful ones, which have been briefly considered in Chapter 4. In this chapter, however, we assume maximisation of profit as a first approximation to the firm's more complex true goals, in the belief that profits play an important role in any situation. We further assume that the firm is maximising its profits in the short run.

For reasons which will become clear later on in this chapter, a firm which is maximising its profits will be vitally concerned with its revenue, or the proceeds which it can get from the sale of its product. The size of a firm's revenue depends on two factors – the amount of output which it sells, and the price at which it sells it. Both of these factors depend upon the demand curve of the consumers of the product, or the market demand curve. We analysed the market demand curve in Chapter 6, and showed it to be a line relating the amount of the commodity consumers were prepared to buy to the price at which the commodity was offered. A typical market demand curve is shown in Fig. 7.1.

Now this is the demand curve for the industry as a whole and not for the individual firms making up the industry. The demand curve for the latter, as we shall see in a later section, may well be a horizontal straight line, as represented in Fig. 7.2. If the firm's demand curve has this form, it means that the firm can sell any

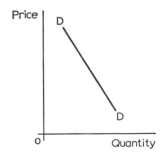

Fig. 7.1   A market demand curve

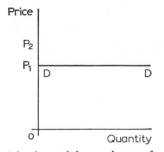

Fig. 7.2 A horizontal demand curve for the firm

amount of the product it desires to sell, at the price represented by P_1. If it were to raise the price to P_2, its sales would be zero. The horizontal or flat shape of the demand curve for this firm tells us this, and also has another important consequence. The firm can sell any extra units of output it chooses at the price at which it sold earlier units. If we define the money the firm will receive for selling one further unit of the commodity as the firm's marginal revenue, we can say that the marginal revenue is constant. Hence the demand curve in Fig. 7.2 can also be labelled the marginal revenue (MR) curve. The price is also, of course, the average revenue (AR) the firm receives per unit of output.

But this is not always so. Suppose the firm's demand curve is sloping downwards, as the demand curve or average revenue curve is in Fig. 7.3. (Note that Fig. 7.3 illustrates a demand curve for a firm, while Fig. 7.1 shows the demand curve for a whole industry.) In this case the firm must lower its price in order to sell more of its output. For example, a firm can sell 2 units of output at a price of £5 per unit, but if it is to sell 3 units, the price must be lowered to £4 per unit. Similarly, to sell 4 units, the price must be lowered to £3 per unit. We assume that as in the normal case the same price is charged for all units of output. In other words there is no price discrimination between different purchases. This means that in order to sell 4 units, the firm will not only get a lower price for the last unit of output, but will also have to take a cut in its revenue from the three earlier units. Thus the extra or marginal revenue the firm receives is lower than the price or average revenue it can charge. This is shown in the following table, from which Fig. 7.3 is drawn.

The top part of Fig. 7.3 shows the firm's average and marginal revenue; the bottom part shows total revenue. Total revenue reaches a peak at an output level of 3½ units (note that the same total revenue is received for 3 and for 4 units). Thereafter, total

Table 7.1

Units sold	Price or average revenue	Total revenue	Marginal revenue
1	6	6	6
2	5	10	4
3	4	12	2
4	3	12	0
5	2	10	−2
6	1	6	−4

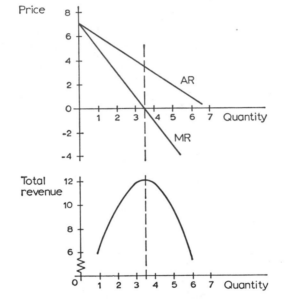

Fig. 7.3   Average revenue (AR), marginal revenue (MR) and total revenue curves

revenue declines, so that the marginal or extra revenue for further sales is negative. To the left of the dotted line in Fig. 7.3, the price elasticity of demand is greater than one. A 1% reduction in price leads to an increase of sales of more than 1%, so that total revenue rises. To the right of the dotted line the price elasticity of demand is less than one. A 1% reduction in price increases sales by less than 1%, so that total revenue falls. At an output level of 3½ the price elasticity of demand is exactly equal to one (the reader should verify these results for himself). This is another illustration of the proposition advanced in Chapter 6 that the price elasticity of demand falls as we move down a straight-line demand curve.

The concept of marginal revenue is one which we shall use extensively in order to show how different pricing and output decisions result from different assumptions about market structure. At this stage the important fact to note is that for a firm with a horizontal or flat demand curve, price (or average revenue) is always equal to marginal revenue, while a firm with a falling demand curve will always find that its marginal revenue is less than its average revenue.

3 Perfect competition – the short run

Four conditions must be satisfied for perfect competition to prevail. Firstly, each participant must be insignificant relative to the market. Second, each firm's product must be identical to the product of every other firm in the industry. Third, resources in the industry must be perfectly mobile and firms must be able to enter and exit the industry (see Section 4 below). Finally, each participant must have perfect knowledge of all market conditions.

The key assumption here is that each firm must be insignificant relative to the market and hence unable to affect the price at which the product sells. The ordinary meaning of competition in a market context is that firms are fighting with one another for custom, rather than agreeing with one another, openly or tacitly, on a joint strategy to take advantage of consumers. If a firm is very small relative to the market as a whole, it is unlikely to want or to be able to enter into collusive relations with other firms. This fact is the basis for the economist's definition of perfect competition. A key requirement for a market to be perfectly competitive is that no firm can influence the price at which the commodity is sold either by supplying less or by supplying more of the product. In other words,

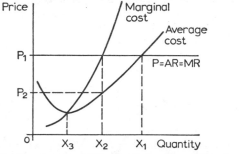

Fig. 7.4 Short-run equilibrium for a competitive firm

the firms must face a demand curve for their output which is flat or horizontal (see Fig. 7.4). The point is often made by saying that the firm is a *price-taker*. At the prevailing market price the firm can sell any amount of output that it likes; if it raises its price it will sell none; if it lowers its price it will attract all the demand for the product which, since the firm is a small unit, it will be unable to satisfy.

This does not mean that the demand curve for the whole industry is flat. The demand curve for the industry will almost invariably be downward sloping, as illustrated in Fig. 7.1. But this is not inconsistent with a horizontal demand curve for the firm, for in perfect competition each firm only supplies a tiny portion of the industry market. Each firm sees only a minute portion of the industry demand curve close to the market price in an enormously magnified form, and since each firm is producing only a tiny fraction of total industry output, that magnified segment of the industry demand curve seems, as it were, horizontal to the individual firm. Indeed it is horizontal, as each firm can sell any units of output at the going price.

We can now examine how the perfectly competitive firm will behave, when faced with a particular horizontal demand curve. Since the price at which the firm can sell is not affected by the level of production, the horizontal demand curve also shows the average revenue the firm receives from the sale of its output, and the marginal, or extra revenue it receives from each successive unit. These are identical as each successive unit is sold at the same price as each of the previous units. We indicate this in Fig. 7.4 by writing:

Price (P) = Average Revenue (AR) = Marginal Revenue (MR).

Fig. 7.4 indicates the revenue the firm receives per unit of output, but the firm's decisions will also be based upon its level of costs. We can illustrate this in Fig. 7.4 by superimposing the firm's short-run average and marginal cost curves. (Remember that in this section we are dealing with the short run only.) We can now show how the firm will choose its output level in the light of the demand curve it faces and the cost conditions under which it operates.

Let us first consider the output level X_1. At that point the firm's average costs are equal to P_1, which is also the average revenue the firm receives. Since average costs and average revenue are the same the firm is just breaking even, making neither a loss nor a profit. This may seem at first glance to be the output level the firm would choose. But let us examine it more closely.

Since the firm can adjust its output level to any desired level, it will want to examine whether its profits would be increased by raising or lowering its output by one unit. If increasing output by one unit will improve the firm's profits, it will provisionally decide to increase its output by one unit, and then, at the higher proposed output level, see if a further increase in output will yield an even larger profit. Now suppose the firm initially selects output level OX_1. By how much will its profit be increased if it increases or decreases production by one unit? We must inspect the firm's marginal cost and marginal revenue at that point, for the extra profit or loss the firm will make is the difference between these two magnitudes. At OX_1, marginal cost is above marginal revenue: this is clear from Fig. 7.4. The firm has made a loss on the last unit it produced. By reducing its output it would eliminate this loss.

A firm will be able to increase profits by reducing production at any point where the marginal cost curve lies above the marginal revenue curve. Conversely, wherever marginal revenue is above marginal cost, the firm will make a larger profit by increasing output. This is true, for example, of the output level OX_3 in Fig. 7.4. There is one point only where the firm cannot increase profits by either increasing or decreasing output; this is the point at which marginal cost and marginal revenue are equal. In Fig. 7.4 this occurs at output level OX_2. By lowering production below this level the firm would forego a possible profit; by increasing production above it the firm would incur a loss on its last unit of output. Hence OX_2 is the best level of output for the profit-maximising firm.

The firm does not consider the average levels of costs and revenue in deciding its output, but the marginal values. This applies to any profit-maximising firm in any situation, perfect competition or monopoly. However we have to look at the average values of costs and revenue to establish the level of profit the firm achieves per unit of output. At the best output level OX_2, average costs are equal to OP_2, while average revenue is OP_1. The firm's profit per unit is therefore P_1-P_2. This can be summarised in two sentences.

Firstly, the best output level for a profit-maximising firm occurs where marginal cost is equal to marginal revenue. Secondly, profit per unit is equal to the difference between average revenue and average cost at that output level.

We assumed the market price of the product to be given, and then analysed how the firm would choose its output level at that price. We must now consider how that price is fixed by the joint action of all suppliers and consumers in the market. In Chapter 6 we showed how the market demand curve was built up from the indidivual demand curves of consumers. We can also build up an aggregate supply curve of firms in perfect competition.

For the individual firm, the quantity supplied is fixed by the principle of setting marginal cost equal to marginal revenue. If the price of the commodity were higher, then, since we are assuming perfect competition, marginal revenue would also be higher, and the firm would set its output level accordingly. This is illustrated in Fig. 7.5. If the price were P_2 instead of P_1, then the firm in setting marginal cost equal to marginal revenue would increase its output from OX_1 to OX_2. Thus the firm's short-run marginal cost curve is its supply curve: it shows how much the firm will supply at different prices. (We are assuming that it is not more profitable for the firm to cease production altogether; in other words, we assume that it is covering its variable costs – see Chapter 5 above.) Now the supply curve for the industry is made up by adding together the supply curves of the individual firms. If, for example, there were 100 firms in an industry, each of them able to supply 1000 units of output at a particular price, then the industry supply at that price would be 100 000 units. In this way the industry supply curve can be built up, by adding together the supplies forthcoming from individual firms. Such an industry supply curve is shown by the curve SS in Fig. 7.6. Since the supply of output from each individual firm rises as price rises, as the marginal cost curve in Fig. 7.5 indicates, the same will be true of the industry supply curve.

Fig. 7.6 also illustrates the market demand curve DD. These two curves together determine market price. At price P_1 demand and supply are equal. Producers will together want to supply OX_1 units at that price, and consumers will demand OX_1. Thus demand will be equal to supply. If the price were P_3, demand would be at level OX_2, and supply at the lower level of OX_3. Producers would offer less than consumers wanted. Similarly at P_2, demand is less than supply. In the former case, with price level P_3, there will be pressure for

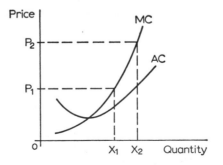

Fig. 7.5   Derivation of the firm's supply curve

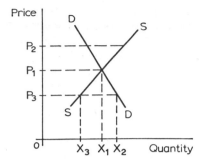

Fig. 7.6 Supply and demand curves for the industry

prices to rise to P_1; in the second case, prices will tend to fall to P_1. Only at P_1 is there no tendency for price to change. Thus P_1 is known as the equilibrium price: once it is established, there will be no pressure in the market to change it. The level of equilibrium price is determined by the sum total of decisions of individual consumers on one hand and of individual producing firms on the other.

The chief distinguishing feature of a perfectly competitive market is that the independent actions of the individual agents in the market jointly determine the price level of the product, while for each individual member taken separately the price level is something which he must take as given. The industry as a whole faces a downward-sloping demand curve, while each individual firm faces a horizontal demand curve. (It is for this reason that we have so carefully distinguished demand curves for the firm and for the industry.) This occurs because of the very large numbers of firms in the industry, none of which is large enough to affect the price of the product by withholding or extending its supply. The economist's technical definition of perfect competition thus merges into the ordinary definition. If no firm can affect price, then no firm can dominate the industry.

4 Perfect competition – the long run

In the previous section we have seen how the output levels of individual firms, and the price level, are determined in a competitive market with a large but fixed number of producers. Firms equate their marginal cost to the given price, and the collective supply curve of all firms taken together determines the price in conjunction with the market demand curve of consumers. Now we relax the assumption that the number of firms operating in the industry is fixed, and see what effect this has on our analysis.

In perfect competition we make the important assumption that there is nothing to prevent firms starting up production of the product and adding their output to that produced by existing firms. In other words, we assume that there are no barriers to entry into the industry. Of course, it takes a certain amount of time for a firm to build a factory, to buy equipment and put it into commission, and to engage a labour force. But in the long run a new firm will be able to complete the process of starting up production, and our long-run analysis should take account of this possibility.

In practice freedom of entry of new firms into particular industries may be restricted or even non-existent. In some industries there may be legal restrictions: for example in the United Kingdom no firm can set up to deliver mail in competition with the Post Office and the patent system operates to prevent some competition. In other industries there may be factors eliminating freedom of entry of a technical kind; for example existing firms may have occupied all the possible sites for a factory. In yet further industries already existing firms may pursue a deliberate policy of restricting entry by economic means, using, for example, a heavy advertising budget to make the costs of entry prohibitively high. (These factors are further discussed in Chapter 8.) However, in perfect competition we assume that the industry already consists of a very large number of small firms, all of which must have started up production at some stage. It is therefore quite logical to assume that entry to the industry is possible in the future.

What factors will attract a new firm to the industry? We are assuming throughout this chapter that the objective of existing firms is maximisation of profit, and we can make the same assumption of firms entering an industry. Firms will enter industries where the level of profits is higher than the normal rate for the economy as a whole. This normal rate is not zero, but it is the payment to businessmen and industrialists which is adequate to compensate them for the risks of investing capital in a business. In fact, this normal rate of profit can be regarded as a component of total costs, in the same way that payment to labour is a component of total costs. Thus when we draw cost curves we should include normal profits as part of costs. (The average cost curves in this chapter and Chapter 5 can be seen as including normal profits.) With this interpretation of the cost curve any extra profit the firm receives is *supernormal* or excess profit, and with free entry into the industry any supernormal profit is an attraction to new firms.

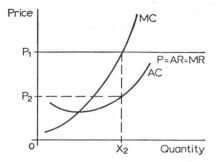

Fig. 7.7 Supernormal profits in the short run

Let us examine once again the short-run equilibrium position of a firm in perfect competition. In Fig. 7.7, equilibrium output level is OX_2, average revenue is OP_1 and average cost (including normal profit) is OP_2. Thus the firm is making a supernormal profit of P_1-P_2 per unit.

The prospect of making a similar profit will attract new firms to the industry. These firms will set up in business and add their output to that of the industry, operating on the same basis as the existing firms. The new firms will set their output level by equating their marginal costs to the price. Thus at any price level, the amount supplied by the industry will be larger than before, as the output of the new firms will swell the industry's total supply. In other words the industry supply curve will shift from S_1S_1 in Fig. 7.8, to S_2S_2. With the demand curve remaining where it was before, the new equilibrium price will be lower, at P_2.

This process will continue until the supernormal profits in the

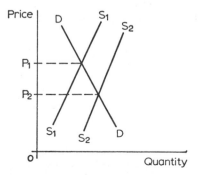

Fig. 7.8 The effect of an increase in industry supply on market price

industry have been eliminated. Until that time is reached new firms will continue to be attracted into the industry; the process will cease only when the price which each firm receives for output is equal to the average cost of production at that output level. But the firm is itself ensuring that price is equal to marginal costs, as this is a consequence of our assumptions that the demand curve for the firm is horizontal, and that the firm maximises its profits. Thus in long-run equilibrium, for the firm in perfect competition, two conditions should be fulfilled: firstly, price must be equal to average cost of production (otherwise new entrants will be attracted to the industry); secondly, price must equal marginal cost (otherwise the firm is not maximising its profits). Taken together these conditions imply that marginal and average costs are equal. We showed in Chapter 5 that this condition is satisfied only at the lowest point on the standard U-shaped average cost-curve. So we have shown that in the long run, the free entry of firms into an industry will ensure that each firm operates on the lowest point of its average cost curve. If the price ever rises above that level, new firms enter the industry and force it back down. The firm's long-run equilibrium position is illustrated in Fig. 7.9. Moreover, the industry supply curve in the long run is horizontal (see Fig. 7.10), as any extra output can be supplied at the same price simply by attracting a new firm into the industry, producing at the same minimum average cost as existing firms.

This is a remarkable result, which goes some way to explain the attraction to economists of the model of perfect competition. We have used a limited number of assumptions, of which the chief ones are that each firm has a U-shaped cost curve, that each firm maximises profit, that each firm faces a horizontal demand curve,

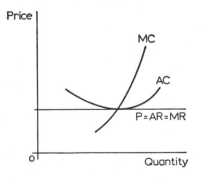

Fig. 7.9   Long-run equilibrium for a competitive firm

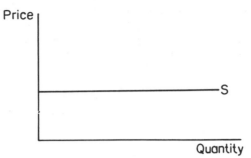

Fig. 7.10 The horizontal long-run supply curve for a competitive industry

and that there is free entry into the industry. On the basis of these assumptions we have shown that in the long run the forces of competition oblige each firm to operate on the lowest point of its average cost curve, as this is the only point where marginal and average cost are equal. From an efficiency point of view it is clearly desirable that commodities be produced as cheaply as possible. Our analysis has shown that in the long run perfect competition achieves this desirable result.

5   The pricing and output decision of a monopolist

Monopoly and perfect competition are the opposite extremes of the possible range of market structures. The perfectly competitive firm is one of a very large number of production units supplying the same market; its market power is non-existent. The monopolist in contrast is the only supplier of his product; the market power a monopolist can exercise is limited only by a combination of consumers of his output. [We ignore here the role of the government in controlling monopolies, which is examined in Chapter 10.] When the monopolist is producing consumer goods for sale to members of the public this opposing power is not organised and the monopolist can set his price or output level at will.

Since the monopolist is the sole supplier of the commodity, his demand curve and the demand curve for the industry are identical. There is no distinction between the demand curve for the firm and the demand curve for the industry, as there is in the case of competition. The monopolist will face a demand curve such as that illustrated in Fig. 7.11. We have seen earlier in this chapter that when the demand curve is sloping downwards the extra revenue the producer receives from selling one extra unit of output is not the same as the price he receives for that unit. This is because to sell one more unit the producer is forced to lower his price, and since he charges the same price for all units of output he loses a small amount of revenue on all his output. Hence the marginal revenue curve lies below the average revenue curve, as illustrated in Fig. 7.11.

We also showed in Section 3 of this chapter that any firm maximising its profits, whatever the market structure, will equate marginal cost to marginal revenue. Otherwise the firm will increase its profits either by raising or by lowering its output level. This is perfectly general, and applies equally to perfect competition as to monopoly. In order to find the output level a monopolist will choose, we must superimpose his marginal cost curve on the same diagram as the marginal revenue curve. This is done in Fig. 7.11.

The conventional U-shaped average cost curve (AC) is shown in Fig. 7.11 with its associated marginal cost curve (MC). The monopolist will choose the output level which makes marginal cost equal to marginal revenue. This is the output level OX. To establish the price the monopolist will charge we look at the average revenue curve (AR), which is the market demand curve. At the price level P_2, demand will be equal to OX. Hence the profit the monopolist achieves per unit of output is equal to $P_2 - P_1$, and the monopolist's super-normal profit is shown by the shaded rectangle in Fig. 7.11. Naturally in a competitive market this level of profits would attract new entrants to the industry, but we are dealing with a situation where there is only one producer and where entry is impossible.

We have now seen how the price level is fixed in a perfectly competitive market and in a monopolistic market. In both cases

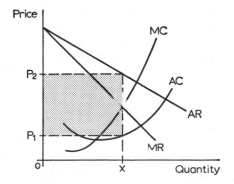

Fig. 7.11   The pricing and output decision of a monopolist

firms maximise their profit and equate marginal revenue to marginal cost, but because of the different shape of the demand curve and the possibility of entry in perfect competition the monopolist is able to gain and keep supernormal profits.

A further difference between competitive and monopolistic markets is the way in which they respond to a change in the basic factors determining the output level, such as the position of the demand curve. We can illustrate this by showing the effects of a shift in the demand curve in competitive and monopolistic markets. Let us deal with monopoly first.

Suppose that demand for the monopolist's product increases at each price level. This situation is shown in Fig. 7.12, where the demand curve has shifted from AR_1 to AR_2. The marginal revenue curve shifts to MR_2. In order to maximise his profits in the new situation the monopolist will again equate his marginal costs to marginal revenue. With the shift in the marginal revenue curve this condition is now satisfied at output level OX_2, instead of OX_1. By referring to the new demand or average revenue curve (AR_2) we see that in order to sell output OX_2, the monopolist will charge a price equal to P_2. This is above the earlier price level P_1. The shift in the demand curve has allowed the monopolist to raise his output and to raise his price.

Now let us consider the sequence of events in a perfectly competitive market. The shift in the demand curve initially causes the equilibrium market price to be raised, as in the short run the intersection of the new demand curve with the short-run supply curve takes place at a higher price and output level. This is illustrated in Fig. 7.13. The new demand curve D_2D_2 intersects the old supply curve at price P_2. However the new price attracts new

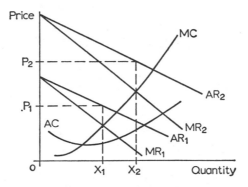

Fig. 7.12   The effect of an increase in demand when there is a monopoly

entrants to the industry, which shifts the supply curve to the right. This process continues as long as the price of the commodity remains above the lowest point of the average cost curve of the firms in the industry, for until this point is reached marginal cost and price lie above average cost, and the firm is making supernormal profits (see Fig. 7.7). Thus eventually the supply curve shifts to the right, as new firms enter the industry, until it intersects the new demand curve at exactly the same price that prevailed before. This position is reached when the supply curve has shifted to S_2S_2, in Fig. 7.13. The result is obtained because the possibility of a continually falling average cost curve (increasing returns to scale) is ruled out as inconsistent with perfect competition. If there were increasing returns to scale a single large firm, or a few such firms, would dominate the industry, as their costs would be lower and they would drive smaller firms out of business. If this happened, of course, the market would cease to be perfectly competitive in the sense intended here, and a different kind of analysis would become appropriate.

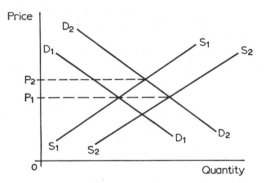

Fig. 7.13 The effect of an increase in demand when there is perfect competition

There is therefore an important difference between perfect competition and monopoly in the response of price to a shift in the demand curve. In perfect competition the price in the long run returns to its original level, which is set by the industry supply curve and based on the underlying cost conditions of the firms in the industry. In a monopolistic market the price is determined by a combination of demand and supply factors. A shift in demand alone is enough to alter the monopolist's equilibrium price.

6 Monopoly with price discrimination

In the analysis of monopoly above, we assumed that the monopolist charged the same price for all units of output. Some monopolists, however, may be in a position to practise *price discrimination*, that is, to charge a different price for different units of the same product.

The most complete form of price discrimination arises where the monopolist can charge a separate price for each unit of output sold (i.e. each purchaser pays different prices for successive units purchased, according to a scale which varies from purchaser to purchaser). If this applies, the monopolist's demand curve is also the marginal revenue curve, as every unit is sold for the maximum price any consumer is prepared to pay. Thus in this case the monopolist would produce at X in Fig. 7.14. Total revenue is the area OAPX and total costs are OSTX, so that profits are SAPT. A different price is charged for each unit.

Such cases of perfect price discrimination are rare. The more common case arises when a monopolist sells the same good at different prices to different types of purchaser. In this case the market consists of a number of submarkets or segments each with its own price. (For example, a producer may sell goods to foreign and domestic buyers.) A different price is charged for different segments of the market, though the price is uniform within each segment.

Fig. 7.15 illustrates this case on the special assumption that marginal costs are constant and identical in two market segments, A and B. Each part of the diagram shows the demand curve (D),

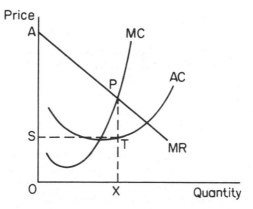

Fig. 7.14 Price and output with perfect price discrimination

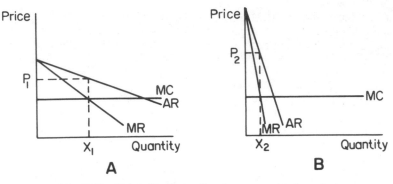

Fig. 7.15   Price discrimination in a segmented market

marginal revenue curve (MR) and marginal cost curve (MC) for the corresponding segment. In segment A, the firm maximises profits by producing X_1 units, which are sold at P_1; in segment B, X_2 units are sold at P_2. Generally P_1 and P_2 are unequal. The price will be lower in the segment where demand is more elastic.

Price discrimination is practised fairly widely. Electricity supply companies charge different rates for commercial and domestic users. Railways and airlines charge different fares at times of the day or week when people travel on business than when they travel for pleasure, or offer reductions in fares for students or retired people. In all these cases the firm exploits the segmentation of its market to earn larger profits.

7   Monopolistic competition

Before finishing this chapter, it is worth giving brief consideration to a market structure given the paradoxical name of *monopolistic competition* by the Harvard economist Edward Chamberlin, who introduced it in 1933. This refers to cases where many different firms produce commodities which are differentiated from each other in at least one respect, so that they are close but not perfect substitutes. Each firm faces the downward-sloping demand curve characteristic of monopoly, rather than the flat demand curve characteristic of perfect competition. At the same time, the products are sufficiently alike for any new entrant to reduce sales of existing firms. Thus each firm has a monopoly of its particular output, but this monopoly is qualified by the possibility that new firms may enter the market with products slightly differentiated from existing ones, which will reduce demand for the output of each existing firm.

This process is illustrated in Fig. 7.16. A firm operating in conditions of monopolistic competition faces a demand curve AR_1 and a corresponding marginal revenue curve MR_1. Its average and marginal cost curves are shown as AC and MC. To maximise profit the firm will produce where marginal cost equals marginal revenue (output level OX_1) and charge the price for that output indicated by the demand curve, OP_1. Since average revenue exceeds average costs, the firm is making supernormal profits.

Thus far the analysis is identical with that of an ordinary monopolist. However under monopolistic competition, new firms will enter the market with slightly differentiated products, and will reduce the sales of our existing firm. Its demand curve will move inwards, and will continue to do so as long as new firms are attracted by the supernormal profits; that is as long as average revenue exceeds average costs. The process ends when the demand curve reaches AR_2, which yields only normal profits at output level OX_2. At this output level it is also true that marginal cost equals marginal revenue, so the firm is maximising its profit.

This analysis carries the interesting implication that under monopolistic competition firms have excess capacity in equilibrium, in the sense that an increase in output would lower unit costs. This can be seen in Fig. 7.16, where the equilibrium output, OX_2, is less than the cost-minimising output. In this sense monopolistic competition

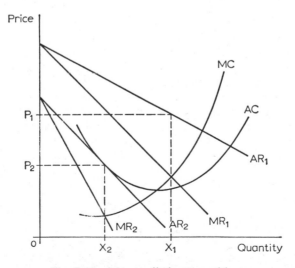

Fig. 7.16 Monopolistic competition

is inherently inefficient, and the source of the inefficiency is product differentiation which gives the firm's demand curves a downward slope. But for this feature, the appropriate analysis would be that of perfect competition given above.

Monopolistic competition is an interesting attempt to combine elements of monopoly and of competition and to bring the analysis closer to the real world of slightly differentiated products whose brand names are impressed upon the public by advertising campaigns. However the assumptions of many small firms and of freedom of entry are open to question, and in the case of many industries it may be more appropriate to recognise explicitly that the market is supplied by a small number of firms. This important case is analysed in the next chapter.

Summary

The demand side of the market is made up of consumers of a product, and the supply side by all the firms producing the particular good or service. These firms can be called the industry, and as a first approximation all firms can be assumed to have profit-maximisation as their objective. The price and output levels of the industry are determined by the interaction of the demand and the supply side of the market, although the outcome depends upon the structure of the market, particularly upon the number of firms which supply the product.

If the number of firms in the industry is so large that no individual firm can influence the price at which the product is sold, then it can be said that there is perfect competition. Each individual firm will fix its output level at the point where the marginal cost is equal to the price, and the price itself is determined by the demand curve and the industry supply curve. But if the price is at a level which gives the firms already operating a rate of profit above the normal rate, new firms enter the market and by increasing supply they lower the price level and restore the level of profits to the normal rate. This process of entry eventually forces all firms to operate at the lowest point on their average cost curves. If demand increases then the number of firms increases and not the amount supplied by each firm. Thus in the long run with freedom of entry the price is fixed by supply conditions, at the lowest point on the firm's average cost curve, and the level of output is determined by the demand curve.

At the opposite end of the scale from perfect competition is monopoly, where there is a single seller in the market. A profit-maximising monopolist will fix his output level at the point where his marginal cost is equal to the marginal revenue he receives from selling an extra unit of output. The marginal revenue is less than the price, because to sell an extra unit of output the firm will have to take a cut in the price it receives on its whole output, and not just on the final unit. The point where marginal cost equals marginal revenue determines the output, and the position of the demand curve then indicates the price which the monopolist can charge. The difference between the price received and average cost shows the extent of monopoly profit per unit. A monopolist who can practise price discrimination and charge different prices for the same output has even greater opportunities of making supernormal profits.

Finally, under monopolistic competition, a large number of firms compete, but with slightly differentiated products. With this market structure, new firms enter the industry if supernormal profits are being made, until the profit rate is restored to the normal one. In equilibrium, each firm operates with excess capacity.

Questions

1 What are the main characteristics of a perfect market? Assuming perfect competition exists, describe and explain the conditions necessary for equilibrium of the firm and industry. (Associated Examining Board, A-Level Economics)

2 How will the equilibrium of the perfectly competitive firm differ from that under monopolistic competition? (Southern Universities Joint Board, A-Level Economics)

3 Distinguish the pricing policy of a business in (*a*) competition, (*b*) monopoly. (Institute of Cost and Management Accountants, Foundation Stage)

4 'The fortunate monopolist can fix what price he chooses. But if he doesn't sell enough he doesn't gain, he loses.' Discuss. (University of London, A-Level Economics)

5 What economic factors would you consider to be most important in determining the price of fresh vegetables (i) in the long run and (ii) in the short run? (University of London, A-Level Economics)

6 In what circumstances is monopolistic price discrimination both practicable and possible? Illustrate your answers with reference to the pricing of first and second class rail travel. (University of London, A-Level Economics)

8

Oligopoly

Introduction

The previous chapter explained the operation of three types of market: the perfectly competitive market in which firms are price takers, the monopolistic market in which the firm is a price fixer and monopolistic competition. Although these models give us useful insights into real life situations, there are many markets in which they are inapplicable. In much of manufacturing the characteristic pattern is one not of many small competing firms or a single monopolist but of a few companies, perhaps half a dozen or so, which are in a prominent position with a major share of the sales, assets and profits in that market. The situation is said to be one of oligopoly, meaning 'few sellers'. The large firms may have the market to themselves or, as is common, share it with numerous smaller firms. Oligopolistic competition may be between firms making virtually identical products – for example the steel and chemical industry, oil refining, etc. – or it may be between products differentiated by advertising and design, such as cars, refrigerators and cigarettes. Each of these markets has its own characteristics, but a feature common to all of them is the interdependence between the actions of the competitors. This poses special problems for the economic analyst.

Measuring market structures

Before looking at the behaviour of firms in oligopoly markets, it will be useful to consider briefly the ways in which economists attempt to measure the characteristics of a market, known as *market structure*.

The possible impact on society of the concentration of market power has been a central theme of writers such as Marx, Schumpeter, Marcuse and Galbraith.[1] In contrasting ways these writers have attempted to analyse the consequences of the growth of large firms as instruments of modern capitalism. Marx saw the eventual breakdown of capitalism stemming in part from the growth of capital-intensive large-scale enterprise, while Schumpeter saw the big firms as ideally suited to the process of innovation and technical change. Marcuse and Galbraith stressed the all-pervasive nature of the modern corporation influencing values and life-styles. Central to these arguments is the question of evidence – the way in which market structures are measured.

As we have explained in the last chapter, market power has many dimensions and the extent to which any firm can exercise it depends upon many factors. It is clear from our discussion of perfect competition and monopoly that a crucial element is the number of firms competing in the market. Nevertheless as an index of competition, the number of suppliers may be misleading. A fifty-firm market may be less competitive than a ten-firm market, if in the former case a single large firm dominates, while in the latter market the competing firms are of equal size and strength. Thus economists studying market structure are concerned with both the number and size distribution of sellers. This measure is known as *market concentration*. The number and size distribution of buyers may also be important but often ignored because information is not available.

Numerous problems surround the construction of concentration indexes. These problems illustrate the difficulties which so often confront the economist in trying to obtain an unambiguous measure of the phenomenon to be studied. The interested reader is referred to Hannah and Kay's excellent study, *Concentration in Modern Industry* (MacMillan 1977). One of the key problems concerns the choice of the unit of measurement. The size of firms may be measured in terms of capital, employment or sales, each of which has limitations. Large firms are likely to be more capital intensive than smaller firms. Thus the capital measure of size will tend to overstate the significance of large firms, while the employment measure gives prominence to smaller firms. Two firms may be of equal size in terms of sales, but one may be in quite a different position because it undertakes the whole process of production, while the other only assembles parts made elsewhere. That part of sales known as net output or value added, which the firm actually produces itself, is a more relevant measure for some studies.

The ideal all-purpose index is yet to be discovered. A crude but commonly used measure is the *concentration ratio*, the percentage share of sales, employment, or some other unit of measurement held by the biggest firms. We distinguish between:

(*i*)   *Aggregate Concentration Ratio* – the share (usually of the 100 largest firms) in, for example, a country's total manufacturing output;

(*ii*)   *Market Concentration Ratio* – the share of the biggest five or six firms in a particular market.

Thus a 'five firm concentration sales ratio of 70%' means that the five largest firms supply 70% of market sales.

Competition among the few?

Both aggregate and market concentration have grown in the UK, although in recent years the levels have stabilised. According to a study by S. J. Prais[2] the share of the hundred largest firms in net output rose from 16% in 1909 to 43% by the 1970s. The importance of oligopoly in particular markets in the UK can be judged from the following figures for market concentration. Other industrial countries also have significant, but somewhat lower levels of concentration.

Table 8.1[3]   % Share of 5 largest firms

Product or product group	Net output	Sales	Employment
Newspapers, periodicals	44	42	42
Brewing	37	50	40
Domestic electrical appliances	50	52	51
Bread, confectionery, biscuits	54	55	47
Basic chemicals	46	50	50
Ice cream, chocolates, cocoa	61	61	55
Tapes, gramophone records	74	75	76
Motor vehicles, cycles, motor cycles	91	91	88
Cigarettes, tobacco	99	99	97

The common characteristic of the markets listed is that the largest five firms have a major share of the market, the rest of which is divided between a few firms or, in some cases, many firms. Since the word oligopoly means 'a few sellers', it might be disputed whether all the markets listed fall into this category. In some cases such as cigarettes there are only a few producers, whereas in the cases of brewing and bread the firms can be numbered in hundreds. Although the usual starting-point in the definition of oligopoly is the emphasis on fewness, it is unlikely that numbers alone would identify an oligopoly market. An oligopoly is most likely to arise when a few firms have a significant market share. Because each of the big firms is sufficiently large to have a major impact on the market, it will need to consider the possible reaction of its larger rivals. This is not to say that the small firms are unimportant. There have been occasions, for example, when the large oil firms lowered petrol prices in an attempt to control the small cut-price oil companies. On the other hand the small firms may be regarded by their larger rivals as not significant enough to justify retaliatory action. It is the pattern of interdependent behaviour among the big firms in an oligopoly market which is the crucial and identifying feature.

Interdependence

In oligopolistic markets the larger firms are certainly not price takers since the size of their output is large enough to have an influence on market size. On the other hand they cannot be described simply as price fixers in the manner of the monopolist discussed in the last chapter. Actions by one firm may well provoke counter-measures by others and each firm will have to watch very closely the sales policy of its rivals. The rival firms are interdependent. We cannot explain the policy of one without considering the policy of the others and the way in which they will interact. Interdependent rivalry is not only common in competitive markets but is also found in fields of activity such as sport, diplomacy and the more serious business of warfare.

The problem which confronts the economic analyst, in trying to explain what a firm will do when its tactics depend upon its assumptions about the strategy of its rivals, is well illustrated by the dilemma which faced the detective Sherlock Holmes in his attempt to escape from his enemy Professor Moriarty. Although this may seem far removed from oligopoly competition, the issues are the same. The detective's plan was to catch a boat from Dover to Calais. Provided he could elude his pursuer at Dover he would be safe once he got to France. Both Holmes and Moriarty had caught the same train from London to Dover. Both rivals, who were sitting in different compartments of a non-corridor train, were aware of this. There was only one stop at Canterbury, which was so brief and the platform so crowded, that it would not be possible to see who had got off or, having alighted, to get back on to the train again. The possible outcomes facing Holmes were: if both he and Moriarty alighted at either Canterbury or Dover, then Moriarty would catch and kill him – a win for Moriarty; if Moriarty got off at Canterbury leaving Holmes on the train then this would be a win for the latter who would get to Dover and escape to France; if Holmes got off at

Canterbury and Moriarty at Dover then this could be looked upon as a draw, for Holmes had temporarily eluded his pursuer. In trying to decide whether to get off at Canterbury or Dover, Holmes might reason as follows: 'if Moriarty gets off at Canterbury then the worst possible outcome – from his point of view – would be a win for me if I was still on the train and went to Dover; whereas if he decides on Dover the worst possible outcome for him would be a draw, if I got off at Canterbury. Therefore he is most likely to go for Dover and my best policy would be to alight at Canterbury.'

The only problem with this strategy is that if Moriarty is equally intelligent, he would deduce Holmes' intentions and also get off at Canterbury! For both opponents the problem remains unresolved. The dilemma of choice facing top management in an oligopoly is no less complex. With a range of competitive weapons to choose from, they have to decide upon a marketing policy in the light of possible rival retaliation.

Game theory

The main weapons of competition are:

1 *retail price*; the competitiveness of this must be judged in relation to the quality and reputation of the product.
2 *trade deals and margins*; the aim is to encourage the distributor by increasing the margin between factory and retail prices or providing incentives such as special discount offers, loyalty bonuses.
3 *advertising and promotions*; to expand the market through persuasion and information, as, for example, with special offers, coupons and distinctive packaging.
4 *design/styling*; modifications and improvements in the product to make it distinctive from competitors.

In their book *Theory of Games and Economic Behaviour*,[4] Neumann and Morgenstern attempt to analyse the consequences of rivalry between two or more competitors and take account of all the competitive weapons that a firm may employ. The object is to provide a systematic way of choosing the best strategy, allowing for retaliations. This is best illustrated by simple examples. A *game* is defined as a set of rules controlling the contest and *strategy* is a method of play planned in advance. Let us assume only two firms A and B and that they each have two strategies open to them: Price Cuts and Trade Deals. Only one strategy can be used at a time. The object of the game is to achieve the maximum market share, which we shall assume is commensurate with increased profits. The outcome of the strategies in terms of the effects on A's and B's market share is shown in the boxes in the tables below (often referred to as a *pay-off matrix*). The figure above the diagonal in each box shows A's percentage share of the market and below the diagonal B's share:

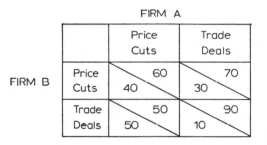

Assume that A and B are both familiar with the information in the table. Starting from the position in the upper left-hand box where both are adopting a strategy of price cuts, this results in a 60% share of the market for A and a 40% share for B. In this situation it will pay B to switch to trade deals which will increase its market share by 10%. A will retaliate by switching from price cuts to trade deals and B will reply by switching back to price cuts, resulting in a 70% share for A and 30% for B. At this point neither of the firms can improve their position by shifting their strategy. The result is a stable combination of strategies and is said to be *strictly determined*. However, if the outcomes were as follows:

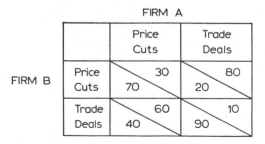

Here the situation is unstable and the game is not strictly determined. If both firms initially adopt price cuts it will pay A to shift to trade deals, which will provoke B to retaliate by also switching to trade deals. This will prompt A to move back to price cuts, which in turn will induce B to revert to price cuts – the original position. Unless the rivals can devise some other strategy such as a random mixture of tactics, then they will continue to chase each other around.

The theory of games can be extended to much more complicated situations involving more than two rivals and a number of different strategies. With rather more complicated mathematics, allowance can be made for a range of pay-offs, or outcomes, in relation to the cost of any given combination of strategies. For the economist studying behaviour in oligopoly markets, the limitation of the game theory approach is that it does not explain how the pay-offs in the boxes actually occur. For a Sales Director trying to use it to devise a marketing policy, the problem is even more basic. Data with which to predict pay-offs may simply not be available. With new products or in rapidly changing market conditions, previous experience may provide no guide to possible outcomes. Moreover, if rival firms are run by managers who are poorly informed or not very clever, then the game theory approach may be irrelevant and unprofitable. Nevertheless it is illuminating for both the businessman and the economist because it shows very clearly the nature of the problems they have to try and analyse, as well as revealing the gaps in their information. For example, it may provide some guide at the market research or test market stage, towards the sort of data that should be gathered or propositions that might be tested.

Furthermore, game theory underlines for the economist a very puzzling feature about oligopoly markets. From the kind of analysis presented in the tables, one would expect oligopoly markets to be characterised by a considerable amount of movement in prices, as rival firms switch from one strategy to another in search of an optimal policy, or because the situation is inherently unstable. In practice the reverse is the case. The common feature of oligopoly markets is not price wars, although these occasionally occur, but price stability. Some economists even refer to the *price rigidity* of oligopoly markets. One possibility is that price is regarded as such a dangerous offensive weapon that, like poison gas or nuclear bombs in warfare, it is not used for fear of equivalent retaliation. It is the most dangerous of the competitive weapons because it works faster than, for example, advertising or changes in product design. The message of a price cut is more immediately apparent to customers than any of the other tactics. For these reasons, when faced with a price cut by a rival, competitors may feel compelled to respond in the same way, which induces further price cuts in turn and triggers off a price war. To avoid this, firms may try to regulate prices or find forms of *non-price competition* such as advertising. Economists are not agreed upon a single theory for the paradox of price stability in oligopoly markets. There are a number of explanations, the most important of which are examined in the following sections.

Kinked demand

An oligopolist in trying to estimate how much more or less he will sell if he lowers or raises his price will try to take account of his competitors' reaction. Let us assume in a particular oligopoly market that the competing firms are selling similar but not identical products, perhaps differentiated by minor differences in design, advertising, after sales service and so on. Thus although the firms are close rivals, their products are not in fact perfect substitutes. This means that if the firm raises its price, it will lose some but not all of its customers. For the same reason, if the firm lowers its prices it will not succeed in luring away all the customers from its rivals. Much will depend upon how they respond with their prices. A possible situation might be as follows: if there is already a price prevailing in the market, giving the firms a satisfactory level of profit, then a price increase by one firm is not likely to be followed by the others. They will actually gain customers by not actually raising their price since their products are now more competitive. However, a price cut by one firm is likely to be followed by the others because if they do not reduce their prices they will lose customers. The impact of this on the demand curve for a single firm is shown in Fig. 8.1 – it has a distinct bend which gives this explanation of oligopoly its title: the theory of kinked demand.

From the diagram it can be seen that if the firm raises its price above the prevailing market level P, it will lose quite a lot of sales. The firm's demand schedule DD above the kink is sensitive to price increases – relatively price elastic. Below the kink the firm will not gain any customers by price cuts because these are matched by rivals – demand is relatively unresponsive or price inelastic. Its best policy is to stick to the price at the kink. Because of the abrupt change in the demand curve, the marginal revenue curve (MR on the diagram) at the point immediately below the kink has a break or what mathematicians call a 'discontinuity' – shown by the vertical dotted line. This may further explain *sticky* (very stable) prices in oligopoly. Remember that the profit-maximising rule (Chapter 7) is to produce at the level of output and price where marginal cost is equal to marginal revenue. It can be seen from the diagram that

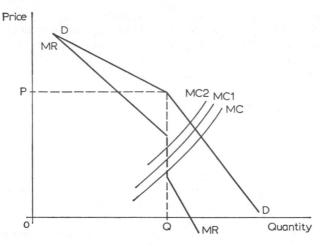

Fig. 8.1   Kinked oligopoly

even if there is a considerable change in costs – shown by the
marginal cost curves MC2, MC1 – the most profitable level of
output remains unchanged at quantity Q and price P.

The theory of kinked demand is an attractive one as it not only
incorporates the realities of interdependent rivalry but also appears
to explain price stability. Once a market price is established, firms
will have little incentive to move from it because of the kink. Price
rigidity is the result. The kink in the demand curve will be sharper
the greater the degree of interdependence in the market – the fewer
the firms and the greater the similarity in the competing products.

The theory is difficult to test satisfactorily.[5] If, for example, one
firm raises its prices and other firms respond by raising theirs, which
is contrary to the predictions of the theory, what does this mean?
There are three possible interpretations:

(*a*) the theory is incorrect; (*b*) because of changed cost or demand
conditions the kink is being established at a new level; (*c*) the firms
are acting in unison to raise prices. Clearly it is insufficient merely to
observe the price behaviour of oligopoly firms in order to test this
theory. It is important to know something about the policies that lie
behind the price moves. The theory also seems to take insufficient
account of the impact of non-price competition. If, because of the
kink, firms decide not to compete on price grounds but direct their
competitive strategies towards design or advertising, this will increase the amount of product differentiation, lessen the amount of
interdependence and eventually weaken the kink.

Oligopoly prices may be 'sticky' for reasons quite unconnected with the kinked demand theory. Firms may, for example, be reluctant to adjust prices frequently because of administrative inconvenience associated with stock revaluation, etc. Lack of knowledge about the shape of their demand curve (elasticity of demand) may also deter firms from price changes. Although a kinked demand offers an explanation of the operation of oligopoly markets under certain circumstances, it is not a general theory of oligopoly.

A further difficulty with the theory is that it starts with the assumption that a prevailing price has already been established. How this happens in an oligopoly market is in fact the major question facing the economic analyst.

Price leadership

As the title suggests, a price is set by one firm in the oligopoly market and then followed by the others. This solves the problem of uncertainty about rival reaction. Each firm does not have to worry about what price to charge and what will happen if prices change. Two different types of price leadership are common in oligopoly markets: (*a*) *dominant firm*; (*b*) *barometric firm*. Dominant-firm price leadership is readily understood. The largest or possibly most efficient firm takes the pricing lead and others follow because they fear that if they do not, a price cutting war would result. They become price takers (page 48). Many industries fit this model, including retailing where major chain stores act as price leaders for some, although not all products, and are followed by smaller independent shops in a locality. The dominance of the huge US Steel corporation (now USX) in the American steel market is also often quoted in textbooks as an example. Some take the view that dominant price leadership is not consistent with the concept of interdependence in oligopoly markets. The leader may have such control of the market that it can ignore rival reaction.

The dominant firm is not necessarily the price leader. General Motors, although in the past dominant in US motor vehicles has not always initiated price changes. Instead this was sometimes done by a smaller firm which acted like a barometer, sensitive to market pressures of supply and demand. Others will find it prudent to follow the price set by the barometric firm. In a study of British industries, Maunder[6] reveals that in the glass bottle, plant-baked bread and sanitary-ware markets, barometric price leadership was evident. The leading firms were similar in size and efficiency and moved in step with price changes. In the UK petroleum industry the barometric price leadership is said to have rotated between the two leading firms.

Collusive pricing

In this situation the price is determined by joint agreement rather than by the action of an individual firm. When the collusion is through a formal agreement, which in some countries such as the United States is illegal, this is known as a *cartel*. Irrespective of whether the agreement is formal or informal it is more likely to work the greater the similarity in firms in terms of products, market shares and production costs. Otherwise a firm with a smaller market share, lower production costs or possibly a distinctive product, may believe it could secure some advantage by breaking the agreement and lowering the prices. Unless there are sanctions which the other firms can invoke, such as getting distributors to boycott the price breaker, then the agreement may collapse.

Entry-limit pricing

It might be thought that the tactics of the colluding firms would be quite straightforward – to set prices so as to maximise the combined profits of the group as a whole. In practice this raises a number of complex issues. The collusive pricing behaviour might be directed at discouraging or totally stopping new competitors from entering the market. This is known as 'entry-limit' pricing. If the collusive price is too high then newcomers may enter the industry and erode the profits and market shares of the existing firms. A price which is too low will simply reduce the insiders' profits unnecessarily. It is a problem of balancing short-run gains against the stream of profits likely to be earned over the long run. Thus the entry-limiting price will usually be less than the price which will maximise short-run profits. Entry limit pricing is not to be confused with *predatory pricing*, which is a disparaging term applied to the, often illegal, process of driving rival firms already in the market out of business by lowering price below full cost.

The potential entrant, looking in from the outside, will consider the likely responses of existing firms. Will they try to maintain their market shares and levels of output, letting prices fall as the extra output of the newcomer increases the total supply? Or will they be more concerned with price stability, allowing some reduction in their output and market shares? If the former tactic is adopted and prices fall to unprofitable levels, the newcomer may be driven out of the market, unless he has sufficient resources to cover his losses. A poker-like game of bluff may be played in these circumstances.

There is an alternative theory known as *open oligopoly* which predicts that firms may do just the reverse. That is to say, they will find it more profitable to set prices higher than an entry deterring level, going for higher short-run profits and accepting a decline in shares of the market as newcomers enter.

Both the entry-limit and open oligopoly theories assume long-run profit maximisation. In deciding which explanation is most appropriate in a particular situation, an important question is that of the time horizon over which firms plan their operations and set their targets. It has been suggested by some economists that the time horizon of smaller firms in a highly precarious market, where survival is uncertain, may be relatively short. Larger firms, who feel more assured about the future, may take a longer run view of their prospects in the market and be more concerned with maximising their income over a greater number of years.

Both theories are difficult to test satisfactorily. Changes in concentration ratios have been used to help assess them. Falling concentration ratios would be consistent with open-oligopoly but not with entry limit pricing. It is said that the open-oligopoly model fits the facts in the American Steel Industry, where the dominant firm, US Steel, accepted a declining share of a growing market. As is so often the case in economics, where controlled experiments are not possible, such evidence is not necessarily conclusive. It could be argued that declining concentration is also the result of other influences such as diversification and government measures to limit the power of large firms. In many industries concentration has significantly increased, while in some it has shown little change or actually declined. As with kinked demand, neither the entry-limit nor the open-oligopoly models provide a general theory of oligopolistic markets, though they may give a useful insight in some cases.

Barriers to entry

The extent to which the firms in the industry can charge a price above the normal competitive level without being challenged by newcomers will depend upon what are known as *barriers to entry*. In a seminal study of twenty industries, Bain (*Barriers to New Competition*, Harvard 1956) concluded that when 'very high' entry barriers exist, firms in the industry may be able to raise prices by 10% or more above average costs (which include normal profit) without attracting new entry.

Three types of barriers were identified which appeared to hamper or block new entry:

(a) Product differentiation
which refers to actual or perceived features which make a product seem distinct from its rivals. Advertising, brand names, design differences and after-sales service all contribute to this. Consequently, a newcomer may have to incur heavy advertising and marketing expenses in order to make his product known. This is likely to occur in oligopoly markets when there is an emphasis on non-price competition, particularly in consumer goods.

(b) Absolute cost barriers
which exist where established firms have advantages due to superior production techniques or favourable access to inputs or finance which are not available on the same terms to other firms.

(c) Scale economy barriers
which occur when the output of a firm of the most efficient size is a significant portion of total market sales. To be competitive, a newcomer would have to produce on a scale that would have a substantial impact on the market and probably provoke retaliatory action from existing firms, unless total demand was growing very rapidly.

The significance of any particular barrier to entry will vary from firm to firm. Companies that are already established with other products may have techniques, marketing skills or financial resources which enable them to diversify into new markets without great difficulty (see Chapter 5; section 6, Multi-product firms). A firm less well placed may find the same barriers much more formidable. Some economists, notably Stigler,[7] have argued that some of the barriers listed, such as economies of scale, are not really barriers at all because they apply equally to all firms inside and outside the industry. They determine the size of firms. Logically this is correct. Any firm could, if it wished to, undertake production on a scale which led to lowest average cost. However, from the practical viewpoint, the Bain definition of barriers is realistic. Even if new firms could raise the necessary finance to produce on the optimum scale, they might not feel they could face a battle with established firms who already had a secure hold over a limited market.

Cost-plus pricing

To understand oligopoly markets, it is not sufficient to explain the way in which price is arrived at, whether by price leadership, collusion or other means. It is also necessary to study the objectives that underlie the price setting. Numerous empirical studies have shown that most oligopolists (and other price fixers) adopt a form of pricing known as cost-plus, which is sometimes called *full cost* or *average cost* pricing. The formula for this is simple: the firm calculates its average direct (variable) costs per unit of output – labour, materials, etc. – and adds to this a percentage to cover its overheads (fixed costs) and to give a profit margin.

At first sight, cost-plus pricing seems a direct contradiction of two important parts of economic theory explaining how market prices are determined. We have shown (in Chapters 2, 3 and 7) that price is determined in a market system by the forces of supply and demand; also that businessmen set prices so as to get maximum profits and will do so at the point where marginal cost is equal to marginal revenue. The cost-plus formula seems to make no reference to demand nor does it refer to marginal cost and marginal revenue. Surveys among businessmen and business accountants have shown that many of them are unfamiliar with the concept of marginal cost and revenue. Some critics have argued that all this evidence completely demolishes price theory as a satisfactory explanation of what happens in oligopoly markets.

The contradictions may be more apparent than real. In setting a price, oligopolists cannot afford to disregard the forces of supply and demand any more than sellers in other types of market. Suppose a firm using the cost-plus formula has overhead costs of £10000. These might consist of fixed payments for rates, rent, interest, etc. In addition let us suppose the firm needs to earn a further £10000 in profit to compensate the owners for the risk and trouble involved in that particular line of business. If the average direct costs (e.g. labour, materials, fuel) work out at £8.00 per unit, the firm will have to decide what percentage to add on to this in order to recover enough revenue to pay for overheads and profits. It can only determine the 'plus' element of its price if it has some idea about the impact of price on the quantity sold – that is to say the nature of the demand curve as discussed in Chapter 6. If, for example, it decides to add 25% to its direct cost of £8.00 per unit, the selling price will be £10.00. If at this price it sells 10000 units (£100000 revenue) then its direct costs will absorb $10000 \times £8.00 =$ £80000 of the £100000 sales revenue. This leaves £20000 to cover overheads and provide an adequate profit, which is exactly what is required. However, it is possible that the firm may have misjudged the strength of demand and at £10.00 is only able to sell 8000 units, then it will earn insufficient revenue to pay for overheads and profits. It may then be forced to consider a smaller percentage mark-up, that is to say lowering the price. If, by lowering the price to £9.00 – a mark-up of 12½% – the demand increases to 20000 units, then the sales revenue will be sufficient to cover direct costs, overheads and profits. In this example we have assumed average direct costs to be constant at £8.00 a unit. If, for reasons outlined in Chapter 5, the unit costs vary, this would have to be taken into account.

Thus we can see that even cost-plus pricing requires sound judgement about demand conditions in the market. In trying to decide what mark-up it should use, the firm in the situation described above is taking account of the concept of price elasticity of demand, as explained in Chapter 6. The Sales Director, unless he has studied economics, may not use this term but it makes no difference. Similarly the fact that businessmen do not describe their operations in terms of marginal cost and marginal revenue, does not invalidate marginal analysis as an explanation of what businessmen may be trying to do when deciding upon their level of price and output. If a reduction in price is contemplated, then businessmen operating in any market are almost certain to compare the extra revenue gained with the extra costs of production. In doing this they are behaving in a manner consistent with the marginal analysis of previous chapters, although they may not be aware of this.

Although the cost-plus formula in the previous example can be reconciled with the marginal approach to pricing, it would be wrong to suggest that it is exactly equivalent to the MC = MR rule, which may in practice be difficult, and sometimes undesirable, to apply. Firms may not aim at a precise equivalent of marginal cost with marginal revenue. There are a number of reasons for this: in order to equate marginal cost with marginal revenue a firm must know the shape of its demand curve – how responsive customers are to changes in price. Yet this may be a matter of great uncertainty despite market research.

Experimental adjustments in price to try and test the nature of demand are not only likely to be unpopular with distributors but in an oligopoly market hazardous because of rival reaction. In these circumstances the oligopoly firm will satisfy itself with an approximate idea of the state of demand, gained from sales research and experience. It is important to remember that price is only one of the competition weapons which a firm may use. Having fixed a price the most sensible strategy for the firm may be to concentrate its efforts on selling, servicing, design, competitive delivery, etc., rather than make a series of complicated price adjustments to establish exactly what is marginal revenue. In an expanding oligopoly market non-price competition may be the safest way of maintaining its market share.

From all this it can be seen that although the cost-plus formula lacks the precision of the MC = MR rule, it is not necessarily inconsistent with the ideas underlying it. In a changing and uncertain oligopoly market, it is seldom possible to set price according to an exact rule. In addition to facts, flair and business intuition are needed; hence the cost formula. The plus element, despite its apparent crudity, reflects business judgements about a number of complex factors – the possible reaction of rivals as well as customers. It must also be remembered that in setting its mark-up, the firm will be thinking of its investment requirements, since as we have explained in Chapter 4, retained profits are a major source of funds. The firm might have to weigh the probable gains from extra investment funds generated by a higher mark-up, against the probable disadvantages associated with a higher price and a less competitive product.

An additional complication is that profit may be one of a number of objectives that the firm is pursuing, which might also include such things as growth, maintaining market share or keeping a design/research team continuously employed. These may constrain or even conflict with the pursuit of maximum profit, at least in the short run. Different combinations of these objectives will have different implications for mark-up policy as well as other forms of non-price competition.

In view of the uncertainties that surround firms, particularly in oligopoly markets, it is hardly surprising that some economists have claimed that firms do not succeed in maximising anything at all. It is suggested that they are not *maximisers* but *satisficers*. Instead of trying to maximise anything they pursue a level of profits, share of the market etc., which is satisfactory. Hence the preference for a fixed percentage mark-up or a certain rate of return on the capital as a target, rather than the use of marginal analysis, MC = MR. This is sometimes compared with looking for a needle in a haystack. The searcher stops when he has found one which is satisfactory, even though it may not be the sharpest. Although the satisficing idea seems realistic in practice it is hard, when looking at firms, to distinguish between satisfying and maximising. To revert to the

haystack analogy, it could be said that when the man stops searching, he does so because he calculates that the gains from finding a
sharper needle will not be sufficient to compensate for the effort and
uncertainty involved. He is therefore in a preferred or maximum
position, even though a sharper needle exists.

It must now be clear that, unlike perfect competition and
monopoly (Chapter 7), there is no single theory of oligopoly which
will fit all cases. Much depends on the type of market. This means
that the economist, whether he is acting as an adviser to a large firm
or a government agency, cannot offer any general prescriptions for
policy. Instead he must study in detail the characteristics of the
particular oligopoly market whose operations he is trying to explain. We conclude with an illustration of this from two oligopoly
markets, which at first looked similar in terms of market concentration but in fact behaved in very different ways.

Two case studies

The heavy electrical equipment and cigarette industries in the
United States are both oligopoly markets. During the 1950s and
early 1960s they both had a similar concentration ratio with the top
four firms accounting for more than 80% of the market. The
electrical equipment industry was characterised by a formal but
illegal price fixing and market sharing agreement, which occasionally broke down and precipitated violent price wars. In 1961 the top
executives of General Electric and Westinghouse, together with
some other large manufacturers of generators, circuit breakers and
turbines, were declared guilty of price fixing and market sharing
agreements arranged in secret meetings over the previous decade.
Where equipment was sold on sealed bids, the firms agreed in
advance which was to get each bid and at what price. Elaborate
precautions were taken to try and disguise these price fixing
arrangements by making them appear competitive. By contrast the
cigarette industry, with a similar concentration ratio, avoided both
illegal cartels and price wars.

There are a number of reasons why such different market practices were developed in the two industries. Firstly, the nature of the
demand: in heavy electrical equipment this varies with the business
cycle and puts firms under severe pressure in slack periods. Faced
with over capacity and high fixed costs associated with substantial
investment in fixed plant and equipment, the temptation to cut
prices in order to keep the factories working is high. Growth in
cigarette demand presents quite a different picture. It is much more

stable and unaffected by the business cycle. The severe price and excess-capacity problems which confronted the electrical industry did not arise. Secondly, cigarette manufacturers were also less likely than electrical manufacturers to use a price as a competitive weapon, because of the differences in the product in the two industries. Because cigarettes are highly standardised and the prices known to everyone, it is an easy matter for a firm to detect any price cutting by a competitor which may break a stable pattern. Formal agreements are unnecessary. No firm would risk price cutting as it would be promptly spotted by its rivals. However, with electrical equipment where offers are made through sealed bids, there is no way to check up on how firms are pricing until the contract is finally made.

In such a situation formal agreement is necessary. The possibility of this was enhanced in the electrical industry as there were effectively only three large firms competing for big orders in heavy equipment. Formal collusion was easier to arrange than in the cigarette industry where there were more firms competing. It was in the lighter electrical equipment where there were more producers that formal collusion was more difficult to arrange and occasionally broke down. The problems among the firms producing the lighter types of equipment were intensified by the entry of newcomers, which put price fixing and market sharing agreements under further strain. The cigarette industry was untroubled by new entrants. Furthermore, a price war was less likely because competitive effort could be directed into non-price forms of competition, particularly advertising, which was not possible in the electrical industry.

These brief comments indicate the complexity of predicting oligopoly price and output behaviour, even when a detailed study is made of particular cases. Often there are strong forces tending towards formal or informal price and market sharing agreements. These are difficult to maintain if demand fluctuates, if there are newcomers, or if the price is much above the competitive level. In these cases there would be a strong incentive to cut prices.

Oligopoly and other market structures

Before concluding with a summary of the points raised in this chapter on oligopoly markets, it will be helpful to compare it with what we have said about the other market structures examined in Chapter 7 – perfect competition, monopoly and oligopolistic competition. This is done on the accompanying table. In the upper half of the table the market structures are listed. Against each of these in the lower half of the table are the corresponding predictions that can be made about the conduct and performance of firms in each market. It must be emphasised these are theoretical models. They have been stripped of many of the details of real-life markets which for the purposes of analysis are felt to be inessential. If it can be shown that there are features that have been overlooked which would influence conduct in these markets, then these features should be included.

This is not an exhaustive list of market structures. For example, we have assumed in the models studied that the number of buyers is so numerous that no one of them is powerful enough to influence the price. If, however, buyers are few or can organise themselves into groups to negotiate with suppliers, then this may significantly modify the predictions made for any of the markets listed. Powerful buyers may be able, where there are few sellers, to influence the seller's price and output policies. This has been described as 'countervailing power',[8] in which the exercise of power by one group in the market is curbed by the existence of other powerful groups. If the number of buyers is few and they are confronted by numerous and boldly organised suppliers, then it may be the buyers that dominate in the market place. Professor Bain has listed fourteen different types of market structures which may influence the price and output policies.[9] Here we have selected some of the more important ones.

The most useful models are those which yield predictions that can be tested. If the facts do not appear to be consistent with the predictions of the models, this tells us one, or more, of a number of things: (i) the theories incorporated in the model are incorrect and should be discarded or modified; (ii) the observations are inaccurate; (iii) the model may be inappropriate for the market under observation. Taking the last point, it could be that a perfectly competitive market has been confused with a monopolisticly competitive market, in which case we should test our data against the appropriate set of predictions.

The market structures listed can be divided into three groups: those in which the firms are price takers, those in which the firms are price fixers and those in which the firms are able to fix prices but only within certain limits. At opposite ends of the spectrum, as far as pricing is concerned, are perfect competition and monopoly. Firms in the perfectly competitive type of market have to accept the prevailing price in the market which is determined by the interaction of all sellers and buyers. By contrast the monopoly firm is a

Table 8.2 Some profit maximising models of market structure

	PRICE TAKERS *perfect competition*	PRICE FIXERS WITHIN LIMITS *monopolistic competition*	*oligopoly*	PRICE FIXERS *pure monopoly*
MARKET STRUCTURE	Large number of firms Identical products No barriers to entry	Many firms Differentiated products No barriers to entry	Typical industry consists of a few big firms with large share + smaller firms (*a*) differentiated products or (*b*) identical products Barriers to entry a common feature	One firm supplies entire market No close substitutes Barriers to entry
PREDICTED CONDUCT AND PERFORMANCE	MC = MR = PRICE In the long-run equilibrium firms earn 'normal profit' and are at lowest point on AC curve	MC = MR < PRICE Long-run 'normal profit' but excess capacity	The policies of firms interrelated. We must make assumptions about reactions of one policy on another. Therefore a variety of oligopoly models and no single prediction about prices and profit levels	(1) MC = MR < PRICE (2) Output likely to be lower and price higher than would be in the case under perfect competition; above normal profits (*ceteris paribus*)

price taker since it can choose the point on the total market demand curve at which it wishes to operate.

Monopolistic competition and oligopoly come somewhere in between these two extremes. Where there are differences in rival products, however slight, then each of the products is in certain aspects unique. Each firm has a slice of the market which is attached to its particular product. Each firm faces its own demand curve and must consider what price it should charge. The freedom to fix prices is, however, restricted. Firms in both types of market will at some point lose customers to their rivals if prices are raised too high. Substitutes become more attractive as the price difference widens. At high prices, cross-elasticity of demand may be increased and firms may simply price themselves out of the market. As we have seen, the oligopoly firm is further restricted in its price-setting activities because it must take account of the possible reaction of large rivals.

Structure – Conduct – Performance

These market models all have two features in common: (*a*) they assume a link between market structure and the way firms behave, and (*b*) they assume that firms will aim to maximise profits. We shall briefly examine the realism of these two assumptions.

The first assumption was formerly stated by E. Mason in the 1930s,[10] although it was implicit in much of the earlier analysis of markets. It rests on the view that the conduct of firms, such as pricing and advertising policies and responsiveness to change, is determined by the market environment in which they operate. According to this view the tactics and manoeuvres of an oligopolist, for example, differ from those of a perfectly competitive firm, not because the oligopolist has a particular lust for power but because of the particular features of its market structure. In both competitive and oligopolistic markets the firms aim to maximise profits. Their conduct differs simply because their market structures are different – the rules of any particular competitive game between firms are determined by the market.

It follows that the conduct of firms will also influence their performance in terms of their efficiency, technological progress and so on. The concept of the structure → conduct → performance relationship has been influential in economic research. Numerous studies have been undertaken to explore the connection between different types of structure and performance. The results of some of these studies are discussed in Chapter 9. The relationship has been influential in the sort of advice given to governments on industrial policy. In the USA, for example, the *White House Task Force Report on Antitrust Policy* called for the break up of industries with concentration ratios of 70% or more and the prevention of mergers where they would take the concentration ratio above that same figure. In the UK if two companies proposing to merge have together more than 25% of the market, the merger may be investigated by the Monopolies and Mergers Commission.

Government policy in practice is examined in Chapter 10. At this point it is sufficient to note that it would be wrong to assume that the structure→conduct→performance models provide a simple set of policy prescriptions. Looking àt Table 8.2 it might be thought that the perfectly competitive structure provided the most desirable conduct and most efficient performance. But such a structure with many small firms may be quite incapable of utilising the most efficient technology, which may require larger units such as those found in a monopoly or oligopoly structure. In different market structures there are losses in efficiency as well as gains which the policy-makers must evaluate.

The models which we have been discussing share the common assumption that managers have only one objective – profit maximisation. There is substantial evidence that firms have also other targets, such as the level of sales: maintaining a particular share of the market. Numerous models have been developed to explore the consequences of alternatives to the objective of profit maximisation. Fig. 8.2 compares a profit maximising (PM) oligopolist with a sales revenue maximising (SRM) oligopolist. TC is the oligopolist's total cost curve and TR measures its total revenue. Remember that this is derived from a downward sloping demand curve, as described in Chapter 7, Fig. 7.3. In order to sell more of the output (assuming no unfavourable rival reaction) the oligopolist must reduce price. Curve TP measures total profits (TR − TC). The line P_A is the level of profits acceptable to shareholders. Presumably, lack of information among shareholders prevents the maximum level of profits becoming the acceptable level. The PM firm will produce output Y_P. The SRM firm will produce at the higher level of output Y_S and consequently have lower prices than the PM firm. It can be seen that, in this example, output Y_S is not at the highest point on the TR curve, because at the corresponding level of output Y_X, profits are below the minimum acceptable level. This is as close as the firm can get to sales revenue maximisation without upsetting the shareholders.

There are other more complex and realistic models specifying *the*

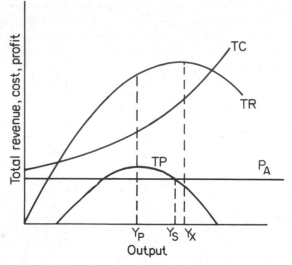

Fig. 8.2   Profit and non profit maximising firms compared

rate of growth – in for example, sales revenues and assets – as an objective. Nevertheless, the evidence suggests that although firms pursue a variety of objectives, profitability is a primary aim, since retained profits substantially finance future investment. Irrespective of the analytical model adopted, the market structure framework is useful. Whatever firms aim to do, they will be influenced by the kind of market in which they operate.

Summary

It might be expected that because of interdependence between rival firms, oligopoly markets would be unstable. In practice they usually exhibit a high degree of price stability, with occasional price wars. Economists have provided various explanations for this:

(*a*)   The emphasis in some markets on *non-price competition*, which avoids the danger of retaliatory price cutting.
(*b*)   Firms sticking to the prevailing market price – the *kinked demand theory*.

   The latter is difficult to test and does not provide an explanation of how price in oligopoly markets is established in the first place. It may be achieved by *price leadership* – with either a dominant competitor or a firm sensitive to market conditions setting the price, which is then followed by others. Alternatively it may be by formal or informal *collusive agreement*. The aims of such agreements may vary: they may be to deter newcomers by charging a moderate price, to achieve a steady level of profits over the long run, or to go for higher prices or profits in the short run, ignoring the subsequent entry of newcomers. The cost-plus pricing formula, used by many oligopolists, is a convenient 'rule of thumb' and is not necessarily just an arbitrary percentage. The 'plus' element requires sound judgement about supply and demand conditions in the market. In contrast to the theories of perfect competition and monopoly, there is no single theory which can explain the operation of all oligopoly markets. The characteristics of each individual market must be studied by the economist.

Questions
1 What is an oligopolistic market? Discuss the main characteristics exhibited by such a market. (Associated Examining Board, A-Level Economics)
2 In what ways can the size of firm be measured? For what purposes does it matter which method of measurement is used? (University of London, A-Level Economics)
3 A manufacturing company determines the price of its products by considering numerous and complex factors. Explain. (Institute of Cost and Management Accountants)
4 'While price-cutting is seldom a feature of oligopolistic markets, near simultaneous price rises are often a characteristic.' How would you explain this tendency? (Institute of Chartered Secretaries and Administrators)
5 (*a*) Explain and give an example of an oligopolistic market structure.
   (*b*) Compare and contrast the goals of profit maximising and non profit maximising oligopolies.
   (Institute of Chartered Accountants in England and Wales, Economic Foundation Examination)

Notes
1 Schumpeter – *Capitalism, Socialism and Democracy* (Allen & Unwin, London 1947); Marcuse – *One-Dimensional Man: Studies in the Ideology of Advanced Industrial Society* (Routledge & Kegan Paul, London 1964); Galbraith – *The New Industrial State* (Pelican Books, London 1969).
2 Prais, S. J., *The Evolution of Giant Firms in Britain* (CUP, 1976).
3 The information for this table is taken from the *Census of Production* (HMSO).

4   Von Neumann, J. C. and Morgenstern, O., *Theory of Games and Economic Behaviour* (Princeton, 1947).
5   Stigler, J., 'Kinky Oligopoly and Rigid Prices' contained in Irwin, R. D., *The Organization of Industry* (New York 1968).
6   Maunder, 'Price Leadership: an appraisal of its character in some British industries' contained in *The Business Economist*, 4 (1972).
7   See Stigler – above, note 5.
8   Galbraith, J. K., *American Capitalism* (Mifflin, New York 1952).
9   Bain, *Essays on Price Theory and Industrial Organization* (Little, Brown, 1972).
10 Mason, E., 'Price Production policies of large-scale enterprises' contained in *American Economic Review* (1932).

9

Markets and Efficiency

Introduction

This chapter examines the performance of the market system of resource allocation. Previous chapters in this book have shown how prices, determined in free markets, play a crucial role in resolving the questions of how, what and for whom, which face all communities when dealing with scarce resources. How efficiently does the market system perform these tasks? In attempting to make an evaluation, we shall be looking at two interrelated questions: (*a*) the connection between competition and efficiency; and (*b*) the efficiency of price as a signal to guide producers and consumers in their decisions. It will be helpful to review briefly the various meanings which economists attach to the word efficiency, since this is a rich source of confusion to the layman.

In general terms when people speak of something as 'efficient' they usually mean that it is the most effective way of reaching a desired objective – i.e. involving the minimum amount of fuss, time, expense and so on. In this sense the idea of efficiency concerns a relationship between means and ends. This is exactly how the economist sees it, though in terms of scarce resources – inputs and outputs. Economic efficiency in input/output relationships must not be confused with technical efficiency. The latter measures output of energy per unit of energy applied, whereas economic efficiency is concerned with cost and value. A technically efficient engine, for example, might convert fuel into brake horsepower, at a very high rate, but it may be economically inefficient, because the costs of its components and materials are so high that no one would be prepared to buy it.

In assessing the economic efficiency of an industry, there are four distinct aspects which would need to be examined:

(*a*) *Cost efficiency*: for any given level of output of a specified quality, is the industry using the best available techniques and producing at the lowest possible cost?

(*b*) *Allocative efficiency*: is the industry producing the right quantity of goods? That is to say, supplying what consumers are prepared to pay for at prices which, without restriction, reflect the underlying conditions of supply and demand in the market.

(*c*) *Innovation:* is the industry capable over a period of time of introducing innovations which either reduce cost or increase the performance of existing products, as well as producing new ones? Unlike the two previous aspects which are *static*, this is a *dynamic* feature of efficiency.

(*d*) *Product range*: does the industry supply an adequate range of alternatives in terms of price/quality/performance from which buyers may choose?

These four aspects of economic efficiency do not exhaust the list, although they are among the most important. Moreover the attainment of efficiency in any one of the four areas noted might be at the expense of others. For example, a reduction in product range might lead to an increase in cost efficiency, with greater standardisation making mass production possible. The interrelationship between the price mechanism and these aspects of efficiency is explored in the following sections.

Prices and efficiency

We have seen in previous chapters how prices have to perform three essential and inter-connected tasks in organising economic activity: firstly they transmit information about scarcity; secondly they provide incentives to both buyers and sellers to make the best use of scarce resources; thirdly they determine the distribution of income – who gets how much of the product. The way in which prices function in a market economy provides the answers to the key questions of *what*, *how* and *for whom*. The classical economists (see pages 30–1) argued strongly that prices were most likely to perform these tasks well if settled by buyers and sellers in unfettered competitive markets.

The idea that competition is linked to efficiency is one that pervades much of economic literature and public policy. The famous economist Marshall in writing his *Principles of Economics* (1890) was much influenced in his examination of the competitive process in the economy, by the biologist Darwin, whose study of the competitive process in nature *Origin of Species* had appeared some years earlier. Social Darwinists saw parallels between the 'survival of the fittest' in the jungle and the struggle for survival in the market. Competition is an attractive idea because it offers buyers choice. Sellers that arc inefficient, in the sense that they do not match the price, quality and standard of delivery of their rivals, will be driven out of business. Such competition also ensures the dispersal of power in the market place. No single firm can dominate.

The precise theoretical connection between competition and efficiency can be seen with reference to the model of perfect competition explained in Chapter 7. We saw that every firm in such a market would, in pursuit of maximum profits, expand its output of the product up to the point where its marginal cost (MC) is just equal to its price (P). The reader can readily appreciate why this is a desirable level of output not only for producers, but also for consumers. The MC of a product measures the extra cost to the community of an additional unit of output. It reflects the opportunity (or alternative use) cost of the resources needed to make that extra unit of output (page 4). If for a particular product $P > MC$, this indicates that consumers place greater value on an extra unit of that product than they place on the resources needed to make it employed in the best alternative use. The price system is giving us a clear signal that more of that good should be produced.

Conversely, if $P < MC$, then this is a signal that output of the product has been pushed too far. The consumers place a higher value, at the margin, on the resources employed in their best alternative use, than employed in making an extra unit of the product in question. Only when $P = MC$ is output at an *efficient* level, in the sense that the extra cost of the output is exactly matched by the value consumers place on it – the price they are willing to pay.

Although lack of space precludes it here, it can be demonstrated that in a society in which all markets are perfectly competitive, *cost* and *allocative* efficiency (explained in the introduction to this chapter) will be achieved for all products.[1] The pressures of competition will be sufficient to ensure that every producer will be making the most effective use of available inputs – cost efficiency. The same market pressures will also push output for every product to the point where $MC = Price$. Thus for any pair of goods A and B:

MC_A = Price A; MC_B = Price B and so MC_A/MC_B = Price A/ Price B. This equality of the ratios of marginal costs to prices indicates an equivalence between the relative costs to society of producing various goods and the relative values which it places on them. In less technical language, the society is producing exactly the mixture and quantities of goods it is prepared to pay for – allocative efficiency.

This appears to be a powerful theoretical argument in favour of perfectly competitive markets, supporting the case for non-interference by Governments – the policy of *laissez-faire*. According to this analysis, the 'hidden hand' as Adam Smith called it, of the competitive market is sufficient by itself to achieve efficiency without an elaborate set of rules administered by a state bureaucracy. The market price system also settles the crucial question of 'for whom' since it determines individual incomes and what people çan afford to buy. Although it produces a socially efficient level of output, it is by no means certain that it will distribute that output in a way which is socially equitable. The elimination of inefficiency does not eliminate poverty and gross inequalities in the distribution of income.

The questions of efficiency we have been examining are testable propositions; matters of positive economics, whereas what is socially equitable clearly raises questions of what *ought* to be, and rests on value judgements. The pricing system has been described by some critics as 'rationing by the purse' and is said to be unfair in circumstances where the wealthy can afford to pay scarcity prices while those with low incomes may be forced to have little or nothing at all. It is beyond the scope of this book to explore these issues further. We simply note that most governments in varying degrees try to mitigate the perceived harshness of the price system through progressive taxation, price subsidies and income supplements for the less well-off.

Market failure

The case for non-interference by the Government in a market system is also made less convincing if it can be shown that real world markets do not always produce efficient answers to the problems of using scarce resources – what is known as 'market failure'. This section examines four kinds of failure: price signals being distorted; providing incomplete information; failing to coordinate or not providing adequate incentives. For the case of *public goods* such as defence and roads, where adequate markets fail to come into existence, the reader is referred to the points raised in Chapter 2, pages 28–9.

1 Structural weaknesses

The existence of powerful firms or coalitions of firms may result in a market structure which distorts the message of the price signal. Market prices may not reflect the true balance of supply and demand, but may be rigged at an artificially high price by a dominant firm or groups of firms acting together. The price is raised by restricting output. Thus the signal reflects a contrived rather than real scarcity, which may lead to an inefficient use of resources. A cartel among fertiliser manufacturers, for example, which restricts output, may raise prices to such an extent that the fertiliser is not being as widely used on farms as it might have been. The possible impact of monopolistic or restrictive output and pricing policies on an industry is shown in Fig. 9.1. If a perfectly competitive industry has (in the long run), constant unit costs, the supply (average and

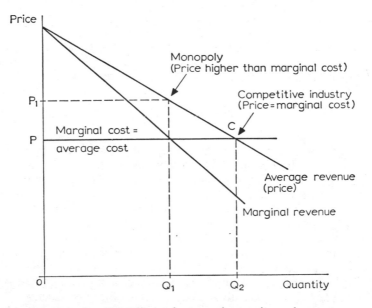

Fig. 9.1 Possible effects of monopoly on price and output

marginal cost) curve will be horizontal (PC in Fig. 9.1). We saw in Chapter 7 how in such a market, competition would ensure that output would be taken to the point Q_2 at which the price (average revenue) P would be exactly equal to average and marginal cost.

If by a series of mergers or a formal agreement this competitive industry was turned overnight into a single firm or cartel, then the price and output might be quite different. The single monopolist or giant cartel is now a price fixer, unlike hundreds of small firms that previously constituted the industry who were price takers. By restricting output, the monopolist can raise prices. If maximum profit is the aim, then the price and output will be determined in the manner described in Chapter 7. The profit-maximising point, where $MC = MR$, is at point Q_1 with a corresponding price P_1. The price is higher and output lower than it was under perfect competition. It will be noted that price P_1 at the lower level of output is higher than marginal cost. This is a measure of the allocative inefficiency caused by the contrived scarcity.

As shown in the diagram a monopoly structure may lead to allocative inefficiency since output may be restricted to a point where $P > MC$. It should be emphasised that this outcome – a higher price and lower output – is not an inevitable consequence of the switch from perfect competition to monopoly. For example the monopolist may not adopt a profit-maximising ($MC = MR$) policy, perhaps to avoid the possibility of government intervention, or because other objectives are being pursued such as maximising market shares. Even if restrictive policies are adopted, there may be compensating advantages because of the economies of large-scale operation. In terms of the diagram, this will lower the level of the supply curve PC, resulting in a lower price and higher output.

2   Externalities

The market mechanism's signals may also be misleading because the price of the commodity may not reflect the full social costs and/or benefits to the community. As a consequence too much or too little of the commodity may be produced. This situation arises because of what are known as *externalities*. Examples of externalities in production are the costs of air or river pollution caused by the manufacturing processes; such costs are not included in the price of the product. These side-effects – ill health, river pollution and so on – when costed and added to the private production costs of the individual factories make up the full social cost of production of any commodity. There may also be external benefits in production. An example of this would be the farmer who in draining his land also benefits adjacent farms. Just as in the former case, where the external cost was not borne by the individual producer, so in this case the external benefit does not accrue as revenue to the farmer. Examples of externalities in consumption are the costs of traffic congestion caused by holiday traffic and the benefits that result from well-kept gardens, which enhance the attractiveness of a neighbourhood and increase the value of other properties.

We can use the supply and demand framework shown in Fig. 9.1 to analyse externalities. We can regard them as additions to (or subtractions from) the private costs and benefits shown in Fig. 9.1. If the firm was polluting the environment, then there would be a cost which is not reflected in the marginal cost curve, which includes only private costs. If the costs of pollution are included this would give a new, higher level of marginal costs than depicted.

This can be pictured as a line lying above PC. Because the external costs are not taken into account, then resources are misallocated. More is produced than would be justified if full social costs were considered. The reader should check this on the diagram to see how a shift in the MC curve will change the desirable level of output – where MC = Price. Similarly benefits in consumption which are not reflected in the demand schedule would have the effect of shifting curves to the right and justifying a higher level of output than would be attained if only private benefits were taken into account. *Cost Benefit Analysis* is a method, using this framework, for the evaluation of investment projects, which takes account of all benefits and costs, both public and private.

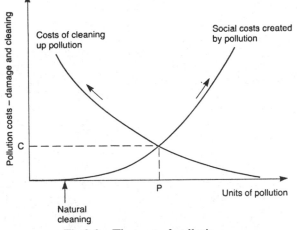

Fig 9.2   The cost of pollution.

162   *Economics*

In Fig. 9.2, the curve sloping up to the right represents the social costs of pollution – the extra cost imposed on the community by an extra or marginal unit of pollution. At high levels of pollution, the marginal damage to the community may be high. For example, at certain effluent levels all fish in a river may die. At very low levels of pollution the cost to the community may be negligible or zero. This is because low concentrations of pollution may be dispersed naturally by wind or water.

The downward sloping curve represents the social costs of avoiding or cleaning up extra or marginal units of pollution. A movement to the left along the curve indicates lower levels of pollution and shows how marginal costs of cleaning may rise. Zero pollution may be very expensive.

The efficient level of pollution is not where there is no pollution at all, but at the point where the marginal cost of cleaning up pollution is just equal to the marginal damage inflicted by pollution (at a level of cost C on the diagram and a pollution level of P). To the right of the point where the curves intersect there is too much pollution – the losses it imposes on the community are greater than the costs of cleaning up. To the left of Point P, the costs of reducing the pollution are greater than the losses it imposes on the community. Because these costs are not reflected in prices, the market gives the wrong signals and inappropriate amounts of resources are allocated to environmental problems. It should be added that for some products such as plutonium, the damage is so great, there is no 'efficient' level of pollution.

3   Instability
A major claim for the merits of free markets is made on the grounds that they coordinate the activities of producers and consumers through the generation of equilibrium or market-clearing prices. Yet in some markets, price signals may fail to coordinate the activities of producers and consumers because they come at the wrong time, or because the market is unable to respond to them. In these circumstances, price may have a de-stabilising rather than a stabilising influence. This is most likely to occur in agriculture where there may be a considerable time-lag between the input of factors and the eventual output. This is particularly noticeable with tree crops and livestock products. A coffee bush may not yield until five years after planting and then will go on bearing for twenty years, while for cattle up to two and a half years may elapse before beef or milk is available. As a consequence, farmers, taken as a whole, may increase their output of a product too much in response to a high

price. Because of the time-lag, the extent of this over-production will not be shown in the price, which will remain high. When the increased supplies eventually come on to the market, the price of the product may fall sharply. There may be heavy losses and some farmers may go out of business. Responding to the price signal, farmers as a whole may then make the mistake of cutting their planting and cattle breeding back by too much. Again because of the time-lag, this may not immediately be reflected in prices, which remain low. Two or three years later, when the reduced output resulting from previous decisions makes its impact on the market, prices will rise sharply and the whole cycle may begin again.

Economists have shown[2] that periodic shortages and surpluses of skilled professionals – doctors, scientists, engineers etc. – are also associated with time-lag problems. There is a substantial lag of several years between high earnings – signalling scarcity – and the emergence of an increased supply of qualified professionals from colleges, universities and training programmes in response to this. The unregulated market economy may also fail to achieve stability at a national level because the price mechanism does not ensure a balance between the total supply of goods and services and the total demand. The market may, for example, fail to coordinate savings and investment decisions. A full analysis of the causes and possible remedies for fluctuations in national income, employment and output is given in Part Two of this book.

4 Rigidity
Even when price signals are correct in their information and timing, there may be certain 'rigidities' in the system which prevent an adequate response on the supply side. In theory, price-signals of the market system provide powerful inducements to ensure that resources are properly allocated. Capital and labour are supposed to move away from those industries where prices and profits are low in search of higher rewards in industries where prices and profits are higher until, in the long run, resources are allocated so that no further gains can be made from change. In practice, however, social and institutional factors may hamper the effectiveness of the price system's incentives. Adjustment of supply and demand to the price mechanism's signals may be a very slow and socially painful process. Experience shows that labour does not move easily from areas with declining industries such as shipbuilding, textiles and coal mining to regions where industries are expanding. High unemployment may persist for many years.

There are numerous reasons for this, including reluctance, especially among the older workers, to pull up roots and start life in a new community. The cost of moving and lack of information about job opportunities together with a shortage of suitable accommodation, are other impediments to the mobility of the labour force. In addition, both organised labour and industry may attempt to distort the proper flow of resources, blocking responses to the price signals by restrictive practices. Both professional organisations and trade unions, by insisting on unnecessarily protracted training and apprenticeship schemes, may deter new entrants. The control of firms over distributive outlets – e.g. brewery ownership of public houses – may discourage new competitors. Barriers to entry, discussed in Chapter 8, can also act as a deterrent.

Competition and efficiency

We have examined the model of a particular type of competitive structure – that of perfect competition. What can be said about competition in general? Does it ensure the survival of the fittest? A firm may be able to survive in times of grave recession simply because it has sufficient bank balances to finance its losses. This may be quite unconnected with its efficiency. A more efficient firm that has perhaps been investing heavily in new product development, may be in a less favourable position and unable to survive a slump. Small firms may also exist because they are under the protective 'umbrella' of a larger firm which, although it is more efficient, allows them to survive in order to give an impression of competition and so avoid government monopoly investigation.

It must also be recognised that a large number of small competing suppliers may be incompatible with the effective exploitation of modern technology, which requires large plants. In motor-vehicle manufacture or petro-chemicals, for example, where the economies of scale are considerable, the market may not be large enough to support more than a few firms. Complex technology of this kind involves large commitments of capital, elaborate organisation and consequently a considerable lapse of time between the initiation of a product at the planning stage and its appearance on the market. The more a firm can control and dominate the environment in which it operates, the less the degree of uncertainty which surrounds its operations. Larger firms in more dominant positions may perhaps be more willing to undertake the long-range planning and commitment of resources for modern technology than small firms in a highly competitive market, where the time-horizon may be much shorter. The combination of economies and the greater degree of uncertainty associated with size is also apparent in the case of research. It is not surprising that in agriculture, which is characterised by a large number of small competing units, it is extremely rare to find any single farmer undertaking his own research and development work, although it is important for farming.

Finally, there are the effects of non-price competition, which is a feature common in oligopolistic markets discussed in the previous chapter. Clearly some of this may help to promote efficiency. Improvements in product design and performance, which provide better value for money, can be just as significant as price cuts. However, some non-price competition may be distinctly wasteful. Frequent but superficial changes in design aimed at creating an impression of being fashionable, may add little to performance but much to cost, especially as the 'new model' is launched with heavy advertising expenses. Some of the possible advantages and disadvantages of advertising were discussed in Chapter 6. While advertising may increase the amount of information buyers have on competing products, and help them to make better choices, it may bring few benefits and add to selling costs, if it is a purely persuasive 'brand X is superior' type of message.

The preceding points are not intended to imply that there is no connection between competition and efficiency. The practical question is not whether competition is desirable, but how much and what kind is desirable. Too much competition may be damaging to efficiency; too little competition may mean that there are no checks on possible abuses by powerful firms, and little incentive for improvement. The intense uncertainty of excessive competition may stunt rather than stimulate enterprise and risk taking, which may only be undertaken by a firm with some control over its environment. As the economist Schumpeter has commented 'one is more likely to drive faster if one has good brakes'.

Market structure and market performance – the evidence

In this and other chapters, we have explained how the extent of competition in a market, sometimes known as market structure, can influence the competitive tactics adopted by firms and hence their efficiency. It is a basic proposition of micro-economics that market structure is likely to have an important influence on market conduct (what firms do) and consequently on market performance (how efficient they are). This concluding section reviews some of the statistical evidence which economists have collected in an attempt to test the connection between structure and performance. It illustrates the difficulties which confront economists in collecting and interpreting data when trying to test theories.

A simple theory of market behaviour suggests that the fewer the firms, the greater the possibility of collusion (informal or formal) to raise prices and hence the greater the level of profits. One way of testing this theory is to compare the level of concentration for different industries with the rate of return on capital (Profits/Capital employed %).

As we have explained in Chapter 8, concentration is the share of the market held by the leading firms. Usually the percentage share of the market held by the leading four or five firms is used. If the theory is correct, one would expect to find that collective agreements to regulate competition, together with a greater return on capital, will be associated with higher levels of concentration. Numerous studies undertaken in the United States and Europe appear to offer some support for the theory. High concentration is often associated with various measures to control the market. The evidence also shows that firms in concentrated markets obtain persistently higher rates of profit than firms in less concentrated markets. This in itself does not prove a causal relationship but it does *suggest* that higher prices are associated with higher levels of concentration.

Although the evidence appears to be consistent with the theory, it would be wrong to assume that it is in any way conclusive. Despite the positive association between concentration and rates of return on capital shown in the studies, the relationship is generally a weak one. That is to say an industry with a concentration level of 80% for the top four firms, does not show rates of return on capital much higher than another industry with a concentration level of only 40%. The degree of association between two variables Y and X – in this case concentration and rates of return – is measured statistically by what is called the *coefficient of determination* R^2. It may range from a value of 1.000, which indicates a perfect positive relationship, to 0, which indicates that none of the variation in Y is explained by the X variable. Coefficients at or near to zero suggest a weak relationship between the two variables. In most of the studies mentioned the coefficients of determination are between +0.20 and +0.50. This means that no more than one-fifth to one-half of the variation in rates of return is associated with differences in concentration. There are a number of possible explanations for this:

1   Collusion depends upon many factors of which concentration is

only one. The reader is referred to the case study in Chapter 8 as an illustration of this. Even when firms do collude, their pricing and output policies may be protective measures against the severities of competition rather than instruments of exploitation.

2   The data is consistent with the view now emerging from economic research that market structures alone do not determine every aspect of pricing conduct and profit levels.[3] How the competitive game is played within any particular structure is important. Recent analysis has also emphasised the influence of potential competition – a point discussed later under 'Contestable Markets'.

We still have to interpret the significance of the fact that average profit levels are higher in some industries than others. It must be remembered that profits are in part a reward for risk taking (pp 69–70). Therefore, to some extent, different profit levels will reflect the compensation for varying degrees of risk between, for example, the uncertainties of an industry in a high technology market – space research or bio-engineering – and a safer established market such as bread and biscuits. In addition to the risk factor, differences in market structure, particularly concentration, explain some but not all of the variation in profit.

Are the observed differences in profits arising from market structure the result of efficiency or inefficiency? The theory has already been presented in this chapter that higher profits in highly concentrated industries may be the result of greater market power which gives the opportunity to fix prices and output. On the other hand it could be argued that economies of scale require a few large firms and hence high concentration levels. Various studies have shown that the average size of the largest firms in the most highly concentrated industries is approximately ten times that of those in the least concentrated.[4] Thus some economists claim that it is the efficiency of large scale production rather than market power which generates higher profit.

This does not put highly concentrated industries beyond suspicion. Those firms fortunate enough to be in such an industry may earn excess profits behind the barriers to entry created by economies of scale. Moreover research indicates that efficiency measured in terms of productivity – output per unit on input – is not significantly higher in concentrated industries.[5] Despite the inconclusive nature of the evidence on the effects of high concentration, it is clear that firms in such markets may have the power to manipulate price and output to the detriment of customers. This fact has influenced government competition policy (described in the following chapter). Mergers which increase concentration and the conduct of firms in concentrated markets are subjected to close scrutiny to see if they operate against the public interest.

As we have seen, differences in average profitability *between* industries can be understood in terms of differences in market structure and variations in the risk associated with operations in different types of market. What appears to be more puzzling are differences in profitability between firms *within* an industry. Firms may find it difficult because of barriers to entry, lack of knowledge, etc., to move from one industry to another in pursuit of higher profits but one would not expect the same difficulties within an industry as the less profitable strive to match their more prosperous rivals.

Many of the intra-industry profit rate studies have used cross-sectional data, which gives a snapshot of the industry at a particular point in time. The profit variations in such a snapshot may be compared with the variation found in a cross-section of trees in a forest. For a given species and with given soil and climate, there may be an optimum size and condition of tree. The cross-section reveals different sizes because some trees are still growing to maturity; others are at their peak and some declining. A cross-section of firms will also reveal similar stages of growth and profitability. If we took a long-term time series of statistics for an industry we would expect to see profit levels tending to converge to an equilibrium level, if there were no disturbances. Using the techniques of inter-firm comparison, for example, the less profitable firms may be able to diagnose their weaknesses and narrow the gap between themselves and their competitors. In practice, equilibrium rarely occurs because innovations in product design manufacturing and marketing techniques will always put some firms temporarily ahead of their rivals.

Market structure and innovation

What is the impact of market structure on the development of technology? Is the modern industry of a few large firms, as Professor Galbraith has claimed, an 'excellent instrument for inducing technological change'?[6] A distinction is made between *invention* – an original idea for something – and *innovation*, when the idea is profitably transformed by a firm into an actual product or process. A further stage of *diffusion* occurs when the manufacture of the new product or use of the new process spreads to other firms.

Large firms spend more on research and development (R&D) than smaller firms. The hundred largest firms in many developed countries account for a major share of R&D – four fifths in the US for example. Despite this, large firms do not always dominate the process of invention. It is calculated that of 64 important inventions in the twentieth-century, only 24 came from the R&D Departments of large firms, while the remaining 40 were the product of individual inventors.[7] However large firms do play a major part in innovation where the resources of large R&D departments are evidently important. Diffusion also appears to be greater in industries with fewer firms, possibly due to the easier transfer of information. There are notable exceptions to both of these general tendencies. The picture that emerges suggests that no single industry structure is ideal for all aspects of technical change. The economist cannot therefore come up with a general prescription on policy for industrialists and governments. In deciding how best to promote improvements in technology, scrupulous attention must be paid to the characteristics of a particular markets.

Contestable markets

Throughout this chapter is the idea that the fewer the firms the less competitive the market. This view has been questioned by Professor Baumol and others in the *theory of contestable markets*.[8+9] According to this, a market with, for example, three firms may be just as competitive as one with three hundred. The position of the three firms, however large and powerful they are, can be contested by new entrants who may also be large firms in other markets, wishing to diversify. They will find it profitable to enter the market as challengers if the three firms have uncompetitively high prices and profits.

It is claimed that contestability depends upon:

1   All firms having equal access to appropriate finance and technology;
2   The type of costs incurred. Although the technology may involve high fixed costs they will not be a barrier to entry, if the costs are not of the sunk (non-recoverable) type. A fixed sunk cost on a railway, for example, would be the expenditure on the construction of tunnels and excavations to accommodate the track, which is lost if the railway closes. Expenditure on the locomotives and carriages is not a sunk fixed cost because the

equipment can be used on other railway lines. It is thought that the smaller sunk costs are, as a proportion of total fixed costs, the lower the barriers to entry and the more contestable the market. Transportation is considered to be a particularly contestable industry because the sunk cost of terminal facilities, such as harbours, airports and roads are shared. Other fixed costs in the form of ships aircraft and trucks are recoverable since they can be shifted from one regional market to another.

Contestable market theory is not universally accepted. Its critics argue that a prompt competitive response by established firms can force newcomers out of the market at a loss before they have time to earn enough to cover their sunk costs. In this situation even small sunk costs can render a market incontestable. Whatever its shortcomings, contestable market theory provides some useful insights. It emphasises the significance of sunk costs and conditions of entry, which may compel even a few firms to be competitive. It is also an important reminder that any government policy intended to encourage competition cannot be based simply on the number of firms in a market.

Summary

The most important aspects of economic efficiency are concerned with cost, allocation, innovation and product range. There is an expected connection between the extent of competition in markets and efficiency: the greater the competition, the more efficient firms need to be in order to survive. However, competition may sometimes impede efficiency; for example, a large number of small competing firms can be incompatible with the effective use of modern technology, which may best be employed where there are only a few large firms; uncertainty may be created by intense competition, discouraging long-range planning and investment. For governments trying to improve the market system, the problem is one of achieving the right balance between too much and too little competition.

Market prices should act as signals to guide the efficient coordination of the activities of producers and consumers but they may not always promote the efficient use of resources. Price signals may be misleading or provide inadequate stimulus because of:

1 Monopolistic and restrictive practices.
2 Social costs not being fully reflected in price.
3 Time-lags in producers' response to price.

4 Social factors hindering the movement of resources between industries and regions.

Evidence from studies on the connection between the nature of competition (market structure) and efficiency indicates a positive but weak correlation between concentration and profit levels. There are considerable problems in interpreting the significance of this; these include the accuracy of data, the possibility of profit levels being connected with other factors and the need to decide what is a normal level of profit for a particular industry. The evidence on the connection between market structure and innovation is also difficult to analyse; it appears that there is no single structure applicable to all industries which is conducive to innovation.

Questions

1 How may a market system malfunction? (Oxford Local Examinations, A-Level Economics)
2 (*a*) Explain, using examples, what you understand by 'divergences between private and social costs and benefits'.
   (*b*) Does the existence of such divergences suggest an economic case for state intervention?
   (Institute of Chartered Accountants in England and Wales)
3 How efficient is the price mechanism as a system for allocating resources in a developed economy? (Institute of Cost and Management Accountants)
4 Why is it considered that perfect competition provides an optimal allocation of resources? (Oxford and Cambridge Schools Examination Board, A-Level Economics)
5 Does economic theory predict that a market economy must, of necessity, arrive at an equilibrium price for each commodity? (Oxford and Cambridge Schools Examination Board, A-Level)
6 How do you account for differences in:
   (*a*) the average profitability of different industries.
   (*b*) the profitability of different firms in the same industry?
   (Associated Examining Board, A-Level Economics)

Notes

1 See Bator, F. M., 'The Simple Analytics of Welfare Maximisation', *American Economic Review* (March 1957), or Morris, D. *The Economic System of the UK* Chapter 6 'Allocation of Resources' (W. Jones).
2 Arrow and Capron, 'Dynamic Shortages: The Engineer-Scientist Case' in Watson, *Price of Theory and its Uses* (Mifflin 1976).

3   Davies, S. et al, *Economics of Industrial Organisation* (Longman 1988).
4   Winn, D. N., *Industrial Market Structure Performance* (Michigan 1975).
5   Davies, S. and Caves, R. E., *Britain's Productivity Lag* (Cambridge University Press 1987).
6   Galbraith, J. K., *American Capitalism: The Concept of Countervailing Power* (Mifflin 1952).
7   Jewkes, J., Sawyers, D. and Stillerman, R., *The Sources of Invention* (Norton 1969).
8   Baumol, W., 'Contestable Markets: An Uprising in the Theory of Industry Structure' *American Economic Review* 72 (March 1982).
9   Davies, G., 'Revolution in Monopoly Theory' *Lloyds Bank Review* No. 153 (July 1984).

10

Markets and Government Policy

Introduction

The preceding chapter has discussed the relationship between different concepts of efficiency, and the way in which the free play of the price system may permit departures from efficiency, or 'market failure'. In this chapter we consider the part the government can play in countering several types of market failure.

The extent of government intervention in advanced Western economies has grown strikingly in the past thirty years. Some government measures are directed at controlling the overall level of activity in the economy: these form the subject of much of the second half of this book. Our concern in this chapter, however, is with a fairly varied set of measures aimed at making the market system operate more efficiently at the level of individual firms or industries. These include policies to regulate monopolies or restrictive practices in private industry (structural policies); policies to take certain industries into public ownership (nationalisation) or, conversely, to return them to the private sector (privatisation); measures to limit pollution and other harmful effects associated with some types of production; and finally policies directed at improving the economic situation of particular regions.

1 Structural policies

Chapters 7 and 8 showed how the outcome in different types of market – the quantity produced and the price at which it is sold – depends on the market structure. From perfect competition through oligopoly to pure monopoly, structure (the number of producers) influences conduct, and may thus affect performance. We also saw in Chapter 8 that many individual industries in Britain and in other Western countries are highly concentrated, and, moreover, that the share of the largest firms in output has risen consistently throughout this century.

The mere existence of concentration in industry does not necessarily mean that prices are kept at an artificially high level to the detriment of consumers. As few as two firms in an industry may compete vigorously with one another. Domestic firms may have been increasingly open to competition from imports in the post-war period, especially as tariff barriers were lowered. Again, a highly concentrated supply side of a market may face an equally highly concentrated demand side, which gives customers a degree of market power equal to that of suppliers. Any or all of these factors may limit the significance of a high level of concentration in a particular case. Nonetheless, concentration does create a danger of abuse of market power which is not present in unconcentrated industries, and this has caused most governments to pass legislation for the control and regulation of concentration.[1]

(a)   British legislation on monopolies and mergers

British legislation on monopolies and mergers dates back to 1948, when an Act was passed setting up the Monopolies Commission. The Commission has two chief functions: to examine industries which are dominated by one or more large firms, and (since 1965) to report on the desirability of mergers involving large companies.

The present institutional framework is as follows. Either the minister in the relevant government department (currently the Department of Trade and Industry) or the Director-General of Fair Trading (a public servant) may refer to the Commission any industry in which a single firm's sales or purchases account for a quarter or more of the market. The Commission first establishes whether a monopoly (as defined by a 25% market share) exists; it then examines the industry's performance and makes appropriate recommendations to the minister. In the case of mergers, only the Secretary of State may make a reference to the Commission, though advice on this issue is given by the Director-General of Fair Trading who consults a Mergers Panel.

When a reference is made, the Commission decides whether the merger is in the public interest, and recommends accordingly. In the case of both monopolies and mergers, however, the final decision is up to the minister, who can overrule recommendations from the Commission. This is unusual in the case of merger references, although in late 1982 the minister did overrule the Commission's majority recommendation that the proposed merger between Charter Consolidated and Anderson Strathclyde should not take place (*Financial Times*, 22 December 1982).

All the British legislation has been rather vague about the criteria on which monopolies should be evaluated, and in practice the Commission has had to develop its own approach, which has varied over the course of its life. Essentially this has consisted of a pragmatic evaluation of the costs and benefits associated with the existence or formation of a dominant firm in a particular market. Many of these costs and benefits are difficult or impossible to quantify precisely, so the issue is decided finally on the judgement of the Commission members. It is hardly surprising therefore that the majority report is often accompanied by a minority report of members who have evaluated the costs and benefits differently.

Let us consider a typical situation where the formation of a dominant firm may be both beneficial and, in other ways, detrimental. Say, for example, that a merger between two firms will give them sufficient market power to raise prices. This brings about allocative inefficiency as defined in the previous chapter. At the same time rationalisation of production lowers costs and permits a higher level of technical efficiency, which is beneficial to the economy. [For evidence on the extent of economies of scale, see Chapter 5.] Moreover, some of the surplus profits may be used for research and development or product innovation, which also benefits the economy, yet which may strengthen the firm's domination. [The influential economist Joseph Schumpeter (1883–1950) argued that the prospect of obtaining high profits through innovation was one of the main factors in the dynamic development of capitalist economies.] The Monopolies Commission has to weigh up the balance of advantages and make a recommendation accordingly.

Where the Commission has been investigating existing monopolies, the range of recommendations made has been wide. Many reports have expressed the view that the existence of a dominant firm or firms has not operated against the public interest, while a number have recommended remedies ranging from a reduction in advertising expenditure to divestiture by a dominant firm of a large shareholding in its major domestic competitor. (In fact the Board of Trade declined to follow up this recommendation.) More draconian remedies which are available in principle but not applied in practice are compulsory dissolution of a dominant firm or nationalisation. This last remedy was proposed in a minority report of the Commission's inquiry into British Oxygen, but was not contained in the majority report nor acted upon by the government. However it remains one possible way of dealing with the problem of achieving technical efficiency in large-scale production without running the risk of there being profiteering by the monopolist with the consequent misallocation of resources. This point is taken up further below.

One indication of a dominant firm's performance which is almost always included in Commission reports is the measurement of the firm's rate of return on capital. A rate of return substantially above the national average may be an indication that a dominant firm is cutting back production in order to raise price and increase profits, in the manner described in the last chapter. However there may be a different explanation. The firm may be run with unusual efficiency which justifies a rate of profit above the average. Conversely an average rate of return is not a definite indication of lack of monopoly power. A dominant firm may tolerate what is known as X-inefficiency, i.e. costs being higher than necessary. The reward for being a monopoly may not necessarily be high profits, but a quiet and undemanding commercial life. Moreover, the Commission has proved willing to consider and in some cases accept the argument that an above average rate of return in some industries is justified either by the high level of risk or by the need to incur heavy expenditures on research and development. Thus the rate of return on capital, though its calculation is an important element in the Commission's procedure, is viewed from a pragmatic standpoint in the light of particular circumstances.

Investigation of mergers follows the same pattern as investigation of dominant firm positions, though naturally such investigations have to be completed with more urgency in order to avoid prolonged uncertainty in the stock market. The merger referral legislation, which makes any merger above a certain size eligible for examination, irrespective of whether or not it creates a dominant firm, gives the Commission an opportunity to pass judgement on situations where absolute concentration is growing, even though concentration in particular markets remains unchanged. The formation of conglomerates is an example of this trend. conglomerates are brought about by mergers or takeovers of other firms in unrelated markets by a single firm. Often the very fact that a merger is referred to the Commission is sufficient to deter the two sides.

In investigating mergers the same criteria are used as in investigating dominant firm positions. At the start of the 1980s, there was a tendency for the Commission to take increasing account of arguments not directly related to competition. In the Charter Consolidated and Anderson Strathclyde case noted above, these included loss of control of a Scottish Company. The suitability of bidders was also a factor. To counteract this trend, in 1984 the Secretary of State for Trade and Industry noted: 'my policy has been and will continue to be to make references (to the MMC) primarily on competition grounds.' Putting this policy into effect has proved difficult, in the light of debates about how the degree of concentration should be defined. For example, to what extent is competition from abroad relevant? Is it enough to avoid a reference that competition is there potentially, if not actually?

For these reasons it has not proved easy to make mergers policy clear, predictable and tied to competition grounds. Merger policy has now been further complicated by developments in the European Community, which are discussed below.

As well as rules governing concentration and mergers, firms are also subject to the Competition Act 1980 which is directed against business practices which might have an anti-competitive effect. An example is refusal to supply to retailers which sell goods at a discount. The Act adopts a flexible approach to such instances which are investigated on a case by case approach, first by the Director-General of Fair Trading and then, if a reference is made to it, by the Monopolies and Mergers Commission. The Act leaves open the possibility that a practice may be found by the MMC to be anti-competitive, but justifiable on other grounds.

(b)   Other approaches to monopoly

The British legislation on monopolies and mergers reflects the view that unregulated markets may operate against the public interest, and that the standard competitive analysis which assumes the possibility of new firms entering profitable or inefficient industries is not an accurate representation of reality in advanced economies. But if the markets operate imperfectly the opposite danger is also present, as there may be cases where increased concentration might on balance operate in the public interest.

It was to meet these cases that the Labour government set up the Industrial Reorganisation Corporation (IRC) in 1966. The purpose of the IRC was to promote mergers where rationalisation of production seemed desirable and to offer financial assistance to firms wishing to expand or modernise. Thus the IRC in some cases acted with the deliberate intention of promoting a dominant firm position. This inevitably led to some conflict of approach between the IRC

and the Monopolies Commission, especially as the two organisations were attached to different ministries.

In the course of its relatively short life, the IRC was involved in
the restructuring of a number of industries, including computers,
motor vehicles, electrical engineering and a number of other key
sectors. Its work was occasionally controversial, as when it took the
side of GEC in a contested merger with AEI to restructure the
electrical industry, though most observers now regard the takeover
as a success. The IRC was also empowered to deal in shares in the
open market in companies in which it was interested.

The IRC was wound up in 1971, by a government with a less
interventionist philosophy. Some of its functions were subsequently
taken over by the National Enterprise Board (NEB), established in
1975 by a subsequent Labour government, but one of the main
purposes of the NEB was to increase the level of government
ownership and control of industry as well as to promote restructuring of the public sector. The change of government in 1979 led to the
abolition of the NEB two years later. These frequent reversals of
policy not only make it difficult or impossible to evaluate the
long-term effects of alternative measures; they also promote uncertainty in industry and discourage long-term planning.

We noted above that both the Monopolies Commission and the
IRC were founded upon the principle of discretionary intervention
and upon examination of each individual case on its merits. This
contrasts with an alternative view that no intervention is necessary
and that the market will regulate itself to achieve maximum efficiency. [Supporters of this view often argue in favour of improving the
amount of information available in the market, through company
disclosure, in order to make the market operate more efficiently.] A
third alternative which has some support favours non-discretionary
intervention. According to this view, action should be taken to
eliminate or prevent the emergence of any dominant firm, irrespective of the circumstances. A maximum market share would be
established and no firm would be allowed to exceed it. This
approach is embodied in anti-trust legislation in the United States,
but it is fair to say that in practice enforcement has been incomplete.

The advantages claimed for this approach are that it saves
expensive inquiries into individual cases and reduces uncertainty –
each firm knows in advance what is the position. But the disadvantages of this approach are so large as to render it virtually unworkable in practice. In the first place, a market must be defined exactly.
We considered this problem in an earlier chapter dealing with
consumer demand and noted that it was difficult to solve. But with a

non-discretionary approach to the control of market power it becomes crucial to define a market precisely in order to establish whether a firm has exceeded the maximum market share permitted under the legislation. Even using the British discretionary approach problems of market definition have hindered the work of the Monopolies Commission. In an inquiry into frozen vegetables, a company asserted that the relevant market for which its share should be calculated was not the market for frozen vegetables, but for vegetables as a whole (including fresh and tinned). With a non-discretionary policy, such problems of market definition would assume a vital importance, as calculation of market shares would lead to automatic action. Even if this problem were solved the legislation would have to lay down maximum market shares, and it is not clear how these would be determined, as by definition in a non-discretionary approach limits would be established irrespective of the extent to which any firm used its market power. Because of these problems British legislation on monopolies and mergers has consistently rejected the non-discretionary approach and adopted instead the discretionary pragmatic approach, described above. This involves weighing up the costs and benefits of any dominant firm position or merger and making a decision on this basis.

(c) The control of restrictive practices

A restrictive practice is an agreement between separate firms to restrict competition between them, without going to the length of a merger or takeover. It may take the form of an agreed division of the market between the firms, with the elimination of price competition (this would be an instance of a cartel). Or it may involve a lesser degree of collusion, such as the exchange of price lists, which still restricts competition by allowing firms to coordinate price rises.

Since the 1956 Restrictive Trade Practices Act, firms have been required to register any such agreements with an official organisation, which since 1973 has been the Office of Fair Trading. Agreements are presumed to be against the public interest, unless the parties to the agreement can convince the Restrictive Practices Court (established by the 1956 Act) that the agreement is beneficial.

If an agreement is to be maintained it must pass through one of seven gateways and also satisfy a consideration known as the *tailpiece*. The seven gateways are as follows:

(i)   that the restriction is needed to protect the public against injury;

(ii)　that removal of the restriction would deny the public advantages;

(iii)　that the restriction is necessary to prevent another person or firm not party to the agreement from restricting competition;

(iv)　that the restriction is necessary to give parties to the agreement sufficient market power to negotiate fair terms with a dominant supplier or customer;

(v)　that removal of the agreement would create serious and persistent unemployment in an area or areas;

(vi)　that removal of the agreement would cause a substantial reduction in export earnings;

(vii)　that the restriction is necessary to maintain another restrictive agreement approved by the Court.

Finally, in the tailpiece, the Court must be satisfied that any advantage accruing under the gateways is large enough to outweigh any harmful effects of the agreement.

It is clear that the nature of the Restrictive Practices legislation differs from that for the control of monopolies in a number of fundamental ways. In the first place, consideration of any agreement coming within the scope of the Act is automatic, and the presumption is made that the agreement is harmful and should be abandoned, unless the parties can prove otherwise. This is quite different from the procedure used for monopolies and mergers, where there is no automatic referral and no presumption of harm. This difference in approach can be justified by the observation that a restrictive agreement among firms, to fix prices and share out markets for example, produces all the harmful effects on allocative efficiency of a monopoly, with none of the potential benefits in technical efficiency from rationalisation of production as the firms continue to operate independently.

Secondly, restrictive practices are considered a subject suitable for court rulings, rather than for consideration by a body not following court-room procedures. Courts are often used to decide policy matters of this kind, within the framework of legislation, but it has been argued that some of the gateways, particularly gateway (ii) above, are so vague as to make the task of the Court almost impossible and to allow inconsistent ruling. A third difference from Monopolies Commission proceedings consists in the fact that court rulings are not subject to negotiation between a minister and the firms involved. Subject to an appeal on matters of law, the Court's ruling is final.

The Court initially took a fairly strong line and this contributed to the abandonment of a large number of agreements before they went through the legal process. Inevitably some cases excited a certain amount of controversy. Among the controversial cases where agreements were maintained were the black bolts and nuts case of 1960 and the net book agreement case of 1962. Both of these agreements were maintained under gateway (ii), on the grounds that they offered the public advantages. In the former case it was argued that price competition would impose a cost of shopping around for the customers; in the latter that price-cutting in the retail book trade would limit outlets and result in detriment to the public. Both these decisions have been disputed by observers.

But agreements successfully defended account for a tiny minority of all agreements registered, and the effect of the 1956 Act was to eliminate formal restrictive agreements, many of them long standing, in many sectors of British industry. What is more difficult to establish is whether the formal agreements have not been replaced by alternative methods of restricting competition. A number of loopholes appeared after 1956, including the growth of information agreements, in which the parties undertook to notify one another of price changes. Later legislation required registration of some agreements of this kind. In addition, the Office of Fair Trading was permitted to investigate concealed agreements, many of which recently came to light. These considerations make it hard to give a simple verdict on British legislation on restrictive practices.

(d)   The impact of European competition law

The European Community is having an increasing impact on the operation of competition law in Britain, as in other member states. For a number of years the Commission has been seeking in particular to develop a community wide policy on merger control.

Articles 85 and 86 of the EC Treaty set out the European position. Article 85 essentially prohibits restrictive agreements which distort trade between Community member states. This provision has been most commonly applied to such practices as market-sharing or price-fixing. Article 86 prohibits abuse of a dominant position affecting trade between member states – the classic example being monopoly pricing.

Until 1989 there was uncertainty about the precise powers granted by Article 86 in respect of control of mergers. Some noted that the Commission was interpreting them in an increasingly elastic way. Thus in the case of the merger between British Airways and British Caledonian in 1986, the Commission was able to use the threat of Article 86 to persuade the companies to alter the terms of the deal even after it was passed by the United Kingdom authorities.

At the end of 1989, however, agreement was reached over the division of responsibility between the national competition policy bodies on one hand and the Commission on the other. National authorities will judge merger proposals involving companies with a worldwide turnover of up to £3.65 billion per year, while the Commission will deal with the 40 or so cases per year above that level. It is not yet clear, however, how the Commission's decisions will be made in practice.

2 Nationalisation, privatisation and regulation

The most extreme form of government intervention occurs when a government takes a firm or an industry into public ownership, and runs it itself, usually as a public corporation. In the whole of the post-war period nationalisation, and its opposite 'privatisation', have been a source of great political controversy. Rather than enter into that controversy here, we will only examine the arguments for and against nationalisation, using the concepts developed in the previous chapter. In other words, we shall ignore the important argument, on the fringes of economics and politics, that public ownership of industry prevents the domination of society by a small group of powerful capitalists, whose economic power is exercised in their own interests rather than in the interests of society as a whole, as well as the counter-argument that nationalisation is harmful because it concentrates within a single organisation – the state – economic power which it may be much better to leave dispersed among individual private owners.

From the standpoint of efficiency, nationalisation is one possible way of combining technical efficiency, which in many industries requires a large scale of production, with allocative efficiency, or the absence of abuse of market power by single dominant producers.

According to this argument a nationalised industry will reap the benefits of large scale production without risking the damage of monopolistic behaviour, as the industry's pricing decisions can be determined and monitored by the government. The argument finds particularly strong application in industries which are *natural monopolies* – that is, industries which by their nature can be supplied efficiently only by a single supplier.

Possible examples of these are the gas and electricity and water distribution networks. It is almost certainly inefficient for two separate sets of pipes to deliver these services to the same areas.

But is nationalisation the only solution? And are the so-called 'natural monopolies' in state ownership in all countries? The answer to the latter question is clearly no. In the United States and, increasingly in other countries, especially the United Kingdom, utilities such as gas, electricity, telecommunications and water supply are in private hands, but their behaviour is circumscribed by government controls, usually implemented by a regulatory agency.

The co-existence of public and private firms in an industry has made it possible to investigate which form of ownership generates greater efficiency in production. The method adopted is to compare costs of production in two or more firms operating in broadly similar conditions. Many studies of this kind have been undertaken in the United States, Europe and elsewhere. A review of them suggests that no unambiguous conclusion can be drawn, although there is some suggestion that private ownership is less costly.

If an industry is a monopoly and not subject to the discipline of competition, some form of regulation will be required whether it is in public or private hands. In the case of a nationalised industry the government is confronted with the difficult problem of fixing a price for its output.

We have seen in the previous chapter that a system of setting price equal to marginal cost has certain desirable effects on efficiency. With marginal cost pricing, consumers make their choice of what to buy on the basis of prices which reflect the marginal cost of producing goods of different kinds, and consumption decisions are thus based on the true (marginal) cost of production to the firm (we now assume that there are no externalities of the kind described on p. 183). We also saw, in Chapter 7, that in competitive markets firms will set their output levels in such a way that their marginal cost is equal to price. Thus in adopting the principle of marginal cost pricing, nationalised industries would be extending to the public sector a system of pricing based on perfect competition.

However there are certain difficulties here. In the first place, it is not easy actually to establish the level of marginal cost, especially from the transport sector: when all the carriages of a train are full, the marginal cost of carrying an extra passenger is large, as a new carriage must be added; however the marginal cost of subsequent passengers fall sharply, until a further carriage is required. In practice, problems of this kind can usually be solved by some kind of averaging procedure.

Secondly, if the industry shows increasing returns to scale (a falling average cost curve), then marginal cost will lie below average cost, and a policy of charging price equal to marginal cost will condemn the industry to inevitable losses, as revenue will not cover cost. This is illustrated in Fig. 10.1, which shows a declining average cost curve AC with the marginal cost curve MC lying beneath it. Given a demand curve DD, marginal cost pricing would imply an output level of X_1 and industry losses equal to the shaded area in the Figure. If it is decided to persist with marginal cost pricing and accept the losses, they could be, and often are, met out of public funds. But the need to raise taxation to cover them may have harmful effects on the economy – on incentives to work, for example. This means that marginal cost pricing is only achieved at the cost of introducing further distortions into the operation of the economic system. The government may therefore prefer to adopt a policy of average cost pricing, represented in the Figure by selling X_2 units at P_2.

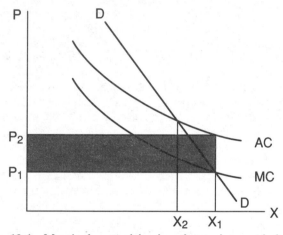

Fig. 10.1 Marginal cost pricing in a decreasing cost industry

In practice, nationalised industries in the United Kingdom have operated under a number of different regimes. The current system requires the industries to earn a 'required rate of return' on their investment programme as a whole. Until 1989, this rate was set at 5%. In 1989, however, it was raised to 8% placing it closer to rates of return earned in the private sector. At the same time, the industries are encouraged to charge prices equal to long-run marginal costs, and to appraise their investment projects in a way calculated to generate the required rate of return on average. In practice, however, UK nationalised industries have not achieved on average even the lower target return of 5%. There are a number of reasons for this, including a tendency for the firms to over-invest and a reluctance on the part of successive governments to promote price rises in home services such as water and electricity.

It is noteworthy that when equivalent industries in the United States have been in private ownership, they have had their prices controlled in a form analogous to the British required rate of return system. The regulatory bodies set up to control them have identified allowed rates of return which the firms can earn, and prices are allowed to rise only when those rates of return are not achieved. It has often been noted that such a system gives firms little incentive to save on costs, as any such savings are passed on to the customer in the form of lower prices rather than kept as profit.

Because of the faulty incentives in rate of return regulation, there has been a move in recent years towards an alternative system known as 'price-capping'. Under this system the regulatory body estimates the reduction in costs, relative to other sectors, which the industry should achieve. It is then allowed to raise its prices up to that limit. If it achieves a larger cost reduction, it makes more profit: if it is inefficient and fails to meet the target, it makes a loss. The critical point is that the firm has an incentive to reduce costs which is absent under rate of return regulation.

As an example, the prices of certain telephone services in the United Kingdom are pegged so that on average they can rise by up to 6¼% less than the overall price rise of consumer goods in the economy – the retail price index (RPI). Other industries have a similar RPI-X formula, the differential price rise (or X factor) differing from case to case. There are obvious difficulties in setting or changing the appropriate value of X, but the system seems to work better than rate of return regulation. It is used in all United Kingdom utilities in one form or another and is increasingly adopted in the United States and elsewhere.

We noted earlier that over the past ten years there has been a shift in the balance of ownership in favour of privatisation of utilities. The trend is most marked in the United Kingdom where by 1990 the telecommunications, airport, water and gas supply industries had been privatised, as had many other firms operating in a more competitive environment, such as British Aerospace, British Steel, British Petroleum and British Leyland. The Government also had plans well advanced to complete the sale of the electricity supply industries. At the end of 1990 total revenue from such sales had exceeded £30bn.

The act of privatisation gives an exceptional opportunity for restructuring in a way intended to promote competition. Some nationalised industries consist of two or more distinct stages of activity which are combined in a single 'vertically integrated' firm. These stages may exhibit economies of scale in different degrees. For example, electricity *generation* at power stations can be organised on a competitive basis, whereas electricity *distribution* is probably a natural monopoly. If these two activities are sold separately, as the British Government has done, regulation can be confined to the distribution companies.

This approach reflects a widely held belief that the form of ownership of assets is less significant than the extent to which firms using them are subject to competition. By this argument, privatisation by itself makes little difference to efficiency, unless it is accompanied by liberalisation.

Finally, it is worth noting that selling state assets also gives governments an opportunity to promote wider share ownership. If shares in the privatised companies are offered at less than their market value, and the rationing system for their allocation favours small investors, the effect on share ownership can be enormous. It is estimated that the privatisations in the UK have increased the number of share owners enormously. This benefit was gained however at the cost of under-pricing the shares sufficiently to make them an attractive investment even for inexperienced investors.

To summarise, there are some industries, particularly those involving distribution networks, which are likely to remain monopolies and to require government intervention of some kind. This may take the form either of nationalisation or of regulation of a privately owned company. In either case there are serious problems in maintaining incentives for efficiency, and there is no clear ranking of options. There is ground, however, for favouring the development of competition wherever possible.

3   Externalities and the price system

Monopolies bring with them the danger of allocative inefficiency, as monopolistic firms may deliberately raise their prices in order to make higher profits, and the consumer pays a price which does not reflect the true economic cost of production. In this section we consider a totally different set of circumstances in which the price paid by consumers fails to reflect the true cost of production, and again, we see a potential role for the government to step in to promote allocative efficiency. As we have seen in Chapter 9 the need for intervention arises because many activities undertaken by a firm or an individual may have repercussions on other organisations within the economy. If a firm discharges an effluent into a river as a by-product in an industrial process, it will affect the composition of the water and may have a harmful effect on another factory downstream which needs pure water for its own production.

In recent years there has been growing concern about the effects of pollution, especially of 'acid rain', the effect of emission of sulphur into the atmosphere especially by coal-burning power stations, and the 'greenhouse effect', the fear that the earth's temperature is rising as a result of damage to the ozone layer, again brought about by emissions of gases. In discussing the effects of externalities we shall concentrate on the illustration of atmospheric pollution. When a firm emits a pollutant into the atmosphere, there are two alternative ways of analysing the problem. It can be said either that the firm is producing in addition to its normal product an additional harmful product, known as a *bad*, which is inflicted on other people in the area; or that the firm uses up in the production an extra input, which is clean air or a clean environment in general. Whichever way the problem is examined, the firm is either using an input for which it is not paying or inflicting on others an output for which it does not compensate them. This analysis suggests one possible solution for the control of pollution and for dealing with externalities in general.

Externalities arise because there is no market or price for the external effect. No one has property rights over the environment and therefore no one has the legal right to seek redress from anyone harming the environment. Under the present legal system only the government can solve the problem. It can do so by levying a tax upon firms or individuals that damage the environment. By doing so the government forces polluters to pay a price for the input which they would otherwise use freely. To look at the problem in the other way – the government forces the polluter to pay for the damage inflicted by the pollutant. The tax would be passed on at least in part to the consumers of the product whose production damages the environment, but this is a good thing since previously consumers of the product were not paying the full economic cost, including pollution cost, of production. The tax should be set at such a level which reduces production to the point where the marginal cost, including external cost, of producing a unit exactly matches the consumer's willingness to pay. Note that this does not mean that pollution is wholly eliminated. The cost of total elimination is usually greater than consumers are willing to bear; in this case a certain level of pollution is desirable. Levying such a tax would eliminate the allocative inefficiency brought about by pollution, and it would do so by using the price system.

Another possible approach is to subsidise anti-pollution measures, such as equipment in power stations to eliminate sulphur dioxide. This has the merit of reducing pollution, but it breaches the 'polluter pays' principle. The price charged for the goods which generate the pollution will exclude pollution cost, which will be picked up by the subsidy.

Of course use of the price system is not the only way of coping with pollution. An alternative, widely practised, is *direct quantitative control*. The government imposes maximum levels on the discharge of harmful effluents into the environment. A firm which breaches these limits is guilty of an offence and may be prosecuted, though the penalties on conviction have until recently been derisively small. This may seem a more straightforward method of controlling pollution, and a quantity limitation can in principle, if set correctly, eliminate the allocative inefficiency brought about by externalities in exactly the same way as an optimal tax. But, as Professor Beckerman has powerfully argued, most resource allocation decisions in capitalist mixed economies are taken through the price system, and there is no obvious reason why control of pollution should be an exception. Secondly, the information required to calculate the optimum level of taxation is no greater than that required to set the optimum level of quantitative control, so the latter method has no advantage in this respect. As Beckerman has argued: 'whatever can be controlled must be measurable; if it is not measurable it is an illusion to believe that it is being controlled. And if it is measurable it can be taxed.'[2]

In practice the argument in favour of control of pollution through the price system has not been accepted by governments, which continue to rely upon quantitative controls. Thus in the UK the burning of certain fuels is prohibited in some areas. More flexibly, Parliament has delegated to various bodies the right to set individual standards in particular cases, either by controlling the emission of pollution (effluent standards) or by limiting the maximum concentration permitted in the environment (ambient standards). Generally, however, the standards have been set on the basis of a complex set of considerations, rather than being derived from economic analysis.

Of course, where the external effect is beneficial, an opposite policy is required; the government should raise the scale of an activity by subsidising it or even by performing the function itself. An example, noted in the previous chapter, of an activity requiring positive government intervention is research and development; this applies particularly in industries such as agriculture which are composed of small units. A scientific discovery made by a single firm will normally benefit other firms in the industry, yet a firm undertaking research does not take into account this external effect. In these cases research should be either sponsored or subsidised by the government.

4 Summary

In this chapter we have analysed the role that governments can play in ensuring technical efficiency and allocative efficiency in an economy. The free play of the price system leads to market failures of various kinds, and creates a potential role for government intervention. Different types of market failure require different forms of intervention.

In the case of monopoly and restrictive practices, the aim of government policy is to prevent abuse of market power by a single supplier or a small group of suppliers, a danger analysed in Chapters 7 and 8. At the same time a government framing monopoly legislation must take into account the advantages in terms of technical efficiency which large scale production may bring. The notion of weighing up the costs and benefits of monopoly positions underlies both British and European Community legislation in this area, though other approaches are possible.

A more comprehensive form of government intervention is through nationalisation. This is one possible method of achieving efficiency in the presence of natural monopoly, but it is not the only method, nor is it guaranteed of success. Disenchantment with nationalised industries is partly responsible for the recent British government policy of privatisation, which often involves transfering public sector assets to the private sector. However, many privatised companies receive government regulation, which may be distorting.

The final form of government intervention considered arises when one firm or individual affects another directly, in a way not accounted for by the price system. Such cases arise, for example, when a factory pollutes the environment. This disrupts allocative efficiency since essentially the factory owner is not paying the full costs of producing output, including the costs of pollution. The problem can be remedied by the government either imposing a tax on the polluter, or imposing quantitative limits on the discharge of harmful effluents. Either policy may in principle restore allocative efficiency, though the latter is generally chosen.

Questions

1   Discuss the view that monopolies lead to a misallocation of resources and should therefore be made illegal. (Associated Examination Board, A-Level Economics)

2   Why have governments found it necessary to introduce laws to control: (*a*) monopolies, (*b*) mergers, (*c*) restrictive practices? Give examples of such laws and discuss individual cases where they have had to be used. (Royal Society of Arts Examination Board, Economics)

3   Is it contradictory for a country to have anti-monopoly legislation at the same time as it seeks to restructure parts of its industry into larger units? (Institute of Secretaries and Administrators, Economic Policies and Problems)

4   Explain the economic advantages of nationalisation. What are the potential disadvantages? (Royal Society of Arts Examination Board, Economics)

5   How can prices be used to control pollution?

6   'If regional policy consists of taking work to areas of higher unemployment, it leads to economic inefficiency. If it tries to move unemployed workers to areas of higher activity it leads to high social costs. The best thing therefore is not to have a regional policy.' Discuss. (Institute of Chartered Secretaries and Administrators, Economic Policies and Problems)

Notes

1   For a fuller account of UK competition policy, see Bennett, P., and Cave, M., *Competition Policy* (Heinemann, 1991).

2   Beckerman, W., *In Defence of Economic Growth* (Cape, 1974), see page 165.

11

Factor Markets and the Distribution of Income

Introduction

In Chapter 5 we analysed the firm's choice of how to combine factors of production in order to produce output at minimum cost. In that chapter we assumed the price of factors of production (for example, the wage rate) to be given. In this chapter we examine the way in which these prices are determined.

Each of the major *factors of production* – labour, capital and land – receives *factor payments* of a different kind. Labour receives wages, capital receives interest and profit, and landowners receive rent. [We also distinguished in Chapter 5 two separate factors of production – loan capital, which earns interest, and entrepreneurship, which earns profit. In this chapter, following the statistical convention we amalgamate the two as 'capital'.] Total national income is divided among these three factors in a way which has changed substantially over time. An individual's income depends upon his ability to supply the three factors of production. Most people, of course, receive income only in the form of wages, as labour is the only factor service they supply. However some individuals may receive factor payments of all three kinds if they work and supply capital services and also receive rent from land.

Since factor payments determine the distribution of income in an economy they are naturally often a highly contentious subject, on which there is substantial disagreement among economists. In this chapter we shall first examine the evidence on the distribution of income. Then we analyse factor payments as an extension of the earlier analyses of production and of markets in Chapters 5 and 7, looking both at competitive *factor markets* and at markets where either the buyers or sellers of *factor services* combine to form a single block.

However, this analysis must be supplemented by wider considerations of the overall position of demand for factors of production in the economy and the role of the government which may seek to intervene directly in factor markets by such means as an incomes policy. In other words we cannot treat labour markets, or factor markets generally, in isolation from the overall position of the economy. This interaction between analysis of the economy as a whole, or macro-economics, and analysis of a particular sector or market, or micro-economics, is a point to which we return in the final section.

1   Factor shares and the distribution of income

In 1988, the gross domestic product of the United Kingdom was broken down into income categories in the following way.[1]

Table 11.1

	£	%
Income from employment	249 775	63.3
Gross trading profits and surpluses of private and public companies (less stock appreciation)	71 342	18.1
Other income (including income from rent and self-employment)	73 489	18.6
	394 606	100.0

Unfortunately, it is impossible to link these categories directly with the shares of labour, capital and land. In fact this subject is a statistical minefield for the unwary, with difficulties and ambiguities lurking at every corner.[2] For example, the category 'income from self-employment' undoubtedly includes the return to or payment of capital inputs both owned and used by a self-employed person. Secondly, *rent* is defined for national accounts purposes as income derived from the ownership of land and buildings, but in cases where a company owns and uses land for production it is very hard to separate the return from land (i.e. rent) and the return from capital (i.e. profit). This sort of problem can only be overcome by patient statistical research. Yet in fact, among those who have done work of this kind, there is almost complete agreement that the trend of factor shares in advanced Western economies is towards an increase in labour's share. For example, Atkinson cites figures indicating that from 1938 to 1968 the share of employee compensation (or labour) in national income grew from 63% to 75%, with a corresponding reduction in the proportions of capital and land.[3] This trend almost certainly continued throughout the 1970s.

The preceding breakdown is known as the *functional distribution of income*, showing how total income is divided among the different factors of production. Another breakdown is given by the *size distribution of income*, which indicates how income is distributed among individuals. It is useful here to make a distinction between the distribution of *original*, *disposable* and *final* household income. Original income consists of earnings from employment and self-employment, pensions, investment income and other income before government intervention. When cash benefits (such as state retirement pensions) are added to this and income tax and employees' national insurance contributions are deducted, we get disposable income. But some items of household expenditure include indirect taxes, such as rates, Value Added Tax, etc. At the same time, households receive benefits in kind like health care, education, etc. When indirect taxes are subtracted from disposable income, and benefits in kind are added, we get final income.

Table 11.2 The distribution of original, disposable and final income
Percentage of Income in 1986 accounted for by

	Bottom Fifth	Next Fifth	Middle Fifth	Next Fifth	Top Fifth
Original income	0.3	5.7	16.4	26.9	50.7
Disposable income	5.9	11.0	16.9	24.1	42.2
Final income	5.9	11.4	17.0	23.9	41.7

Table 11.1 shows the distribution of original income, disposable income, and final income among different groups of households. The Table shows the proportion of each kind of income which goes to each 'fifth' (quintile group) of the population in 1986. Thus the Table shows that the bottom fifth of households in 1986 received 0.3% of original income but 5.9% of final income. The tax and benefit system redistributes some original income in their favour. The Table also shows that the top fifth of the population in 1986

received 50.7% of original income and 41.7% of final income. Data have been collected in this form for a number of years, and they show that between 1976 and 1986 the proportion of final income accounted for by the bottom fifth of households fell while that accounted for by the top fifth rose.

2 The firm's demand for factors of production

The previous section has described how total income is divided among the factors of production, and how the personal distribution of income is determined as the result of the quantity of factors of production supplied by an individual, by the price at which these factors are traded, and by the government's transfer payments. It is now time to examine the forces which determine the quantity of factors supplied and the price paid for them.

We begin by examining the demand for factors of production. When we considered the demand for consumer goods and services, the source of the demand was the household and the supplier was the firm. In the case of factors of production the supplier is the household and the source of the demand is the firm. So the roles of firm and household are reversed. There is another important difference. Consumer goods directly satisfy the wants of the household, while the firm does not engage the services of factors of production for their own sake, but as a means to satisfy demand for output. In other words the demand for factors of production is based upon the demand for goods. Hence it is known as a *derived demand*.

Let us recall the discussion in Chapter 7 of the objectives of the firm. There it was assumed that the firm's motive in setting its output level and, where it has the opportunity, the price of the output, was maximisation of profit. What implication does this objective have for a firm deciding how much of a factor to use? Initially we assume that the input levels of all factors of production except one are fixed. In other words, there is a single variable factor and the issue faced by the firm is how much of it to employ. This situation may arise in the short run if a firm can only vary the size of its workforce, and its other factors of production, such as plant and equipment, are fixed.

A firm in this position will use extra units of the single variable factor provided that the marginal cost to the firm of an extra unit is less than the value of the extra output the firm gains. Suppose that the variable factor is labour and that the marginal cost to the firm of employing one more worker is £100 per week. A profit-maximising firm will then employ an extra man provided that by doing so the firm increases its revenue by more than £100, and it will continue to employ extra workers until the increase in revenue contributed by the last or marginal worker is £100. The contribution made by the last unit of a factor of production can be called its *marginal value product*, or the value of its marginal product. Thus a profit-maximising firm will increase its use of the variable factor if its marginal cost is less than its marginal value product; if the marginal cost of the factor exceeds its marginal value product, the firm will increase profits by cutting down on the use of the factor. Profits will only be maximised if the marginal cost of the factor is exactly equal to the marginal value product. Denoting the marginal cost of the factor by MCf and the marginal value product by MVPf, we can say that a firm is employing the right quantity of a single variable factor when:

$$MCf = MVPf.$$

We can now consider the factors which determine the marginal value product. The MVPf is the value of the extra output the firm will get by employing one further unit of the factor. It is thus made up of two parts: firstly, the physical quantity of extra output, or the marginal physical product of the factor (MPPf); and, secondly, the extra revenue the firm gets from selling a single extra unit of output. This is the marginal revenue (MR) introduced in Chapter 7. This relation can be expressed as follows:

$$MVPf = MPPf \times MR.$$

For example, suppose labour is the single variable factor and that the marginal physical product of labour in a steelworks is half a ton per week. Suppose further that the marginal revenue per ton of steel is £500. Then the marginal value of product of labour is calculated as follows:

$$MVPf = \frac{1}{2} \times £500$$
$$= £250 \text{ per week.}$$

The marginal value product has now been broken down into two components, each of which can be considered separately. Let us first examine the marginal physical product of a factor. How will this vary as the quantity of the factor varies?

The relevant concept here is the law of diminishing returns. We have already encountered this law in Chapter 5. It states that beyond a certain point successive units of a factor of production yield smaller and smaller increases in total output. In other words the marginal physical product is declining, as illustrated in Fig. 11.1, which shows the quantity of the variable factor on the horizontal

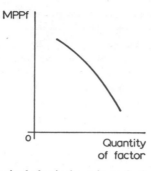

Fig. 11.1 The marginal physical product of a factor of production

axis and the marginal physical product of the factor on the vertical axis.

If the firm is operating in a competitive market for its output, then the marginal revenue it receives for its output is constant and equal to the price. (This is the formal definition of a competitive market, that no firm can affect the price at which the output is sold, and each must take it as given – see Chapter 7.)

We have now identified the two components of the marginal value product of a factor (MVPf): the marginal physical product (MPPf) which is declining, and the marginal revenue to the firm of selling output (MR) which is constant if the firm is a competitive one. As we have seen:

$$\text{MVPf} = \text{MPPf} \times \text{MR}.$$

The MVPf is equal to a constant (MR) multiplied by a magnitude (MPPf), which declines as more of the factor is used. This means that the MVPf as a whole is declining as shown in Fig. 11.2. This is

Fig. 11.2 The firm's demand curve (marginal value product curve) for a factor

the curve we have been looking for – the demand curve of the individual firm for a single variable factor.

Now suppose that the firm had been a monopolist instead of a competitive firm. What difference would this have made to our analysis? The marginal value product of a single variable factor employed by a monopolist would still be made up of the two components of marginal physical product of the factor and the marginal revenue of output. The marginal physical product of the factor which reflects the basic technological conditions of production and is independent of market structure, would still be as illustrated in Fig. 11.2. But the marginal revenue of a monopolist is not constant and equal to the price of output, but falling and less than the price, as shown in Fig. 7.11. Thus the marginal value product of a factor to a monopolist is equal to the marginal physical product of the factor, which declines as more of the factor is used, and the marginal revenue of output, which also declines as more output is produced by increasing the quantity of the variable factor. Since we are multiplying two quantities which are declining, the product of them must also be declining. Thus the demand curve of a monopolist for a factor is downward sloping as shown in Fig. 11.2. Other things being equal, it will tend to slope more steeply downwards than will the demand curve of a competitive firm. This is because in a competitive market the single reason for a firm's demand curve for a factor to slope downwards is the law of diminishing returns, or declining marginal physical product of the factor. In a monopolistic market this tendency is supplemented by another: not only do successive units of a factor yield smaller increases in output, but also in a monopolistic market this output can be sold only by lowering the price, not merely on the last unit but on all output sold.

3 The pricing of factors of production

We have now identified the shape of the firm's demand curve for a single variable factor on the assumption of perfect competition or of monopoly in the market for the good which the firm produces. Now we must consider the nature of the market for the factor. We have previously been able to postpone this issue as we have concentrated on only one side of the market, the demand side, and on the level of a single firm.

Let us take the case of labour. The first question is, what is the labour market, and how narrowly should it be defined? This is the same sort of problem as that which we faced in Chapter 7 over the definition of an industry. We noted there that in theory an industry should be described as a group of firms making products which could be substituted for one another in their uses, but that in practice industries were defined according to other more practical criteria. The same problem arises in the case of defining a labour market. Obviously, all men and all women cannot perform all jobs equally well. There is no single labour market including the whole workforce; some divisions are necessary, by age, by skills and qualification, and by sex (in those rare cases where men and women cannot equally well perform the same tasks). There are also local or regional divisions: a bricklayer in the south-east of England is not in the same labour market as a bricklayer in Scotland, if neither of them is prepared to move. Equally important is the internal labour market which most organisations create. Workers who are already employed are not in competition for their existing jobs with other possibly better qualified candidates from outside. The only competition is between outsiders seeking employment with the firm. Moreover, many organisations only promote internal candidates, i.e. present employees, to certain positions. The effect of these internal labour markets is to segment the market and restrict the number of jobs for which workers are eligible.

The problem arises because the separate labour markets are not entirely insulated from one another. If the rate for bricklaying in the south-east of England is very high compared with that in Scotland, then there will be some movement of workers from Scotland to the south-east. There is usually some overspill of this kind from one market to the other so that the task of identifying a particular labour market is one of exercising a careful, practical judgement, rather than applying straightforward theoretical principles. Experienced researchers have been able to identify and analyse particular labour markets, and so the task is not an impossible one. In the case of capital the problem is not such an acute one since investible funds can usually be employed anywhere and thus the market is much wider.

We now assume that the labour market has been identified, and can go on to consider the range of possible market structures. One possibility is that both sides in the market, the supply and the demand side, can consist of a large number of independent agents, none of which individually can set the price of labour, or the wage rate. This is the case of a perfectly competitive market. Alternatively, there may be a single employer while members of the workforce may act independently; this is an example of *monopsony* (a single buyer). Or the workforce may act jointly, probably through a union, while there are a large number of independent employers: this is the case of *monopoly* (a single seller). Another possibility is that each side may act in concert, so that a single seller faces a single buyer: this situation is known as *bilateral monopoly*. Finally, there is another range of possibilities in which each side of the market is neither competitive nor monopolised, but at some intermediate stage, with a limited number of buyers or of sellers. We can examine in detail only a few of these possible cases: the reader will be able to analyse other possibilities for himself.

We begin with the competitive case. A large number of firms employ labour of a certain kind, and each of them has an individual demand curve, as illustrated in Fig. 11.2. The total demand curve of all the firms will be formed by summing the individual demand curves of the firms in rather the same way that the total demand curve for a product is formed by summing the demand curves of individual consumers. [There is a difference in that for the market as a whole extra output can only be sold at the cost of a reduction in price. This means that as more of the variable factor is employed in the industry, the price falls, and with it the marginal value product of the factor. This tends to make the total demand curve for the factor slope downwards more steeply than do the demand curves of the individual competitive firms.] Thus the total demand curve for the factor slopes downwards as illustrated by line DD in Fig. 11.3.

The supply curve of the factor is also illustrated in Fig. 11.3 by the line SS. This line slopes upwards, on the assumption that the higher the reward offered to a factor, the larger is the supply of that factor. (This need not always be so and the possibility of other cases is discussed below.) The supply curve and demand curve for the factor jointly determine the equilibrium price (Pf* in Fig. 11.3). Since we have assumed that the market for the factor is perfectly competitive,

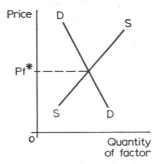

Fig. 11.3   The determination of factor price

each firm can employ as much of the factor as it wishes to at the price Pf*; in other words, although the supply curve for the industry is upward sloping, as in Fig. 11.3, the supply curve for the firm is a horizontal line, as shown by ss in Fig. 11.4. This curve, together with the firm's demand curve for the factor, dd in Fig. 11.4, determines the amount of the factor employed by the individual firm. The reader will notice the close similarity between the reasoning used here and that used to illustrate how prices for goods are determined in a perfectly competitive goods market.

Thus in the competitive case, the level of factor payments is determined by the intersection of the demand curve and the supply curve for factors of production. Since the profit-maximising firm will always choose a point on its demand curve, and since the latter is the marginal value product curve, this theory of factor payments is often known as the *marginal productivity theory*. If the assumptions on which the theory is based are satisfied, it is possible to explain the relative earnings of different factors in terms of differences in the shape and position of the marginal value productivity curves on one hand and their supply curves on the other. Thus if one type of labour earns more than another it is simply because the marginal contribution to the value of output made by workers of the first type is greater than the marginal contribution of another and has nothing to do with the relative bargaining strengths of the two groups *vis-à-vis* the employer. But note that the assumptions both of profit-maximising behaviour by firms and of competitive factor markets are necessary to achieve this result. If either condition is not satisfied, then the marginal productivity theory falls to the ground.

Let us now assume that there is a single buyer of the factor of production. The total demand curve for the factor will be the same as the individual demand curve, Dd in Fig. 11.5. The supply curve we assume is upward sloping, for example SS in Fig. 11.5. How will the price of the factor be determined? The intersection of the demand and supply curves is at P_1, but this is not the equilibrium price. The single employer will realise that if he employs one extra unit of the factor, not only will he have to offer a higher payment to that unit, but he will also have to raise the payment to all other units of the factor, since he cannot discriminate between them by offering different payments. The marginal cost of employing a factor will thus be higher than the supply price of that factor. Units of the factor will be employed up to the point where marginal value product equals marginal cost. This is the quantity Q^*, in Fig. 11.5. The factor will be paid P_2, which the supply curve SS shows to be the

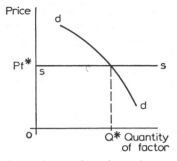

Fig. 11.4   A firm's demand curve for a factor in a competitive market

payment necessary to bring forth the desired supply of the factor. Again the reader will note the similarities between the analysis here and that of the monopolistic seller of commodities, outlined in Chapter 7.

The final form of factor market to be analysed is one in which the suppliers of the factor collude to form a single unit and negotiate jointly with the users. The obvious example of this is a trade union. However, an analysis of this will first be preceded by a closer look at the shape of the supply curve of a factor and its implications.

4   The supply curve of a factor and economic rent

In the previous section we assumed that the supply curve of a factor slopes upwards; in other words that a larger supply is forthcoming as the price paid for it rises. This was illustrated in Fig. 11.3, by the curve SS. But is this always the case?

It is not difficult to think of circumstances when the supply curve

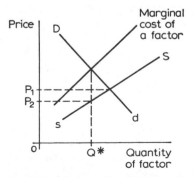

Fig. 11.5   Determination of factor price; the case of a single employer

will have a different shape. Consider the supply curve of labour for example. An upward-sloping supply curve indicates that to raise the wage rate will bring forth more labour, either because the existing labour force will work longer hours (if the length of the working week is not fixed) or because more men and women will be attracted into the occupation. Let us suppose that the number of hours can only be increased by the existing labour force working longer hours. Will they do so in response to a rise in the wage rate?

Now it is true that in advanced industrial societies most people get little satisfaction from their jobs. Work is just a means of earning money, to be spent in leisure time, and leisure is something enjoyed for its own sake. At some levels of wages, an increase in the wage rate will stimulate workers to work longer hours, as they will be prepared to forgo leisure in order to enjoy the higher standard of living which longer hours at higher wages will provide. This corresponds to the rising part of the supply curve in Fig. 11.6. But after a certain point workers may be reluctant to forgo more leisure by working longer hours at higher wage rates. If they have a target level of money income which they will work to achieve but which they do not want to exceed, then at higher wages this target level of income is achieved by working fewer hours. The higher is the wage rate, the less the number of hours worked. This is illustrated by the section S_2S_3 in Fig. 11.6. This phenomenon is known as the *backward-bending supply curve of labour*. There is strong evidence of the supply curve taking this shape both in fairly primitive societies and also in advanced industrial societies, particularly in certain hard and disagreeable occupations.

A different situation arises with factors which are in fixed supply. The obvious example is land. Apart from reclamation, the total

Fig. 11.6   The backward-bending supply curve of labour

supply of land is fixed, and the supply of land of a particular type – land suitable for building in a city centre, for example – cannot be increased, nor can such land normally be used for any other purpose, such as farming. In this case the supply curve will be vertical; the same amount will be forthcoming whatever the price. This situation is illustrated by the curve SS in Fig. 11.7. If the demand curve is shown by DD in the same figure, then the equilibrium price is Pf*.

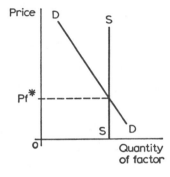

Fig. 11.7   The price of a factor in fixed supply

In this situation, the factor would be supplied at a price very close to zero, as its owner has no alternative use for it, and is willing to take any income for it. But because of demand conditions, the factor receives a substantial reward. The difference between what a factor receives and the price at which it would be supplied is called *economic rent*. Rent is of course the term used to describe the income which goes to owners of land and natural resources. This is no accident as this category of income does consist almost entirely of economic rent in the sense given above, i.e. the difference between the price paid to a factor and the price at which it would be supplied. But whenever there is an upward-sloping supply curve factor rewards contain an element of economic rent. In Fig. 11.8 the shaded area above the supply curve is economic rent, which is that part of the factor reward in excess of the price at which the factor would be supplied.

The other part, below the supply curve, is called the *transfer earnings*, as it is the price which successive units of the factor would actually have to be paid to transfer them from other activities.

In practice it may be difficult exactly to establish the size of the rent component in an observed factor payment, as it is difficult or

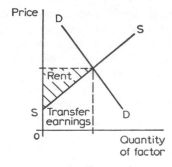

Fig. 11.8   Economic rent

impossible to identify the supply curve. But the existence of rent
does have consequences for government taxation policy. Suppose
the supply curve for a block of land is vertical or nearly vertical, as in
Fig. 11.7. The price of the land is determined by the position of the
demand curve; the same quantity is available whatever the price.
The government can therefore tax the whole of the payment
received by the land-owner without affecting the amount of land
made available. Economic rent can always be appropriated in this
way, though identification is difficult. This principle underlies the
policy of taxing building land or taking it into ownership at a price
lower than the market price and roughly equal to its value for
agricultural use. The aim of this measure is to appropriate the large
economic rent which would otherwise go to a landowner who may
have purchased the property for speculative reasons immediately
before the final sale and done nothing to improve its value. But a
policy of this type will only work if landowners are not able to hoard
land in the expectation of a reversal of policy by a new government.

5   How satisfactory are micro-economic explanations of factor payments? – the case of trade unions

The focus of this chapter has been how the distribution of income
between persons is made up of the quantities of factors of production which individuals can supply and the price paid for those factors
of production. The analysis has been micro-economic: we have
looked at the source of demand for factors in individual firms and
the supply of factors by individual households and shown how
supply and demand are brought into balance at an equilibrium
price. Our approach has been to discuss partial equilibrium. We
have looked at equilibrium prices in factor markets only, and have

not considered how the prices established in factor markets may affect, for example, the demand for goods and thus indirectly the derived demand for factors of production. We have also ignored other influences on factor prices, such as government incomes policy which may prevent a factor market from reaching its equilibrium level. These points can be illustrated by looking at the influence of unions in the labour market.

Collective bargaining by unions on behalf of their members has been a feature of economic life for over one hundred years, but the growth in union membership and the extension of unions in recent years to 'white-collar' workers have further increased both economic and political union power. We begin by analysing the role of unions along the lines of the argument in the previous two sections, restricting our treatment to a particular labour market. Suppose the demand curve for a type of labour is shown by the curve DD in Fig. 11.9. The supply curve is SS and the equilibrium wage is W^*. Now suppose the workers form a union, which sets a minimum wage of W_1. The supply curve now becomes $S_3S_4S_2$. The new wage is W_1, and the level of employment drops from E^* to E_1. [If there is a single employer who behaves monopsonistically as in Fig. 11.5 above, then the formation of a union may both increase wages and employment. But this is a special case.] However at the wage W_1, more people want to work than there are vacancies. There is an excess supply equal to E_1E_2. [Note that some government legislation may have a similar effect. If a legal minimum wage is fixed it may cut back employment and create excess supply by preventing firms from paying the lower, equilibrium, level of wages. Such legislation also shifts the supply curve from S_1S_2 to $S_3S_4S_2$ if the minimum wage is W_1.]

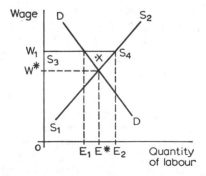

Fig. 11.9 The impact of a union on the levels of wages and employment

The extent of the excess supply demands upon the slopes of the demand and supply curves. The flatter the curves the larger the excess supply, and the harder it is to maintain the higher wage, as many people without a job would be prepared to undercut the rate established by the union. The supply curve will be steep in the short run if the job in question requires a lengthy period of training; it will remain steep in the long run if the union is able to restrict entry to the occupation, as, for example, the American Medical Association is able to do in the United States by limiting the number of doctors in training. The slope of the demand curve for a factor of production depends upon a number of considerations, examined earlier. Demand for a particular factor by an industry will be inelastic (the slope of the demand curve will tend to be steep), in the following circumstances:

(a)   if it is difficult to substitute other factors for the factor in question;
(b)   if the demand for the product is inelastic;
(c)   if the proportion of total costs accounted for by the factor is small.

These three propositions can be illustrated quite simply. Firstly, if a particular kind of labour is indispensable to a production process or activity, then the demand curve will be steeper than for a factor which can be easily substituted. This tends to make the demand curve steep, in the short run at least, for employees such as airline pilots who are obviously indispensable to the operation of an airline. Secondly, if the demand for the product is inelastic (its demand curve is steeply-sloped) then the demand curve for a factor producing it will also be steep; this arises because if the price of the factor of production increases, and the price of output rises as a result, the reduction in demand for the product is limited; hence the reduction in derived demand for the factor is also limited. This consideration may go some way to explaining the industrial strength of miners. If demand for coal is inelastic, then so will be the demand for the labour of miners; even a large increase in miners' wages will not reduce employment substantially.

The third and final proposition is sometimes known as 'the importance of being unimportant'. If a group of workers account for only a small proportion of total costs, an employer can grant a substantial wage increase without increasing substantially the price of output. The wage increase does not lead to a large reduction either in demand for output or in demand for the factors used in its production. Any specialist group of workers has its industrial power enhanced by this, although in practice a rise for a small group of workers in a factory may be the signal for all other workers to seek compensating increases to restore differentials. If this is the case, all wage rates move together and no group is 'unimportant'.

In exceptional cases a union may be able to compel the employer to accept a point such as X in Fig. 11.9 which is not even on the employer's demand curve. This can only occur if the union is strong enough to bargain with employers over both wages and employment levels. When it does happen, employers are forced to accept over-manning, i.e. the employment of more labour than they would choose to accept at existing wage rates.

We have seen that in theory trade unions can raise wages for their members, but does the evidence bear this out? In practice it is extremely difficult to arrive at a definite answer to this question, for a number of reasons. In the first place, one cannot simply compare the wages of unionised and non-unionised workers, as these two groups differ in other respects. For example, unskilled workers and women are less likely to belong to unions than skilled male workers, and since skilled workers earn more than unskilled and men earn more than women, these two factors explain part of the differential in wages of union over non-union members. Secondly, many workers are covered by collective agreements even though they do not belong to a union themselves.

Efforts have been made to isolate the effects of union membership alone from those of other factors. For the UK, evidence has been presented that in 1964 membership of trade unions produced a wage differential of from 0% to 10%, and evidence from the United States corroborates this. However, it is estimated that in 1973, in the UK, coverage by a collective agreement, usually reached through bargaining by a trade union, conferred a differential of about one-quarter: those covered by such an agreement would earn 26% more than similar workers not covered.[5] However, there is good evidence that the differential varies substantially over time.

But has this increase been achieved at the expense of employment? In particular industries it probably has, but can this be said about the level of the economy as a whole? Has the trade union movement been forced to sacrifice employment for the sake of higher wages for those in work?

These questions raise an important issue in economics. Can arguments which apply to particular sections in the economy – in this case individual labour markets – be applied to the economy as a whole? At first sight it might appear that they can, for how can an analysis which applies to each individual part in the economy not also apply to the whole? But the problem is not so simple. Certainly it is true that in discussing particular sections of the labour market we can take the overall level of demand for goods, and thus the derived demand for factors, as being fixed independently of the price of our particular type of labour. However, at the level of the labour market as a whole we cannot do so. A general increase in wages will increase the demand for goods as workers spend their wages, and thus indirectly it will increase the demand for labour. The demand curve for labour shifts in response to changes in the wage rate, and we cannot use the analysis of the earlier sections of this chapter as the only means of explaining the determination of factor rewards.

In other words we must look at the overall level of demand in the economy, which affects and is in turn affected by the level and distribution of income. This depends to a large extent on government policy. In the 1960s and 1970s, unions were able to exploit the commitment to full employment of post-war governments by forcing up wages in the expectation that government policy would prevent the emergence of substantial unemployment. As a result, the share of labour in national income rose, at the expense of the shares of capital and land. However, this process also generated inflation, which in turn encouraged governments to intervene in labour markets with such measures as incomes policies. In the 1980s, the government's willingness to accept inflation diminished and this had a major impact on labour markets, with unemployment increasing dramatically.

These issues of inflation, unemployment and the role of unions are discussed in more detail in the second half of this book. We end this discussion simply by noting that neither partial analysis of particular factor markets nor aggregate analysis of the economy as a whole can provide a complete and satisfactory explanation of factor prices.

Summary

In this chapter we have examined how prices are determined for the factors of production which households supply to firms. The analysis has been conducted on the same basis as the analysis of the determination of goods prices in Chapter 7. We have examined influences on the supply of factors of production and influences on demand. Supply depends upon the willingness of households to provide factor services and demand is derived from the demand for final goods and services, because if the latter demand is to be satisfied, then factors of production will be needed to produce the required goods and services. The price in factor markets is determined, in the same way as the price in goods markets, by the interaction of supply and demand.

As in the case of goods markets, the way in which factor supply and factor demand interact depends upon the market structure. A number of different market structures have been examined, ranging from perfect competition, in which there are large numbers of independent suppliers and employers of factor services, to situations where either the demand side or the supply side of the market consists of a single person or a group acting in concert. This last example, where the suppliers of a factor act together, corresponds to a labour market with an active union representing workers.

The initial analysis of unions suggests that their effect is to raise wages and to lower employment in the particular labour markets concerned, but at the level of the economy as a whole, the position is more ambiguous. The demand curve for a particular factor of production, derived from the demand for final goods and services, has been drawn on the basis of a given overall level of demand in the economy. But that level of demand depends, among other things, on the size and distribution of factor incomes. Thus the markets for goods and factors are interdependent. If unions collectively achieve wage increases, the increase in the price of different types of labour may tend to lower demand for labour, but this will be counteracted by the greater level of overall demand in the economy as workers spend their higher incomes. This illustrates the interaction between the particular markets and the economy as a whole. Analysis at neither of these levels can provide a complete answer.

Questions

1 What is the marginal productivity theory of wages? Assess the validity of the theory in explaining wage levels in the United Kingdom economy. (Associated Examination Board, A-Level Economics)
2 Examine the likely effect of the requirement that women should receive equal pay for equal work on: (*a*) the demand for female labour, (*b*) the supply of female labour, and (*c*) the level of final earnings. (Institute of Chartered Accountants in England and Wales, Foundation Exam)
3 A trade union negotiates increased real wage rates for the employees of a particular industry. What factors determine whether the total wages paid by this industry will subsequently

increase or decrease? (Welsh Joint Education Committee, A-Level Economics)

4   Why is the market for labour regarded as imperfect? How does this affect wages? (Institute of Cost and Management Accountants, Foundation Stage)

5   Explain why the earnings of famous entertainers are mainly economic rent. (Institute of Chartered Secretaries and Administrators, Principles of Economics)

Notes

1   The information for this table is taken from *Economic Trends Annual Supplement* 1990 Edition (HMSO, London), see Table 4.

2   The statistical conventions used and the problems encountered in compiling the accounts are discussed in Maurice, R. (ed), *National Income Statistics: Sources and Methods* (HMSO, London, 1968).

3   Atkinson, A. B., *The Economics of Inequality* (Oxford University Press, 1975), see page 167.

4   Social Trends 19 (HMSO, London, 1989), page 97.

5   See Mulvey, C., pages 419–27 in *Economica* (November 1976).

PART TWO

The Economy as a Whole

Introduction: Macro-economics

The first part of this book was devoted largely to the study of *micro-economics*; we studied the behaviour of individual households, firms and industries. We saw how relative prices are determined and how consumption and production decisions respond to changes in those prices. Throughout, average price levels were simply taken as given, as were average levels of wages, employment and of economic activity generally. Yet readers will be aware that each micro-economic unit functions within the context of an entire economy and is therefore closely affected by the performance of that economy. It is to this latter aspect – to the branch of economics known as *macro-economics* (from the Greek word 'makros' meaning 'large') – that we now turn.

The distinction between macro- and micro-economics is a somewhat arbitrary one but it serves to emphasise the differing preoccupations and approaches of the two branches. In micro-economics we approach the problem of allocating scarce resources with a theory of price determination based upon the interaction of supply and demand. In macro-economics we employ the theory of the *circular flow of income* in order to analyse the overall behaviour of the economy.

The circular flow of income, as the phrase suggests, pictures an economy as a closed system with income flowing between the two basic spending units – households and firms. Households pay money to firms in return for goods and services produced by the firms, and firms close the circuit by paying money to households in return for the use of factors of production – land, labour and capital – owned by the households. This is obviously a gross over-simplification of what actually occurs. Nevertheless we shall have much to say about the circular flow model in Chapters 12 and 13 because, with suitable modifications, it allows us to discover why economic activity expands and contracts as it does.

In macro-economics we are therefore concerned with aggregate levels of output, income, employment and prices, and with their respective fluctuations. We shall consider how the above aggregates are influenced by foreign trade, and how they are influenced by the way the resources of an economy are distributed between consumption and investment. We shall also have to consider the role of government in determining the flow of income because governments command a large proportion of total expenditure and investment in modern economies. And the explicit inclusion of government in our model illustrates another distinction between micro and macro-economics. In micro-economics the emphasis is on the working or market forces mediated by the government. On the other hand, macro-economics is predominantly policy-oriented. It is about government intervention.

State intervention is now an accepted fact in broad areas of economic life. It is, however, a relatively recent phenomenon which owes its development to the experience of the inter-war depression (1921–39). During that period of historically unprecedented industrial slump, when the UK unemployment rate averaged 14%, considerable doubts arose about the ability of an unregulated economy to achieve full employment. These doubts were crystallised by John Maynard Keynes in *The General Theory of Employment, Interest and Money*, published in 1936. In this book Keynes concentrated mainly on the determination of output and employment and, unlike his predecessors, he argued that there was indeed no natural tendency for an economy to achieve full employment. *The General Theory*, 'with its happy combination of intellectual excitement and promise of social improvement', has probably had more influence on the management of Western economies than any other work and we shall be discussing some of the theories contained in it in Chapters 13 and 14.

The 1960s saw the development of what has become known as monetarism, associated primarily with Professor Milton Friedman at the University of Chicago. Monetarism has its roots in the economic theory attacked by Keynes and suggests that altering the level of demand in the economy affects only the rate of inflation and not output and employment. Monetarism became increasingly influential in economic policy during the 1970s and 1980s.

But governments have not only confined themselves to general economic management, they have become enmeshed in the detailed workings of the system as well. Governments now intervene in all economic sectors – in agriculture, in industry, in the labour market, in trade. They police restrictive practices and monopolies in order to ensure free competition; they are responsible for defence and law and order; they supply the economic infrastructure of transport systems, energy, posts and telecommunications; and they provide a wide range of social services and facilities. The dissatisfaction with the role of government at the macro-economic level was matched in many countries in the 1980s with a greater emphasis on the operation of markets free of unnecessary government intervention.

Governments have four basic economic objectives: full employment, price stability, balance of payments equilibrium, and economic growth. These objectives are just as applicable to governments of developing countries as to those of developed countries, though the latter have minuscule problems to solve in comparison to the problems facing developing countries. We will now have a brief look at each of the four objectives of government economic policy.

1 Full employment
Unemployment implies that the full productive potential of the economy is not being utilised. Able-bodied men and women are idle when they could be producing goods and services and this is an obvious waste in a world characterised by scarcity. Secondly, unemployment is an unpleasant experience for the individual no matter how high the social security benefits are. If suffered for any length of time, unemployment results in despair and declining morale because, in industrial countries at any rate, there is a psychological need to work. As countries develop and urbanise, and as traditional family ties, religions and cultures break up, people become increasingly identified with – and identifiable by – the sort of work they do. Work becomes an integral part of a person's identity and if work is denied or is unavailable then the identity suffers as well. Finally, high and continuing levels of unemployment are an indictment of the economic system. The unemployed will feel they have little stake in the society and therefore no responsibility towards it. Consequently, consensus politics of the type necessary for democracies to function will be put at risk. It is no wonder therefore that the unemployment rate has become of abiding concern to governments as an indicator of general economic and political well-being.

In developing countries the problem of unemployment is on a totally different scale. Rates of population growth are in general much higher than in developed countries and persistent unemployment rates ranging from 10% to as high as 30% of the working population are commonplace. And these figures are probably underestimates since in the absence of unemployment benefits there will be little incentive to register as unemployed. There are also even larger proportions of the working population who are 'underemployed', i.e. who are either irregularly employed or who are doing jobs like shoe cleaning or petty retail trading which add little to total output.

2   Price stability

Governments are concerned with price stability because changes in prices directly affect living standards. If a man's money income increases by 10% in a year but prices rise over the same period by 12% then that man has suffered a 2% drop in *real income* (or his standard of living). Thus governments are concerned with changes in prices, known as *inflation* if prices are rising and *deflation* if they are falling. Most of the discussion in Part Two of this book will be in terms of inflation since it now seems to be a permanent feature of most market economies.

Inflation would not be such a problem if it affected everyone equally, however in real life this is not the case. Some people, such as members of strong trades unions, can bid-up their money wages to keep pace with, or even exceed, the rate of inflation whereas others less fortunately placed (especially those on fixed incomes) will see their living standards eroded. Inflation therefore redistributes income haphazardly, in a way which may be contrary to the requirements of social justice. (The causes and effects of inflation will be discussed further in Chapter 19.)

Inflation can also damage the balance of payments. If, for example, the UK has an inflation rate higher than that of its foreign competitors this means (with a fixed exchange rate – see Chapter 18) that the UK's goods are becoming increasingly expensive in relation to goods produced elsewhere. The UK's exports will therefore decline and its imports increase creating a deficit in the balance of payments. Under a floating exchange rate system (see Chapter 18) the UK's divergent inflation rate will be reflected in a continuing deterioration in sterling's external value.

For all the above reasons inflation is a problem in developing countries. It is also endemic in such countries because governments have a tendency to expand demand along Keynesian lines at a greater rate than can be coped with by the productive structure. Increased demand for an unchanging amount of goods naturally results in rising prices. It is possible that industrialists and farmers may be induced by the rising prices to invest in new techniques, which is the reason why some governments deliberately indulge in *inflation financing* as it is called. Too often, however, such a policy merely results in inflation getting out of control (*galloping inflation*) and a rising demand for imports.

3 Balance of payments equilibrium

The UK is said to be an *open economy* because it relies heavily on foreign trade to supply the bulk of its raw materials and foodstuffs. And to all such open economies the balance of payments is of vital concern. A country must pay for its imports with foreign exchange earned by its exports of goods and services, and a country cannot continue to import more than it exports without running into serious difficulties. The underlying cause of the imbalance between imports and exports is that the country is consuming more than it is producing and the correction of this situation, by whatever means, necessarily results in a reduction of living standards.

The developing countries face severe problems in trying to achieve a balance of payments equilibrium. They are usually vulnerable open economies relying heavily on exports of a narrow range of agricultural products and mineral raw materials, known collectively as *primary products*. Their payments problems stem from the fact that the prices of those products on the world market tend to decline over time in relation to the prices of the manufactured products of developed countries. This is both because world demand for primary products expands slowly and because supply grows as a result of improved production methods. The result is that developing countries have to export larger and larger quantities to buy an unchanged volume of imports. And if these countries succeed in a measure of industrialisation and seek to export the results it is highly likely that the developed world will erect trade barriers against them on the grounds that the exports will 'unfairly' compete with domestically produced goods. Trade and the balance of payments will be discussed in Chapters 17 and 18.

4 Economic growth

Growth is desirable because the faster the economy grows the more goods and services there are to distribute and the faster standards of living will be improved. Fast economic growth in itself does not mean that all will benefit equally but at least it facilitates a redistribution via taxation from the richer to the poorer sections of the community. Generally, it has been found easier to redistribute portions of a growing product when all are experiencing absolute increases in living standards than to improve the relative position of the poorer sections of the community at the expense of the better-off in times of economic stagnation.

More growth is obviously preferable to less growth – look at the relative living standards of Britain and West Germany for proof of this. However it has been increasingly realised that growth is not without its costs – pollution of the environment and the waste of non-renewable resources are just two examples of these. This is the result of a misallocation of resources rather than of economic growth as such. Since no one owns property rights in the environment factors such as clean air and water have no price and there is no incentive to economise on their use. The halting of economic growth will do nothing to relieve the environmental problem. There is also a related school of thought which warns that if present rates of economic growth continue for much longer world catastrophe and collapse is inevitable because of the exhaustion of the planet's natural resources. Most of the claims made in this direction have however probably been much exaggerated.

There are no such qualms about economic growth in developing countries. In these countries, where malnutrition and starvation are the norm, growth rates can be measured in terms of lives. Developing countries will not wish to see the developed world deliberately reducing its rates of growth either. When world trade is in recession primary product prices fall and then growth rates suffer. But if the desirability of economic growth is not at issue in developing countries the type of growth chosen certainly is. Too often governments have tried to emulate the experience of developed countries (including the USSR) by trying to industrialise at the expense of the agricultural sector, where the bulk of the population is engaged. The industrial technology has to be imported from the developed world where labour is scarce and capital is abundant. The result in developing countries is an industrial sector that economises on labour – the abundant factor in these countries – and depends heavily on scarce capital. The result of this *industrially biased* strategy can sometimes be rapid economic growth rates but it is also often synonymous with a stagnant, even declining, number of jobs and increasingly unequal income distribution especially between urban and rural areas. Economic growth – its meaning, measurement and causes – will be discussed in Chapters 12 and 14.

The discussion of these major themes is organised in Part Two of this book as follows: Chapter 12 is concerned with measuring economic activity and its components. Without detailed knowledge of what is happening in an economy, it would not be possible for governments to intervene effectively in pursuit of their objectives. In Chapter 13 the basic principles of the Keynesian model are introduced. In Chapter 14 the analysis of the Keynesian model is extended to look in greater detail at how and why different sectors of the domestic economy may behave. Chapters 15 and 16 are devoted to monetary aspects. In Chapter 15 the functions of money and the organisation of the UK financial system are described. Chapter 16 discusses whether the conclusions of the Keynesian model need to be modified to incorporate monetary factors, and whether independent monetary control is possible. The following two chapters are concerned with external influences on the economy. In Chapter 17 the problems of international trade for both developing and developed countries are discussed. Chapter 18 deals with the balance of payments and its adjustment. Finally, Chapter 19 brings together recent developments in macro-economics in an extension and synthesis of Keynesian and monetarist approaches. Current problems of economic policy-making are also examined.

12

The National Income

All governments have macro-economic objectives such as full employment, price stability, balance of payments equilibrium and economic growth. These objectives can seldom be achieved without a degree of government intervention in the economy, and governments must therefore have a clear picture of economic activity in their countries. They will need to know whether people's incomes and expenditure are rising or falling and why they are doing so in order to devise appropriate policies. The most basic requirement for policy-making therefore is a measure of economic activity and its components. The National Income is such a measure, and in this chapter we shall be discussing the way it is estimated and what it can and cannot tell us.

In the first section we shall use the circular flow of income model to demonstrate the principles of National Income Accounting as the process of measuring economic activity is known.

1 National income accounting

The national income is the basic measure of economic activity. It represents the total of all incomes earned by the factors of production land, labour and capital over some time period, and the total of all goods and services produced over the same time period. National income accounting refers to the process of classifying the millions of economic transactions that occur each day in order to measure the national income and its components. We shall start by analysing the national income of a very simple economy and then use this model to explore the principles of national income accounting.

The circular flow of income

The simple economy (see Fig. 12.1) comprises two economic units, firms and households, and two flows, 'real' flows of goods and services (the continuous line) and money flows of expenditure and incomes (the dotted line) in the opposite direction. Firms pay incomes to households in the form of wages, rent, interest and profits, in return for the use of labour services, land and capital owned by households. Households in turn spend their incomes on goods and services produced by firms. Assuming that households spend all their incomes on the purchase of goods and services; that firms keep production exactly equal to sales; and that firms pay out to households all the money they receive from the sale of goods and services, the economy will be in equilibrium with total output = total income = total expenditure.

It is obvious that these assumptions are very restrictive and that therefore the model represents a gross over-simplification of reality. Households generally save fractions of their incomes for various reasons; firms keep stocks of finished goods to meet short-term fluctuations in demand; and firms may retain part of their profits to finance future investment programmes. And of course there is foreign trade and government intervention. Expenditures on goods and services produced abroad will reduce the domestic circular flow of incomes, and foreigners' purchases of domestically produced goods and services will enhance it. Taxation and government expenditure will have similar results. These *injections* into and *withdrawals* from the circular flow and their effects upon levels of output and employment will be discussed in the next chapter.

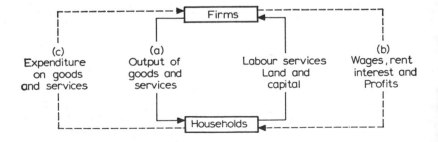

Fig. 12.1 The circular flow of income

Three ways of measuring national income
The simple circular flow model is however useful for demonstrating the principles of national income accounting. We have seen that output, income and expenditure totals are all equal in our model economy, and we can use any one of these aggregates to measure that economy's total output. We can count all output at point (*a*) in Fig. 12.1, all incomes at point (*b*), or all expenditures at point (*c*), and all three methods will give us the same answer. These methods form the basis of national income accounting, but before applying them to the complex world of reality we must discuss them in greater detail to ensure that we know exactly which transactions enter the accounts and which do not. It is important to remember that the national income accountant is trying to measure only those activities which contribute to the flow of goods and services.

(*a*) *the output method*: this involves totalling the money-value of output of all goods and services produced by the economy. We must however avoid the error of double-counting which would occur if all intermediate inputs and final products are simply lumped together. For example: industry A sells £50 of steel to industry B; B shapes this steel into a car body and sells it to industry C for £80; C completes the car and sells it for £100. Now, only the final figure, £100, must be included in the accounts otherwise we would be counting the intermediate inputs twice. Therefore only the 'value-added' by each industry must be counted. In our example this is £50 + £30 + £20 = £100, which is equal to the value of final sales to the consumer.

(*b*) *the income method*: all money paid for goods and services must eventually pass into the pockets, safes and bank accounts of people and organisations as profits, interest, rent and wages. Thus the total of incomes received must be equal to total output. However we must again exercise caution when computing total incomes in order to avoid double-counting. For example, a father might distribute his income to his children in the form of pocket-money and to his wife in the form of a housekeeping allowance. We must not include these latter incomes otherwise we would be counting part of the same income twice.

More generally, only those incomes which are received for work done or for services rendered by property and equipment can be included in the accounts. Incomes which are not earned in this way are known as *transfer payments*, because they are transferred (usually by taxation) from one group of people to another without goods and services – 'real' flows – moving in the opposite direction. Thus gifts of money, social security benefits, students' grants and earnings from gambling are all forms of transfer payment and must be excluded from the accounts.

(*c*) *the expenditure method*: with this method all final sales to the consumer are counted. Some final products are not sold but are added to a firm's stocks. In this case, the national income accountant treats the output as if it had been sold and values it at the relevant market price. Thus, the total of all expenditures (including the hypothetical expenditure on stocks) = total output = total incomes.

The three methods in practice

We have established the basic principles of national income accounting and we are now in a position to see how they are applied in practice. We shall be using UK data drawn from the *National Income and Expenditure Blue Book* which is published annually by the Central Statistical Office. We shall begin with the income method.[1]

Table 12.1   Gross National Product by category of income, 1987

		£m
1	Income from employment	226343
2	Income from self-employment*	32959
3	Gross trading profits of companies*	65596
4	Gross trading surplus of public corporations*	6623
5	Gross trading surplus of general government enterprises*	− 177
6	Rent†	24798
7	Imputed charge for consumption of non-trading capital	3235
8	Total domestic income*	359377
9	Less stock appreciation	− 4858
10	Statistical discrepancies	− 2282
11	Gross Domestic Product at factor cost	352237
12	Net property income from abroad	5523
13	Gross National Product	357760
14	Less capital consumption	− 48238
15	National Income	309522

*Before providing for depreciation and stock appreciation (for an explanation of these terms see below).
†Before providing for depreciation and including imputed charge for consumption of non-trading capital.

Rows 1–7 in Table 12.1 show all the incomes accruing to factors of production in the UK in 1987, which together comprise *total domestic income* (row 8). However, this income total will not correspond to the true total of incomes earned from contributing to the national product without the exclusion of stock appreciation. *Stock appreciation* (or inventory profits) are particularly significant in times of inflation. For example, a firm buys a ton of metal for £50 at the beginning of the year. During the year the value of the metal rises to £75 thus making an inventory profit of £25 which would be included in the profits shown in the company tax returns. This profit (row 9) must be deducted from trading profits because, like transfer payments, it does not contribute a reward to a factor of production.

An amount called the *statistical discrepancies* (row 10) allows for errors and omissions. The scope for errors and omissions is clearly enormous, given the millions of transactions that enter the accounts. It should be realised that the central statistics-gathering machine was not designed with the national income accounts in mind, but rather for the administrative purposes of government. For example, income figures are derived from income tax assessments and do not therefore cover those beneath the income tax threshold. Such incomes have to be estimated and, in addition, there is a certain amount of tax evasion. It should always be remembered that all estimation procedures are highly fallible, which of course makes it worthwhile to use the different methods for computing the UK's output as cross-checks.

The result of making these adjustments is *Gross Domestic Product* (GDP) at *factor cost* (row 11). 'Factor cost' means that the total is valued in terms of the incomes received by the factors of production. All national income totals with the prefix 'domestic' are connected with income, expenditure or output taking place within a country's boundaries. There are, however, other sources of incomes and outgoings to consider. Some firms in the UK (and some properties) are wholly or partly owned by overseas residents – e.g. Ford, IBM – and part of the income earned by these firms will be sent abroad in the form of interest and profits. Similarly investment and profits flow to residents of this country as a result of previous investments overseas. The difference between the two flows is called *Net property income from abroad* (row 12) and when added to GDP it gives us *Gross National Product* (GNP).

There is one last adjustment that we can make. Capital – that is, plant, machinery and equiment – wears out or becomes obsolete during the production process and has to be replaced. Money spent maintaining existing productivity capacity is known as *capital con-*

sumption or *depreciation* and when this is deducted from GNP (row 14) it leaves us with *National Net Product* (NNP) or *National Income* (row 15). It must be emphasised, however, that capital consumption can only be estimated very crudely, and GNP is usually taken as the most reliable aggregate with which to work.

We have seen how the income method is employed to estimate GNP, and how to make allowance for stock appreciation, for errors and omissions, and for property income from abroad. The income data can also be re-arranged to give the breakdown of GDP by industry.

Table 12.2   Gross Domestic Product by industry, 1987

	£m
Agriculture, forestry and fishing	5901
Energy and water supply	24184
Manufacturing	85552
Construction	21524
Distribution	48963
Transport	16227
Communication	9638
Banking, finance, insurance*	43408
Ownership of dwellings – rent	20180
Public Administration	24895
Education and Health services	31681
Other services	22366
Total	354519
Statistical discrepancy	− 2282
GDP at factor cost	352237

*Includes adjustment for financial services.

An alternative way of calculating national income is the output method, which requires us simply to total the value added by each industry to arrive at a figure for total domestic output. Whereas the income and expenditure measures are expressed in value terms (so many millions of pounds), the output measure is only available as an index number showing changes in output relative to a given year (currently 1985).

Finally, we examine the expenditure method.

To calculate total domestic expenditure we add together consumers' expenditure (row 1); general government final consumption (row 2) and all expenditure maintaining or increasing the capital stock – the total amount of capital goods – of the country (row 3). We must also add the value of the physical increase in stocks and work in progress (row 4). Stocks are purchased and therefore constitute an item of expenditure. Similarly a bridge may take many years to complete and expenditure on it will occur while construction work is in progress.

Table 12.3 Gross Domestic Product by category of expenditure, 1987

		£m
1	Consumers' expenditure	258431
2	General government final consumption	85772
3	Gross domestic fixed capital formation	70767
4	Value of physical increase in stocks and work in progress	− 627
5	Total domestic expenditure at market prices	415597
6	Exports of goods and services	107506
7	Less imports of goods and services	−112030
8	Less taxes on expenditure	− 67980
9	Plus subsidies	5762
10	GDP at factor cost (expenditure based)	348855
11	Statistical discrepancy	3382
12	GDP at factor cost	352237

years to complete and expenditure on it will occur while construction work is in progress.

We have now arrived at a figure for total domestic expenditure at market prices (row 5) which does not coincide with the previous measures of domestic output and income. There are two reasons for this. Firstly, some of the goods and services sold in the UK are produced abroad. Thus expenditure on these items will create incomes in other countries and we must deduct this amount from total expenditure (row 7). Conversely, if the UK sells exports overseas and the proceeds augment domestic incomes, then they must be added to total expenditure (row 6).

Secondly, the prices paid for the sales of goods and services are not equal to the income received from their sale because of indirect taxes and subsidies. For example, a bottle of whisky may cost £7.00 in the shops, but of that total only £1.70, say, may go to the distributor and manufacturer, with the remainder going to the government as duty and VAT. Clearly these expenditure taxes must be deducted (row 8) to bring the expenditure measure into line with the income measure. But this is not the whole story. Subsidies also affect market prices − indeed that is their purpose. Fertiliser, for example, may be sold to farmers at £1.00 a ton, while the cost of producing the fertiliser to the manufacturer may be £1.50 a ton. The difference – 50p – is paid to the manufacturer by the government as a subsidy in order to encourage farmers to use fertiliser. The subsidies must therefore be added to total expenditure (row 9) to bring the latter into line with income. The result is a figure for GDP at factor cost (row 10) which matches that produced by the other two methods.

By definition, the three methods of estimating national product will produce the same result. In practice, however, we have seen that the inclusion of a residual error term is necessary to compensate for the errors and omissions that inevitably occur in any statistics-gathering exercise of this magnitude. Under the circumstances it is perhaps surprising that the residual error only amounted to an annual average of 1% of GNP between 1971 and 1981. The marginally differing results produced by the different methods are presented in *Economic Trends*, published monthly by the Central Statistical Office. The three estimates can be averaged and the resulting figure is known as the *compromise* or *average estimate*.

We have discussed the various ways that the output of an economy can be computed for any one year. For the purposes of analysis and policy-making, however, economists need to know how the economic aggregates change, and how they compare with those of other countries. We now turn to comparing an economy's performance over time and space.

2 Comparisons over time

Current prices and constant prices
The first problem we face in comparing GNP and its components over a number of years is that we need to make allowances for changes in prices. *Inflation* describes a rise in the general price level, as opposed to an increase in the price of a particular good or service. Conversely, *deflation* is a sustained fall in the general price

Table 12.4   GNP at current and constant prices (£m)

	1981	1982	1983	1984	1985	1986	1987
GNP (current prices)	219019	238743	262604	283486	307535	327300	357760
GNP (1985 prices)	275057	280182	291886	298147	307535	319230	332724
GNP deflator (1955 = 100)	79.6	85.2	89.9	95.1	100	102.5	107.5

level. Historically inflation has been the predominant type of general price movement. A change in GNP will reflect both changes in prices and changes in production. If GNP increases by 10% and prices also increase by 10%, then the volume of output remains unchanged. Without knowledge of price movements we can say nothing about changes in production, and it is changes in production that affect living standards.

We must talk in 'real' terms if we are to make valid comparisons over time. This is done by valuing GNP at the prices ruling in a particular year, or, put another way, expressing GNP at *constant prices*. The conversion of current to constant prices is known as *deflating* and yields the *GNP deflator* which shows how much prices have changed.

Table 12.4 shows both current and constant price estimates of GNP (the GNP deflator is obtained by dividing current price GNP by constant price GNP and multiplying by 100). Between 1981 and 1987, current price GNP rose by 63%; constant price (or real) GNP (measured at 1985 prices) rose by 21%, and the GNP deflator (or prices) increased by 35%.

The movement of prices over time affects people in different ways – consumers are primarily interested in retail prices, while manufacturers will be concerned about the prices of inputs such as raw materials and fuel. Official statistics therefore present a variety of price indices or measures of inflation. The best known of these is the Retail Price Index (RPI), which like other price indices is not a simple average of price increases but 'weighted' so as to reflect the pattern of spending on a basket of 600 goods and services purchased by a typical household. The RPI unlike the GNP deflator, measures only the price of final goods and services. It does not include intermediate products.

Per capita measures

GNP series on their own are of obvious relevance to an assessment of an economy's performance over time. However, if we wish to see how living standards change over time, we should look at *per capita* GNP figures – GNP divided by the number of people in the population. This will tell us how the average volume of goods and services at the disposal of each member of the population changes. Obviously, a population that is growing at the same rate as GNP will not be experiencing, on average, any improvement in living standards. This is one of the problems that affects many developing countries.

Rising real output *per capita* is some indication that living standards generally are rising, but this cannot be taken for granted.

Output *per capita* is only an average measure which can conceal major disparities in income distribution. Real GDP *per capita* (at 1975 prices) may have increased by 92% in the UK between 1948 and 1981 (from £921 to £1764), but it is certain that not all the population benefited equally. There are still pockets of extreme poverty in even the most advanced and fast-growing countries and this will be overlooked if we confine ourselves to average measures. It is especially important to look at the way income is distributed in developing countries when assessing their economic performance over time. Typically, in such countries, incomes are exceedingly unequally distributed and only a small proportion of the population materially benefits from economic growth.

Quality changes

A particularly intractable problem connected with interpreting GNP statistics over time is that of quality changes in what is produced. Information on quantity is normally expressed in simple units such as number, weight, volume or area but these units may conceal big differences in quality which will affect prices, costs and welfare. Over time products may change markedly in quality, making it difficult for us to decide whether increasing numbers of them have contributed to total welfare or not. At least one economist is in little doubt about this. In *The Costs of Economic Growth* Mishan argues that GNP ought to be divided into 'expendables, luxuries, regrettables, frustratables and neo-garbage'. We shall have more to say about the relationship between economic growth and welfare in Section 4.[2]

Services also change in quality over time and there is no way we can include this fact in the national income accounts. Indeed, deteriorating services might conceivably cause an increase in GNP although it is quite clear that welfare has declined. Suppose car servicing deteriorates in quality from some given standard – a not unrealistic assumption. Car owners will therefore have to have their vehicles serviced more times to achieve that standard and the extra servicing will be reflected in the accounts as additional expenditure, income and output.

The public sector

An even more difficult problem emerges when we contemplate the services of the public sector, such as education, health, defence and domestic security. We have no way at all of judging the quality of public services. If more children are staying longer at school and more people are being treated at hospitals can we say that total welfare is increasing? Clearly not without some judgement about the quality of the education and health care. In the accounts the output of public services is valued simply by adding up the various items that enter into their production.

The coverage of the statistics

Finally, we must have some idea about the coverage of national income statistics if we are to equate changes in GNP with changes in living standards. Only activities that are marketed are included in the accounts, so all do-it-yourself activities and housewives' services are omitted, whereas the activities of builders, decorators and cleaners are included, therefore the GNP measure may well understate true living standards. Illegal activities are also omitted from the statistics. The classic example comes from the 1920s when the production and sale of alcoholic drinks in the US was prohibited and the whole industry had to go underground. Of course when prohibition was lifted, the industry was once more included in the accounts, imparting a spurious increase to the GNP figures. In recent years attention has focused on the 'black economy' – those transactions not recorded in the GNP figures because of tax evasion. Estimates of the size of the black economy in the UK vary between 2% and 8% of GDP.

The coverage of national income statistics is more of a problem for developing countries. These countries tend to have inefficient data-gathering agencies anyway and their difficulties are increased by the fact that major sectors of their economies are *non-monetised*; in other words, transactions take the form of barter or inter-family exchange, with no money involved. Economies that are divided into a *monetised* and a *non-monetised* or *subsistence* sector are known as *dual economies*, and we shall discuss the problems they present for making comparisons between countries in the next section. It is sufficient in this context to note that as data collection improves, and as the monetised sector expands, so that the share of output covered by the statistics increases, the GNP figures will be given an upward bias.

3 Comparisons between countries

Comparisons of economic growth and living standards between countries are fraught with problems. The most obvious problem is the already mentioned differences in the degree of statistical sophistication between countries. Allied to this is a lack of international uniformity in categorising and classifying national accounts; this prevails despite the efforts of international institutions such as the IMF and the OECD. All economic aggregate figures of developing countries with 'dual economies' should be regarded with the greatest possible scepticism, since they are based upon estimates of the subsistence sector's product which have often proved to be exceedingly unreliable.

Per capita income

The commonest method of comparing living standards between countries is nevertheless by reference to their respective *per capita* incomes. This only provides a rough indication of relative living standards, as we shall see, though it does broadly group countries according to their level of development. Thus countries with relatively low *per capita* incomes can be expected to have such characteristics in common as: a low capacity to produce and consume; relatively high birth and infantile mortality rates; relatively low life expectancy rates; poor nutrition standards; predominantly rural based populations, and so on.

Many development economists are extremely critical of the use of *per capita* income as a measure of economic progress. They claim that exclusive focus on such statistics has blinded Western economists to the fact that in most Third World countries rising national income has gone hand in hand with increasing unemployment and inequality. These economists are concerned with the conditions necessary for the realisation of the human personality's potential. Accordingly they stress the absolute necessity for food, a job and for equality as well as for such non-economic factors as education, freedom of speech and national independence. National income is therefore seen as being merely an indicator of development potential which has to be complemented with other indicators such as infant mortality rates, consumption of meat *per capita*, number of cars and telephones and cement and steel consumption *per capita* to produce a true picture of economic progress.

Measures of 'real' purchasing power

Conventional national income statistics are inadequate for measuring economic progress for the reasons stated above and, furthermore, they only provide a starting-point for classifying levels of development. The reason is that GNP totals cannot simply be converted into some common currency, say the US dollar, and the resulting figures compared because this assumes that $1 will buy the equivalent amount of goods and services in each country. The assumption is unsatisfactory because either official exchange rates are artificially managed (see p. 345), or they are allowed to float freely (i.e. the supply of, and demand for, currencies are allowed to determine their relative values (see p. 345). In the former case, internal price changes are not reflected in exchange rate changes. In the latter case, exchange rate movements only reflect the price changes of internationally traded goods, and the price gap between traded and non-traded goods tends to be wider in developing countries than in developed countries. The purchasing power of a currency over domestic goods therefore may be completely different from that over foreign goods. An Indian might be able to sustain himself and his family perfectly adequately on the equivalent of $100 a year whereas that total in the USA would not even permit him to keep himself alive.

Different climates, life-styles and customs ensure that different nations have different needs. For example, the climatic extremes in the USA make central heating and air conditioning a virtual necessity. The demand for these will increase the USA's GNP as compared with countries with more moderate climates, but we cannot necessarily infer from this that the Americans experience higher standards of living as a result. Different life-styles also produce different consumption patterns which are not easily comparable. The potato, for example, satisfies the same need in the West as does rice in the East.

The only complete solution to the problem of comparing living standards is to derive 'real' exchange rates which take into account differences in the internal price level and in consumption patterns. This involves extensive and expensive fieldwork to ascertain exactly what commodities people consume in different countries and how much they spend on them. The UN International Comparison Project has been engaged on such an undertaking and the results show that simple conversions of GNP via official exchange rates do understate 'real' *per capita* income, relative to that of the US, in all the countries sampled – and especially so in developing countries. In 1970, India's real *per capita* product was found to be three times that suggested by the official dollar exchange rate and in the case of Kenya, two times.

4 Economic growth and its costs

We turn finally to the subject of economic growth and its costs. Many equate rising GNP with a deteriorating quality of life. They see economic growth causing pollution of the environment, exhaustion of non-renewable resources and destruction of privacy as, for example, increasing affluence brings crowds into previously un-spoiled beauty spots and holiday resorts. As Mishan has put it, 'economic growth is the snatching of any technological innovation that proves marketable with no respect for the social consequences'. These feelings have much to justify them, but before echoing them ourselves, it is worth briefly considering the issues involved.

GNP as a measure of welfare

No one would claim that GNP measures total welfare. If the same GNP is produced with fewer hours of labour input, then leisure and, presumably, welfare will have increased. Since leisure has no price, however, this will not be reflected in the statistics. GNP measures only that part of economic activity that is expressed in terms of money. It is therefore only one part of economic welfare, which is in turn only one part of total welfare. The economist merely assumes that more economic welfare is better than less, because it contributes to total welfare. He does not necessarily have to view Man as being motivated solely by a lust for material goods.

GNP growth and environmental issues

The debate about the problems created by growth is one of reflection of growing public concern (at least among the developed countries) with the future of industrial society, and with the physical possibility and social desirability of continuous economic growth.

That concern has been stimulated by the work of ecologists and natural scientists rather than economists. Their research makes it clear that almost every activity of mankind – including city dwelling, factories, traffic and agriculture – produces gases which can damage the capacity of the atmosphere to support human life. It is now well known that these pollutants include the so-called 'greenhouse' gases, especially carbon dioxide, from burning fossil fuel, which can contribute to global warming. This clearly has potentially devastating consequences for the world climate and food output.

In addition many gases (such as CFCs used in refrigerators and aerosols) not only add to the greenhouse effect, but also erode the upper atmosphere's ozone layer which filters out injurious radiations from the sun. Some gases also contribute to acid rain and photo-chemical smog, both damaging to plant and human life. To this gloomy list of threats to the world's environment must be added the impact of toxic waste and the destruction of forests and other habitats.

Scientists are not in agreement about the significance of these threats or the exact way in which environmental changes occur. Whatever its differences on these issues, the scientific community is however unanimous about the potential threat to the environment caused by industrialisation and technological change. Paradoxically, the pursuit of high living standards in the short run may result in a permanent lowering of living standards in the future. What are the implications of this for the growth of GNP? It might be argued that, since it is productive activities and certain forms of consumption which contribute to pollution, growth in GNP should be reduced. Some even advocate a zero growth rate in GNP.

Against this is the view that zero growth is no solution, because we would have fewer resources to clean up the present environmental problems created by past growth. Some supporters of this view would therefore claim that increasing the growth rate of GNP would actually contribute to the solution of environmental problems, instead of causing them.

The economist's response to this is that both the zero and maximum growth advocates miss the point that pollution is the result of the mis-allocation of resources rather than growth itself. Whatever its growth rate, a community can be engaged in environmentally damaging production and consumption activities. As we have explained elsewhere (pages 161 and 183), this can occur because of *externalities* and the absence of well defined property rights in the environment. As a result, inputs are wasted and goods and services produced without regard to their true costs.

Sustainable GNP growth?

A group of economists from the London Environmental Economic Centre (LEEC) – Pearce, Barbier, Markandya – present a case, not for minimum or maximum GNP growth, but for moving the world's economies on to *sustainable development* paths.[2] This means, for every country, growth in GNP which can be maintained without harming the world's life support systems. This implies: avoiding damage to world ecosystems; ensuring that harvesting takes place at sustainable yields; exploiting non-renewable resources at rates which permit the development of replacement technologies.

It is argued by the LEEC Group that current GNP growth is not sustainable because markets fail to allocate resources properly. The remedies therefore lie in adjusting market prices for environmental effects. This might for example be done through taxation (page 183). Also proposed is the restructuring of national accounts to ensure that natural resource gains and losses are included in measures of GDP. In these and other ways, including cost benefit analysis (page 161), environmental values will be incorporated in private and public sector decisions, thus ensuring that the right amount of resources are allocated to achieve the sustainable development.

Most conservationists support such proposals. However, some emphasise that government action to correct price distortions still leaves unresolved the question of who bears the burden of solving our environmental problems. The impact on consumers and tax-payers is of great importance. As the economist John Bowers has said 'too large a burden on the consumer is likely to be regressive and carries the risk of increasing consumer resistance to environmental improvements'.[3] These are questions of equity or fairness rather than efficiency, not solved by market prices. For example, how much of a burden should be borne by current generations for the benefit of future generations? The question of 'who pays?' also arises in the debate over the conservation of tropical rain forests. Third World countries argue, quite understandably, that they should not be expected to forfeit the gains from economic development of their natural resources simply for the benefit of richer nations.

Natural resources and limits to GNP growth
How long will natural resources last? Two influential studies of this question – the *Limits to Growth* (Meadows, et al); *Mankind and the Turning Point* (Mesarovic and Pestel)[4] – were financed by the Club of Rome which was founded in 1968 to promote the study of long term future world trends. The authors of these works predicted, on the basis of a computer model of the world, that the continuous economic and population growth would lead to world catastrophe and collapse because of the depletion of natural resources.

The basic assumption was that growth (of population, rates of consumption and natural resources and so on) proceeded *exponentially* – that is to say, by a constant percentage of the whole over a constant time period. And it is a feature of such an assumption, allied to that of fixed physical limits (to petroleum and coal supplies, cultivable land, etc.) that those limits are approached over a very short space of time.

The Club of Rome forecasters – sometimes known as 'Doom-watchers' – proved to be unduly pessimistic. Thus the authors of the *Limits of Growth* forecast that demand for crude petroleum would exceed supply by 1990. It is instructive to see how these excessively gloomy forecasts were made. Firstly, the use of the exponential growth assumption, left no room for a price system to transmit economic messages about relative scarcities. The world was expected to continue consuming natural resources at the then current rates, until depletion and collapse intervened. The doom-watchers failed to see that as things get scarcer, so they become more expensive, and research is stimulated to find substitutes. They also neglected the role of continuous technological progress, which is an odd omission since it has certainly been a feature of past economic growth, and there is no reason why it should not continue to be so in the future.

For example, to produce a dollar of real GNP, industrial economies now use 40% less oil than they did in 1973. Higher oil prices have encouraged consumers to shift to other fuels and to more energy-efficient cars and machines; the microchip also means that industry consumes less of all commodities, including energy.

Secondly the doom-watchers committed the very basic and very common error of using a static concept of resources (of coal, oil, iron ore, and so on), rather than a dynamic one. Known reserves have always been measured in terms of decades, simply because it is not profitable at any one time, under prevailing market conditions and technology, to prospect for more. However, over time, prices rise, technology improves and new reserves become economically exploitable.

5 Summary

In this chapter, we were concerned with the measurement of economic activity. Firstly, the basic principles of national income accounting were established with the circular flow of income model which showed us that output = income = expenditure.

The three methods of measuring national income – the output method, the income method and the expenditure method – were then discussed in greater detail to ensure that errors, such as double-counting or the inclusion of transfer payments, were eliminated. We proceeded to an examination of UK national income accounts where we saw the methods employed in practice.

The problem connected with making GNP comparisons over time formed the subject of Section 2. The necessity for making comparisons in terms of constant rather than current prices was stressed, as was the value of *per capita* measures. GNP measures proved unable to incorporate quality changes satisfactorily, especially with regard to public services. We noted that GNP omitted all non-traded activities including do-it-yourself work, housewives' services and barter.

Section 3 was devoted to comparisons of living standards between countries. The problems were seen to be legion. They included the inaccuracy of the statistics, the inadequacy of national income as an indicator of economic progress and, more fundamentally, the differing purchasing powers of currencies over domestic and foreign goods. This latter factor made it impossible to compare GNPs directly via conversions at official exchange rates, and we saw that the problem could only be solved after intensive study of the consumption patterns and price levels prevailing in individual countries.

In the final section we discussed the emotive subject of economic growth and its costs. The maximum versus zero growth debate was examined. The concept of sustainable development, which adjusts economic activity so as to maintain the world's life support capacity, was presented as an alternative. Because markets fail to allocate resources properly, ways must be found of including environmental values in decisions on resource use. Finally, we examined the shortcomings of Club of Rome predictions on the depletion of non-renewable resources.

Questions

1 *Country A*   *£m*
    Gross Domestic Product   87 000
    Gross National Product at
        factor cost   97 000
    Gross National Product at
        market prices   110 000
    Net National Product   90 000

(*a*) With reference to the above figures, explain carefully the distinction between:
    (i) GDP and GNP
    (ii) GNP at factor cost and GNP at market prices
    (iii) GNP and NNP.

(*b*) Explain what is meant by the terms:
    (i) Economic growth
    (ii) Real National Income.

(Royal Society of Arts, Single-Subject Examination, Stage II)

2 In what ways can national income be measured? How are taxes and subsidies dealt with in these different ways of measurement?
(The Institute of Chartered Secretaries and Administrators)

3 Consider the significance of each of the following for measuring the national income:
(*a*) the existence of owner-occupied houses,

    (*b*)   interest payments received by the owners of government securities,

    (*c*)   changes in the monetary value of stocks held by trading enterprises,

    (*d*)   the depreciation of capital equipment.

    (Welsh Joint Education Committee, GCE A-Level.)

4   Between 1971 and 1987, National Income in the United Kingdom rose from £45 163m to £309 522m. What reservations would you have in concluding that this represents an increase in economic welfare in this period?

5   To what extent are international comparisons of Gross National Product satisfactory indicators of relative standards of living in different countries? (Associated Examining Board, GCE, A-Level.)

Notes

1   The information for this table and the following tables is taken from *National Income and Expenditure*, (HMSO, 1988).

2   See also Misham, E. J., 'GNP – Measurement or Mirage?', *National Westminster Bank Quarterly Review* (November 1984).

3   Pearce, D. et al.: *Blueprint for a Green Economy* (Earthscan, 1990).

4   Bowers, J.: *The Conservationists' Response to the Pearce Report* (BANC, 1990).

5   *New Statesman*, (8 January 1971).

6   Meadows, D. et al.: *The Limits to Growth*, (Earth Island, London 1972) and Mesarovic, M. and Pestel, E.: *Mankind at the Turning Point* (Dutton, New York 1974).

13

The Level of Output and Employment

Introduction

This chapter introduces the elements of what has come to be known as the 'Keynesian' macro-economic model, after its originator, John Maynard Keynes. As we saw in the introduction, the inter-war depression, with its massive and continuing unemployment, led to a revision of earlier views that market mechanisms would automatically ensure full employment. Keynes' 'General Theory of Employment, Interest and Money' attempted to explain the paradox of how large numbers of people willing and able to work could remain idle while at the same time there was an obvious need for a wide range of commodities to be produced. The emphasis is therefore on what determines the level of national income at any given moment. That is to say, we are concerned with the short-run problem of the degree of use made of the *existing* factors of production of the economy. This chapter therefore leaves aside the longer-term problems of economic growth and development, which are concerned with how to increase both the productivity and the supply of factor resources, and these equally important issues will be discussed in Chapters 14 and 19.

The causes of involuntary unemployment

If we make the reasonable assumption that most people offer factor services – i.e. they work or hire out assets such as land and capital – in order to be able to purchase goods and services, then it seems difficult at first sight to see how any *involuntary* unemployment of resources could take place. People only offer their services because they want to buy the goods which will be produced as a result. The amount of factor services they offer indicates the quantity of goods and services they want to consume. This principle can be seen most clearly in a primitive subsistence economy in which there is absolutely no specialisation or division of labour. An individual who wants to consume more can do so only by increasing his factor inputs – if he wants more food, he must himself cultivate land or hunt to get it. How much use he makes of his factor resources is entirely up to him, beyond the bare necessity for survival. There is no question of his being 'unemployed' in the sense of being willing to work but without anything to do.

Now it is obvious that in modern, economically developed economies this is no longer true. Probably the most publicised economic statistic in the modern world is the percentage of unemployment, and the fact that this varies significantly is pretty clear evidence that full employment of economic resources does not take place automatically. There are two overriding reasons why this is so. Firstly, the individual no longer produces what he consumes, so that if he wishes to increase his consumption he will only be able to do so if there is a potential market for the goods or services he himself produces. Correspondingly, producers of the goods that he wants more of will have to be induced to increase their output. There may be individuals who are prepared to offer labour services, but in the short term at least are unable to provide the type of services for which demand exists.

Secondly, modern economies function through the medium of money. The simultaneous, two-sided, decision by households that they want both to offer their services and at the same time demand output has to be communicated to firms. And the communications 'medium' in a modern economy is money. Firms will not increase output (and hence their demand for inputs) unless there is an increase in money demand for that output. And households can only increase their demand for output once their offer of additional inputs has been recognised, accepted and paid for. There may well be on occasion a communications failure, either stemming directly from the monetary system, which we shall examine in Chapters 15 and 16, or as a result of imbalances in the factor and goods market which we examine here.

Disturbances to the circular flow of national income

The concept of the circular flow of national income has already been introduced in Chapter 12. Fig. 12.1 in the previous chapter depicted a very basic two-sector (firms and households) model of the economy in order to demonstrate the way in which the flow of national income is identical to national output and expenditure. The economy is said to be in equilibrium when this flow remains undisturbed from one period to another, in other words when national income and expenditure do not fluctuate upwards or downwards.

Clearly this is not normal, since historically all economies have tended to fluctuate between boom periods when output is high and unemployment is low, and slumps when output and employment are both low. The Keynesian model analyses the causes of such disturbances, which can conveniently be grouped into pairs – savings and investment, taxes and government expenditure, and imports and exports. Fig. 13.1 shows the effects of these influences on the level of GNP added to the circular flow diagram (Fig. 13.1). Arrows pointing away from the flow represent factors which will reduce the national income flow in money terms – these factors are savings, and taxation and imports, which are referred to as *withdrawals* from the flow. Arrows pointing into the circular flow represent *injections*, that is to say investment, government expenditure and exports, all of which have the effect of increasing the income flow.

The income flow can be seen to be in static equilibrium; i.e. it is unchanged from one period to another, when total injections are equal to total withdrawals. In this situation any disturbances to the flow cancel each other out, and the level of national income is constant.

As a starting-point, then, it is important to examine what determines an 'injection' and a 'withdrawal', and in order to do so we will

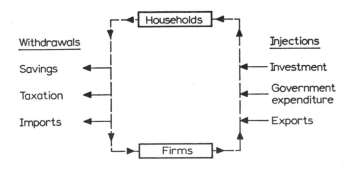

Fig. 13.1   Disturbances to the circular flow of income

group together savings and investment, taxes and government expenditure, and imports and exports.

Savings and investment

The first point to note is that *saving* is defined as 'not spending' – a broader definition than the normal use of the term which includes not only conscious acts of putting aside resources for future use – depositing money in a building society or purchasing saving certificates, bonds or shares and so on – but also any reduction in spending, temporary or permanent, for whatever reason. Thus saving represents a 'leakage' which reduces the income flow – and makes national income smaller. Now this seems at first sight paradoxical, and is known as the *Paradox of Thrift* – increased savings, which for the individual are a prudent and sensible way of providing for the future, will actually result in lower expenditure, national income and employment. What is good for the individual may be bad for the economy as a whole. Note however that this paradox is true only when saving is *not* translated into investment. When savings *are* invested in the construction of capital equipment this not only maintains present national income, but also increases its future potential.

Investment is also defined more broadly than in normal usage, and here refers to any domestic non-governmental injection of purchasing power into the circular flow process. We can distinguish between savers, who are spending less than their current income, and investors, who are spending more than current income. Investors borrow funds from savers. If total saving is exactly equal to total investment, no disturbance to the circular flow results. But in practice this is most unlikely to be the case. This can be seen most clearly where savers simply hoard money. The pound notes stuffed into a mattress or kept in a jar on the mantelpiece are completely removed from circulation and are obviously a withdrawal from the circular flow.

This may not be as apparent in the case of savings deposited with a financial institution such as a Building Society. Such institutions exist in order to bring together net savers and net borrowers. Ideally they should match the two identically, in which case the circular flow would be uninterrupted. But in practice it is not possible to equalise the amount of saving and the amount of investment that takes place at any given time, and the flow is inevitably disturbed. If, for example, consumers decide to delay purchasing new cars for a year, consumer expenditure on cars drops, and thus savings rise. There will be an immediate fall in sales, and subsequently in output and employment in the car industry. If the resulting savings are deposited with a Building Society, the society will be able to expand its lending activity – leading ultimately to increased investment in housing. However a lag will inevitably occur while this is arranged, during which the circular flow has been reduced, and total expenditure in the economy fallen. And even when increased lending does take place, the immediate result is that demand for housing is increased. Since the supply of housing is inelastic in the short term, the immediate effect will be to raise house prices. This will not raise employment at all. Subsequently, as a result of higher house prices, more new houses are likely to be built, which will increase employment directly. But in the meantime, the immediate impact of the increased saving has reduced output and employment, without any offsetting rise in investment.

This example illustrates two basic causes of domestic disequilibrium, lags between the act of saving and the act of investment, and large-scale changes in demand between differing sectors of the economy.

Prior to Keynes, there was a widespread belief that domestic disturbances between savings and investment would be eliminated by interest rate movements. Fig. 13.2 shows the relationship between the supply of loans (saving) and the demand for loans (investment) and the rate of interest.

As the rate of interest, on the vertical axis, increases, the supply of loans increases. This is depicted by the supply schedule 'S' (for savings). Conversely the demand for loans, shown by the investment curve, I, declines. The interest rate adjusts to ensure equilibrium at the intersection of the supply and demand schedules. If this were, in fact, the case, equilibrium would always be assured and

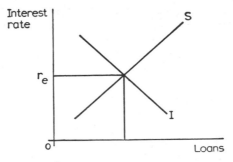

Fig. 13.2 Supply of savings and demand for investment

savings would equal investment. But in practice the interest rate is only one of a number of factors likely to influence savings and investment. And even if the rate does alter rapidly to take account of imbalances caused by these other factors, both saving and investment may respond in the fashion traced out by the curves in Fig. 13.2 (though it is by no means clear that they will always do so), but only very slowly. In the long run the interest rate may ensure equilibrium, but in the short and middle term (which may be a matter of years), imbalance between saving and investment may disturb the circular flow and generate either unemployment or inflation, as we shall see in a moment. 'In the long run we are all dead,' was Keynes' response to critics who argued that equilibrium would be restored automatically. Even if the interest rate could bring about an adjustment eventually, governments might not be prepared to wait – particularly if an election was imminent.

Exports and imports

Exports represent a net injection of expenditure into the income flow, raising the equilibrium value of national income. Payment for goods sent abroad results in an inflow of purchasing power into the economy. Conversely, imports, which entail expenditure overseas, result in a leakage of purchasing power from the domestic economy – so that the equilibrium value of national income is reduced.

Again, just as with savings and investment, if exports and imports are exactly equal, there will be no net effect on the economy. Export injections and import leakages cancel one another out. It is only when there is a net deficit – a surplus of imports over exports – that a leakage occurs, and vice versa. Everyone knows nowadays that the balance of trade very rarely balances. (It would be more correct in this context to refer to the balance of payments – the distinction will be discussed in Chapter 18.) In practice it swings from deficit to surplus, with some countries tending to have persistent surpluses, others persistent deficits. As in the case of the interest rate, there is a mechanism, the exchange rate, which operates generally to restore balance of payments equilibrium, but like the interest rate, its effects take a long time to work through and at least in the short term may be overwhelmed by other factors. Chapter 18 examines the problem in more detail, but again the conclusion is that exports and imports are unlikely to be equal at any given time, so that total expenditure in the economy will tend to be increased or reduced directly by trade surpluses and deficits.

Government expenditure and taxation

Government expenditure and revenue activities differ from those of private individuals in one very important respect as far as the income flow process is concerned. The private individual can only spend in excess of his income by running down past savings or by persuading another individual to reduce his spending and lend him the balance.

Governments on the other hand are in a position consistently to spend more than they receive in revenue, if they decide to do so, whether or not people are prepared to reduce their own expenditure correspondingly. They can do this because they can finance deficits, in the last resort, by *creating money* as we shall see in Chapters 15 and 16. For this reason it is possible to separate the effects of government expenditure and of taxation on the circular flow: net expenditure (a budget deficit) raises national expenditure and the equilibrium value of national income. Net taxation (a budget surplus) reduces total expenditure and lowers equilibrium national income. In this case there is no mechanism such as the interest or exchange rate to assist in restoring eventual equilibrium. The decision on whether a government should balance its budget or increase or reduce total spending by deficit or surplus is largely a political decision. However we shall see shortly that economic policy considerations offer some general guidelines, since the budget tends to be used to try to stabilise aggregate expenditure by counteracting unwanted injections or withdrawals which occur as a result of changes in both savings and investment, and in exports and imports.

The determination of equilibrium output – the 'Keynesian Cross'

In order to find out what does determine the actual level of national income it is necessary to make some working assumptions about what determines the level of injections and withdrawals. The assumptions we make here are simplified so that we can construct a model of the economy which will illustrate the principles involved. We could complicate the issue by bringing in a variety of other factors which may influence the level of injections and withdrawals, and indeed if we wish to construct a model which will enable us to *forecast* with any degree of accuracy the movements of national income in the real world, we would have to do so. However, forecasting is not our purpose here – we are concerned only with illustrating the principles involved. Therefore we make a number of simplifying assumptions to avoid confusing detail, following the model-building principles outlined in Chapter 1.

At this stage, then, we will treat the injections into the circular flow as being *autonomous*, or *exogenously determined*. All this means is that they are decided independently of any of the other variables in our model – off-stage, so to speak. So we will treat government expenditure (G), investment (I) and exports (X) as already given. If we *did* want to decide what in turn determines these items, we would have to examine a variety of other factors: the political make-up of the government, rates of profit and other countries' demand for our exports would be examples of such factors, but for the moment we will take these as given, leaving a more detailed analysis until the following chapter.

Withdrawals on the other hand will more accurately be represented as *dependent*, or *income induced*. Taxes (T), savings (S) and imports (M) all depend to a considerable extent on the level of national income – they all tend to rise systematically with national income, at least in the short run, and the model would be seriously deficient if it ignored this fact.

We depict these assumptions on a simple diagrammatic model of the determination of national income in Fig. 13.3, which is known as the *Keynesian Cross* since it embodies the principles set out in his General Theory.

Income, Y, is plotted on the horizontal axis, and the various disturbances to the income flow on the vertical, labelled J and W for injections and withdrawals. The withdrawals line depends on the level of income. Other things being equal, savings, imports and taxation tend to rise as income rises, and this is shown by the line

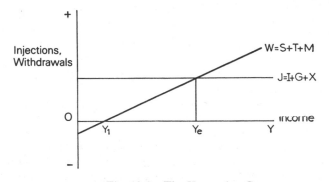

Fig. 13.3 The Keynesian Cross

labelled W = S + T + M. The fact that the withdrawals function, S + T + M, has a negative value between income of zero and Y_1 is sometimes a source of confusion.

It is drawn thus because at very low levels of income, savings become negative; this means that people spend more than their income, or *dis-save*. People live off their past savings, but obviously only as long as they last. However, it is possible that in years when national income is exceptionally low (in the Depression for example) the nation as a whole could temporarily dis-save, by running down assets previously accumulated.

Injections, in this simplified model, are taken as autonomous and are shown by the horizontal line, I + G + X, which is independent of the level of income.

The point at which the two functions, injections (J) and withdrawals (W), intersect is the equilibrium level of income, Y_e. At this point, where J = W, the disturbances to the circular flow process that we have been examining above exactly offset each other, and this determines the equilibrium level of national income. Thus the diagram illustrates the basic principle of the Keynesian model – that in the short run the level of national income depends on the behaviour of the disturbances, injections and withdrawals, to the circular flow process.

Chapter 14 examines in detail the problem of how these disturbances come about in practice. We will now reinforce the basic principles by an alternative presentation of the elements of the Keynesian model known as the '45° diagram', shown in Fig. 13.4. Income is shown on the horizontal axis and expenditure on the vertical axis. A 45° line is drawn from the origin to show all points at which the distance on the vertical axis equals the distance on the

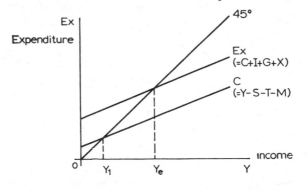

Fig. 13.4 The Keynesian 45° diagram

horizontal – i.e. all points where total income equals total expenditure.

The line labelled 'C' shows the level of consumption expenditure and how this varies with income. Consumption expenditure is defined here as spending on domestically produced goods and services; C therefore represents all income that rejoins the circular flow process outlined in Fig. 13.1 after withdrawals for savings, imports and taxes have taken place. Hence,

$$C = Y - S - T - M.$$

As before we assume that these withdrawals are dependent on the level of national income, so our domestic consumption line slopes upward to show that it rises systematically with income. As before, at very low income levels, withdrawals may temporarily be negative, which means that expenditure will exceed income (as past savings are run down). That will occur to the left of Y_1 on the diagram.

Again, as in the Keynesian Cross, injections are assumed autonomous – they do not vary with income. Injections add to consumption expenditure, so a line labelled Ex is drawn parallel to C – parallel to show that injections remain constant regardless of income. Thus the vertical distance between the 'C' line and the 'Ex' line represents the total value of injections. Hence,

$$Ex = C + I + G + X.$$

The equilibrium level of income is where total expenditure $(C + I + X + G)$ is exactly equal to total income, Y. This is shown by the point where the expenditure function cuts the 45° line, and corresponds to an income level of Y_e on the diagram. At this point, national income will remain unchanged from one period to the next (i.e. it is in equilibrium). This point corresponds exactly to Y_e on the Keynesian Cross.

The relationship between the two alternative diagrams is shown in Fig. 13.5. Income level Y_1 in A is the point at which total withdrawals from income are zero. This is the point at which the withdrawals function cuts the income axis, at Y_1, in Fig. 13.5B. Equilibrium income in A is where total expenditure equals total income (Y_e), which is also the point at which total withdrawals equal total injections on the Keynesian Cross of Fig. 13.5B – labelled Y_e again.

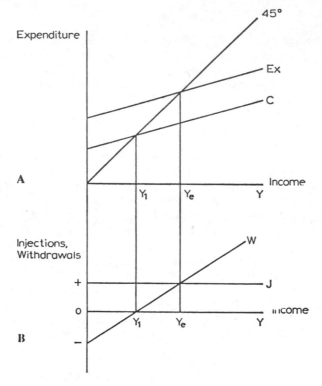

Fig. 13.5   The relationship between the Keynesian Cross and the 45°
diagram

The effect of changes in injections and withdrawals

It is obvious from the diagrams that any change in expenditure leads
to a change in national income. Fig. 13.6 shows a Keynesian Cross in
which autonomous expenditure (injections) shift upwards from J to
J_1. This could occur as a result of an increase in investment,
government expenditure or exports, all of which may vary in the
short term as we have noted. The upward shift in injections results
in the equilibrium income level, given by the intersection of the
injections (J) and withdrawals (W) functions, rising from Y to Y_1.

Similarly any change in withdrawals will also have a direct impact
on national income. If tax rates are raised, for example, then
withdrawals associated with any given level of income will rise,
shown by a new withdrawals function, W_2. Higher withdrawals

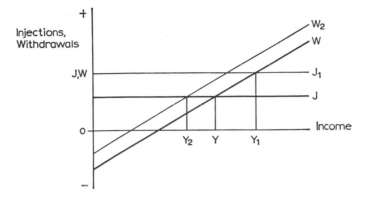

Fig. 13.6 The effects of changes in injections and withdrawals on the National Income

reduce the circular flow and lead to income falling from Y to Y_2, with the original level of injections, 'J'.

The size of income changes – the multiplier

So far we have seen that changes in net injections or withdrawals lead to corresponding changes in national income. This may seem fairly obvious – higher expenditure leads to higher national income. What is not so immediately obvious is that any given change in injections or withdrawals has a magnified impact on national income, and the way this takes place is known as the *Multiplier* process.

If, for example, the government spends an additional £100m on road-building, without increasing taxation, this initial injection of £100m autonomous expenditure raises the GDP. However the rise is not confined to the initial £100m extra spending. National income will eventually rise by a multiple of the initial injection.

In the case of road-building, the initial £100m expenditure generates incomes for all those concerned with the construction; for the labour force, the suppliers of materials, the managers, and ultimately the shareholders in the firms involved. However the story does not end here. When incomes rise, people are likely to spend part of the rise in their income. And this expenditure obviously gives rise to income for another group of individuals in the economy, which will also partly be re-spent and in turn generate income for others, leading to further expenditure, and so on.

The same is true of a drop in autonomous expenditure – it not only immediately affects those selling products no longer being bought, but also those whose livelihood depends on the expenditure of the first group. Politicians have long been well aware of the impact of the multiplier though they may never have heard of the term. Local MPs from Bristol and Toulouse, for example, were strong supporters of the Concorde, regardless of its overall merits or demerits, mainly because they fully understood that ending the project affected not only the aircraft industry employees but all their constituents whose income depended on aircraft workers' expenditure.

The amount of additional expenditure generated by a given rise in income is determined by the *marginal propensity to consume* (MPC). The MPC is simply the ratio of a change in income to the change in consumption spending that is associated with it, i.e.

$$\text{MPC} = \frac{\Delta C}{\Delta Y} \quad \text{where } \Delta C = \text{change in consumption and}$$
$$\Delta Y = \text{change in income}$$

Consumption in this context, it should be emphasised, refers to consumption of *domestically produced* output. We are concerned with expenditure that is returned to the circular flow of domestic income – obviously spending on imports represents a leakage from this flow, as we have already seen, and so is not included.

In Table 13.1 we have assumed that in Stage 1 autonomous expenditure rises by £100m. The marginal propensity to consume domestic output is 0.5. For simplicity, consumption is dependent on current income, while current consumption determines next time period's income. Thus in the first stage, the £100m autonomous expenditure increase, multiplied by the MPC, 0.5, generates a rise in consumption of £50m.

Table 13.1

	Income (Y)	Consumption (C)	Withdrawals (W)
Stage 1	+100	+50	+50
Stage 2	+50	+25	+25
Stage 3	+25	+12.5	+12.5
Stage 4	+12.5	+6.25	+6.25
Stage 'n'	+0	+0	+0
Final sum of all stages	+200	+100	+100

In Stage 2 the previous stage increase in consumption means that incomes have risen by that amount (£50m). Of this, half (£25m) will be consumed, half withdrawn in the form of savings, imports and so on. This generates income in Stage 3 of £25m, of which £12.5m is consumed, £12.5m withdrawn and so on. We have not continued beyond the fourth round, but it is clear that since the increase in income, consumption and withdrawals in each period is being halved, eventually it will become small enough to be insignificant. The sum to which the columns will tend is shown in the final line of Table 13.1 – income will rise by £200m, consumption by £100m and withdrawals by £100m. Our equilibrium condition is when J = W. Injections rise by £100m, therefore equilibrium will occur when withdrawals equal £100m. So national income, as shown in the table, continues to rise until total withdrawals equal £100m, at which point equilibrium is restored.

In other words, after the initial impact of increased *autonomous* expenditure, ΔJ, in Stage 1, there were further *induced* rises in expenditure as a result of the increased income it generated. Thus at stage 2, income of $\Delta J \times MPC$ was generated. At Stage 3, half of the latter increased income was re-spent, i.e. income rose by $\Delta J \times MPC \times MPC$ or $\Delta J \times MPC^2$. Similarly half of this was re-spent to generate a further rise in income at stage 4 or $\Delta J \times MPC^2 \times MPC$ or $\Delta J \times MPC^3$.

The sum of all the stages can be summarised as $Y = (\Delta J) + (\Delta J \times MPC) + (\Delta J \times MPC^2) + (\Delta J \times MPC^3) + \ldots (\Delta J \times MPC^n)$. This type of series is known by mathematicians as a *Geometric Progression*, and the formula for obtaining the sum of it, in this context is,

$$Y = J \times \frac{1}{1 - C}$$

where the multiplier $= \dfrac{1}{1 - C}$

Since we have defined consumption as whatever is returned to the domestic flow of income, anything not consumed is a withdrawal. Hence,

$$1 - C = W$$

and therefore $\dfrac{1}{1 - C}$ can be written as $\dfrac{1}{W}$ as an alternative formula for the multiplier.

In the example we used above, the MPC = 0.5; thus, using K as a symbol to represent the multiplier,

$$K = \frac{1}{1 - \frac{1}{2}} = \frac{1}{\frac{1}{2}} = 2.$$

As a further example, if the MPC = 0.75, then

$$K = \frac{1}{1 - \frac{3}{4}} = \frac{1}{\frac{1}{4}} = 4.$$

In general, then, the multiplier is given by the reciprocal of the marginal withdrawals from the circular flow. It may also be depicted by the Keynesian Cross diagram. Referring back to Fig. 13.6, the multiplier effect of any change in injections can be seen when we shift the aggregate injection function up from J to J^1. Here we have drawn the withdrawals function with a slope of 0.5 – i.e. a rise of 1 unit along the income axis is associated with a rise of 0.5 units along the injections and withdrawals axis. Thus when the injection schedule moves up from J to J^1, income rises by twice that amount, from Y to Y^1.

It is very important to note that in practice, the sum of withdrawals (W) from the circular flow at each 'round' of expenditure can be quite large. When account is taken of savings, direct and indirect taxation, imports, and other miscellaneous withdrawals, the proportion of expenditure that is directly re-spent *domestically* in the multiplier process is quite low. Recent estimates suggest that of every £100 net expenditure 'injected' into the circular flow, two-thirds or more will be immediately withdrawn in this way, giving a 'domestic' MPC of only $\frac{1}{3}$. Thus in practice, the multiplier as it affects domestic output would be calculated as follows:

$$K = \frac{1}{1 - \frac{1}{3}} = \frac{1}{\frac{2}{3}} = \frac{3}{2} = 1.5$$

'Real world' estimates of the multiplier used by the Treasury and other economic forecasters are in fact around this level, or even less. This contrasts sharply with the misleadingly high multiplier obtained by concentrating on the marginal propensity to *save* as the only withdrawal. The following chapter examines the factors affecting the size of the multiplier and the level of demand in greater detail.

Full employment and the inflationary and deflationary gap

The Keynesian model shows us how the equilibrium level of income is determined. The critical role is played by shifts in injections and withdrawals. As we have seen, in the short term these may change significantly, particularly in the case of investment, which is notoriously volatile. Given the operation of the multiplier, national income may therefore fluctuate quite substantially.

On the other hand, the size of the labour force changes only very slowly. It therefore follows that the level of national income which is generated when the labour force is 'fully employed' may well not be the equilibrium level of income determined in the short run by the pattern of injections and withdrawals. [The rather indefinite concept of full employment is discussed further in Chapter 19.]

If total expenditure (and thus national income) is relatively low, unemployment is likely to result. On the other hand if total expenditure is very high, and is actually higher than the potential output of the economy when all factors are fully utilised, employment and the real volume of output will be physically limited by the capacity of the economy at any given time. Since the real volume of goods and services cannot be increased, total expenditure in excess of capacity can only result in an increase in the prices at which the output is sold. Spending over and above the productive capacity of the economy at existing prices has the effect of raising the general price level. In Fig. 13.7 the effect of full employment constraint on aggregate expenditure is shown.

In Fig. 13.7A the solid line through Y_{fe} shows the full employment income level. This is greater than the equilibrium level of income Y_e shown by the dotted line. Thus total expenditure falls short of full employment expenditure. It would require additional expenditure equal to the distance ab on Fig. 13.7A to generate full

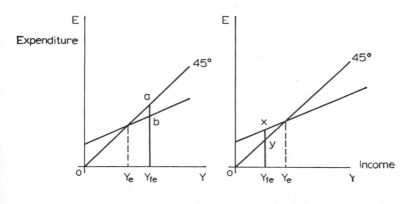

Fig. 13.7   A   Deflationary gap   B   Inflationary gap

employment income. The distance ab is known as the *deflationary gap* – the difference between actual expenditure and expenditure necessary to generate full employment.

Conversely, Fig. 13.7B shows an *inflationary gap*, xy. With real capacity limited by full employment, giving income of Y_{fe}, an equilibrium income of Y_e generates an excess of expenditure over real output equal to xy. This results in inflation.

In order to bring the equilibrium income level into line with the full employment income level, governments may attempt to adjust their own tax and expenditure policies to offset fluctuations occurring elsewhere. Chapter 14 examines in detail the sources of economic fluctuations in the framework of the Keynesian model, notably in savings and investment, and also looks at government taxes and expenditure, while fluctuations in the balance of payments are analysed in Chapter 18.

Summary

Taking existing resources as given, we have examined what determines the equilibrium level of output in the economy. Using a simple two-sector version of the Keynesian model consisting of firms and households, we have illustrated the principle of the circular flow of income. In advanced monetary economies, there is no presumption that this will tend quickly towards a full employment equilibrium. The income flow is liable to be disturbed by injections and withdrawals, which can be grouped together as investment and savings, exports and imports, and government expenditure and revenues. Withdrawals tend to depend on the level of income, while injections are autonomous and liable to considerable fluctuation.

Although there may be mechanisms to equate injections and withdrawals, such as interest rates and exchange rates, these alone are unlikely to bring about equilibrium quickly, and substantial changes in national income are likely to result in the meantime. The impact of fluctuations in autonomous expenditure is magnified by the operation of the multiplier process, since an initial expenditure change has substantial further repercussions on the income flow.

Thus aggregate demand, and hence national income in money terms, can vary substantially. On the other hand, productive capacity, and the size of the labour force, is fixed in the short run. Hence a substantial drop in aggregate demand leads to unemployment and the existence of a deflationary gap, while if aggregate demand exceeds the full employment level, an inflationary gap exists, and the price level will tend to rise.

Questions

1 Distinguish the equilibrium level of National Income from the full employment level of National Income. Why may they differ? (University of London, A-Level Economics)

2 Explain carefully what is meant by 'the multiplier'. Show how the multiplier concept can be extended from a closed economy with no government sector to an open economy with a government sector. (The Associated Examining Board, A-Level Economics)

3 Decisions to save and to invest are made by different groups of people for different reasons. What factors influence these decisions and what economic consequences result? (The Institute of Cost and Management Accountants, Professional Stage, Part I)

4 It has been estimated that, for the United Kingdom, the marginal propensity to save is about 0.1 and the value of the full multiplier is about 1.5.

   (a) What is meant by the 'marginal propensity to save' and the 'full multiplier'?

   (b) Why is the full multiplier smaller in the UK than in the USA?

   (The Institute of Chartered Accountants in England and Wales, Foundation Examination)

5 'Savings and investment will always tend to equality, but the point of equality will not necessarily be the point of full employment. This is the essence of the Keynesian revolution.' Explain, making clear the main features of the Keynesian analysis. (The Institute of Cost and Management Accountants, Professional Stage, Part I)

14

The Components of Demand

Introduction

The last chapter was devoted to an outline of the Keynesian model. We saw that the level of national income is in equilibrium when withdrawals equal injections or, in other words, when desired aggregate demand (expenditure) equals aggregate supply (national income). All injections – investment, exports and government expenditure – were assumed to be exogenously determined, i.e. outside the model, and all withdrawals – taxes, savings and imports – were assumed to be endogenously determined, i.e. within the model. These working assumptions must now be modified since such clear-cut distinctions cannot be made in practice. Accordingly, in this chapter we shall be considering the behaviour of the components of aggregate domestic demand – consumption, investment and government expenditure – in greater detail. Foreign trade will be discussed in Chapters 17 and 18.

1 Consumption

Consumers' expenditure is the largest single component of aggregate demand, representing roughly one half of total expenditure in the UK. Its fluctuations, therefore, even though traditionally small in percentage terms, have significant consequence for output and employment. Suppose, for example, that consumer expenditure were to decline by 2%. This would reduce Total Final Expenditure (total domestic expenditure plus exports) by 1% (given that consumers' expenditure is 47% of TFE) and, via the estimated UK multiplier of 1.4, would reduce national income by 1.4%, with serious consequences for the level of unemployment. Governments dedicated to the maintenance of full employment may try to offset such fluctuations with tax and expenditure policies, which is why it is so important to be able to explain and predict consumers' behaviour. In this section we shall be looking at the determinants of consumption at the micro-level of the household and then at the macro-level of the economy.

The household consumption function

Keynes argued in the General Theory that consumption is determined mainly by income. This is obviously a reasonable argument. A household earning £10000 a year can be expected to consume more goods and services than one earning £5000 a year. Thus we can say that a household's *real consumption* is a function of (i.e. is related to) its *real disposable income*. (Disposable income is defined as personal income after payment of income tax.) Keynes went further. He stated that 'the fundamental psychological law, upon which we are entitled to depend with great confidence both *a priori* from our knowledge of human nature and from the detailed facts of experience is that men are disposed, as a rule and on average, to increase their consumption as their income increases, but not by as much as the increase in their income'. Again this is a reasonable argument. Both logic and observation suggest that when a household receives additional income, it will spend a part but not all of that income and save the difference.

We can represent Keynes' two hypotheses in terms of the 45° diagram already used in the last chapter (see Fig. 13.4). Note, however, that consumption here refers to consumers' expenditure on all goods and services (i.e. including imports) and not just on those, as in the previous chapter, that are domestically produced.

The line marked C in Fig. 14.1 is the consumption function and it shows us what annual household consumption would be for alternative rates of household income. As in Chapter 13, we include the 45° line for reference. Anywhere along the line consumption equals disposable income; thus, the 45° line could be called the consumption function if the household's consumption always increased by the same amount as its income. However, the fact that the slope of the consumption function C is flatter than the 45° line reflects the hypothesis that the household's consumption increases less rapidly than income.

A household can only do two things with its income: spend it or save it. Hence the difference between disposable income and consumption expenditure is savings, and we can represent this

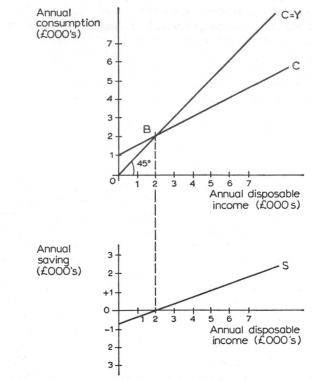

Fig. 14.1 Consumption and saving functions

relationship in Fig. 14.1A as the difference between C and the 45°
line or in Fig. 14.1B as a distinct savings function, S. Note in Fig.
14.1A that saving is zero where C and the 45° line intersect at B,
when consumption equals income. This is shown in Fig. 14.1B
where the savings function intersects with the horizontal axis. Thus
if income drops below £2000 per annum, our household will spend
more than its income by dissaving or borrowing. Of course if income
were to stay below £2000 for long, the household would exhaust all
its assets and credit facilities. This suggests a difference between the
long run and the short run that we shall pursue later.

Propensities to consume and save
We can further our understanding of the relationship between
consumption and income by developing the concepts of the *marginal propensities to consume* and *to save* (MPC and MPS) and the

average propensity to consume and *to save* (APC and APS). We are already familiar with the MPC from the last chapter where it was seen to be important in the derivation of the multiplier. The MPC was defined as the ratio of the change in disposable income to the change in consumption. Geometrically the MPC is the slope of the consumption function (the change in consumption divided by the change in income) and is constant in Fig. 14.1A since C is drawn as a straight line. This need not be necessarily true in reality. The marginal propensity to save is the proportion of the increased income which is saved. Since additional disposable income must either be spent or saved MPC + MPS = 1.

The APC is the proportion of disposable income which is spent on consumption, while the APS is the proportion of it which is saved. For any income level APC + APS = 1, so, for example, if a household spends £8000 out of an income of £10000 its APC will be 8000/10000 or 0.8 and its APS will be 2000/10000 or 0.2.

We are now in a position to re-phrase Keynes' 'psychological law' more concisely. The law states that a household's MPC will on average be positive but less than one. Further, Keynes hypothesised that as disposable income increases and as the basic necessities of food, clothing and shelter are satisfied a greater proportion of income will be saved as real income increases. In other words, as disposable income increases APC falls and APS rises. These relationships are illustrated in Fig. 14.1A above but it might help to clarify the concepts if they are also presented numerically. Table 14.1 presents the consumption schedule of our sample household. The relationship between disposable income and consumption in columns 1 and 2 is the same as that depicted by the consumption function in Fig. 14.1A.

The MPC is assumed to be a constant 0.67 but despite this the APC can be seen to fall steadily as disposable income rises. The APC is greater than one at income levels under £2000 because the household is consuming in excess of its income, and consequently net dissaving is occurring. After the £2000 break-even point saving becomes positive and the APS steadily rises.

The aggregate consumption function

We have seen how a household allocates its income between consumption and saving, but for macro-economic analysis we are interested in the aggregate of consumer expenditure. An aggregate consumption function is illustrated in Fig. 14.2. It is similar to that of the household except that the units are now in millions rather than in thousands. The area under the consumption function to the left of

Table 14.1 Consumption schedule of sample household (£ per year)

1 Disposable income	2 Consumption expenditure	3 MPC	4 APC	5 Net saving	6 MPS	7 APS
0	667		—	− 667		—
		0.67			0.33	
1000	1333		1.33	−333		−0.33
		0.67			0.33	
2000	2000		1	0		0
		0.67			0.33	
3000	2667		0.89	333		0.11
		0.67			0.33	
4000	3333		0.83	667		0.17
		0.67			0.33	
6000	4667		0.78	1333		0.22
		0.67			0.33	
7000	5333		0.76	1667		0.24

the break-even point B is of little practical significance at the macro-level since dissaving has only once occurred during modern times, and that was at the bottom of the Great Depression in 1932–3 in the USA.

The aggregate consumption function portrays the relationship between the consumption and the disposable income of the economy as a whole. Its position therefore depends upon the sum of all the individual household consumption functions and upon the distribution of aggregate disposable income between households. The distribution of income would not matter if all households had similar MPCs, but such is not the case for a variety of reasons. To

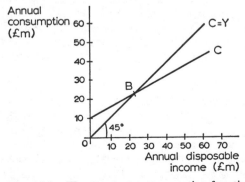

Fig. 14.2 The aggregate consumption function

take a simple example, there will be a marked difference in behaviour between a very rich household and a very poor household towards an extra £100 of disposable income. The rich household, whose wants are satisfied, will have a relatively low MPC of, say, 0.5 whereas the poor household will seize upon the money to buy necessities and consequently have an MPC equal or close to one. Differing characteristics of households with similar incomes may also lead them to consume different proportions of their incomes. They may differ in the size of their asset holdings (wealth); in their expectations about future job prospects; in ages and family size; and in their degree of foresight.

Shifts in and along the consumption function

We have seen that consumption is a function of the level of disposable income, of the distribution of that income between households, and of the differing characteristics of households. We can thus envisage movements occurring along the function as a result of changes in the level of aggregate disposable income; similarly we can anticipate shifts in the slope of the function as a result of changes in the propensity to consume. The former changes are much easier to engineer than the latter. Governments can, and frequently do, use fiscal policies comprising tax and expenditure measures to alter aggregate disposable income in order to offset inflationary or deflationary gaps. (These gaps were discussed in the previous chapter.) We shall have more to say about the use of fiscal policy in the last section of this chapter.

On the other hand, the determinants of the propensity to consume are complex, as we have seen, and consequently are difficult to influence deliberately. Alterations in the personal attributes of households, in their asset holdings, or in their perceptions of the future lie outside the immediate scope of government. Changes in the distribution of income will alter the aggregate consumption level associated with a given level of disposable income but such changes, though theoretically within the range of government action, occur only very slowly in practice. Price expectations will also influence expenditure patterns. For example, the belief that an inflation is imminent may induce households to purchase now what they were planning to purchase some time in the future. There remains the availability of credit, and especially of credit for financing purchases of durable goods, such as cars, washing-machines, etc., which can be directly controlled by government. The problem however with, say, stiffening credit (hire purchase) terms is that this merely causes households to postpone their purchases of durables until such time as the terms are eased when there is a resurgence of credit-financed expenditure. In the UK, the MPC has in fact fluctuated considerably since the Second World War. On two occasions, 1957 and 1962, it was greater than unity – a finding which refutes the first part of Keynes' psychological law. The average MPC 1955–70 was 0.90 with values ranging from 1.2 to 0.63, and between 1976 and 1980 the average estimated MPC was 0.84 with the lowest value – 0.74 – occurring in 1978.

The long-run consumption function

The consumption function that we have been discussing reflects short-term changes in consumer spending in response to short-term fluctuations in disposable income. It does not show us what happens to spending as income grows over time. Keynes hypothesised that the APC should fall as income rises but this has not turned out to be the case in reality. Since the Second World War in the USA, where most consumer research has been done, the APC has been found to be virtually constant, fluctuating in a narrow range between 0.90 –0.95.

In the UK the APC fell through the 1950s from high post-war levels and stabilised around the 0.91–0.93 range from 1962 onwards. Between 1970 and 1980 the average APC declined to 0.88, and reached 0.84 by 1980; i.e. the average propensity to save increased. This, however, was probably due more to households' desires to restore the value of their inflation-eroded assets and to provide for possible unemployment than to any 'Keynesian' reason. By contrast, throughout most of the 1980s, when prices were rising less quickly, the APC rose, reaching 0.95 in 1988. It should not however be assumed that there is a precise relationship between inflation and consumption/saving behaviour.

Some explanation for variation in the APC can be found if we interpret the consumption functions in Figs. 14.1 and 14.2 as short-run functions, on the reasonable assumption that spending habits are fixed in the short term and therefore unresponsive to short-run income fluctuations. For example, if a household experiences a 40% drop in its disposable income which it believes to be temporary it will cut back, say, 10–20% of its expenditure and make up the difference by dissaving. Similarly a household experiencing a 40% increase in income in a given year will be reluctant to increase its expenditure by the full 40% if it believes that income will fall to its original level the following year.

Over the long run, however, adjustments will be made to income changes if the latter are expected to be permanent. As households get richer so former luxuries, such as televisions, for example, come to be regarded as necessities and advertising and new products stimulate desires. In the long run consumption increases in proportion to income and this can be seen as an upward shift in the short-run consumption function. C, C_1, C_2 and C_3 in Fig. 14.3 below

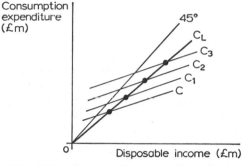

Fig. 14.3 Consumption expenditure (£m)

represent such upward shifts in the function over time. The heavy dots represent the normal level of income in each period and when these are joined up the resulting line, C_L, forms the long-term consumption function.

There are many theories why the consumption function shifts upwards in such a fashion. The two most prominent theories are the *permanent income hypothesis* which is associated with Professor Friedman and the *relative income hypothesis* of Professor Duesenberry. Friedman thinks that households have a view of their expected lifetime earnings – or permanent income – and thus hold their APCs constant in relation to permanent rather than current income. Duesenberry thinks that households base their consumption patterns on relative rather than absolute income. If all incomes increase by 20% then the *keeping-up-with-the-Jones'-effect* will ensure that all consumption expenditures are adjusted by the same proportion. Both theories have implications for government policy, as we shall see in section 3 of this chapter.

2   Investment

We now move on to discuss the second major component of the Keynesian model, investment. It will be recalled that the term *investment* is applied to the process of adding to the real capital stock of an economy. It thus comprises plant and machinery and must not be confused with investment in financial assets. In the

1978–1987 period Gross Domestic Fixed Capital Formation amounted on average to 17% of Gross Domestic Product, but this figure belies its importance. Investment in productive capital is central to the process of economic growth. Investment, being volatile, also contributes to fluctuations in the economy in general.

We shall be examining various theories of investment behaviour, but readers should not be surprised to discover that none yield a completely satisfactory explanation of observed fluctuations in investment. Such is the diverse nature of Gross Domestic Fixed Capital Formation (GDFCF) – comprising investment in dwellings (19.6% of GDFCF in 1988), investment in other new buildings (30.1%), investment in plant and machinery (40.3%) and investment in vehicles, aircraft and ships (10.1%), all of which have been public or private – that it is most unlikely that a single theory could account for all the differing motivations behind investment decisions.

The marginal efficiency of investment

The first theory we are going to examine is that investment is a function of the rate of interest. Assume that we are dealing with a businessman who is considering investing in a new machine, and assume further that he is a profit maximiser. He knows the cost of the machine, but in order to estimate the profitability of the venture he must have some idea of the net returns to be produced by the machine during its useful economic life. Obviously he will not invest unless the net returns exceed the cost. The problem the businessman faces however is that the net returns lie in the future therefore he can only forecast them with a degree of uncertainty. Similarly, he cannot be sure about the useful economic life of the machine since tastes can change or technology advance, thus rendering his machine obsolete. The resulting expected rate of return on the machine is known as the *Marginal Efficiency of Investment* (MEI).

Having estimated the Marginal Efficiency of Investment the businessman must now determine whether the investment is profitable or not. Assuming that he has to borrow the funds with which to purchase the machine then he will have to pay a rate of interest on those borrowed funds. We can say therefore that our businessman will only invest if the rate of return on the new machine exceeds the rate of interest he has to pay on the borrowed funds. For example if, by borrowing £20000 at 5%, he can purchase a machine yielding a forecast rate of return of 10% then it will pay him to make the investment. We can also see that the higher the rate of interest the higher the MEI will have to be before an investment is worth considering and therefore the lower the amount of actual investment that will be carried out. In other words investment is inversely related to the rate of interest.

The investment decision is clearly risky since it is dependent upon estimates of the future which are, by their nature, subjective and uncertain. The risk also increases as the firm invests because a larger proportion of the firm's assets will become dependent upon estimates of future yields. The firm will react to this increased risk by making larger allowances for it when considering a new investment, and this will reduce the MEI. The same applies at a macro-economic level, and will be augmented by other forces tending to depress the MEI. Firstly, an increasing rate of investment will raise the demand for new capital goods and possibly force up the latters' price thus depressing the expected rate of return. Secondly, continuing investment will lead to more and more capital being combined with the existing labour force. As with all other factors of production, diminishing returns will set in and the marginal product of each additional unit of capital will decline and with it the MEI. For all the above reasons the MEI schedule for the economy as a whole, when plotted graphically in relation to the rate of interest (Fig. 14.4) slopes downwards. The steepness of the schedule will depend upon the interest elasticity of investment, i.e. the responsiveness of investment to interest rate changes. The equilibrium level of gross investment can therefore be determined and is the point where the MEI schedule cuts the line representing the rate of interest (I in Fig. 14.4).

The theory tells us that annual investment is determined by the rate of interest and the factors that comprise the MEI. Thus investment will be stimulated by a decline in the rate of interest or

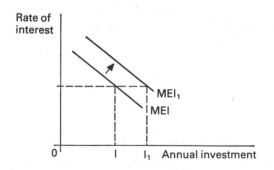

Fig. 14.4   The Marginal Efficiency of Investment schedule

an upwards shift of the MEI schedule (MEI_1 in Fig. 14.4). The latter could occur as a result of a fall in the cost of capital goods, an improvement in technology, or an increase in business confidence, and it means that there will be more investment forthcoming at each interest rate than before (e.g. I^1 in Fig. 14.4).

The accelerator principle

Most empirical evidence suggests that changes in the level of demand are a more important determinant of investment than the rate of interest. Businessmen will be, understandably, more optimistic about the future during periods when demand is expanding, and they will also be able to maximise their output and the profits out of which investment can be financed.

The accelerator principle stresses the relationship between the level of net investment and changes in National Income. In its simplest form the principle states that net investment (I) is determined by the change in income (Δ) multiplied by a fixed quantity – the accelerator coefficient (v) – which is the amount of investment necessary to produce an extra unit of output. For example, if a machine costs £20 000 and produces annually £10 000 worth of output the coefficient will be $\frac{20\,000}{10\,000} = 2$. The principle can be expressed symbolically:

$$I_t = v\Delta Y \text{ (where } I_t \text{ is current investment)}$$

Now let us see how the theory works. Assume at the outset that income is constant; and that the existing capital stock is working at full capacity and is simply being kept intact by replacement investment. There is therefore no net investment. If income starts to rise demand will increase putting pressure on manufacturers to expand their capacity in order to meet that demand. The resulting new net investment will be a multiple of the change in income because in our example above it takes £2 of investment to produce £1 of extra output. This process will continue as long as income rises at the same rate or faster. However if the rate of growth of income should decline then the absolute level of net investment will fall. A numerical example will help to clarify this point.

We assume an accelerator coefficient of 2. In Year 1 income increases by 10% and net investment rises from zero to 200 (100 × 2). In Year 2 income again increases by 10% as does investment. However thereafter the rate of change of income declines. It is still rising – by 6% in Year 3, 4% in Year 4 and 2% in Year 5 – but the growth rate is progressively lower. Meanwhile the absolute level of net investment declines throughout and becomes zero when income

Table 14.2 The Accelerator Principle

Year	Y	ΔY	Net I (excluding replacement)
0	1000	0	0
1	1100	100	200
2	1210	110	220
3	1282	72	144
4	1333	51	102
5	1360	27	54
6	1360	0	0

ceases to grow at all in Year 6. In sum therefore the accelerator principle tells us that net investment depends on the rate of growth of income not the absolute level, that changes in the rate of growth of income produce magnified changes in investment, and that when the rate of increase of income falls the absolute level of net investment falls. The accelerator process thus generates fluctuations in investment, and sharp fluctuations are indeed a feature of investment behaviour.

Criticisms of the accelerator
There are many criticisms of the principle. Perhaps the most telling is that the accelerator relationship will not apply when the economy is operating below capacity. If such is the case investment will only respond after income has been rising for some time; there will be a *lagged response*. Criticism has also been levelled at the excessive rigidity of the technical relationship between investment and output. It is argued that manufacturers experiencing increased demand for their products may make more intensive use of existing capacity by increasing shifts, working overtime and so on, rather than by investing. And they may not invest at all if the increase in demand is thought to be only temporary. The principle avoids all the problems connected with the supply and cost of investment funds and profitability, and it also assumes that the capital goods industry can expand its output when required. Finally, the principle assumes that manufacturers have no expectations, that they simply respond automatically to a rise in demand, and that they only invest to meet that demand and for no other reason; for example they do not, says the principle, invest in new techniques to lower production costs.

We have said enough about the accelerator principle to show that such a simple mechanical relationship will not by itself satisfactorily explain investment behaviour. However an allied principle, the *capital stock adjustment principle*, seems to provide a more accept-able explanation of manufacturing investment. The latter principle is similar to the accelerator in that it proposes a fixed relationship between income and net investment but it also allows for the underutilisation of capacity by including the existing capital stock as a variable. The current level of investment (I_t) is related directly to the level of income in the previous period (Y_{t-1}) and inversely to the capital stock in the previous period (K_{t-1}). Thus,

$$I_t = aY_{t-1} - bK_{t-1}$$

where a and b are constants. In other words net investment depends on income, and since increases in the capital stock are involved, it will also depend on the quantity of capital stock in existence.

As we have said the capital stock adjustment principle seems to explain manufacturing investment better than the simple accelera-tor. But it cannot explain other business fixed-investment so well, perhaps because capital is not such an important component of this; for instance, the principle does not attempt to explain investment in dwellings. Economists are therefore a long way from being able to construct a satisfactory model of the determination of gross fixed investment. Proof of this lies in the fact that official forecasters still rely heavily on surveys and questionnaires for their investment predictions.

In conclusion the role of expectations must be re-emphasised since they are probably the most important determinant of invest-ment. Despite the development of advanced management tech-niques and sophisticated computer forecasts, investment still remains an act of faith dependent upon a fundamental optimism about the future. Recent UK experience shows that no amount of inducement, either verbal or financial, by the government can overcome the private investor's pessimism about the future. Thus a sort of 'band-wagon' effect may help to explain observed investment fluctuations. When demand is growing strongly the business climate is bright and all rush to invest. Conversely when things are going badly, business pessimism is apparent and no one invests.

3   Government

The budget
Finally, we must consider the role of government in the determina-tion of aggregate demand. That role is likely to be a significant one since most Western governments command a significant proportion

of their nations' economic resources through their expenditure and taxation policies. In 1987 the UK General Government expenditure (Central and Local government) accounted for 21% of Gross Domestic Product. With the above policies – jointly known as fiscal or budgetary policy – governments can therefore try deliberately to alter the course of the economy in chosen directions. They may, for example, endeavour to achieve a high and sustained level of employment by offsetting fluctuations in aggregate demand. This activity is known as *stabilisation*. Thus the government will try to counteract a fall in aggregate demand (a deflationary gap) by increasing its net injections into the circular flow. Assuming that the budget is balanced to begin with, with revenue equal to expenditure, this implies that expenditure should be increased and revenue (taxation) maintained at the same level. Expenditure will now exceed revenue and we can speak of the government running a budget deficit.

Conversely, if aggregate demand grows at a rate faster than the productive sector of the economy can cope with, causing balance of payments problems and inflation (an inflationary gap), then the government will try to mitigate this by increasing its net withdrawals. Assuming once again that the budget is balanced at the outset, this will entail running a budget surplus; the government will spend less than it receives in revenue. The financing of budget deficits has important monetary implications and these will be discussed in Chapter 17.

Until the Second World War it was an item of conventional economic wisdom that budgets should always be balanced. Governments, it was argued, should behave like households and balance their books. After being largely disregarded for some 20 years following the War, this view of budgetary conduct has now returned to the centre of policy debate. The reasons for this are manifold. They include a growing disillusionment with traditional Keynesian economic remedies for inflation and unemployment; an ideological distrust of all public – as opposed to private – expenditure; and the theory that public expenditure simply replaces private expenditure with little impact on the overall level of aggregate demand. This latter is known as the *crowding out effect* and we shall have more to say about it in Chapter 16.

Most economists would however accept that the government can influence the level of domestic economic activity to some extent, and it must be remembered that the blanket requirement for budgetary balance means that governments must cut their expenditures during recessions when tax revenue falls. This will reduce injections into the circular flow and further worsen the recession. It was one of the central insights of Keynes' General Theory that governments could use the budget to stabilise the economy by acting 'counter-cyclically'. Even partial acceptance of this view implies a governmental willingness to tolerate rising budget deficits during recessions.

The effects of budget deficits and surpluses on national income

The government has two strategies at its disposal to eliminate inflationary and deflationary gaps. It can either alter tax revenues or it can alter expenditures. What strategy should the government adopt? We shall discuss the problem with reference to the familiar deflationary gap.

The government can either reduce taxes or raise its expenditure to increase injections to the desired level. However it will require a larger budget deficit to achieve a given income with tax reductions than with increased government expenditure. In order, for example, to raise national income by £4m and with a multiplier of 2, the government simply has to raise its expenditure by £2m. However a reduction in tax revenue of £2m, having the same effect on the budget deficit, will not result in the desired increase in national income. This is because only a proportion of the £2m of disposable income in people's hands will be passed on in increased expenditures. The remainder will leak out of the circular flow in the form of savings. If the propensity to consume is 0.8, an extra £2m of disposable income will increase expenditure by £1.6m and with a multiplier of 2, raise national income by only £3.2m. In order, therefore, to achieve the required £4m increase in national income the tax revenue would have to be reduced by £2.5m. The converse is true for dealing with an inflationary gap. Government expenditure would have to be cut by a smaller amount than tax revenue would have to be raised.

The balanced budget multiplier

The differing effects of expenditure and tax changes lie at the heart of the balanced budget multiplier. This shows that an increase in the size of the budget, even though revenue and expenditure are kept in balance, will exert an expansionary pull on the economy. A rise in government expenditure, of, say, £1m will be fully passed on into the circular flow. Whereas a £1m increase in tax revenue will reduce consumption expenditure by less than the full amount because some of the extra tax payments will come out of savings. Thus, if 80% of the tax revenue would have been used for consumption expenditures, and tax revenues and government expenditure are each increased by £1m the net effect will be an increase in total expenditure of £0.2m, and national income will rise by £0.4m (given a multiplier of 2).

Fluctuations in economic activity

It will probably be clear by now that cycles of boom and recession are a feature of economic life, at any rate in capitalist economies. Since the War, output and living standards have tended to rise over time but there have been marked variations in their rates of growth from year to year. But why do these fluctuations occur? We can attempt an explanation using the theories now at our disposal. Assume initially that the circular flow of income is in equilibrium (injections = withdrawals) at less than full employment. Assume further that there is an injection into the circular flow caused by an autonomous increase in investment. This will raise national income by more than an equivalent amount because of the effect of the multiplier. Rising national income will then produce a more than proportionate increase in investment, because of the effect of the accelerator, which will in turn cause incomes to rise more than proportionately – and so on. The cumulative growth of income will continue until the economy's full employment 'ceiling' is reached. Then the process goes into reverse. The growth rate of income levels off causing, as we saw in Table 14.2 above, an 'accelerated' decline in the absolute level of net investment, followed by a 'multiplied' reduction in income – and so on. The bottom – or 'floor' – of the recession will come when withdrawals once more equal the reduced level of injections. At worst this could be when saving and investment are zero leaving consumption equal to income. And another autonomous injection will start the whole cycle moving again.

The simple multiplier-accelerator model, though of course lacking the complexity of reality, does yield some real insights into economic fluctuations. Investment in the UK has indeed been volatile, and this has undoubtedly contributed to fluctuations in the level of total demand. However investment has not been the only source of instability. The UK is an *open economy*, highly dependent on overseas trade, and therefore vulnerable to changes in foreign demand for UK exports. Exports have been the most volatile of the main expenditure components; also government consumption tends to fluctuate counter-cyclically, rising as consumers' expenditure falls, and vice versa.

Built-in stabilisers and discretionary fiscal policy

There are two distinct types of fiscal policy measures: *built-in stabilisers* which are automatic in operation, and *discretionary measures* – so-called because they are introduced at the discretion of the government. Built-in stabilisers do not require explicit policy decisions and they operate counter-cyclically to stabilise the economy by increasing government injections during depressions and withdrawals during booms. Most tax systems work in this fashion. Expenditure taxes, like VAT, yield more revenue as expenditure rises and less revenue when expenditure falls. A progressive incomes tax system does likewise. As income rises a progressive tax system takes larger and larger proportions of that increased income; when income falls, tax revenue drops more than proportionately. Other built-in stabilisers are unemployment benefits and virtually all welfare schemes because expenditures on these rise and fall with the unemployment rate.

Built-in stabilisers provide modern economies with more stability than they had in the past. The fluctuations in the UK economy have, in general, been less extreme than they were before the First World War. However, the cycle has not disappeared, and the government has felt obliged to intervene with discretionary changes in tax rates and expenditure to stabilise the economy.

Fiscal policy in practice

We have seen that the manipulation of government expenditure is a more direct strategy than tax alterations. In practice, however, government expenditure changes are too cumbersome to be used with any precision because their impact on the economy is long-delayed. Expenditures on major projects such as roads, bridges and hospitals, are difficult to adjust in midstream and such tactics have only really been used in the UK as panic responses to short-term crises (normally concerning sterling).

Taxes, on the other hand, are relatively easy to manipulate and they do have an immediate effect upon disposable income. This takes us back to the first section of this chapter – the consumption function. If the consumption function is of the simple Keynesian type then a change in disposable income will result in a change in current expenditure. If, however, households determine their consumption patterns in the light of their permanent (or lifetime's) income, as Friedman suggests, then they will disregard what they consider to be short-term tax changes. They will respond to higher taxes by running down savings, making injections (drops in savings) once more equal to withdrawals (tax increase), and national income will be unaffected. Duesenberry's relative income hypothesis predicts a similar response since households will strive to maintain their living standards in the face of short-term tax increases. The nature of the consumption function therefore has serious implications for the effectiveness of short-term stabilisation policies.

We have already mentioned that economies are in continual cyclical motion, oscillating from relative boom to relative depression and back again. We have not however considered what effect this has on policy formulation. Stabilisation in a static economy is simply a matter of eliminating inflationary or deflationary gaps by adjusting the level of national income. On the other hand, stabilising an economy in cyclical motion involves controlling rates of change and this is an altogether different proposition, given the imperfect state of the science of economics.

Economic statistics are always out of date when they are published. Employment figures, for example, are published one month after they are collected and other statistics can be even more delayed. We can never know about the current state of the economy, only its state in the past. There is therefore a lag, known as the *recognition lag*, between the onset of a problem and its identification. Policies then have to be devised to solve the problem, and this may take anything up to six months, before being passed through Parliament, which may take a further three months. This is called the *decision lag*. Finally the policy takes time to come into full effect – the *operation lag*. As much as one year may therefore elapse between the recognition of a problem and its solution. Under these circumstances it is essential to have forecasts, so that the government can act well ahead of events. If these forecasts are not accurate, as they have not been on several important occasions, then it is entirely possible for a government to find itself acting *perversely*, that is to say, amplifying the cycle (by acting procyclically) rather than dampening it (by acting counter-cyclically).

Inflation and unemployment
So far we have been assuming that the government's sole aim is to stabilise the economy around the full employment level. However there are other objectives – balance of payments equilibrium and price stability for example – which may well conflict with the maintenance of full employment levels of demand. The balance of payments will be discussed in Chapter 18 but it is worth noting here that the consequence of high domestic demand may be high imports and balance of payments deficits.

As far as price stability is concerned we have already seen that there may be a relationship between aggregate demand, the price level and employment. The Keynesian model described in the last chapter showed us that inflation will occur when the equilibrium level of income exceeds the full employment level (i.e. when there is an inflationary gap). An examination of the above relationship has given rise to one of the best-known observations in macro-economic analysis – the Phillips curve. The curve, named after its originator A. W. Phillips, is shown in Fig. 14.5. The level of unemployment is registered on the horizontal axis, the rate of change of wages on the vertical. The level of unemployment is used as an indicator of the pressure of aggregate demand, low unemployment being associated with high demand and vice versa. Thus, when unemployment is low (and demand for goods is high) wages can be expected to increase rapidly because firms will be bidding up wage rates to attract labour and thereby increase their output. In addition, if trade unions are active they will find employers willing and able to grant wage increases during times of high demand. When unemployment is high, however, the demand for goods will be low and employers' resistance to wage increases will be greater. Wages will then tend to rise more slowly.

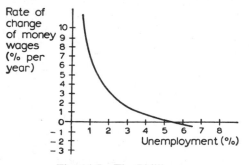

Fig. 14.5   The Phillips curve

Phillips observed that a highly stable relationship existed between the level of unemployment and the rate of change of wages. We can see in Fig. 14.5 that as unemployment decreases towards the origin (aggregate demand increases) the curve becomes steeper, i.e. inflation gradually accelerates. This is because full employment is unlikely to occur in all industries at the same time. As industries run out of capacity they will attempt to increase it by hiring more labour, bidding up wages. As the level of total demand increases, more and more industries find themselves in this situation. Hence the pressure on the labour market increases and the rate of increase of wages accelerates.

Conversely, as unemployment rises, the curve flattens out – particularly after it cuts the horizontal axis. This is likely to be due to the resistance of unions to actual wage cuts. Thus it takes very much larger percentage increases in unemployment to get wages to fall than it does to moderate their rise.

The Phillips curve, fitted to pre-1913 UK data, yielded remarkably good predictions of inflation rates from its date of publication in 1958 until 1966–7. For example, in 1960 unemployment was at 1.6% and money wage rates rose by 4.1%. For that level of unemployment the Phillips curve (see Fig. 14.5) predicts an identical rise in wage rates. It is not surprising therefore that the Phillips curve had a substantial influence on economic policy-makers during the 1960s and early 1970s. However, after 1966–7 observations of inflation increasingly diverged from their predicted values and the original Phillips relationship is now deemed to have broken down. We shall examine attempted modifications of the relationship in some detail in the final chapter.

Comments on UK stabilisation policy

Post-war UK stabilisation policies have been the object of much criticism. It is widely thought that governments de-stabilised the economy with their mis-timed and excessive corrections. There is now widespread scepticism about a government's ability to 'fine-tune' an economy to deliver both low inflation and full employment. This scepticism has found its fullest expression in the writings of 'monetarist' economists – so called because they hold that changes in the money supply cause changes in national income. We shall have more to say about the Keynesian vs. monetarist debate in Chapter 16, but it is worth noting in this context that the disagreement between the two schools of thought is fundamentally rooted in differing perceptions about the way an economy works. The monetarists believe that economies are self-regulating. The minimum of governmental interference is thus required and policy, they argue, should be limited to setting a constant annual monetary growth rate target in order to eliminate exogenous shocks to the economy. Keynesians, on the other hand, believe that the self-regulating mechanism of an economy is weak and unresponsive. Stabilisation policies are thus required, in their opinion, to augment the regulatory mechanism if inflationary or deflationary gaps are not to be endured for long periods of time.

The debate is far from being resolved. Fluctuations have certainly not been eliminated but it is not possible to say whether these have been caused by failures of economic knowledge, conflicts in policy objectives or misguided aims. For instance, it is now clear that the emphasis on achieving full employment encouraged UK governments to maintain a higher level of domestic activity than was compatible with balance of payments equilibrium and price stability. As the latter objectives came under threat so governments had to alter the desired level of demand and to sacrifice the full employment objective. It would be surprising therefore if the frequent policy variations had not contributed to the instability of the economy.

Economic growth

In these last two chapters we have shared Keynes' preoccupation with the short-term problem of the utilisation of existing factors of production. There is, however, the equally important but longer-term problem of achieving economic growth by increasing the quantity and quality of those factors and by improving the efficiency with which they are combined. This has been the objective of most governments since the Second World War.

Keynesian fiscal policies can influence the rate of growth of an economy by altering the level of aggregate demand. But, as we have seen, demand cannot be expanded indefinitely without meeting constraints as the economy nears its level of full capacity working. These constraints take the form of increasing inflation and balance of payments disequilibria and they signify that the domestic economy can no longer meet the demands placed upon it.

' The peak of an economy's capacity is known as its *level of productive potential*, which is defined as that rate of growth which can be maintained at a constant level of unemployment. Productive potential is usually measured by adding the rate of growth of labour supply to the recent trend rate of growth of *labour productivity* (output per man). For the UK it is usually said to be around 3% which means that GDP will have to rise by 3% p.a. to keep unemployment unchanged.

A successful economic growth policy must raise the economy's 'ceiling' by increasing its productive potential. The problem is that it is still far from clear how this can be done. The labour supply is virtually decided by the birth rate though it is also affected by changes in hours worked, holidays, and by internal and external migration. There is a considerable body of evidence to suggest that France and Germany owe their relatively fast post-war growth rates to the movement of labour from the agricultural to the industrial sectors. The fact that this shift had been accomplished in the UK by the beginning of the post-war period has been suggested as the cause of the UK's relatively slow growth rate. The quality of the labour force is also of obvious importance. It must be suitably educated and trained to make it easily adaptable to new techniques.

The rate of growth of capital formation is important for economic growth because it affects the size and quality of the capital stock. The more capital there is to work with the more the output per man will tend to rise; and the newer the capital stock, according to one plausible view, the more it will embody the latest technology. Inventions and innovations are of no economic value unless they are embodied in capital equipment. It is often argued that the Germans owe their high growth rates to the opportunity that war-time devastation gave them to renew their capital stock with the latest machinery.

By focusing on the quantity and quality of factors of production, in other words on the supply side, we have so far ignored the role that demand plays in economic growth. If demand is weak, existing capacity will be under-utilised and there will be no incentive to improve factor utilisation. Equally, weak demand implies low profits which in turn imply low investment. Conversely, when demand is strong profits and optimism will be high and investment and innovation encouraged. And it is not just the relative strength of demand that matters; it is also its variability. If demand fluctuates sharply, as some argue has been the case in the UK, it may discourage investment by holding down overall profitability. The knowledge that recession follows swiftly on expansion may prove a disincentive to the enlargement of productive capacity.

Enough has been said to show that economic growth is the result of a very complex series of interactions between supply and demand factors. Economists are still unclear about the relative contribution that each factor makes to economic growth and thus about the reasons why some economies grow faster than others. It follows therefore that there are no certain measures that governments can take to influence growth rates.

Summary

In the first section the determinants of consumption were considered. The Keynesian short-term consumption function was derived from the 'fundamental psychological law' that the MPC will always be positive but less than one and that the APC falls as disposable income rises. We saw that the position of the aggregate consumption function depends upon the summation of all the individual household's functions and upon the distribution of income. We also saw that deliberate shifts in the function can be engineered with greater ease by altering the level of disposable income than by trying to change the propensity to consume. The short-term function was found to be unable to explain long-term consumption behaviour and two alternative hypotheses were discussed.

The second section was devoted to investment. The theory that investment is inversely related to the rate of interest was found to be only a partial explanation. The accelerator principle, based on a fixed relationship between net investment and changes in national income, was also found to have limited applications. The role of expectations was emphasised and re-emphasised. The conclusion was that no single explanation of investment behaviour is sufficient in itself. All yield valuable insights but it is extremely difficult to forecast which of the various influences will predominate and the precise way in which they will interact.

In the final section we considered the role of government. We saw that it could eliminate inflationary and deflationary gaps with budget surpluses and deficits respectively, and that government expenditure changes have different budgetary implications from tax changes.

A simple multiplier-accelerator model was used to show why capitalist economies might fluctuate and we saw that both built-in stabilisers and discretionary fiscal policies were necessary to try to counteract the fluctuations. The pursuit of an effective stabilisation policy was seen to be hampered by imperfect information and conflicting objectives, and one such conflict, between unemployment and price stability, was studied in detail with the use of the Phillips curve. Finally, economic growth was seen to be the result of a series of interactions between supply and demand factors that are so complex that neither governments nor economists are presently able to devise effective growth policies.

Questions
1 'The rate of interest has little influence on the decision making of firms'. Discuss. (University of London, A-Level Economics)
2 How does economic theory account for fluctuations in investment demand? (Institute of Chartered Accountants in England and Wales)
3 Discuss the inter-relationships between income, consumption and investment and show how a change in each of them might

affect the other two. (University of London, A-Level Economics)

4 How does the introduction of the acceleration principle alter the determination of equilibrium national income in the simple Keynesian model? (Oxford and Cambridge, A-Level Economics)

5 What determines the level of, and changes in the level of, consumption in an individual and an economy? (Institute of Chartered Secretaries and Administrators)

15

Money and Banking

Introduction

Money can only be defined in terms of what it does, rather than be recognised by its physical characteristics. Anything can act as money if it is generally accepted by people as money. In Britain, and all advanced economies, the greater part of the supply of money consists of deposits in bank accounts, rather than notes and coins. The size of this quantity of bank money is influenced by the *reserves* that the banks hold, and an increase or decrease in reserves will tend to result in a magnified increase or decrease in the total quantity of money.

Banking institutions in this country have evolved over centuries, and the organisation of the banking system plays an important part in determining the extent of the Bank of England's control over the monetary system.

What is money?

So far in this book we have not unreasonably assumed that the reader is thoroughly familiar with the concept of money, and used monetary units without going into any explanation of what is meant by them. However it is important for economists carefully to examine the role of money. Money is basically the communications medium of the economic system, the means by which transactors indicate their wants, and their preparedness to offer supplies of economic goods. Any major imbalance in the monetary system can therefore have a disruptive effect on the workings of the 'real' world of production.

Over the years the role of money has been formalised as providing three distinct functions, the provision of a *medium of exchange*,
of a *unit of account* and of a *store of value*. We shall examine these in
turn.

A medium of exchange
The use of money as a medium of exchange is as fundamental to the
development of economic systems as the invention of the wheel was
for transport. Unless there is some commodity (money) that people
are prepared to accept both for the sale of their own output, and to
purchase that of others, transactions are limited to barter, the direct
exchange of goods for goods. Barter is an extremely clumsy and
inefficient way of doing business. Not only must I find a seller who is
offering the goods that I want, but that particular seller who will
accept whatever it is I can produce in exchange. This is referred to
as a *double coincidence of wants*.

I would be a very hungry writer of economics textbooks if I had to
rely for goods on grocers with an interest in economics and engage
in barter transactions to stock my larder, since this would be an
unusual double coincidence of wants. [This should not be interpreted as any adverse judgement on the usefulness of producing
economics textbooks. The argument applies to any pair of goods.
Which does not necessarily vindicate textbook writers, however!]

Store of value
To act as an efficient medium of exchange, money must also
function as a store of value. Barter requires that goods must be
exchanged for each other at the same time. With money, the act of
purchase can be separated from the act of sale. I can now sell my
textbook, hold the purchasing power in the form of money, and
then buy whatever goods I want, as and when I please, directly
from their sellers. Money then acts as a temporary means of
holding purchasing power.

When the overall price level is stable, or even falling, money can
be more than a temporary store of value. The opportunity cost (see
Chapter 1) of holding money is low, and even negative when prices
drop, so people may decide to hold a proportion of their wealth in
the form of money, the medium of exchange, rather than as other
financial or real assets, such as building society shares, or property.
However, even in periods of quite rapid inflation people continue to
hold money, however briefly, in order to carry out transactions,
because of the great convenience it allows. Once they stop doing so
at all, then what was money can no longer be called by that name,

because it is no longer generally acceptable. At this point a substitute is invariably found.

Although there may be better stores of value available than the medium of exchange, they lack the *liquidity* (i.e. the ability to be used directly to make purchases) which is the definitional characteristic of money. Other assets may appear to be better stores of value, but to a greater or lesser extent they are illiquid and cannot be converted into purchasing power without some cost – either a direct monetary cost, as in the case of a brokerage fee, or a cost in terms of time and trouble involved in selling a real asset. In addition, the less liquid an asset is, the less certainty there is as to the capital value realised by its sale. Because of these two factors (transactions cost and uncertainty of capital value), the less liquid an asset is, the higher the return that it must yield in order to induce people to hold it. Conversely, the more liquid an asset is, the lower its yield – down to zero in the case of money.

Unit of account, standard for deferred payment

Money also acts as a measuring unit to assess the relative values of different commodities. This is distinct from its function as a medium of exchange, because a unit of account could in principle be used merely to assign prices rather than act as a means of payment. For example the guinea is still used as a unit of account in many of London's prestigious auction rooms, yet there is no such thing as a guinea note or coin for actual use in transactions.

Money also performs this measurement function over time, when it becomes a *standard for deferred payment*. If I wish to borrow a given sum now, an interest charge will be added to it so that I know how much I will have to repay in the future. Contracts can also be made now for delivery of goods in the future, and the monetary cost assigned. Once again, inflation erodes the usefulness of money in this role. It helps a person little to know in advance the monetary value of a debt obligation if the future purchasing power of that money is uncertain.

Characteristics of money

So far we have looked at the jobs that money should ideally be able to perform, its functions, without discussing either what money is in practice or the characteristics that have led us to adopt certain commodities as money. In the past all kinds of items have been adopted as money, ranging from cowrie shells to cows, and from cigarettes to coffee. The only characteristic that these items had in common, and the only essential characteristic of money, is that they were widely *accepted* by people in payment for goods and services and for settling other business obligations. In fact, virtually any commodity could be used as money, provided that it was accepted as such by the population.

Having said this, it is still clear that there are a number of desirable practical features that a commodity should possess in order to function efficiently as money. One of the foremost requirements for acceptability is that the item should be *limited* in supply. If its supply can be readily increased, then its price in terms of other goods will decline (its purchasing power will fall), which would be highly inconvenient. The supply of the monetary unit should also be relatively *stable*, since variations would tend to cause upward and downward movements in its purchasing power, again inconvenient, because of the uncertainty it causes. People will waste a lot of time ensuring that they are altering their prices in line with the changing value of money, and they will be reluctant to enter long-term contracts expressed in monetary terms.

From the convenience point of view it is desirable that money should be *portable* and *durable*, and also *homogeneous* – variations in the quality of money units also make life very awkward. Finally money should be *high in value*, in relation to its bulk and weight, yet also *divisible into small units* for minor transactions. It is easy to see from the above list why cows have gone out of fashion as a monetary unit!

Money in practice

In Britain, the most obvious form of money is the currency in circulation, known as *Legal Tender*. We are required by law to accept Bank of England notes in settlement of financial obligations, and also coins, though there is a limit on the amount of coin that must be accepted for a single transaction. However, in fact much the greater part of the supply of money consists of *Bank Money*, money deposited by individuals with commercial banks, and held in accounts which may be drawn on by cheque. Bank accounts qualify as money because cheques are widely accepted as a means of payment, particularly for larger transactions. Because individuals are confident that cheques will be encashed for legal tender if required, they are generally prepared to allow transfers of funds within the banking system, from the account of buyer to the account of seller, to act as a medium of exchange. Bank cards and credit cards have had the effect of extending the acceptability of bank accounts as money, since they are a means by which banks guarantee to traders that their customers' cheques will be honoured.

In addition to bank current accounts and cash, which are clearly money in the sense of being widely accepted media of exchange, there are a number of other assets known as *near money*. These are highly liquid – they are easily convertible into the medium of exchange at low cost and without uncertainty as to capital value, as seen above. Bank deposit accounts, building society deposits and post office savings accounts all come into this category – they can all be turned into cash or current bank deposits at minimal notice and without fear of financial loss. There are arguments in favour of including assets such as these in the total money supply, but we defer consideration of these points until Chapter 16. Concentrating on money as a 'medium of exchange' focuses on what is directly available for transactions – notes and coin, and bank current accounts. However, some building societies have now started to offer limited banking facilities. At present they are on a small scale, but as they expand, then the working definition of the money supply will be enlarged accordingly. Such changes have taken place recently in the United States and Britain, and have made it difficult to interpret the meaning of money supply figures for some time while they occur. (This problem is also examined in the following chapter.)

The modern development of money

Prior to the use of paper money, gold and silver were the most widely used currency, since they generally met the convenience requirements outlined above, and above all were widely accepted because of the natural limitations on their supply. Gradually, because of the difficulties of storage and the risk of robbery, gold owners began to leave their wealth in the custody of trustworthy professional guardians, or 'bankers' who would safeguard it. Early bankers were usually goldsmiths, already experienced in providing secure safekeeping for their own stocks, who would issue a receipt stating the amount deposited and its ownership.

It soon became clear that it was simpler to transfer the goldsmith's receipt for the metal than to go to the bother of each individual removing his stock and handing it over in a transaction, which would end with the recipient redepositing the metal in the vault – possibly the same one. Thus individuals began to use those gold certificates as money, confident that they could always exchange them for gold itself when they so wished. For convenience, goldsmiths' certificates were issued in specific denominations rather than the total sum deposited, and certificates for £1 or £5 worth of gold, still redeemable for gold on demand, were the forerunners of modern bank notes.

The next development was that bankers, as they had now become, realised that as long as they retained the trust of their depositors, they could 'lend' money by issuing notes in excess of the gold in their vaults, receiving an interest payment in the process. As long as they were prudent and made sure that they always kept enough gold to redeem notes on demand, depositors would be happy to hold notes. But if depositors lost confidence, they would all try to return their notes for gold at once in a 'run' on the bank, which would collapse. The bank would have loans outstanding which would eventually be repaid with interest (as long as the banker had lent wisely), but these could not be recalled immediately, and it would fail. However as long as bankers kept a sufficient gold reserve to meet any foreseeable withdrawals, they could expand the money stock (in the form of gold certificates). This led to a rise in total purchasing power which, in the 'Keynesian' terms of the previous chapter, would shift up the aggregate expenditure function and result in a multiplied rise in national income.

The process was carried a stage further when people also began to deposit holdings of bankers notes for safekeeping, and transfer these by cheque. New bank note reserves of 100% of total deposits became unnecessary, and again any excess was lent out to earn interest. The danger in this situation was that although bankers were professionally used to treating potential borrowers' prospects with scepticism, they tended to be as optimistic as would be clients when limiting their own activities. The result was that the supply of money fluctuated, expanding while confidence was high, contracting when bank collapses took place. Clearly this was not conducive to the smooth development of trade (and was tough on depositors, too!).

The result was that bankers became increasingly regulated by the state. The Bank Charter Act of 1844 made the Bank of England – then a private institution, but closely associated with government since it managed state borrowing – the sole note issuer in England and Wales. For nearly a century gold sovereigns and Bank of England notes circulated together, but gradually paper took over, and by the end of the Second World War convertibility of Bank of England notes into gold was ended. The note issue is now entirely *fiat* money – meaning that it derives its status as money from the legal authority of the state. The gold reserves now held by the Bank of England are purely for settling international transactions, and have no relationship to the domestic money supply at all.

The banking system and the creation of money

Since the greater part of the money supply now consists of bank deposits, it is clearly very important to examine in detail the way in which total bank deposits may increase (or decrease) and the factors limiting their expansion. The basic limiting factor is the supply of reserves available to the banking system.

In most countries, commercial banks are required by governments to hold a given percentage of their total liabilities in the form of *liquid assets* – assets that can be readily exchanged for cash. In Britain, at the time of writing, there is no longer a *legal* reserve ratio as such. However, banks still need to hold a cash reserve to meet their customers' varying demand for cash. The banks themselves decide the size of the reserve, on commercial considerations, but cash is nevertheless the reserve base of the system. To understand the principles governing the way that the banking system is able to expand or contract the supply of money, constrained by its holding of reserves, an elementary model is useful.

We start by making two major simplifying assumptions in order to illustrate the basic principles involved. Firstly, banks are required to hold a reserve of 10% *cash* against their total deposit liabilities. Secondly, only bank deposits are used as money, so that when bank loans are spent, all the proceeds are transferred between accounts within the banking system – no currency is held outside the banks.

A single-bank system

Initially we simplify further by taking for an example a closed economy served by only one (monopoly) bank. Given our assumptions above, for every £1000m deposit liabilities, the bank must hold £100m in the form of cash reserves. The remaining £900m will be held in the form of whatever assets the bank finds most profitable – which we shall simply refer to as *loans* at the moment. The actual composition of banks' balance sheets will be examined later in the chapter. Here we are using 10% cash as the reserve ratio for arithmetic simplicity. [The working of the structure in practice is discussed in Chapter 16.] This is shown in Table 15.1.

Thus the bank is in equilibrium in that its assets equal its liabilities and its reserve holdings are minimised.

Table 15.1   Single bank system (£m)

Assets		Liabilities	
Cash	100	Deposits	1000
Loans	900		
Total	1000	Total	1000

Now let us assume that a change in reserves takes place, and examine its effect. If the government engineers a rise of £10m in cash deposits for our banking system, the immediate effect is that the bank will be holding more cash than it needs to. In a single-bank system this can be remedied very simply. In order to expand deposits (and thus create money) the bank simply grants loans to customers so that its total liabilities again become ten times its reserves. In this case, reserves have risen by £10m, so the bank makes loans to customers of £90m, doing so by opening accounts on behalf of the customers, on which they may draw for expenditure (in other words, the granting of a loan automatically creates a deposit). This is shown in Table 15.2.

Table 15.2   Changes in reserves in a single-bank system (£m)

Assets		Liabilities	
Cash	+10	Deposits	+100
Loans	+90		
Total	+100	Total	+100

Because we have assumed no leakage of cash from the system, and because there is only one bank, the newly created money circulates by being transferred between the accounts of the bank customers.

Money creation in a multi-bank system
In a multi-bank system, the end result of a similar increase in reserves is identical with that in the single-bank model. However the way in which that result is achieved differs significantly.

If one bank, say 'A', receives the net £10m cash deposit, it could not simply create loans of nine times the value of the reserve. If it did so, it would find itself short of cash, because once its customers spent money with customers of other banks, deposits would be transferred to the latter. These banks would then ask for cash from bank 'A' both to satisfy their reserve requirements and to enable them to increase their own lending. Bank 'A' having retained only 10% cash backing for its loans would be unable to comply. So Table 15.2, which applies to a single monopoly bank, cannot apply to one bank in a multi-bank system.

However, bank 'A' would obviously not take a £10m cash deposit and hold it entirely idle. It cannot create deposits of ten times the value of its cash reserves, but it can reduce its cash to one-tenth of its loans. It does this by retaining £1m cash and lending out the remaining £9m (cash), which when spent will be transferred to accounts held with a second round of banks in the system (again assuming no cash leakage).

So at this second stage, the £9m cash *on-lent* by bank 'A' will end up with a number of banks, all of which will have additional deposits, fully backed by cash. There is no reason for these banks, either, to back their new deposits with 100% cash. They, too, like bank 'A', will retain 10% of the £9m as reserve, and on-lend the remaining £8.1m to clients. We now enter a third stage. A third group of banks will find themselves receiving a net cash deposit of £8.1m. They will retain £.81m as a reserve against these deposits, and loan out the remaining £7.29m. At each stage one-tenth of the fresh deposit is held as reserve, nine-tenths are lent, and appear as fresh cash deposits. The process will be continued in a fourth stage, a fifth, and so on until the total value of deposits created reaches the limit permitted by the reserve ratio. Table 15.3 summarises the process.

Table 15.3   Creation of money in a multi-bank system

STAGE ONE   (a) Bank A receives net cash deposit £10m.

Assets		*Liabilities*	
Cash	+10	Deposits	+10

(b) To maximise profit and eliminate excess reserves, it retains 10% only for reserves, lends out the remainder.

Assets		*Liabilities*	
Cash	+1	Deposits	+10
Loans	+9		

STAGE TWO   (a) A second round of banks receive cash proceeds of loans spent by borrowers from bank 'A'.

Assets		*Liabilities*	
Cash	+9	Deposits	+9

(b) They also reduce reserves to a minimum by lending on any excess cash.

Assets		*Liabilities*	
Cash	+0.9	Deposits	+9
Loans	+8.1		

STAGE THREE   (a) Third-round banks receive cash proceeds of loans made by second round.

Assets	*Liabilities*
Cash +8.1	Deposits +8.1

(b) They reduce reserves to a minimum and lend on remaining cash.

Assets	*Liabilities*
Cash +0.81	Deposits +8.1
Loans +7.29	

STAGE FOUR   Fourth-round banks receive deposits, reduce reserves to a minimum, and lend on remainder.

STAGE FIVE   Fifth-round banks do as above and so on.

FINAL STAGE   *Final sum of total of all stages*

Assets	*Liabilities*
Cash +10	Deposits +100
Loans +90	

Thus Table 15.3 shows that in a multi-bank system no one bank can automatically create new deposits from new reserves in the way that a monopoly bank can. Nevertheless, as long as any new loans made by each bank are redeposited with the banking system as a whole, the end result will be the same as for a monopoly bank. Ultimately new reserves will generate new deposits by a multiple given by the reserve ratio. In this case with a reserve ratio of 10%, for every £1 of new reserves, deposits will increase by £10, a factor of 10. If the reserve ratio is 12½% (one-eighth), every £1 of new reserves ultimately generates deposits worth £8.

Qualifications to the basic model
The model on which we have based our analysis of bank deposits creation is a highly simplified one, and a number of qualifications are necessary.

1 *Banks' reserves.* We are assuming that bank reserves consist of cash, which is a reasonable approximation to the current UK system. However, we are also assuming that the central bank acts to control the amount of cash in circulation. In Britain, the Bank of England generally chooses to control the *price* at which it will supply cash to banks – that is, the *interest rate*. It does not attempt to control the quantity of cash in the system directly. This point is examined in the next chapter.

2 *Public's cash holdings.* Our model assumed that *all* loans made by banks are redeposited in the banks – i.e. that all transactions are made by transferring bank deposits from one account to another

within the banking system. This is obviously unrealistic, since a portion of the average loan will be held as cash, outside the banks. However as long as this demand for cash is a reasonably constant proportion of the total bank deposits (which it is, in practice), it can be incorporated into our model quite simply by regarding it as an additional reserve requirement for banks.

For example, if banks know that in addition to having to hold their 10% legal reserves, they will also have to hold a further 10% of any loan they make available to satisfy the demand for cash. The effective reserve requirement for a bank becomes 20%, or one-fifth, and new reserves will now support deposits equal to five times their value, rather than ten times as before.

3 *Profit maximisation.* We have implicitly assumed in our model that banks will attempt to maximise profits. They do so by expanding their (profitable) loans as far as they are permitted by their reserve requirements (and the public's propensity to hold cash). In practice banks tend to hold reserves in excess of the legal minimum requirement. However holding an additional 1–2% of reserves is simply a safety margin for banks, since it might be very costly for them to have to respond instantly to minor changes in reserves. So although banks do tend to hold some excess reserves, this is usually a constant small percentage of total deposits which can be incorporated in our model very easily.

4 *Adequate demand for loans.* A very important qualification to our simple model is that it may not always be possible for banks to expand their lending up to the reserve limit, as we assumed above. There may be times when business confidence is low, or fears of unemployment exist, which could lead to people being unwilling to borrow all that banks are prepared to lend. If the banks are able to collude to prevent competition between themselves, they may find it more profitable to keep interest rates up and hold excess reserves, than to allow them to fall sufficiently to expand loans to the maximum feasible limit. Alternatively, banks could simply be unable to find enough borrowers they consider to be creditworthy, and again hold excess reserves instead of making doubtful loans.

The significance of the above qualifications is that they show that the money multiplier process should not be regarded as a purely mechanical one, because in some circumstances a given change in reserves will not be automatically followed by a multiple expansion in deposits. This is particularly true when activity and expectations are depressed and loan demand is low.

The UK monetary system

Before we turn to an examination of the ways in which the supply of money can be controlled, and the effects of such control on the economy, it is essential to sketch in details of the principal institutions involved in the process, and to describe the characteristics of the various types of financial assets in which they trade.

The Bank of England

Overall control of the monetary system is exercised by the *Central Bank*, which in the UK is the Bank of England. The primary responsibilities of a central bank are as follows:

1 Control of the money supply
2 Management of the National Debt
3 'Lender of last resort' and guarantor of stability to the banking system
4 Banker to the banking system, and to government.

The Bank of England is divided into two departments; the *Issue Department* is broadly responsible for the first two functions, the *Banking Department* for the latter two.

Control of the money supply. This has two aspects; the first is the regulation of currency issue (the actual notes and coin used for smaller transactions), and the second, and more important from the economist's viewpoint, is the control of the total money stock, including the level of commercial bank deposits.

New currency to replace that worn out, and to meet additional demands, is produced by the Royal Mint and supplied to the commercial banks on demand. The banks pay for any additional notes they require by means of the accounts that they hold with the Bank of England. Thus any net increase in the currency issue yields a profit to the Bank of England, equal to the face value of the currency issued less the costs of producing it, known technically as 'seignorage'.

The actual printing of money normally only alters the composition of the money stock [the exception is in times of hyperinflation, when governments may literally print currency in order to pay their bills], shifting the balance between currency and bank deposits. As we have seen the major factors determining the size of the *total* money stock are the reserves available to the banking system, and the reserve requirement. The way in which the Bank of England can influence these, and other instruments of control over the monetary system, are discussed in detail in the next chapter.

Management of the National Debt. The National Debt is the accumulated net borrowing that the government has undertaken in the past in order to finance expenditure greater than its receipts from tax revenues, duties and other forms of income. The National Debt has been rising since its inception in 1694, occasional reductions in the total being more than offset by increases, with periods of rapid acceleration taking place during wars, as governments borrowed heavily to finance military expenditures.

Governments in general are able to keep borrowing from their subjects because they are an excellent credit risk. This stems from the fact that they have the legal power to levy taxes to finance interest payments on their debts, which means that there is very little likelihood of default on their borrowings. As long as interest continues to be paid on loans, people will be content to allow debt to accumulate, though inflation poses difficulties, as we shall see below.

Government borrowing can be divided into two categories, short term and long term, the former being achieved by issuing bills, notably Treasury Bills, the latter by bonds, also known as *gilt-edged*.

A Treasury Bill is simply a certificate stating that the government will pay the holder, after a period of ninety-one days, a fixed sum of money, for example £100. The government makes a weekly sale of bills to meet short-term cash needs (a gap between tax receipts and expenditure for example). Lenders to the government pay a price below the face value of the bill (i.e. the bill is sold at a 'discount') which determines the interest rate obtained. So, for example, if a (three month) £100 bill is sold for £97, this would represent a 3% interest rate for three months, an annual interest rate of 12%. Because the cash value of a Treasury Bill in the near future is certain (it will be redeemed at face value in not more than three months) it represents a very liquid asset, and a highly developed market exists for the resale of bills, which form an important component of commercial banks reserves.

Longer term borrowing is achieved by the sale of securities known as *government stocks* sometimes referred to as *gilt-edged*. The government issues a certificate known as a bond, which states its *par value* or monetary value when redeemed, the *coupon* or interest rate that will be paid annually (again expressed in monetary terms) and the date at which it can be redeemed at 'par' or face value. So, for example, 'Treasury 5% 1996' means a certificate issued by the Treasury which gives an interest of 5% of the 'par' value, and is redeemable in 1996. A person who bought such a bond with a par value £100 on issue, would receive £5 per year interest every year until 1996. However, there is also an active re-sale market in stocks and the current 'market' re-sale price need not be the par value. If an existing bond has a coupon of 5% and the Treasury is currently issuing new bonds with a similar par value of £100, but with a coupon of 10% and a similar maturity date, the market price of the old bond will fall to about half its nominal par value. [Its price will of course rise as it approaches maturity, because it will then be redeemed at par value.] Thus existing bond prices respond inversely to changes in interest rates being offered on new bonds – as current interest rates rise, existing bond prices fall, and vice versa. Because the trend of interest rates since the Second World War has been upwards, bond prices have tended to fall – though because interest rates may fall in the short term, speculative profits may still be made on the resulting market price rises. If you had bought a long-dated bond in January 1977, for example, as interest rates fell, by September you could have sold it at a profit of over 25%.

Quite apart from any additional borrowing, the size of the outstanding debt, a portion of which is maturing at any given time, means that the task of debt management is a complex one. The central bank has to ensure that the interest rate of new issues is sufficiently attractive to ensure buyers, but if this means higher rates, existing bonds fall in market capital value, which may inhibit future sales. In a time of inflation the real value of both bond 'coupons' and 'par' values for redemption, being fixed in money terms, tends to be severely eroded. A striking illustration of this is the way the ratio of National Debt to GNP has declined recently. In 1965, National Debt was 75% of GNP, whereas by 1989 the figure had fallen to 35%, mainly due to the fact that existing debt issued is fixed in money terms, whereas GNP in money terms has risen sharply due to inflation.

Individuals are naturally reluctant to purchase long-dated securities with fixed money yields in a time of inflation. One solution in Britain has been the sale of index-linked bonds, but even so, debt management is a difficult task, making monetary control in the short term hard to achieve.

Lender of last resort The central bank in all countries has to act to guarantee the financial stability of the banking system. As we saw from our discussion of the historical development of banking, commercial banks operate on a *fractional reserve* basis. That is, they hold reserves of currency sufficient to meet the largest expected withdrawals that customers will make. Should they for any reason be called upon to provide more than the reserves they hold (for example, by an old-fashioned 'run on the bank'), it is the central bank that must provide currency to prevent the insolvency of financial institutions and a breakdown of confidence in the economy. It does this by lending to the banking system, either directly, as in most countries, or in the case of the UK, via the Discount Market, which we examine in a moment.

To avert a collapse, the Bank of England in the 1970s organised an operation to support certain 'secondary' banks (defined on page 299) which were suffering large-scale deposit withdrawals because of their involvement in losses on property dealing. These losses led to a collapse of confidence, and the risk of a run on these banks. The Bank of England found itself forced to intervene. It set up a support scheme (which came to be known as the 'Lifeboat' operation) to assist those banks which were in fact judged to be fundamentally sound (i.e. their total assets exceeded liabilities, though some assets were illiquid). In situations such as this, the Bank of England is forced to act in its role of 'lender of last resort'. This obligation may conflict at times with its task of controlling the money supply.

Banker to the banking system, and to government Finally, the Bank of England acts like a commercial bank to government, managing their revenues and expenditure, and arranging to cover any short-fall by borrowing. It also acts as 'banker' to the commercial banks, which maintain balances with government in order to make payments on their clients' behalf, and to make payments between themselves.

The Discount Market

Between the Bank of England and the commercial banks, there are, in Britain alone, a group of institutions known collectively as *the London Money Market* or *the Discount Market*. This consists mainly of the Discount Houses, but also includes some Discount Brokers, and the money trading departments of the large commercial banks. The Discount Market acts as an intermediary between the Bank of England and the commercial banks. It operates by borrowing money from the commercial banks at very short notice – in fact much of its borrowings are repayable 'at call' – literally when asked for, and without notice. This borrowed 'call money' is then used to purchase part of the Bank of England's weekly sale of Treasury Bills. It is a feature of the system that the Discount Market agrees to bid a price at which they will accept whatever the Treasury wishes to offer – though they are of course free to set that price themselves. In other words the government is assured that the entire bill issue will be taken up. In return for this, the Discount Market is granted sole access to the Bank's facilities as 'lender of last resort', so that any institution wishing to obtain cash from the Bank must do so via the Discount Market. The activities of the Discount Market are illustrated in Fig. 15.1.

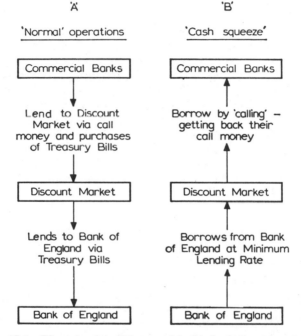

Fig. 15.1   The role of the Discount Market in the banking system

The left-hand side of the figure, under column 'A', shows the normal working relationships between the Bank of England, the Discount Market and the commercial banks. The commercial banks make short-term loans to the Bank of England. However, instead of doing so by the direct purchase of Treasury Bills, as in the case of most economies, commercial banks in Britain lend initially to the Discount Market. They do so by lending *call money* – loans that are literally repayable when 'called', or requested back. The Discount Market then passes on these funds to the Bank of England by purchasing Treasury Bills at a discount. The Discount Market makes an operating profit because the rate of interest it pays for call loans is slightly lower than the rate it receives from the government for the purchase of Treasury Bills.

In addition to providing call money, the Discount Market also acts as a middleman in the sale of Treasury Bills: it resells some of its bill purchases to the banks, again making a small profit on the transaction by borrowing at a slightly lower rate than at which it is lending. In the case of Treasury Bills discounted, this means that the Discount Market pays a slightly lower price for the bill to the government than it receives from the banks.

The case of a cash shortage or 'squeeze' is shown in column 'B' of Fig. 15.1. If the commercial banks require cash, they 'call' their loans to the Discount Market. The Discount Market in turn obtains cash from the Bank of England. In the past, it could do so by borrowing directly from the Bank at Minimum Lending Rate (MLR) – also described earlier as 'bank rate'. Under recently revised arrangements, the Discount Market now normally obtains cash by re-selling either Treasury Bills or equivalent commercial bills to the Bank of England.

In itself this is not a vital change. The important thing is that the Bank of England does provide the Discount Market with cash in order to repay call money to the commercial banks. It makes very little practical difference whether the cash is loaned directly (at MLR) or indirectly (by buying bills from the money market at a discount, which means making a charge for the loan – effectively the same as charging interest directly). What is important is that the Bank of England, as before, can choose the interest rate at which it will relieve immediate shortages of cash. The Bank of England therefore retains very considerable control over the level of short-term interest rates under the new system.

As the Treasury Bill rate rises, this raises with it all other short-term interest rates (since other borrowers must compete with the Treasury rate.) Thus the Discount Market is the intermediary in the process of both the marketing of Treasury Bills, and the provision of last resort lending facilities to the commercial banks.

Commercial banks

Banks, like many other financial institutions, operate by 'mediating' between lenders and borrowers. We saw above how banking originally came about, and the operating principles have not fundamentally changed. Banks attract deposits, either by paying interest on them, or by offering security and convenient payment facilities, and then lend the proceeds out to borrowers on payment of interest. A given reserve is held back to ensure that any feasible deposit withdrawals can be met on demand.

In Britain commercial banks can be divided into two broad groups, the *clearing banks*, or *clearers*, members of the bankers clearing house through which all transactions between customers' accounts are processed, and the *secondary banks*. 'Clearers' are 'retail' bankers, dealing directly with the public to provide day-to-day transaction facilities, and include the banking 'big-four', Barclays, Lloyds, Midland and National Westminster, and now also the Trustee Savings Bank.

Building societies are now legally permitted to compete in the provision of many retail banking services. *Secondary* banks are 'wholesale' bankers, who bid for large deposits, either from the retail banks, or from companies, and lend them again to commercial borrowers. In many cases they provide a range of services, such as advice on takeover bids and financial management generally. Increased competition in domestic banking means that the dividing line between 'clearing' and 'secondary' banks has become blurred, with banks tending to deal in both 'retail' and 'wholesale' markets.

All banks are regulated by the Bank of England. Regulation is now mainly in the form of scrutiny and monitoring of the banks' capital structure and the nature of their balance sheets. There is no longer a legal 'reserve ratio', as was the case in the past. All banks are required to maintain an account with the Bank of England with a balance equal to half of one per cent of their total deposit liabilities. However, this 'cash ratio' is intended only to provide the Bank of England with a working balance for its own operations in the bill markets, described above. Banks are also required to hold 6% of their total deposit liabilities in the form of call money with the Discount Market and associated money market institutions. Again this is not a reserve base, since the Bank of England is not attempting to restrict the amount of call money available. It is intended only to guarantee that there is enough call money to ensure that the Discount Market's dealings in bills are large enough to enable the Bank of England to operate on short-term interest rates effectively.

A simplified clearing bank balance sheet would be as follows:

Liabilities	*Assets*
'Sight' deposits	1 Cash (consisting of till money, and ½% of liabilities deposited with the Bank of England).
'Time' deposits	2 Call money with discount market (6% of liabilities).
	3 'Investments'.
	4 Advances.

On the liabilities side, 'sight' deposits can be withdrawn without notice. These are mainly current (chequeing) accounts, but some interest-bearing deposits also come into this category. 'Time' deposits are interest-bearing deposits, for which some notice of withdrawal is required in principle by the bank, although this requirement is not always enforced.

On the assets side, *cash* includes the 'till money' that bankers require for working balances to meet fluctuations in the demand for cash by the public, as well as the ½% deposit required by the Bank of England. Since cash earns no interest, banks attempt to minimise their holdings of it. *Call money* holdings are explained above. *Investments* is the name given to holdings of government stocks, which being longer term than reserves, normally yield a higher return. Finally, *advances* are the bank's loans, the most profitable part of its portfolio of assets. Commercial banks are the instruments of money creation outlined in our model on page 290 and this money creation can be seen operating on the asset side of their balance sheets. If banks as a whole are able to increase their holdings of 'cash' reserves, then after making an allowance for 'till money' the system as a whole can expand advances to customers. Part of the proceeds of these loans will be held as cash by the public, outside the banks, but a part will be redeposited with the banking system, and will be available for re-lending, so that the effect of an initial increase in reserves will be to permit a multiple increase in deposits, just as in our simple model.

Non-bank financial intermediaries

We have already referred to banks as a form of 'financial intermediary', borrowing by taking deposits, lending by advances. There are many other institutions that operate in a similar way, ranging from building societies to pension funds and insurance companies. They all take deposits from the public, in return issuing interest-bearing liabilities, and re-lend the proceeds to ultimate borrowers. The crucial distinction between banks and 'non-bank' intermediaries is that the former issue liabilities (bank deposits) which are directly spendable – i.e. they are money – whereas the latter do not. This means that non-bank intermediaries cannot 'create deposits' as banks can, because their advances are not redeposited with themselves. In addition, changes in non-bank intermediaries' liabilities do not directly affect the level of purchasing power, only the pattern of expenditure. For example, if building society deposits rise, purchasing power does not alter; though it is switched from day-to-day consumer expenditure to the housing market, the total is unchanged. If total bank deposits rise, however, purchasing power immediately rises, and in addition the banking system will be able to generate loans which will be redeposited, leading to a further multiple expansion of purchasing power. As building societies increasingly offer banking facilities, including cheque accounts, this distinction becomes blurred, and they become more like banks in their ability to 'create' deposits.

Although non-bank intermediaries have no direct effect on purchasing power, by providing a range of liquid assets alternative to money, they may cause people to reduce their money holdings somewhat. This may have the effect of permitting a given stock of money to finance a greater number of transactions, a possibility examined in the next chapter.

Summary

In this chapter we have examined the three major functions of money, acting as a medium of exchange, a store of value, and a unit of account. Money is whatever is generally acceptable in order to perform these functions, and has taken the form of a variety of commodities in the past, though precious metals have tended to be favoured because of a number of convenient physical character-istics, above all the fact that they are limited in supply. With the development of banks, paper currency has come to succeed precious metals as the medium of exchange, initially in the form of gold receipts, and subsequently as central bank notes, backed by the authority of government. Nowadays bank deposits are generally accepted as money, and form the greater part of the money supply.

The fractional reserve system of banking operated in developed countries means that banks can expand their deposits by a multiple of reserves, subject to certain qualifications, notably that adequate demand for loans exists.

The banking system consists of a number of institutions, with the Bank of England playing a crucial role in regulating the supply of money and influencing interest rates, as well as overseeing the operations of commercial banks. The Bank of England also man-ages the National Debt, which entails the sale of longer-dated fixed interest bonds, and short-term Treasury Bills. The latter are purch-ased by the Discount Market, using 'call money' borrowed from the commercial banks. The Bank of England can influence short-term interest rates by varying the price at which it will provide cash through its purchases of bills via the Discount Market.

Commercial banks fall into two groups, 'clearing' and 'secondary' banks. In common with other commercial institutions, they operate by acting as financial intermediaries, borrowing money in order to re-lend it, which they are able to do profitably because of their specialised knowledge of financial markets. Banks are distinguished from other intermediaries by the fact that their liabilities (bank deposits) can be spent directly as money, which makes them the focus of monetary policy, as we see in the following chapter.

Questions

1　(*a*)　Why is there no single definition of the money supply?

　　(*b*)　Describe the way in which a bank can create money. Illustrate your answer with a numerical example.

　　(The Institute of Chartered Accountants in England and Wales, Foundation Examination)

2　(*a*)　The following figures relate to a simplified account of the balance sheet of a commercial bank:

	Liabilities £m		*Assets £m*
Total Deposits	500	Reserve Assets	80
		Other Assets (Including Advances)	420
	500		500

　　　　(*i*)　What are Reserve Assets?

　　　　(*ii*)　What is the Reserve Assets ratio of this bank?

　　　　(*iii*)　What is the purpose of a minimum Reserve Assets ratio?

　　(*b*)　Explain why a Central Bank sometimes has to control bank lending. (The Royal Society of Arts Examinations Board, Economics, Stage II (Intermediate))

3　Explain how banks are able to create credit, and discuss the factors which currently limit their ability to do so. (The Society of Company and Commercial Accountants, Part I, Economics)

4　'Commercial banks cannot simply create money by the liberal use of fountain pens (or computers); they can only make advances or buy assets with cash they have received from depositors and thus cannot "create" anything'. Discuss. (Welsh Joint Education Committee, GCE, A-Level Economics)

5　Some of the functions of money are performed by other liquid assets. What are these assets? Why are they often held in preference to bank notes and bank deposits in the performance of these functions? (The Institute of Bankers, Economics, Stage 2)

16

The Control of the Monetary System

Introduction

This chapter deals with the way monetary policy affects the economy, and the techniques available to governments to implement monetary policy. We start by examining the quantity theory of money, which describes the relationship between the money stock and the level of GNP, from which 'monetarist' economists infer that control of the money supply will directly influence GNP as measured in money – by changing the level of prices, or output, or both. We then examine carefully the reasoning behind the monetarist argument in the context of the controversy between 'Monetarists' and 'Keynesians', outlining the major points of dispute and assessing the validity of the respective arguments. We conclude that monetary policy does have an independent influence on the economy, and that control should be exercised over the rate of change of the money supply. We then examine in detail the techniques available to monetary authorities to exercise such control, and the practical problems involved in implementing monetary policy.

The quantity theory of money

The quantity theory of money, as its name implies, is concerned with the way changes in the quantity of money (the money supply) affect price levels and output in the economy. One of its originators was the Scotsman David Hume, who observed the effect of the gold (money), brought to Europe by the Spanish Conquistadors, in generating inflation in Europe in the seventeenth century. The theory was elaborated at the beginning of the twentieth century by the American economist, Irving Fisher, and the term *quantity theory* is applied to his formulation of the equation

$$MV = PT$$

M refers to the money stock, defined as whatever is generally used as the medium of exchange. V is the velocity of circulation, meaning the rate at which money changes hands. A monetary unit, say £1, will change hands several times in a given period, so that it finances spending worth several times its own value as it passes from hand to hand. Thus for example an economy which has £1m of money in existence, which changes hands on average three times per year (V = 3), will have total spending equal to £3m. P is the price level, represented in practice by a price index, which assigns 'weights' to different commodity prices according to their relative importance in overall spending, as explained in Chapter 12. T is the number of transactions that take place in a given period. In Fisher's version this refers to every transaction, including second-hand sales and sales of intermediate goods from one firm to another. In practice, information on such a wide range of transactions is not available, so it is now approximated by substituting Y, national output, for T, so that the equation becomes MV = PY. As we saw in Chapter 12, Y measures only net output. However, in practice the relationship between T and Y is unlikely to change significantly in the short term, so Y is an acceptable substitute.

The quantity theory states that the money stock, multiplied by its velocity of circulation, M × V, must equal the price level, multiplied by national output, P × Y. In fact this must always be true, since the left-hand side corresponds to total money expenditure in a given period, while the right is total money receipts. Expenditure must equal receipts, by definition, so strictly speaking, the quantity theory is an identity rather than an equation.

The Monetarist–Keynesian controversy

The relevance of the quantity theory for monetary policy has aroused considerable controversy in recent years. Keynes' General Theory was interpreted as diminishing the importance of monetary policy, particularly with respect to the money supply, and this view influenced policy-makers in Britain up to the early 1970s. Since then, however, there has been a widespread revival of interest in the version of the quantity theory advanced by 'monetarist' economists, led by Professor Milton Friedman of the University of Chicago. The main points of dispute between 'Keynesian' and 'monetarist' economists can be listed as follows.

1 The question of how much the velocity of circulation (demand for money) fluctuates.
2 Whether changes in the money stock *cause* changes in PY (money national income) or whether they *result from* changes in PY.
3 Whether attempts to control a defined stock of 'money' will result in the uncontrolled development of money substitutes.

1 Changes in the velocity of circulation

If the velocity of circulation, V, is not stable, then a rise in money stock, M, could be offset by a fall in V, leaving national income, PY, unchanged. The velocity of circulation depends on how much money people 'hold', and for how long. If average money holdings increase, the velocity of circulation drops – money is changing hands more slowly – it is being 'held' rather than 'spent'. We refer to people's desire to hold money as the *demand for money*. It is also sometimes referred to as *liquidity preference*. So if the demand for money drops, people decide to hold less of it, so spending, and the velocity of circulation, rise. The demand for money is influenced by a number of factors, but we are only concerned with those that affect the economy as a whole, and with those that may vary significantly in a short time.

Both monetarist and Keynesian economists accept that the principal influence on the amount of money people wish to 'hold' (i.e. the demand for money) is what Keynes referred to as the *transactions demand*. As its name implies, this consists of the amount of money people wish to hold in order to undertake their day-to-day transactions. This depends primarily on the volume of goods they buy, and on the price level, so in aggregate it will be determined by the level of national income measured in current prices. The transactions demand may alter as a result of a number of factors, such as the increased use of bank accounts, credit cards, and payment by cheque rather than in cash, but such developments are likely to be gradual, and the principal short-term determinant is the level of national income.

So far, monetarists and Keynesians would not disagree. The area of dispute concerns the nature of the response to changes in the interest rate. Keynes argued that changes in expectations in the economy could result in the demand for money becoming unstable. If an investor believes that the price of government bonds, or the price of shares, is about to fall, he will tend to sell these assets and hold money instead. The demand for money increases in an unpredictable way due to speculative factors. Keynes referred to

this as the *speculative demand* for money. Changes in interest rates
will affect this speculative demand for money because interest rates
are inversely related to the market price of government bonds (see
page 294).

Monetarists on the other hand, view this speculation as unimportant in the overall demand for money. They agree that interest rates
affect the demand for money, but argue that this takes place in a
stable and predictable way. If interest rates rise, this increases the
opportunity cost of holding money. Investors will tend to buy more
interest-bearing assets, and hold less (non-interest bearing)
money. Lower interest rates make holding money less costly.

In the monetarist view, the quantity theory equation is useful,
because changes in velocity of circulation (resulting from changes
in the demand for money) are predictably related to changes in
interest rates. Keynesians argue that, on the contrary, changes in
interest rates can cause changes in speculative expectations which
bring about large and unstable changes in velocity of circulation. If
this is so, then control of the supply of money may not increase the
stability of the price level, and the economy in general.

Ultimately, the question of the stability or otherwise of velocity
can only be resolved by empirical studies. What these show for
Britain is that although changes in velocity could be reasonably well
predicted prior to the 1970s, since then the demand for money has
fluctuated unexpectedly. However, it has been argued that this is
because of the somewhat erratic shifts in the institutional regulation of the banking system that have occurred in recent years. Some
economists argue that if allowance is made for these changes, the
demand for money can still be regarded as stable and predictable,
as the monetarist view contends.

Whether this is the case or not, there is no question of the
demand for money fluctuating so far as to offset completely the sort
of changes in money supply that may have occurred in recent years.
Changes in velocity certainly do occur, but not on a scale that
renders the effects of a large monetary change completely unpredictable.

2   The question of monetary cause and effect

The fact that the money supply and the level of money income tend
to move together does not necessarily mean, however, that an
inflationary rise in national income is *caused* by a rise in the money
supply. It could be due to a completely separate factor – militant
trade unions might be forcing up wage rates, leading firms to raise

prices, and the money supply may be responding directly to this – the cause of which has nothing to do with the money supply itself.

Again, it has been argued that changes in the money supply reflect a response to changes in 'real' economic activity, which are the *cause* of the monetary change, rather than the *effect* of them. Firms deciding to invest more will seek loans from the banking system, which will cause the money supply to expand. If firms cut down on their expenditure, the demand for loans will drop, and this may result in a contraction of the money supply. Remember the qualification added to our discussion of the ways banks in a reserve banking system create money – there must be adequate loan demand to ensure that bank reserves are fully employed and that lending is maximised. It is conceivable that if loan demand drops sharply as a result of some 'external' factor, then this will cause the money supply to drop.

Nobody has yet been able to prove conclusively that causation runs either from money to national income, or from national income to money. However, there is a good deal of circumstantial evidence, particularly for the United States, where monetary policy has been pursued actively for some time, that when control is exercised over the money stock, national income does respond to control, after a delay. Some evidence on whether causation does run from money to income can be found by examining a period when the rate of change of the money stock has been deliberately altered as a result of a policy decision (either upwards or downwards), and by then determining whether the association between money and GNP still holds. If it does, then GNP must have altered in response to the change in the money stock, unless by some coincidence an external factor happens to have intervened to alter GNP in the same direction as the money stock. There are enough examples of GNP change following deliberate policy-induced monetary changes in the United States to make it very unlikely indeed that they are purely coincidental.

In Britain, active government control of the money supply has only been adopted in recent years, so there is little reliable historical evidence of cause and effect. However, recent policy leaves little doubt that monetary changes do lead to rather than result from changes in economic activity in the short term (which can be interpreted as at least two years).

On balance, although 'reverse causation' from GNP changes to monetary changes may exist in principle, and occur in practice on occasions, there is strong evidence that a policy of controlling the money supply will directly affect GNP. In particular, where monetary growth is restricted, inflation is most unlikely to be sustained (though the process of stopping it may result in substantial unemployment). Where monetary growth is accelerated, there is likely to be a rise in either real output or prices, although it is possible that where business confidence is particularly weak, raising the money supply may have little effect in raising expenditure and hence GNP.

3 Operational definitions of money

A number of alternative statistical definitions of 'money' exist. These range from M_0, the narrowest UK definition, to PSL_2, which is a very broad definition. M_0, Sterling M_3 and PSL_2 are most widely used. M_0 consists of notes and coin in public circulation, plus the banks' working balances with the Bank of England. This in effect represents the 'cash base' of the banking system. Sterling M_3 consists of notes and coins plus all sterling bank deposits held by UK private sector residents, and is a wide definition of 'bank money'. PSL_2 basically adds to $£M_3$ most building society deposits, plus National Savings Bank deposits. This definition aims to provide an indication of the overall level of liquidity of the economy.

The problem posed by a range of definitions of money is that it is not clear which is the appropriate 'target' for monetary policy. Different monetary measures grow at different rates. Broad definitions such as PSL_2 usually grow more rapidly than a narrow definition such as M_0. In the context of the quantity theory of money, MV = PY, it is essential to determine whether M is represented by M_0 or by $£M_3$ or even PSL_2.

In Britain, official monetary targets used to be expressed in terms of $£M_3$ but more recently the emphasis has been on M_0. The general practice has been to establish a range of growth rates within which monetary expansion will be contained. Targets are normally set for a twelve-month period. However, these targets have more often been missed than achieved, despite the degree of flexibility built into them. When the target has been overshot, the tendency has been to base the following year's target on the money supply figure actually achieved, rather than the upper limit of the figure that has been aimed for. This practice is known as *base drift*. It results in cumulative monetary growth over a number of years being substantially greater than would be implied by the original target percentages.

The relative lack of success in setting realistic monetary targets has led some economists, and on occasion the Bank of England, to argue that M_0 is a better target than $£M_3$. Monetarists argue that the appropriate objective should be to ensure that the supply of money rises sufficiently to finance the 'real' potential growth rate of the economy. This would imply that the 'money' to be used in the target should, on theoretical grounds, be whatever definition most closely accords to the 'medium of exchange'. In practice, monetarists such as Milton Friedman have generally adopted an 'empirical' definition of money. They advocate controlling whichever of the alternative monetary aggregates most closely correlates in the long run with national income. The trouble with this is that in the short run (which may last a number of years), such correlation may break down, especially if the techniques of monetary control distort the relationship.

4 Techniques of monetary policy

(*a*) *Open-market operations*. We have already seen that a sizeable national debt exists in Britain and this is true in virtually all countries, though generally on a smaller scale. In countries where a large and efficient market exists for the re-sale of this debt, an investor who purchases a bond with a distant maturity date can sell it in advance of redemption to anyone who wants to take it over. By operating in this market (hence *open-market operations*), the central bank can influence the quantity of money in circulation. If the aim is to reduce or limit the supply of money, the central bank makes additional sales of government securities (without spending the proceeds). That is to say, it borrows more from the public. The money lent to the central bank is thus removed from circulation, and the public hold securities rather than money. Moreover, the initial impact is multiplied by the effect of the change on the banks' reserves. When the public make loans to the government they do so, for the most part, by transferring funds from their private bank accounts to the government; in effect they write out cheques to the central bank. This means that the commercial banks, instead of transferring funds between their customers' accounts, as in the case of a normal transaction, now have to make a payment to the government which results in a net reduction in the money supply. And this payment will only be accepted by government in the form of cash, since the government will not be willing to leave its funds in the form of commercial bank deposits – it will transfer them to its own account with the central bank.

The upshot is that the increased government borrowing results in a reduction in private bank deposits, which in turn leads directly to a reduction in the commercial banking system's cash reserves. Given the assumptions of the analysis of Chapter 15, a reduction in cash reserves will lead to a multiple reduction in bank lending, and hence bank deposits. So the final consequence of the increased government open-market borrowing is a multiplied reduction in the level of bank deposits, and thus the supply of money.

The process operates in reverse for an increase in the supply of money. The central bank can make net repayments of existing debt by buying back its own debt from existing holders of it (again in the 'open market' for government securities). These net payments direct from the central bank increase the cash reserves of the commercial banks and permit them to expand their lending via the multiplier process shown in Chapter 15.

So by sale or redemption of its own debt, the central bank has a powerful means of influencing the size of the money supply. However, open-market operations are likely to affect interest rates. If the supply of money is to be reduced, more government securities must be sold. In order to make such sales, it is probable that the interest rate on new securities will have to be raised, to make the public increase their purchases of bonds, and hence reduce investments or expenditure elsewhere. If the interest rate paid on new bonds is raised, then the price of existing bonds will fall until its yield is in line with new offers (see pages 294–5 for a review of this process). Conversely, the government purchase of its own securities to expand the money supply will tend to bid up bond prices with the result that interest rates fall.

To summarise, then, the use of open-market operations in order to raise demand in the economy requires the government to purchase its own debt, leading to a multiple increase in bank deposits, and a fall in interest rates. The rise in the money supply would tend to increase all expenditure via the quantity effect, while the 'interest' effect would tend to raise investment expenditure in particular. The reverse is true for open-market issue of securities; the money supply is reduced and the interest rate rises, so that both overall expenditure and investment expenditure in particular will be reduced, and demand is thus 'dampened' or reduced.

(b)   Control of interest rates

As an alternative to controlling the supply of money, monetary policy may focus on controlling the level of interest rates. If this is done, the authorities are choosing as their 'target' the price of money, rather than the quantity supplied. As we have just noted, open-market operations affect both the reserves of the banking system, and the level of interest rates simultaneously. Higher interest rates are achieved by selling more debt, which also reduces the banks' reserves, and thus the money supply. It could fairly be argued then, as it is by the Bank of England, that it makes absolutely no difference whether the authorities choose set targets for interest rates, or directly for the reserves of the banking system. The end result will be the same.

However, it must be strongly emphasised that the above paragraph would be a misleading description of the way interest rate and monetary base controls operate in Britain. The crucial difference centres upon the authorities' attitude towards the banks' reserve ratios. These are *not* used as the basis for control in the UK system. On the contrary, if banks became short of reserves, in the British system they are always supplied, by the Bank of England, with the reserves that they demand – as long as they are willing to pay the interest rate demanded by the Bank of England.

This feature of the British system, which the Bank of England has termed *practical monetarism*, breaks the identity between the consequences of interest rate control and monetary base control outlined above. Thus a policy of raising interest rates via open-market operations is achieved in Britain by additional issue and sales of government debt, which as before cause bond prices to fall, in response to increased supply. As above, the additional bond sales result in customers drawing cheques on their commercial bank accounts in order to make payment to the Bank of England. This reduces the commercial banks' reserves.

However, after that, practical monetarism differs sharply from a true 'monetary base' system. In Britain, the commercial banks' shortage of reserves (cash under the present system) is generally relieved by the Bank of England. Cash reserves are supplied to the banks either by direct loans, or indirectly by Bank of England re-purchase of treasury bills or commercial bills, as explained in the previous chapter. As we stated there, the fact that MLR (minimum lending rate) has been abolished has not really changed the situation, as the Bank of England is always ready to supply the reserves the system requires, but it controls the interest rate it will charge.

Under practical monetarism there is no direct rationing of the quantity of reserves, as in the case of a reserve base system. Banks are not forced to control their lending by a shortage of reserve assets, as would be the case in a 'textbook' reserve base system of the type outlined in the previous chapter, which operates in other countries, such as the USA.

It therefore makes sense to regard interest rate control as something quite separate from money supply control in the British system, because the Bank of England does act to influence interest rates *without* at the same time operating on the banks' reserves directly.

In order to achieve a given money supply target the authorities raise interest rates to a point at which it is judged that banks will be unable to expand their lending, because the cost is too high. It is the effect of interest rates alone, the cost of funds, that is relied upon to restrain monetary growth. In a reserve base system, the reserves of the banking system are fixed at a level which will achieve the target monetary growth, and changes in interest rates are a by-product of this target.

(c)   *Changes in reserve requirements: special deposits*

An additional weapon of monetary control used in Britain is the mechanism of *special deposits*. These are used to alter the reserve requirement of the banking system. The Bank of England issues a requirement to the commercial banks that they must place a given percentage of their total liabilities in deposit with the Bank of England. These 'special' deposits must be paid over in cash, and are not counted as part of a bank's reserves, though interest is paid on them at the current treasury bill rate.

This means that if, for example, the cash ratio is ½%, and then special deposits of a further ½% are required, the effective reserve ratio becomes 1%. In a reserve base system, special deposits are therefore a very effective way of curbing bank lending. If reserves are not under tight control, special deposits still have the effect of forcing the commercial banks to borrow more cash reserves. This enables the Bank of England to enforce its policy of interest rate control, by increasing the cost of the reserves supplied. In this way, special deposits also enhance the Bank of England's control over interest rates.

(d)   *Direct controls*

In Britain, a number of administrative regulations designed to influence the availability and cost of credit have been used to supplement, and at times to replace, the more conventional measures described above. These can be roughly divided into four categories: ceilings and directives on bank lending, the supplementary deposit scheme, consumer credit regulations, and interest rate regulations.

During the 1960s, much use was made of ceilings on bank lending, i.e. instructions to the banks to limit the increase in their total lending to a given percentage. As a policy this was not particularly successful, because they were generally unaccompanied by restrictions on the total money supply. This meant that the clearing banks, which were mainly affected by ceilings, tended to lose business to other financial institutions not subject to such close restriction. For this and a number of other reasons, lending ceilings have been largely abandoned. Directives to the banks to favour specific categories of customer, such as exporters or industrial investors, or not to lend to others, such as the property market, have also been used in the past. However, these also have drawbacks, in that if borrowers are prepared to pay market interest rates for funds, they will usually be supplied somehow, and, conversely, the banks are unlikely to welcome the implied suggestion that they should offer credit at preferential rates to specific customers. This conflict with the banks' role as profit maximisers, together with the difficulties in categorising borrowers and attaching figures to such directives, has meant in the past that they have been little more than political window-dressing.

The supplementary deposit scheme operated from 1974 to 1980. It was devised to prevent banks from competing aggressively with each other for deposits by bidding up interest rates. Specific ceilings were attached to the growth of banks' interest-bearing deposits, and failure to keep borrowing within these limits resulted in progressively more costly financial penalties which rapidly became prohibitive. The overall effect of the measure was to limit growth both of the banks' interest-bearing deposits and of the interest rates paid on such deposits.

Direct restrictions have also been used extensively in the market for consumer credit, notably hire purchase controls. These take the form of requirements for minimum deposits or down payments, and limits on the time taken to repay loans. The short-term effect of such measures is considerable, but they suffer from the defect of penalising certain industries, notably cars and consumer durables. The resulting violent policy-induced fluctuations in the sales performance of these industries has tended to impair their investment programmes and thus leave them particularly vulnerable to foreign competition. As a result, hire purchase restrictions have fallen from favour, though they could still be employed in a crisis, as an extreme measure to alter consumer demand quickly.

(e) *Moral suasion*

Mention should also be made of the supposed influence of *moral suasion* in the operation of the monetary system. This magnificent nineteenth-century expression has been used to describe the influence of appeals by the Bank of England to the banking system to behave in a proper fashion, and in the national interest. Such 'advice' used to be backed up by the implied threat of more formal regulation if the Bank's directives were ignored. This system operated in the days when banking in the City of London was a closed shop with a relatively small number of institutions.

In recent years competition in all aspects of the financial markets has increased greatly, and entry barriers to the London markets have been sharply reduced. With large numbers of new 'players' attracted from all over the world, the 'gentleman's' idea of a club that could be persuaded by the Governor of the Bank of England to act in the moral interest of the nation has become unworkable, although the Bank retains a very powerful influence over the institutions, backed up by its regulatory powers.

5   The effectiveness of monetary policy instruments

All the techniques of monetary control have side-effects of one kind or another that the monetary authorities may regard as undesirable, particularly when policy is acting in a deflationary way. Fundamentally these side-effects result from conflicts between the policy aims of the monetary authorities, such as when their role of managing the National Debt conflicts with the need to control the money supply.

The major problem of recent years has been the conflict between fiscal and monetary policy. We have already seen that government fiscal policy as outlined in Chapters 13 and 14, works by altering the balance of government revenue and expenditure. Aggregate demand can be increased either by raising government expenditure, or by reducing taxation, or by some combination of the two. However, these 'fiscal' decisions then influence the size of the government's overall surplus or deficit, known as the *Public Sector Borrowing Requirement* (PSBR), which in turn affects monetary policy.

The PSBR must be financed in some way. If government spending overall exceeds its tax and other revenues, it must pay for the difference somehow. Basically it can do so in three ways:

(*a*)   Expand the money supply
(*b*)   Borrow from the non-bank private sector
(*c*)   Borrow from abroad

To some extent, all governments have used the first option. The simplest way of increasing its own net expenditure is for the government to create more money. It does so by borrowing directly from the banking system, which results in an equivalent rise in the money supply. (In extreme cases, such as the hyperinflations that occurred in European countries in the inter-war period, it simply speeds up the printing presses and mints more money.) The problem with this option is obvious – it is likely to be inflationary, and since most governments have adopted money supply targets, it cannot be used to finance a large PSBR.

Option (*b*) is equally simple. If it is decided not to create more money, then government must finance its deficit by borrowing directly from the non-bank private sector. It does so by selling more government bonds to the public – using open-market operations as described on page 309. Again, however, problems arise. As we have seen, to sell more debt (borrow more) the government must pay higher interest rates. Higher interest rates deter private sector investment, so unless there are 'surplus' savings, if the government wants to borrow more, the private sector must borrow less. This is known as *crowding out*. Given the adverse effects of government borrowing on interest rates and private investment, option (*b*) does not resolve the problems of funding the PSBR.

Option (*c*) is to borrow from overseas. The public sector obtains finance when the country is running a balance of payments deficit. But clearly no government will want to finance its expenditure by running up a balance of payments deficit, at least not on a large scale. Note that in general, a balance of payments defiicit has the effect of decreasing the money supply, while a surplus results in the money supply increasing.

Clearly then, all the above options for financing the PSBR have drawbacks. The larger the PSBR, the more difficult it is to achieve a given money supply target without the unwanted side-effects each option brings. Finally, we should note that the money supply is independently influenced by what happens to bank lending in the private sector. The more loans banks make, the larger is the supply of money – a new bank loan is made by crediting the borrower's bank account, so the money supply rises correspondingly. Bank lending can be controlled by any of the methods explained above – open-market operations on the reserve base, or on interest rates, special deposits and direct controls, or possibly even by moral suasion. But as we noted, not all methods are equally effective, and depending on the institutional arrangements, bank lending may not in practice be tightly controlled by the authorities.

We can summarise the influences on the money supply as follows:

Increase in money supply = Increase in bank lending to the
                                               private sector
                                          + PSBR (which can be offset by:)
                                          − Government borrowing from the non-
                                               bank private sector
                                          − Balance of payments deficit
                                               (or + balance of payments surplus).

Even in years when fiscal policy resulted in a budget surplus, or
Public Sector Debt Repayment (PSDR), money supply growth has
been rapid. This has generally been due to a lack of effective
controls on the banking system's creation of new credit. In the
absence of an operating reserve base system in the UK, the only
policy instrument available to control bank lending has been the
level of interest rates. This operates on the demand for credit, not
directly on the banks' supply of money. Since the demand for credit
may not respond quickly and predictably to changes in interest
rates, monetary growth in the UK has tended to be more rapid and
less predictable than in other industrialised countries.

6   Conclusion

Finally, it may be argued that the principal difference between
monetarist and Keynesian economists lies in their attitude towards
government intervention in the economy. Monetarists generally do
not accept the Keynesian proposition that it is desirable to manage
aggregate demand to ensure full employment. They believe that the
economy will find its own natural level of full employment as a result
of market forces. The problems of timing Keynesian fiscal policy to
offset fluctuations in activity lead only to making such fluctuations
worse, not better. This viewpoint is discussed in some detail in the
concluding chapter. In the meantime, at the risk of oversimplifying
a lengthy and complex controversy, we can at least venture some
general conclusions on the role of monetary policy. Although there
is a distinct possibility that a number of factors, discussed above,
will obscure any direct link between rate of change of the money
stock and rate of change of money GNP, nevertheless the situation
would have to be very unusual indeed for a large change − say 10%
per annum − in the money supply *not* to affect prices and output.

Frequently changes have been much larger than this − in 1972–3
M_3 rose by over 27%. Figures such as this cannot fail to be reflected
in the inflation rates of subsequent years.

Thus there is a very strong case for monitoring the growth of the
money supply and ensuring that fluctuations beyond a certain range

do not occur. Such growth may be due to changes in banking regulations (which were at least partly to blame for the 1972 figure), or to deficits stemming from expansionary fiscal policy (which has frequently been the case). But whatever the cause, the central bank should use the techniques available to it to offset such major disturbances. This is not to say that monetary policy should be used as an alternative to fiscal policy to 'fine-tune' aggregate demand, since its operation is far too imprecise for this purpose. Nor is it to deny that where a major failure of business confidence takes place – perhaps as a result of a speculative stock market collapse, as in the United States in the aftermath of 1929 – the resulting cumulative depression may be beyond the power of monetary policy to correct, as Keynes argued. When people lose confidence, and are unwilling to spend, increasing the money supply may simply result in more money being held and in a fall in the velocity of circulation. When this happens, Keynesian fiscal policy may be the only answer. The Government must undertake expenditure itself, in order to set off a multiplier process to raise income, and restore confidence and, ultimately, full employment.

Summary

We opened the chapter with an examination of the quantity theory of money, $MV = PY$. The 'monetarist' implication that changes in the supply of money affect GNP is subject to a number of qualifications which constitute the 'Keynesian' objections to this theory. These include the question of whether the velocity of circulation is stable, the issue of cause and effect, and the possibility of alternative money substitutes emerging.

There is a variety of techniques available to central banks to control the monetary system, of which open-market operations are the most important and the most pervasive in their effects. The extent to which these monetary control methods can be employed may be limited in practice by the problems of financing the Public Sector Borrowing Requirement, regardless of which means is chosen – monetary expansion, or borrowing, either domestically or externally. Control of bank lending by means of interest rates is also not always pursued effectively. However, our overall conclusion is that monetary policy, and in particular control of the money supply, will have a significant effect on national income. Whether that effect falls mainly on real output or on the price level depends on a complex web of factors, notably the level of employment and price expectations, which we shall examine in Chapter 19.

Questions

1 How does the government influence the supply of money in the UK? Explain how monetary policy can be used to reduce the level of aggregate demand. (Joint Matriculation Board, GCE, A-Level Economics)

2 Explain why it is argued that inflation is a consequence of allowing money supply to expand faster than the growth of output. On what grounds has this view been criticised? (The Institute of Chartered Secretaries and Administrators, Economics)

3 (*a*) Why is the current British Government trying to reduce the public sector borrowing requirement (PSBR)?

   (*b*) Discuss the difficulties involved in attempts to reduce the PSBR.

   (*c*) How does the government finance the PSBR?

   (The Institute of Chartered Accountants in England and Wales, Foundation Examination)

4 What different techniques are available to the monetary authorities when seeking to control the money supply? Assess critically the effectiveness of each type of control. (The Institute of Bankers, Economics, Stage 2)

5 Compare and contrast the main issues in the Keynesian and monetarist debate over the implementation of public policy. (University of London, GCE, A-Level Economics)

17

International Trade

Introduction

International trade merits special attention because it differs in several crucial respects from the exchanges of goods and services that take place within a country. First, there are more obvious barriers to trade between countries than to trade within countries. These can be simply the result of differences in economic structure, tradition, language or natural resources, or they can be deliberate restrictions imposed by governments on the movement of imports, exports, labour and capital. Secondly, different countries use different currencies, and trade is only possible where the currency of one country can be exchanged for the currency of another. This fact alone is of little consequence where the relationship between currencies is fixed, but in practice the relative values of currencies often change, presenting us with a whole series of additional economic problems. Finally, economic conditions and government policies normally vary more significantly between countries than they do between regions of a country. Thus buoyant demand in the UK might cause the purchase of more goods and services from abroad than foreigners buy from the UK, resulting in balance of payments problems in the UK.

This chapter examines the determinants of international trade, the potential gains from free trade, and the arguments for protecting domestic industry against foreign competition. We shall discuss exchange rates and the balance of payments in the next chapter.

1 Comparative advantage

The classical theory of international trade is associated mainly with the names of David Ricardo (1772–1833) and Adam Smith (1723 –90). Adam Smith argued in his Theory of the Division of Labour that all economic units, from individuals to countries, should concentrate on whatever they are able to produce most cheaply, and then exchange the result with goods produced at a lower cost elsewhere. To take a simple example; a man may be particularly skilled at producing cloth, but in the absence of trade he has to spend part of his time producing food for himself as well. According to Smith's theory, the man would be better advised to concentrate on producing cloth – the activity he does best – and to buy his foodstuffs from a farming specialist. All that is necessary for this system to work is the existence of *absolute difference in costs*.

But is this the whole story? Ricardo thought not, and by refining Smith's principle he showed that gains from trade are still possible even when one country can manufacture everything more cheaply than another. Ricardo saw that it is not absolute but *comparative* differences in cost that are decisive. Under these circumstances it would pay a country to concentrate on the commodities that it produces most efficiently – relatively speaking – and to leave those commodity-lines in which it is relatively less efficient to other countries. Many have difficulty with this principle although the idea is simple enough. Suppose that a medical doctor can also type, file and take shorthand better than his secretary. All we are saying is that the doctor will maximise his earnings by concentrating on tending the sick where his comparative advantage over the secretary is greatest.

The law of comparative advantage explains *why* countries trade and *what* they trade, and can be illustrated in the following simple example. Assume that there are only two countries in the world – the USA and Argentina – each producing only two goods – steel and wheat.

Table 17.1 shows that the production possibilities of the USA allow it to produce 1 unit of steel with 4 units of input or 1 unit of wheat with 2 units of input. Similarly, Argentina can produce 1 unit of steel with 12 inputs or 1 unit of wheat with 4 inputs. The USA is clearly more efficient at producing both commodities, yet it will still pay to specialise since the comparative advantages differ. The opportunity cost of producing 1 unit of steel in the USA is 2 units of

Table 17.1

	USA	Argentina
Steel	4	12
Wheat	2	4

wheat, whereas in Argentina it is 3 units of wheat. The USA will therefore concentrate on the manufacture and export of steel since by doing so only 2 units of wheat are lost. If Argentina tries to specialise in steel production 3 units of wheat will be lost. Turning the calculation around, we find that ½ unit of steel will be lost for every unit of wheat produced by the USA; but only ⅓ unit of steel will be lost for every unit of wheat produced by Argentina. Argentina therefore has a comparative advantage in the production of wheat.

If each country concentrates on producing the good it makes relatively cheaply then the two countries together can make more of *both* goods. We now have the boundaries within which trade can take place. The USA must obtain more than 2 units of wheat for every 1 steel and Argentina must obtain more than 1 unit of steel for every 3 of wheat. Gains from trade are always available wherever opportunity costs are different. However, for a satisfactory explanation of trade flows we need to know not only that gains from trade are possible where comparative advantages or production possibilities differ, but also why such production possibilities should differ between countries.

(a) The Hecksher–Ohlin theory
In the first half of this century two Swedish economists, Eli Hecksher and Bertil Ohlin, attempted to answer the above question by suggesting that the main source of comparative advantage lies in the differing factors of production that countries possess. A country well endowed with capital (such as the USA) would export capital intensive goods, whilst a country with an abundant labour supply (such as India) would export labour-intensive goods.

The Hecksher–Ohlin theory has been extensively tested – most notably for the USA by Wassily Leontief[1] – and these tests have revealed that care must be taken in the definitions of labour and capital, neither of which is a homogeneous factor. Labour can be either skilled or unskilled and a country abundant in skilled labour (or 'human capital', so-called because it represents investment in education and training) will export different goods than one abundant in unskilled labour. Similarly, capital consists of both tangible items, such as machines, and intangible items, such as knowledge, which are much more difficult to measure. When adjustments are made for the different types of capital and labour, the Hecksher –Ohlin theory is a reasonably good explanation of trade, particularly the trade of developing countries.

(b)   The technological gap and product cycle theories

One major problem of the Hecksher–Ohlin theory is that it does not explain why trade patterns change over time. More recent theories of trade emphasise the role of technological innovation in displacing old products and introducing new ones.

The 'technological gap' model sees certain countries (particularly the USA) as having a special talent for innovation and tending to develop and export new products. As time passes, other countries imitate the innovation, and production and exports shift away from the innovating country. The 'product cycle' model explains the speed with which the production of new products spreads to other countries in terms of the changes that occur in the input requirements of a new product as it becomes established. For a new product, production runs are likely to be short, because of uncertainty about how successful the product will be, and require large quantities of skilled labour. However, as the product becomes established, mass production techniques become possible, less skilled labour is required, and production shifts to countries with relatively low labour costs.

The radio is often given as an example of the technological gap and product cycle theories. The US developed the radio, but became increasingly vulnerable to Japanese competition as the technology became known and standardised, allowing the Japanese to exploit their low labour costs. The development of the transistor gave the US another temporary advantage in world markets until transistor technology spread to Japan. Similar processes seem to be at work in the modern computer industry.

(c)   Intra-industry trade

Another problem with the Hecksher–Ohlin theory is that it does not explain why the majority of world trade takes place between countries with *similar* factor endowments. Although the theory explains why the UK might export cars to India in exchange for textiles, it does not explain why the UK and Germany export cars to each other. A different theory is needed to explain trade in goods within the same industry, or so called intra-industry trade (as opposed to inter-industry trade). Economists have identified two important influences on intra-industry trade. The first is that consumers prefer to have a wide variety of goods available to them. The second is that there are likely to be economies of scale in the production of many goods so that it will be advantageous for an economy to specialise in particular types of good.

Studies of intra-industry trade in the industrial countries have shown that, as expected, such trade is more important in relatively sophisticated manufactured goods (such as cars) than for primary commodities (for example, fuels) or unsophisticated manufactured products (such as iron and steel). The degree of intra-industry trade also varies between countries. Japan has much less intra-industry trade than the European Community.

2 Terms of trade

We have seen that gains from trade are possible when comparative costs differ, and that the size of the overall gain and how it is distributed between countries will depend on the prices at which trade takes place. These prices (the terms of trade) will depend on the demand and supply for products of international trade. The country with the most highly-desired goods on offer will receive the most advantageous terms of trade.

We define a country's terms of trade as the quantity of that country's exports that have to be sold per unit of imports. The terms are expressed as an index, and they are estimated by comparing the average price of exports with the average price of imports. Thus:

$$T = \frac{px}{pm} \times 100$$

where T = terms of trade, px = an index of the average price of exports and pm = an index of the average price of imports.

An 'improvement' in the terms of trade means that the country concerned is able to obtain more imports for a given quantity of exports than before. On the face of it, this appears to be a good thing, but a country's export prices can be driven up either by strong foreign demand or by domestic inflation. The former reason is wholly beneficial and can be regarded as a genuine improvement in that country's external position. However, if prices are running ahead of other countries' export prices, the benefits to be gained from the 'improving' terms of trade will be short-lived, as ultimately the country's goods will be priced out of the international market, with serious consequences for its balance of payments.

Conversely, a 'deterioration' in the terms of trade means that a country is able to buy less imports per unit of exports. Once again, however, this statement cannot be taken simply at face value. A 'deterioration' can be organised deliberately by a policy of currency depreciation which lowers the price of exports and raises the price of imports. Exports are therefore encouraged and imports discouraged sufficiently, it is hoped, to cure a balance of payments deficit. (Depreciation will be discussed in greater detail in Chapter 18).

3 Protection

The principle of comparative advantage demonstrates that trade allows countries to obtain more goods and services than would be possible without trade, yet restrictions on trade are the rule rather than the exception. This section examines the methods of protection used by governments, and the reasons why governments seek to impose protection.

(a) Methods
There are various methods of protection available to governments:

(i) *Tariffs* are taxes placed on imports in order to make them more expensive, and therefore to discourage their purchase and encourage the production of domestic substitutes. Tariffs also yield revenue to the government. The effectiveness of tariffs depends upon their size (the tariff *height*), the elasticity of domestic demand for the particular category of imports, (i.e. the way consumer demand reacts to the higher priced imports), and the elasticity of domestic supply of goods competing with the imports.

(ii) *Quotas* are specific limits placed on either the quantity or the value of imports allowed into a country. Because the supply of imports is restricted, quotas raise import prices and are, in this respect, similar to tariffs. However, unlike a tariff, quotas need not yield revenue to the government. The usual way of enforcing quotas is by issuing licences to importers, who gain from the higher prices of imports. If the government wishes to obtain revenue it must auction the licences to the highest bidders.

The above two categories are the most obvious forms of protection but there are other less obvious methods which are becoming increasingly important as tariffs are reduced by international agreement (see section (*c*) below).

(iii) *Government subsidies* can be granted to particular industries to help them maintain their international competitiveness. These can take the form of generous depreciation allowances, straight cash grants, or periods free of tax which are known as *tax holidays*. An important difference between tariffs and subsidies is that tariffs raise the price of imports to domestic consumers, whereas subsidies do not. For this reason, many economists prefer subsidies to tariffs as a way of protecting domestic industry, although subsidies have to be financed.

(iv) *Voluntary restrictions on exports (VERs)* can be imposed by the exporting country at the request of the importing country. In fact this sort of agreement is usually voluntary in name only and represents the application of considerable economic and diplomatic pressure. Voluntary export restrictions have been used in recent years to reduce imports of steel and non-cotton textiles into the United States, and of Japanese cars and other consumer goods into Britain and other European countries.

VERs are often seen as a costless way of protecting domestic industry. This is not so. As with tariffs and quotas, VERs raise the price of imported goods by restricting the supply but, whereas a tariff yields revenue to the government of the importing country and a quota yields profit to the importer (unless the government auctions off the licences), a VER yields revenue to the exporting country which represents a further loss associated with the restriction.

(v) *Currency controls* limit the availability of foreign currency. An importer therefore has to apply to the central bank for the necessary currency before he can buy foreign goods. Currency controls are widely used as a form of protection in developing countries.

(vi) *Administrative regulations* can be every bit as effective as tariffs in limiting imports. Governments can specify complicated and lengthy bureaucratic procedures or systems of advanced payments; they can insist upon a minimum domestic product content or special marketing standards; and they can specify special safety provisions and health regulations which few foreign manufacturers are able to meet.

(b) Arguments for protection
Protection imposes costs on the domestic economy by limiting the supply of cheaper and/or better foreign goods. Arguments for protection suggest that there are benefits from restricting trade

which more than offset these losses. Unfortunately, the majority of arguments for protection are either fallacious or really arguments for some other economic policy.

(i)   Probably the most popular (and most misused) argument for protection is the *infant industry* argument. A new industry, although it may have a potential comparative advantage, takes time to establish this advantage and in the interim is very vulnerable to foreign competition. It is therefore argued that temporary protection is required until production is well underway and the infant is mature enough to compete on equal terms in the international market.

To be valid, the infant industry argument must demonstrate that the industry would not be established without protection. It is not sufficient to argue that costs will be high in the short term, because the whole justification for protecting the industry is that long-term benefits exceed short-term costs, and in this case it can be asked why, if they recognise this, private entrepreneurs are not willing to establish the industry and bear short-term costs in anticipation of long-term benefits. The argument for protection must be that there are benefits to society that private entrepreneurs will not perceive. In other words, there must be *externalities*. For example, the infant industry may raise the skill level of the labour force bringing long-term benefits to society.

Nor is the infant industry argument necessarily a justification for tariffs rather than other forms of protection, such as subsidies to particular industries.

(ii)   The *optimum tariff* argument states that tariffs may be used to improve a country's terms of trade. A tariff on imports reduces demand for imports and may lead importers to cut their prices, thereby improving the terms of trade. The optimum tariff is one which balances the improvement in the terms of trade against the loss from a decrease in trade. This argument is of theoretical rather than practical importance, since few countries possess sufficient market power to influence the price of their imports, and, in any event, the calculation of the optimum tariff would be extremely difficult.

(iii)   Tariffs may also be used to raise *government revenue*. This is a particularly important argument for protection in developing countries, many of which have poorly developed taxation systems. A study of 10 developing countries found that, on average, in the early 1970s, 20% of total government revenue came from taxes on trade.[2] It must be stressed, however, that the government is obtaining revenue at the cost of some of the gains from international trade.

(iv)   It is often argued that protection can encourage the use of unemployed *factors of production* (for example, labour), and improve the *balance of payments*, by causing demand to be switched from foreign goods to domestic produce. The same results could be obtained, without losing the benefits from international trade, by expanding domestic demand and/or by allowing a depreciation of the exchange rate (see Chapter 18).

(v)   International trade frequently involves *changes in the structure* of particular industries. Such changes are rarely painless and frequently have adverse social consequences. For example, textile production and shipbuilding in the North of England has suffered from foreign competition. However, attempting to prevent such changes – which result from changes in comparative advantage – by protection is both pointless and expensive. It is far better to ease the process of adjusting to such changes by, for example, increased expenditure on retraining schemes.

(vi)   Home producers frequently argue that tariffs are needed to protect them from *cheap foreign labour*. This argument is fundamentally flawed because the whole point of trade is to take advantage of differences in production costs.

(vii)   Finally, protection is sometimes used to prevent *dumping* by foreign producers. Dumping occurs when goods are exported at below their marginal production costs. There have been several well publicised disputes on this matter between the EC and Japan and between the US and the EC in recent years. Once again, the argument is not as straightforward as it may at first appear since a country will benefit if it can permanently import goods at a lower price. However, the lower price may only be temporary so that once domestic firms have been driven out of business foreign suppliers may raise their prices. Such predatory behaviour by foreign suppliers might indeed justify some form of protection but great care must be taken to avoid the dumping argument being used to stifle legitimate competition.

Both overt and non-tariff methods of protection are facts of international life, but before concluding we should note the considerable efforts made by GATT to introduce freer world trading conditions.

(c)   The General Agreement on Tariffs and Trade (GATT)

The dangers of protection were illustrated in the 1930s. Faced with high unemployment and balance of payments difficulties, many countries imposed a battery of protective measures with the result that by 1933 the value of exports from the main industrial countries was only one quarter of the 1929 level.

The experience of the 1930s led to the signing of the GATT on 30 October 1947. Under GATT's provisions, every form of discrimination between the signatories is prohibited and all quantitative restrictions are banned. These conditions can however be waived for developing countries, and for other countries experiencing short-term crises. In addition, customs duties can only be altered after negotiation with the countries concerned and all subsidies influencing foreign trade must be notified to the GATT Secretariat.

The major achievement of GATT has been the successive rounds of tariff reductions which have taken place since 1947. The most famous of these was the Kennedy Round, completed in 1967, which produced tariff cuts averaging 35%. The Tokyo Round, completed in 1979, secured agreement to cut tariffs by another third over an eight year period.

The reduction in tariff barriers has been accompanied by increased non-tariff barriers to trade. The Tokyo Round produced agreement on a code of conduct to restrain the growth of non-tariff barriers but the effectiveness of this code remains debatable and concern over the growth of such barriers remains very real.

Non-tariff barriers are often targeted at particular countries (especially Japan and the more advanced developing countries) and at particular sectors and industries such as basic commodities, foodstuffs and basic manufacturers (footwear, clothing and textiles). Increasingly, non-tariff barriers have been used to restrict trade in more technologically advanced products (video tape recorders).

Concern over the growth of non-tariff barriers was one factor leading to the launch of the Uruguay Round of trade negotiations in 1986. Other factors which were important in this launch of the Uruguay Round were the fact that agricultural trade remained highly restricted and that previous rounds of trade negotiations had not dealt with barriers to trade in services such as insurance and banking.

4 Free trade and developing countries

All the arguments raised so far appear heavily biased towards the principle of free trade. The developing countries have long been sceptical of the argument for free trade, which they believe ignores the question of how the gains from free trade are distributed between rich and poor countries.

Many developing countries are highly dependent on one or two products for their exports. These products are often primary commodities – for example, copper in Zambia and cocoa in Ghana. The terms of trade for many primary commodities have deteriorated over the last twenty years reflecting both increased supply and reduced demand as artificial substitutes have been developed. Moreover, the price of many primary commodities is highly volatile. As a consequence, many developing countries have sought to diversify away from primary commodities by establishing their own manufacturing industries.

Feeling that competition from the industrialised countries would prevent them from developing their own manufacturing industries, many developing countries adopted highly protectionist economic strategies in the 1950s and 1960s. Average tariff rates of 100% on imported manufactures were not uncommon, and extensive use was also made of quotas and other trade barriers. High levels of protection were often justified by the 'infant industry' argument.

The results of these protectionist policies were in many cases disappointing. Infant industries have often been slow to grow up and have continued to produce at high cost. In turn, high domestic costs have made it difficult to export, and have discouraged foreign investment.

Moreover, protected firms have become near monopolists in truncated domestic markets leading to reduced pressures for efficiency.

In recent years, many less developed countries – in particular, the so-called newly industrialised countries – have moved towards more export orientated policies, often with spectacular results. A recent study by the World Bank of the trade policies of 41 less developed countries over the period 1963–1985 found that there was a strong relationship between what the Bank termed 'outward orientated' trade policies and growth. The countries with the highest rates of growth – Singapore, South Korea – had the most liberal trade policies. Conversely, countries with import substituting trade policies – such as Ghana, Peru and Zambia – had some of the lowest rates of growth, often experiencing absolute falls in national income between 1973 and 1985.

Despite the apparent advantages of following export orientated trade policies, developing countries face formidable barriers in increasing their exports of manufactured goods. Their comparative advantage generally lies in labour intensive products, and yet it is precisely those products which attract the highest rates of protection in the developed countries.

5   Economic integration

There has been a marked global trend since the Second World War towards economic integration, with the formation of customs unions and free trade areas. The essential distinction between these two measures is that, in the former, member countries must reduce tariffs on each others' goods while erecting a common external tariff against the products of non-member countries; in the latter, however, member countries must similarly lower internal tariffs but are free to decide on their own tariff levels against non-members. GATT allows customs unions and free trade areas provided, among other things, that the common external tariff of the customs union does not increase existing restrictions.

Advantages and disadvantages of economic integration
The gains from integration can be usefully considered under two headings: *static*, applying to those gains that occur simply by switching existing trade from external to internal sources; and *dynamic*, applying to those that occur from the impetus given to trade by the integrated economies.

(*a*)   *Static:* if countries group together in a customs union (and this also applies to a free trade area) there are two results. Firstly, trade is said to have been 'created' if the removal of tariffs within the union allows member countries to transfer their external purchases from high cost to low cost suppliers. Secondly, trade is said to have been 'diverted' if a member country's sources of supply are switched from low-cost foreign producers to high-cost customs union sources.

(*b*)   *Dynamic:* a country expands the size of its potential market by joining a customs union and this enables industry to operate at optimum capacity and achieve economies of scale. At the same time increased external competition will force monopolies to innovate and to reduce profit margins; smaller inefficient companies will have to merge, become more efficient, or go bankrupt, and all this to the benefit of the consumer.

We now turn to the most important integration movement – the European Communities.

(i)   The European Communities (EC)

This is the collective name given to three organisations created to promote various aspects of European cooperation – the European Coal and Steel Community (ECSC), the European Atomic Energy Community (EAEC) and, most significant of all, the European Economic Community (EEC). In 1967, the executive bodies of the three were merged under a single Commission of the European Communities, although the whole organisation is still popularly referred to as the EEC.

All this is a major advance in economic integration and arose for two reasons: firstly, revulsion at the way nationalism had precipitated two world wars, which encouraged Europeans to seek some sort of Union to avoid future conflicts; secondly, it became obvious by the end of the Second World War that European economies were not individually large enough to enable modern, technologically advanced industries to produce at maximum efficiency. Integration was necessary if these industries were to survive against foreign competition.

Drawing on their experience of the ECSC, started in 1951, the six founder members – France, West Germany, Italy, Belgium, Holland and Luxembourg – signed the 1957 Treaty of Rome establishing the EEC, whose object was to promote 'harmonious development of economic activity within the Community, continuous and balanced expansion, greater stability, a steady improvement in living standards and closer relations between member states'. Britain, Denmark and Eire joined in 1973; Greece in 1981; Spain and Portugal in 1985. Starting from a customs union, the aim was to progress to economic, monetary and eventually political union.

The organisation of the Community is based on the following institutions:

1   *The Council of Ministers* which has the power to make decisions on all community matters. Each member country sends one delegate.
2   *The Commission*, with seventeen commissioners and a permanent staff of over 9000, is the executive arm of the Council responsible for the day-to-day running of the EC, and assisting the Council with recommendations and advice. The Commission is in turn

assisted by an Economic and Social Committee with advisory functions.

3   *The Committee of Permanent Representatives (COREPER)* which comprises the ambassadors of the member states appointed to the Community, considers all Commission proposals in detail and undertakes preliminary negotiations before they are passed to the Ministers. It is commonly said 'the Commission proposes, COREPER haggles and the Ministers decide'.

4   *The European Parliament* has 528 elected representatives from the member states, but its role is largely consultative and advisory although it has some budgetary control, with the power – so far never exercised – to dismiss the Commission.

5   *The Court of Justice* where disputes over the working of the Treaty are resolved.

The most notable achievement of the EC to date is the establishment of a common external tariff and the elimination of internal customs duties. It is now the world's largest trading bloc, accounting for more than a third of world exports. The original six member states carried out 34% of their trade with each other in 1957. By 1982, with the enlarged community of ten, this had risen to 51%. Much of this increase was the result of trade 'creation' rather than trade 'diversion'. It is, however, difficult to estimate precisely what the trade effects of the Community have been, because we cannot say what would have happened in the absence of the EC. Certainly trade within the Community has grown enormously, but the trend was already visible before the foundation of the EC.

As for the objective of economic union – common economic policies – the most substantial and controversial attainment so far is the common agricultural policy (CAP) discussed in Chapter 3. There is also a common policy for the steel industry covering output levels and pricing and a common fisheries policy. Anti-competitive behaviour, which may affect trade between member states if subject to Community Law, which gives the Commission power to stop certain restrictive practices and to impose fines on firms guilty of infringement. However, the Community budget is too small to have any real impact, and economic policy is largely determined at national level by the governments of individual member states. Progress towards monetary union through the European Monetary System (EMS), examined in the following chapter, has been very slow and difficult.

The most important development in the Community in recent years has been the Single European Act (SEA) which came into force in July 1987. The SEA was a response to the feeling that the impctus towards economic union was failing and that there were many non-tariff barriers to trade between member states. The SEA was the first comprehensive revision of the Treaty of Rome and committed member states to removing all remaining barriers to trade, thereby completing what has become known as the internal market, by 1992.

The SEA had its origins in the Commission's White Paper (sometimes known as the Cockfield White Paper after the Commissioner responsible) of June 1985 which outlined 300 proposals to eliminate barriers to the completion of the internal market. These barriers were classified as physical (border controls and formalities), technical (e.g. differing product standards enforced by member states) and fiscal (differing national rates and coverage of indirect taxes).

There has been a great deal of controversy about the impact of the completion of the internal market on the Community. Critics have argued that the economic benefits from the original formation of the Community were small, so that completing the internal market will have a similarly small effect. In response to its critics, the Commission published in 1988 its own study into the 'costs of non-Europe'. This study (also known as the Cecchini Report) suggested that the Community stands to gain between 4 and 6½% of GDP from completing the internal market. Half of this gain would come from the direct reduction in costs as a result of removing barriers to trade and the remainder from better exploitation of economies of scale and increased competition.

(ii) The other countries
The United States and Canada reached agreement on the formation of a free trade area in 1988.

There have also been attempts to form common markets in countries of the Third World – two examples are the Andean Common Market and the East African Federation. Their aims all concern the stimulation of economic growth through access to larger external markets. The difference between these attempts and those of Europe is that the developing countries are aiming more to divert purchases from the rest of the world to member states than simply to create trade. However, their problems are much greater than they are for Europe. Their economies are typically competitive rather than complementary, and it is therefore hard for them to form a unified community. It is particularly difficult for them to parcel out major industries, such as steel, to the most efficient producer country within the group. Economic logic notwithstanding, the allocation of a steel mill to one country means that the others must do without, and this is naturally a divisive issue.

Summary

The law of comparative advantage was established as a central element of any explanation of trade flows. The law states that two countries will gain from trade as long as their comparative costs differ, but we were unable to locate the origin of these differences with any certainty. A country's endowment of factors of production is obviously an important determinant of trade patterns, but this view must be interpreted with care and does not explain why so much trade takes place between similarly endowed countries. We suggested that cost differences might be caused by the varying technological abilities of countries.

The law of comparative advantage only deals with the supply side of international trade and gives us therefore only the outer limits of exchange between two countries. A concept from the demand side – the terms of trade – needed to be introduced to enable us to say something about actual quantities traded and the distribution of gains.

In the previous section we examined the various ways in which countries seek to restrict trade, and the costs and benefits of protection. We argued that the objectives of protection are generally achieved at lower cost by other economic policies.

We considered the rate of developing countries in the world trading system and suggested that economic policies designed to encourage exports have been more effective in promoting development than more traditional policies of import substitution.

Finally, we gave a brief history of the European Community and discussed the origins and impact of the Single European Act.

Questions

1

	Steel (tonnes)	Wheat (tonnes)
Urbania	10	40
Ruralia	2	30

The table shows the opportunity cost of wheat in terms of steel, or vice versa, before the opening of trade. Assume that these costs remain constant for all levels of output and that there are no transport costs. Which of the following conforms to the principle of comparative advantage?

(a)   Urbania will export steel
(b)   Ruralia will export steel
(c)   Urbania will export both steel and wheat
(d)   Urbania will export steel and Ruralia will export wheat
(e)   It is impossible to predict until the terms of trade are known.

2   What are the terms of trade and how might changes in them affect the balance of trade? (The Institute of Chartered Secretaries and Surveyors)

3   What are the gains from international trade? (Oxford Local Examinations, GCE, A-Level.)

4   (a)   For what reasons do governments often take measures to assist domestic industries faced with foreign competition?
    (b)   Consider the merits and demerits of the following protective measures:
          (i)   tariffs
          (ii)   quotas
          (iii)   direct financial subsidies from domestic producers.
    (Welsh Joint Education Committee, GCE, A-Level.)

5   The growth of developing countries is hindered by the particular problems which they meet in international trade. Consider these problems and suggest possible solutions. (The Institute of Cost and Management Accountants)

Notes

1   Wassily Leontief: 'Domestic Production and Foreign Trade: The American Capital Position Re-examined', *Economia Internationale* (1954). This article contains the so-called 'Leontief Paradox' that the US exported labour intensive goods. The Paradox was resolved by recognising the importance of different types of labour and capital.

18

The Balance of Payments, Exchange Rates and the International Monetary System

Introduction

International trade gives rise to flows of money between countries, and this chapter examines the consequences of these flows. It begins by showing how monetary flows are recorded in a country's balance of payment accounts and discusses the circumstances in which the balance of payments might be a problem. Trade requires the exchange of national currencies and the chapter examines the factors determining exchange rates, the usefulness of exchange rates as instruments of economic policy, and the debate about floating exchange rates. It concludes with a description of the main features of the international monetary system.

1 The Balance of Payments

The UK's balance of payments accounts are a record of all transactions between residents of the UK and residents of the rest of the world during some period of time (e.g. a year). Transactions are classified in two ways, with a distinction being drawn between credit and debit items, and between the type of transaction. Any transaction which increases the demand for sterling (e.g. when a UK exporter sells a car to Germany and so German marks are exchanged for sterling) is treated as a *credit* item, whilst any transaction which increases the demand for foreign currency (e.g. the purchase of foreign goods by UK residents) is treated as a *debit* item. There have been a number of changes in the presentation of the accounts in recent years and transactions are now divided into two main groups: current account, and transactions in UK external assets and liabilities (sometimes called the capital account). The construction of the accounts can best be appreciated by examining Table 18.1.

Table 18.1   Summary of the UK Balance of Payments 1987[1]

			£m
A		*Current account*	
	1	Exports (f.o.b.)*	79 422
	2	Imports (f.o.b.)*	89 584
	3	Visible balance (1 + 2)	−10 162
	4	Services (net)	+ 5 638
	5	Interest, profits and dividends (net)	+ 5 523
	6	Transfers (net)	− 3 503
	7	Invisible balance (4 + 5 + 6)	+ 7 658
	8	Current balance (3 + 7)	− 2 504
B		*Transactions in UK external assets and liabilities*	
	9	UK direct investment overseas	−15 372
	10	Overseas direct investment: the UK	+ 5 953
	11	UK portfolio investment overseas	+ 6 463
	12	Overseas portfolio investment: the UK	+10 805
	13	Lending etc. to overseas residents by UK banks	−50 264
	14	Borrowing etc. from overseas residents by UK banks	+52 789
	15	Deposits and lending overseas by UK residents other than banks and general government	− 3 112
	16	Borrowing from overseas by UK residents other than banks and general government	+ 2 985
	17	Official reserves	−12 012
	18	Other external assets of central government	− 797
	19	Other external liabilities of general government	+ 1 523
	20	Net transactions in UK external assets and liabilities (total rows 9–19)	− 1 039
	21	Balancing items† (21 + 20 + 8 = 0)	3 543

*F.o.b. indicates free-on-board, i.e. goods are valued at the time they arrive on-board ship (or aeroplane). Sometimes imports are valued on a c.i.f. basis which means that the 'cost of insurance and freight' is included.
†The balancing item represents the sum of all errors and omissions made during the compilation of the accounts.

(a) The current account

The current account records all exports and imports of goods and services and a distinction is drawn between visible trade and invisible trade.

Visible trade (rows 1 and 2) refers to the export and import of goods. In 1987 there was a visible trade deficit, as commodity imports exceeded exports by £10162m.

Invisible trade comprises transactions involving the provision of services (row 4) by both the public and private sector (shipping, civil aviation, tourism, banking, insurance and other financial services), flows of interest, profits and dividends from previous investments (row 5) and private and government transfers (row 6), such as foreign military expenditure, aid, transfers to and from the EC and other international organisations. Overall, invisible trade normally displays a surplus, although transfers always show a large deficit. The visible and invisible balances together make up the current balance (row 8), which showed a deficit of £2504m in 1987.

(b) The capital account

The capital account records all transactions between residents and non-residents involving assets. It includes, for example, direct investment (the purchase of factories etc.), portfolio investment (the purchase of stocks and shares) as well as, amongst other things, the holding of bank deposits. An important point to note about the capital account is that inflows of capital (e.g. the purchase of a factory in the UK by a French company) are treated as credit items, whereas capital outflows (e.g. UK investment overseas) are treated as debit items.

Put another way, any transaction which increases UK assets is treated as a debit item and any transaction which increases UK liabilities is treated as a credit. The reason for this is that an increase in UK external assets involves an outflow of sterling whereas an increase in UK liabilities is associated with an inflow of sterling.

The capital account also includes changes in official gold and foreign currency reserves (row 17) and overseas borrowing and lending by the UK government. The sum of rows 17–19 gives the total of official financing. An *increase* in UK reserves is given a *negative* sign in the accounts because it represents an increase in UK assets in the same way as an increase in UK investment overseas. An overall rise in the UK's net external assets (row 20) is shown by a negative sign. For example, in 1987 there was an overall increase in the UKs net assets of £1039m.

(c)   The balance of payments always balances

It will be readily understood that, overall, the balance of payments always balances. A simple analogy will make this clear. A household cannot spend more than it receives in any one year without financing its over-expenditure by drawing on its savings or borrowing from the bank or some other creditor. The amount borrowed or dis-saved, plus the household's income, must equal the household's outgoings. Similarly, a country's total outgoings must equal its total receipts. A current account surplus must be matched by a rise in net external assets and a current account deficit by a fall.

In reality, the two sides of the account are seldom equal because of the imperfect nature of data collection. For this reason a balancing item (row 21) is inserted which is simply the difference between the known total of official financing and the recorded currency flows. (A residual error is similarly used to reconcile the three national income estimates – see Chapter 12.) The balancing item thus represents the sum of all errors and omissions made during compilation of the accounts. Between 1972 and 1981 the average balancing item was £750m, a small sum in the context of the total monetary flows involved. However, in some years the balancing item has been very large – in 1976 it was over £3bn and in 1978 over £2bn.

(d)   Equilibrium and disequilibrium in the balance of payments

We have seen that the overall balance of payments always balances because of the way the accounts are constructed. This does not, however, imply that the balance of payments is always in equilibrium. For example, a country cannot indefinitely finance a deficit on the balance for official financing by borrowing and/or running down reserves, because its reserves and creditworthiness will ultimately be exhausted. Conversely, a country running a persistent surplus on the balance for official financing is forgoing consumption or investment in exchange for building up reserves. Consequently the traditional definition of balance of payments equilibrium is where the balance for official financing is zero when averaged over a number of years (to eliminate special factors and to allow for the repayment of past debts).

While this definition is simple enough in theory, in practice it proves to be rather complex, and is subject to a number of qualifications. The first qualification is that if we concentrate on the equilibrium of the balance for official financing, we may overlook the stability of that equilibrium. Clearly, an equilibrium founded upon inflows of long-term capital will be much more stable than an equilibrium based upon short-term 'hot money' flows which can reverse themselves at a moment's notice, with drastic consequences for the reserves. Similarly, an equilibrium based on a strong current account will probably be more stable than one based on capital inflows. Second, an equilibrium of the balance for official financing may only be achieved at the cost of forgoing some other objective of policy. For example, the balance of payments can often be improved by reducing domestic expenditure and hence imports, but reducing expenditure will create unemployment. High interest rates can attract capital inflows, but will harm domestic investment. Similarly, import controls might be used to help the balance of payments but would infringe international agreements (GATT, EC, etc.). Finally, with a freely floating exchange rate (discussed on page 345) the balance for official financing would be zero, by definition, and so there could be no disequilibrium in the balance of payments. Nevertheless, governments might then worry about movements in the exchange rate, so that a balance of payments problem would have been transformed into an exchange rate problem.

(e)   Some recent history

Table 18.2 presents details of the UK balance of payments over the decade since 1978. During this period the UK generally ran a deficit on visible trade (the exceptions were the years 1980 to 1982) although this was often more than offset by the persistent surplus on invisible trade so that the current account was in surplus for seven of the ten years. The UK increased its net overseas assets in every year of the period.

In assessing the behaviour of the UK balance of payments, it should be noted that the balancing item has sometimes been substantial during the period (particularly in 1986) and has often exceeded the current account balance. If, as is sometimes argued, the majority of the error and omissions in the balance of payments accounts occur in the current account, it is possible that the UK's current account position was rather better than indicated.

The UK's balance of payments during this period has been influenced by a number of factors, the most important of which have been the emergence of the UK as a major oil producer, the competitiveness of UK goods and services, and relative rates of growth in the UK and overseas.

The UK began to exploit the large reserves of oil that had been discovered in the North Sea in the late 1970s and the importance of North Sea oil was increased by the doubling of oil prices in 1979–

Table 18.2 UK Balance of Payments and Exchange Rate: Summary (£m)

	1978	1979	1980	1981	1982	1983	1984	1985	1986	1987
Visible balance	−1593	−3398	1353	3350	2218	−1075	−4850	−2346	−8716	−10162
Invisible balance	2557	2902	1769	3586	2467	4907	6602	5683	8517	7658
Current balance	964	−496	3122	6936	4685	3832	2022	3337	−199	−2504
Net transactions in UK external assets and liabilities	−2871	−743	−3872	−7395	−2328	−4310	−7664	−9074	−14200	−1039
Balancing item	1907	1044	570	301	−2357	478	5642	5737	14399	2543
Sterling exchange rate index	N/A	N/A	117.7	119.0	113.7	105.3	100.6	100	91.5	90.1
Real exchange rate*	83.3	99.0	122.5	124.8	115.4	104.3	100.5	100	93.8	93.1

* Measured by relative unit labour costs in manufactures

1980. The impact of oil on the balance of payments, and indeed on the economy in general, has been the subject of much debate. One school of thought is that the emergence of a substantial deficit on trade in manufactured goods in the 1980s shows that oil has simply masked underlying balance of payments problems which will therefore be revealed as oil production tails off in the 1990s. This view ignores the fact that the balance of payments must always balance so that an improvement in one part of the accounts must be offset by a deterioration elsewhere as a result of a rise in the exchange rate (discussed further below). In the UK the surplus on oil trade was accompanied by a larger deficit on manufactured trade and, very importantly, by greater outflows of capital increasing the UK's external assets.

The second influence on the balance of payments during the period was the international competitiveness of UK goods and services. Competitiveness declined substantially between 1978 and 1981 (the real exchange rate – see below – rose by 50%) making it much harder for the UK producers to compete with foreign producers. Part of the decline in competitiveness was a result of the rise in the exchange rate associated with the increased importance of North Sea oil, but UK inflation was also much higher than in other major countries. After 1982 competitiveness began to improve as both sterling and the UK's relative rate of inflation started to fall.

The final influence on the balance of payments was the rate of growth in the UK relative to the rest of the world. The recession in the UK in the early 1980s held down the growth of imports but the subsequent recovery in output put pressure on the current account as imports began to grow faster than exports.

2   The exchange rate

International trade is accompanied by the exchange of national currencies and this exchange takes place in the foreign exchange market (in reality a network of professional foreign exchange dealers situated in the world's financial centres and linked by telecommunications) where the relative prices of different currencies – the *exchange rates* – are established.

(a)   Measuring exchange rates
Exchange rates are measured in three different ways – bi-lateral, effective and real. A *bi-lateral* exchange rate is simply the price of one currency in terms of another. In the UK, bi-lateral rates are expressed as the number of units of foreign currency which can be

bought for one pound (e.g. the sterling–dollar exchange rate might be $2 = £1), and sterling is said to have depreciated when fewer units of foreign currency can be bought. (In other countries bilateral rates are expressed as the number of units of domestic currency per unit of foreign currency.)

An *effective* exchange rate expresses the average price of one currency in terms of several other currencies. It is therefore a more general measure of a country's exchange rate and is particularly useful when currencies are floating (see page 345). In the UK the effective exchange rate (known as the 'sterling exchange rate index' – see Table 18.2) is calculated by taking a weighted average of sterling's value against a number of other major currencies, with the weights determined by the importance of the countries involved in UK trade (hence it is sometimes called the trade-weighted exchange rate), and expressing the results as a percentage of sterling's value in 1985 (given the value 100). A fall in the effective exchange rate indicates an overall depreciation of sterling.

The effective exchange rate shows how misleading it can be to focus on one particular bi-lateral rate (e.g. the sterling–dollar rate) when assessing exchange rate performance. For example, between 1985 and 1987 sterling appreciated by 26% against the dollar but depreciated by 15% against the French franc and 22% against the German mark. The overall change, measured by the effective exchange rate, was a depreciation of 10%. $\dfrac{90.1 - 100}{100} \times 100$

A *real* exchange rate is the effective exchange rate adjusted for price movements at home and abroad and is therefore a measure of the competitiveness of a country's goods. A rise in the real exchange rate (which may be caused by an appreciation of the effective exchange rate and/or higher inflation at home than abroad) means that domestic goods are becoming more expensive relative to foreign goods. A number of different measures of the real exchange rate are calculated and published for the UK, using various indicators of price movements. The most commonly quoted measure uses unit labour costs in manufacturing (i.e. labour costs per unit of output) to indicate price movements (Table 18.2).

(b) Exchange rate regimes

The exchange rate is simply the *price* of a currency, and, in the absence of government intervention, will be determined in the foreign exchange market by the interaction of supply and demand. The *demand* for a country's currency arises from the credit items in the balance of payments (exports of goods and services and inflows of capital), and the *supply* from the debit items (import of goods and services and capital outflows). If demand exceeds supply at a given exchange rate, then the currency appreciates, and if supply exceeds demand, the currency depreciates. When there is no government intervention in the foreign exchange market, a country is said to have a *freely floating exchange rate* and the balance for official financing must always be zero.

At the opposite extreme is the *fixed exchange rate*. In this case the exchange rate is fixed at a certain level by the government and can only be altered by government decision. To maintain a fixed exchange rate, a government must intervene in the foreign exchange market to ensure that the supply of, and demand for, its currency are equal at the desired exchange rate. If demand exceeds supply, the government must sell its own currency to maintain the exchange rate, and must buy its own currency if supply exceeds demand. For this purpose it must hold stocks of foreign currency and/or be prepared to borrow abroad.

In between these two extremes is the case of *managed floating* (sometimes called 'dirty floating') where the government intervenes to influence the exchange rate determined in the foreign exchange market.

In the 1950s and 1960s fixed exchange rates were the norm, but the 1970s saw major changes in the exchange rate regime (see page 341), and the present system is a mixture of managed floating and fixed rates. There is much debate about the best exchange rate regime for countries to adopt. The main arguments, together with the empirical evidence, are discussed on pages 349–51.

(c)   The determinants of exchange rates

Since the move to floating exchange rates in the early 1970s, economists have investigated the determinants of exchange rate movements. This involves examining the factors which lie behind the supply of, and demand for, a particular currency.

The first important determinant of exchange rates are rates of inflation. The theory of *purchasing power parity* (PPP) states that if a country has a higher rate of inflation than its competitors, then its industries will become less competitive in world markets, and the demand for its currency will fall, causing a depreciation. Conversely, a lower than average inflation rate will cause an appreciation. A study of eight major currencies by Graham Haache and John Townend of the Bank of England[4] found that PPP performed rather badly as an explanation of exchange rate movements in the 1970s. For example, PPP explained some part of sterling's fall between 1972 and 1976, because inflation was very high in the UK, but it failed to explain the appreciation of sterling between 1979 and 1981, when inflation in the UK was still higher than the world average.

Capital movements are also of great importance in determining exchange rates, particularly in the short run. Interest rates are one determinant of capital flows. If a country has interest rates higher than the world average, then capital will tend to flow into the country and raise the exchange rate, while lower than average interest rates will cause capital outflows and lower the exchange rate. High interest rates in the UK between 1979 and 1981 helped to raise the value of sterling, while the rise in US interest rates in 1981 and 1982 was responsible for the strength of the dollar in those years. Expectations of exchange rate changes are also important. If the dollar is expected to appreciate against sterling, UK residents can make a capital gain by changing sterling into dollars, and the extra demand will induce an actual appreciation of the dollar. Expected appreciations encourage capital flows, and hence actual appreciation, while expected depreciations have the opposite effect. For example, in 1976 holders of sterling thought that the UK government was pursuing inflationary policies which would cause sterling to depreciate, and therefore withdrew funds from London producing an actual depreciation. A similar process operated for the French franc in 1982.

Special factors also influence exchange rates. In the case of the UK, North Sea Oil was one cause of sterling's appreciation between 1979 and 1981, because it improved the current account, increasing demand for sterling, and because it increased confidence in the British economy and stimulated the inflow of capital. Sterling's status as a petro-currency means that it is influenced by actual, and even anticipated, changes in the price of oil. The fall in world oil prices at the end of 1985 therefore led to a fall in the value of sterling.

Finally, exchange rates have also been affected, under the present system of managed floating, by government intervention in foreign exchange markets. For example, the UK authorities bought pounds and borrowed abroad to support sterling in 1976, and in 1977 sold pounds to keep the exchange rate down (UK reserves of gold and foreign currencies rose by £10bn in 1977 as the authorities sold pounds and bought other currencies).

(d)   Exchange rate changes and the domestic economy

How do changes in exchange rates affect the domestic economy? The traditional view is that exchange rate depreciation can be used to improve a country's balance of payments and boost domestic output. This was the reason the Bretton Woods agreement (see page 351) allowed countries in severe balance of payments difficulties to alter their exchange rates, and why the UK devalued sterling in 1967 and allowed sterling to depreciate between 1972 and 1976.

The basic assumption is that changes in exchange rates affect international competitiveness, which in turn influences the balance of payments and output. Consider the situation where sterling depreciates from $4 = £1 to $2 = £1. An item made in the UK for £100 will drop in price in the US from $400 to $200, whereas a good made in the US for $100 will rise in price in the UK from £25 to £50. The depreciation lowers export prices (in dollars) and raises import prices (in sterling), making UK goods more competitive. An appreciation would have the opposite effect.

The impact on the balance of payments and output depends on how people respond to the price changes, or in other words, on the price elasticity of demand for exports and imports. The *Marshall –Lerner* condition states that depreciation will *improve* a country's balance of payments if the sum of the demand elasticities (ignoring + and − signs) is greater than one. Thus, if the elasticity of demand for exports is zero, and that of imports is greater than one, there will be no change in the domestic currency value of exports, but the domestic currency value of imports will fall and the balance of payments improve. Conversely, if the elasticity of demand for imports were less than one, the balance of payments would have deteriorated. An improvement in the balance of payments will raise domestic output for the reasons explained in Chapter 12. Recently the IMF found the Marshall–Lerner condition was satisfied for ten out of fourteen major industrial countries.[5]

There are four criticisms of the above analysis. First, the effects of currency depreciation are not instantaneous. Foreign and domestic demand and domestic suppliers take time to respond to the new price regime, while import values increase immediately by the full extent of the depreciation. The balance of payments is therefore likely to worsen before it improves – the so-called 'J' curve effect. This effect was noticed after the 1967 devaluation of sterling and the 1971 devaluation of the dollar. A reverse 'J' curve may follow currency appreciation.

Second, when the economy is at full employment, exchange rate depreciation alone cannot improve the balance of payments. This is because resources are not available to increase production of exports and domestic substitutes for imports, and in these circumstances an improvement in the balance of payments will only come about if resources are freed by appropriate monetary and fiscal measures.

Third, the ability to compete in world markets depends not only on the competitiveness of price at which goods are sold, but also on the competitiveness of quality, reliability, after sales service, and so on, and exchange rates have little impact in this area. Non-price factors were important reasons why Germany, Japan and Switzerland were able to combine a strong trading performance with currency appreciation in the 1970s.

The final, and most important, criticism is that depreciation cannot improve price competitiveness for any substantial period of time because it raises import prices and the cost of living. If the increase in the cost of living raises expectations of inflation and leads to demands for higher wages to compensate for the increase, then firms will find that they have to raise prices further (which leads to further wage demands). Ultimately any gain in competitiveness is eroded, so the depreciation ceases to affect the balance of payments or output, and only serves to raise the rate of inflation. In contrast, an appreciation can reduce inflation by lowering import prices and inflationary expectations, and by making it unnecessary for employers to grant large wage increases. The reduction in inflation, if large enough, can offset the adverse effects of appreciation on competitiveness.

The evidence from models of the UK economy suggests that depreciations no longer have a long term effect on the balance of payments because of their impact on domestic inflation. There is, however, controversy about the length of time it takes for inflation to offset the impact of a depreciation.

3   Have floating exchange rates been a success?

Economists have long debated the theoretical advantages and disadvantages of floating rates, and the experience of floating rates since 1973 provides an opportunity to see how they have behaved in practice. In this section we examine the performance of floating rates in four key areas.[6]

(a)   Balance of payments adjustment
The main argument in favour of freely floating rates is that they automatically correct imbalances in the balance of payments. Gov-

ernments are therefore free to concentrate on other policy objectives, for example, full employment. In practice, current account imbalances have persisted despite large movements in exchange rates (e.g. between 1973 and 1978 the German current account surplus rose from $4.7bn to $9.3bn despite a 40% appreciation of the mark). This partly reflects the fact that exchange rates have been managed, but also shows the time lags involved in balance of payments adjustment and the importance of factors other than price.

(b)   Uncertainty

An argument often heard against floating rates is that they will cause business uncertainty and harm international trade and investment. However, there is no real reason why this should be so unless fluctuations are excessively wild. Exchange rates can be covered by 'hedging' – that is buying currency 'forward' – in the foreign exchange market. To do this, the trader enters into a contract to buy a quantity of currency in, say, three months time, but at a rate determined now. The trade has therefore effectively insured against the exchange risk, and the cost of that insurance equals the difference between the 'forward' rate and the 'spot' rate – the latter being the rate for immediate currency dealings. There is no evidence that floating rates have reduced trade and investment.

(c)   Speculation

The possibility of de-stabilising speculation is often cited as a major disadvantage of floating rates. This argument portrays the foreign exchange market as being subject to waves of optimism and pessimism about appropriate trends in currency rates. A depreciating currency will create expectations of further falls, and appropriate speculation will ensure that a fall takes place. If it is realised that depreciation has gone too far, the speculation may suddenly reverse itself, causing the exchange rate to appreciate suddenly. Thus, it is argued, speculation will cause self-reinforcing gyrations in exchange rate, out of all proportion to the economic performance of the country concerned.

Alternatively, it is equally possible to view speculation as a stabilising activity. If foreign exchange dealers sell a currency when they consider its rate is too high and buy when it seems too low, they will help to stabilise and smooth out temporary fluctuations.

Exchange rate movements have been very large since 1973, but this does not necessarily mean there has been de-stabilising speculation. Exchange rates moved to compensate for differing inflation and interest rates and for the oil price shocks. Nevertheless, there is some evidence of de-stabilising speculation in the behaviour of sterling in 1976, when it depreciated by over 20% against the dollar in the first ten months of the year.

(d) Inflation

Another major criticism made of floating rates is that they are inflationary. Critics argue that a fixed rate system places a constraint on the pursuit of inflationary economic policies, because if a country has a higher rate of inflation than its competitors, it will experience a balance of payments deficit and will have to take measures to reduce the inflation rate. Floating rates, however, remove the discipline of the balance of payments. Critics point to the rise in world inflation since 1973 as support for their argument.

The issue is not as clear-cut as this. Some of the rise in world inflation since 1973 can clearly be attributed to the oil price increases of 1973 and 1979, and in any event world inflation was rising before the move to floating. Furthermore, it can be argued that under a floating rate system the consequences of domestic inflationary policies are more clearly and more quickly apparent, because an exchange rate depreciation is more obvious than a deficit in the balance of payments, and because a depreciation raises import prices and the cost of living.

The available evidence suggests that there is truth in both arguments. In the early years of floating, some countries, most notably the UK, did follow highly inflationary domestic economic policies because they were no longer constrained by fears of deficits in the balance of payments. However, it is also true that the very large fall in sterling in 1976 prompted the British government to adopt strict anti-inflationary policies.

The overall conclusion must be that floating rates have neither lived up to all expectations, nor performed as badly as some critics have suggested. It would not be correct to say that they have failed because it is by no means obvious that a system of fixed rates could have operated in the 1970s.

4 The international monetary system

In the final section of the chapter we examine the arrangements which govern payments between countries – the international monetary system and the problems faced by it in recent years.

(a)   The International Monetary Fund

The IMF is the central institution of the international monetary system. It was established following a conference of allied nations held at Bretton Woods, USA in 1944, and in 1982 had 146 member countries. The most important non-members are Switzerland and most major communist countries with the exception of China, Yugoslavia, Romania and Hungary. It has both a supervisory and a financial role.

The IMF supervises the balance of payments and exchange rate policies of member countries. It can be regarded as the twin institution of GATT (see Chapter 17) which supervises trade matters.

To enforce its supervisory role the IMF has consultations with members on economic policy and can ultimately refuse to lend to a country if it does not approve of its economic policies. This has led to the criticism that the IMF has greater control over countries in debt than over those in credit.

The IMF also provides borrowing facilities for member countries to finance *temporary* deficits in the balance of payments. The most important credit facility provided by the IMF is credit tranch borrowing.

Loans from the IMF are conditional on the adoption of satisfactory economic policies and this has led to complaints from developing countries that the IMF does not pay enough attention to their particular problems when it makes loans. The IMF has, however, special borrowing facilities for primary producing countries – the compensatory financing facility and the buffer stock financing facility – and, in any event, is not concerned with long-term finance for the purpose of development or economic restructuring. Loans for this purpose are the responsibility of the International Bank for Reconstruction and Development (more commonly known as the World Bank).

The financial role of the IMF became much more important after 1973 when the rise in the price of oil posed particular problems for the world monetary system by creating massive current account surpluses for the oil producers and correspondingly large deficits for the oil-importing countries. The IMF responded to the problem by operating a temporary oil facility in 1974 and 1975, and two additional borrowing facilities – the extended facility (1974) and the supplementary financing facility (1979) – were established to provide assistance to members with severe balance of payments difficulties (often developing countries), in greater amounts and for longer periods than normal credit tranche borrowing allowed.

Beside the borrowing facilities outlined above, the IMF is also responsible for the operation of *Special Drawing Rights*. SDRs are a form of international money created by book-keeping transactions at the IMF. The IMF credits member countries with a certain number of SDRs which can be used to finance deficits in the balance of payments.

(b) The move to floating exchange rates

Under the original Bretton Woods agreement, member countries were required to declare 'par values' for their currencies against the US dollar, or gold, and to keep the exchange rate to within 1% above or below par (widened to 2¼% in 1971). Changes in par values were only allowed in cases of severe balance of payments problems. This 'adjustable peg' system (as it came to be known) contained a basic flaw – it ignored speculation. When speculators thought a country was about to devalue, or revalue, its currency, they sold, or bought, the currency accordingly, thereby forcing the authorities to intervene to maintain the exchange rate. Speculative pressures became increasingly strong in the late 1960s and a massive speculative attack on the dollar in 1971 (when there was a $1bn capital outflow during one day in May) ushered in a period of floating exchange rates. Although the Smithsonian agreement of 1971 tried to re-establish a system of par values, by 1973 the major trading nations had once again let their currencies float.

The movement to floating rates necessitated a change in IMF rules and this was brought about by the Jamaica agreement of 1976 which led, in 1978, to the Second Amendment to the IMF Articles of Agreement. Countries are now free, under IMF rules, to adopt whatever exchange rate system they like, and the IMF has drawn up guidelines for the operation of floating rates that member countries should follow. The guidelines are very broad – many economists think they are too broad – and require members to avoid manipulating exchange rates to achieve an unfair competitive advantage, to take action to moderate 'excessive' exchange rate movements, and to consider other countries' interests when determining exchange rate policies.

There was a move towards greater co-operation on exchange rates policy between the major industrial countries during the 1980s, prompted by persistent current account imbalances and, in particular, the current account deficit of the United States. In September 1985 the main industrial countries reached the Plaza Agreement to take co-ordinated action to reduce the value of the dollar. The Louvre Accord of February 1987 led to action by the same countries to seek to stabilise the international values of their currencies within (undisclosed) limits.

(c)   The international debt problem

In the 1970s many developing countries faced difficulties in repaying the large loans which they obtained from international banks in the 1970s. The problem first came to prominence in 1982 when Mexico announced that it could not meet its debt obligations.

The origins of the debt problem lie in the two oil price shocks of 1973 and 1979/80. The 1973 oil price rise increased the current account deficits of the non-oil producing developing countries both by increasing the price of imports and by leading to slower growth in export markets. Rather than reduce these deficits by restricting domestic economic growth, many developing countries financed the increased deficit by borrowing from international commercial banks. In turn, the banks were willing to lend because many oil producers put their increased export earnings into bank deposits.

Following the second oil price shock, developing countries again attempted to finance their increased deficits by borrowing more. However, the industrial countries reacted to the second oil price shock by tightening domestic economic policies so as to reduce the inflationary impact of higher oil prices. These restrictive economic policies led to higher interest rates (particularly in the United States) and an appreciation of the dollar which, since some four-fifths of the debt of developing countries is denominated in dollars, together raised the cost of servicing debts. At the same time slower growth in the industrial countries made it harder for developing countries to sell more exports to repay their debts.

In 1982 Western banks were owed more than $300bn by developing countries and there were fears that a default by a major debtor would undermine the world banking system since several of the biggest American banks had lent more than their capital to Latin America alone. Since 1982 progress towards solving the debt problem has been slow and total debt rose to over $1000bn by 1988 of which one quarter was owed by three countries (Brazil, Mexico and Argentina). Policy has been based on restricting new lending to developing countries and making new lending conditions and changes in their economic policies to encourage export growth. Critics have argued that the developed countries need to do more to help developing countries export by reducing trade barriers.

(d) The European Monetary System[7]

The European Monetary System was established in March 1979. It is an arrangement whereby member countries (Belgium, Denmark, Spain, France, West Germany, Luxembourg, Ireland, Italy, the Netherlands) maintain fixed exchange rates between themselves, but have floating exchange rates with non-member countries, so that the EMS currencies move as a unit against, for example, the dollar. Each currency is assigned a value against other member currencies and the members of the EMS have to keep exchange rates within $\pm 2\frac{1}{4}$ of the central rate (exceptionally, fluctuations of $\pm 6\%$ are allowed for some members), although occasional changes in central rates can be made by mutual agreement. Borrowing facilities are provided for countries that experience severe balance of payments problems as a consequence of adopting fixed rates.

There were both political and economic motives behind the formation of the EMS. Politically, the EMS was seen as providing a further step towards European unity and increasing the influence of Europe in international monetary affairs. Fixed exchange rates were thought to bring economic benefits by promoting trade and by forcing member countries to keep their inflation rates in line with each other.

The economic benefits of the EMS have been the subject of much debate. The EMS has been unable to prevent large movements in the US dollar against the EMS currencies and there have been frequent exchange rate changes within the EMS, with eleven realignments by March 1989. Nevertheless, the EMS does seem to have acted as a discipline against inflation within member countries.

The UK joined the exchange rate mechanism (ERM) of the European Monetary System in October 1990, hoping that this would eventually contribute to more stable exchange rates with its European partners, lower interest rates and lower inflation. However, participation in the ERM is not necessarily an easy remedy for economic problems. It might involve difficult and painful interim costs for the UK in terms of higher unemployment and high and volatile exchange rates, before the benefits are achieved.

Summary

A country's balance of payments accounts record all transactions between domestic residents and residents of the rest of the world. The accounts can be split into the current and capital accounts and official financing. Overall, the balance of payments must always balance, but that does not mean that there is always balance of payments equilibrium.

An exchange rate is the price of one currency in terms of another (a bi-lateral exchange rate), or several others (an effective exchange rate). Exchange rates can be allowed to float (with or without government intervention) or fixed by government policy. Under a system of floating rates, exchange rates are determined by rates of inflation, capital flows and special factors. There is a debate about the impact of changes in exchange rates on the domestic economy. Some economists think that exchange rates affect the balance of payments and output, others that the effect is solely on inflation.

Floating exchange rates have long been a subject of academic debate and the widespread adoption of floating exchange rates in the 1970s has allowed theories to be tested in practice. The overall conclusion is that floating rates have neither lived up to all expectations nor performed as badly as some critics have suggested.

Questions
1 When does the balance of payments become a problem? Explain the steps that can be taken to remedy the situation. (Institute of Chartered Secretaries and Administrators, Principles of Economics)
2 With particular reference to the United Kingdom experience over the past ten years, explain those factors which determine the exchange rate for sterling. (Southern Universities Joint Board, GCE, A-Level.)
3 What advice would you give to the United Kingdom Government on its future exchange rate policy? (Oxford Local Examinations, GCE, A-Level.)
4 Discuss the case for and against floating exchange rates. (Associated Examining Board, GCE, A-Level.)
5 Evaluate the role of the International Monetary Fund in the last two decades. (Oxford and Cambridge Schools Examination Board, GCE, A-Level.)

Notes

1 The figures for this table are taken from *Economic Trends*.
2 Ibid.
3 The figures in this table are taken from *Economic Trends*. Daily effective exchange rates are published in the *Financial Times*.
4 Graham Haach and John Townend: 'A Broad Look at Exchange Rate Movements for Eight Currencies, 1972–80', *Bank of England Quarterly Bulletin*, December 1981.
5 Michael C. Deppler and Duncan Ripley: 'The World Trade Model: Merchandise Flows', *IMF Staff Papers*, March 1978. See also, Brian Kettell 'The Importance of the Marshall–Lerner Conditions in Predicting the Impact on the Trade Balance of Devaluation', *Economics*, Winter 1979.
6 For a fuller discussion of these issues see David Higham: 'Have Floating Rates Been a Success?', *Economics*, Spring 1983.
7 The background to, and the future of, the EMS are discussed in M. Sumner and G. Zis: 'Whither European Monetary Union?', *National Westminster Bank Quarterly Review*, February 1981, and David F. Lomax: 'Prospects for the European Monetary System', *National Westminster Bank Quarterly Review*, May 1983.

19

Managing the Economy: The Problems of Macro-economic Policy

Introduction

In the introduction to Part Two of this book we set out the four principal policy objectives of macro-economic management: economic growth, full employment, price stability and balance of payments equilibrium. These aims, as we have argued, are now common to most governments, but the degree of emphasis placed on each objective varies considerably. In particular, the nature of the problems facing developing countries is fundamentally different from those confronting the industrialised nations, due to the former's acute shortage of capital. This point will be examined later in the chapter, but we start by taking the problems of economic management in the industrialised countries and focusing on the major preoccupation of recent years, the paradoxical rise in both inflation and unemployment. The 'demand-pull' view of inflation, which can be held by both 'monetarist' and 'Keynesian' economists, is contrasted with the 'cost-push' view, in which the role of trade unions is emphasised. The addition of the concept of inflationary expectations to the 'Phillips curve' analysis of Chapter 14 provides an explanation of why the process of eliminating inflation proves to be so slow and costly in terms of high unemployment and lost growth of the economy. This concept also provides an explanation for the reluctance of governments to adopt 'Keynesian' policies of stimulating demand, even when unemployment remains high.

1 The similarities between 'Keynesian' and 'Monetarist' theories of inflation

The Keynesian view of inflation examined in Chapters 13 and 14 focuses attention on aggregate demand via the individual components of total expenditure, consumption, investment, government activity and net exports $(C + I + G + X - M)$, and analyses the situation in terms of an inflationary or deflationary gap between total expenditure and the 'full employment' level of national income. The monetarist position stems from the 'quantity theory', seen in Chapter 16, and regards the total money supply as the prime influence on the level of aggregate expenditure, without having particular concern about how individual components are affected. This view stresses that growth of the money stock in excess of the growth of capacity will generate inflation.

Essentially both theories are 'demand-pull' theories in that inflation is seen as a problem of excess demand in relation to productive capacity. Frequently the similarity of approach becomes more than that, and in practice amounts to two different ways of looking at the same thing.

This will be the case where inflation is due to (or augmented by) excess demand emanating from the government sector. Where expenditure is greater than tax revenues, this fiscal deficit gives rise to a borrowing requirement which, as we saw in Chapter 16, places limits on the ease with which the supply of money can be controlled. In Britain, one of the major causes of monetary expansion in the past was unwillingness to accept the higher interest rates which would result from borrowing from the public to finance deficits. So, from a Keynesian viewpoint, inflation is created by excess government expenditure (over-expansionary fiscal policy), while from the monetarist side, inflation is generated by the resulting increase in the money supply – to unscramble separate and distinct effects of fiscal versus monetary policy is impossible, because they are two aspects of the same policy.

In recent years, British governments have adopted money supply targets, which has broken the simple link between fiscal deficits and monetary expansion. In order to avoid financing deficits by creating money, large-scale borrowing from the non-bank private sector has taken place. This borrowing, carried out by additional sales of government bonds, has resulted in very high levels of real interest rates.

Although both monetarist and Keynesian explanations of inflation agree that excess demand is the fundamental cause, excess demand alone cannot explain recent events. The notion of excess demand implies that productive capacity is fully used, yet clearly recent inflation has been accompanied by relatively high unemployment of labour (at least in the post-war context) and excess productive capacity. We have already noted that the Phillips curve relationship has broken down completely in recent years and, in order to explain this, alternative explanations of inflation have been sought.

Cost-push theories of inflation

Perhaps the most widely held view is that trade unions have caused inflation. This is the so-called *cost-push theory*. But note that 'cost-push' is strictly speaking a more general term, since it also includes the effects of rising import prices on inflation. The argument is that trade unions can force employers to grant wage demands which can only be met by raising product prices, if the firm concerned is not to go out of business. Resulting price rises then give rise to further wage demands, generating further price increases, and an inflationary spiral develops.

Although the futility of this process seems self-evident from the viewpoint of society as a whole, militancy could be a perfectly rational policy for the individual union. Inflation redistributes income, most powerfully against those on incomes fixed in money terms (private pensioners for example). More generally, any group whose incomes manage to keep ahead of the average inflation rate gains in relative terms. Thus any union has an incentive to attempt not only to match, but to stay ahead of, the average inflation rate.

Conversely, if a group does not keep up with the average inflation rate, its relative income drops. So even if a union comes to regard the process as destructive and futile, it will harm the interests of its own members if it alone opts out of the spiral.

It is this reasoning which has been one of the arguments in favour of incomes policies. If inflation is maintained by trade unions, who have to run to stay in the same place as far as relative incomes are concerned, then a general agreement to stop the race will be acceptable to most. (This does not apply to the strongest unions, who by this arguement have most to gain from inflation.)

A refinement of the cost inflation theme is the concept of *Real Wage Resistance* developed by Sir John Hicks. Briefly, the argument is that the labour force has attempted to maintain the recent growth of real personal income. When this is threatened by tax increases or price rises due to devaluation, for example, the response is to compensate by bidding up money wage rates. For example, when oil prices rose sharply in 1973–4 and the UK import bill rose (which required a corresponding increase in exports and a consequent drop in real domestic consumption) inflation accelerated as people tried to maintain their standard of living with wage rises.

Monetarist economists have strongly disputed the role of unions in generating inflation. Their argument is that even if it were true that powerful unions could force employers to grant wage increases, government action is also necessary if inflation is to continue. If governments hold the level of aggregate demand constant – by restraining the expansion of the money supply for example – then, ultimately, rising prices could only lead to unemployment.

Referring back to the quantity equation of Chapter 16, $MV = PY$, monetarists agree that if prices of goods, P, are raised, a larger money stock, M, will be required to finance the same volume of output. Offsetting changes in V, the velocity of circulation, might enable inflation to continue briefly, but in practice, a limit would soon be reached. If demand is held constant and prices rise, then the volume of output must fall. It is therefore necessary for money demand to be expanded to permit union-inspired price rises to be passed on without reducing the volume of output. If it is not, output drops and unemployment increases.

The monetarist conclusion, then, is that even if unions do attempt to push up their wage rates, this cannot lead to continuing inflation unless the government raises aggregate demand. If governments refuse to do so, but unions persist, unemployment is generated. Continued union action is then seen to be self-defeating and, with unemployment mounting, is abandoned. Monetary expansion is a *necessary* condition to permit even union-initiated inflation to continue, and it is also a *sufficient* condition to generate inflation independently of the actions of trades unions. The conclusion is that it is excess monetary demand which is the root cause of inflation.

Although the argument may be valid in principle, other factors may alter the conclusion. Governments often have an electoral commitment to 'full employment'. If unemployment rises above some politically acceptable level (which may fluctuate according to circumstance), steps will be taken to reduce it. If trade union demands do lead to inflation, governments are unlikely, initially at any rate, to sit tight and let unemployment rise sufficiently for prices to stop rising. Even if a government did take this course of action, the length of time and the level of unemployment necessary to abate trades union pressure are unknown quantities.

Trade union militancy alone is not a sufficient explanation of inflation, but in practice constraints may prevent governments from exercising their ultimate ability to call a halt to the process. It can also be argued that at the beginning of such an inflation, governments will be more concerned to minimise unemployment than to control inflation, and will not resort to restrictive policies until inflation has accelerated. This means that union militancy will initially have met with success, at least in the sense of having driven up money wages without raising unemployment. Initial successs may result in greater militancy, which would not have occurred if demand had been controlled at the start.

Nevertheless, experience in the 1980s in Britain does seem to suggest that trade union 'militancy' is not sufficient in itself to generate inflation. Given the very high levels of unemployment experienced in the 1980s, trade unions do not appear to have been able to force up money wages independently. Individual unions in particularly strong bargaining positions still appear able to raise their own wages by the threat of strike action (although the miners' strike of 1984-5 suggests that there are limits to this power). But there seems to be at least a partial recognition by unions that when the government refuses to raise aggregate demand, 'cost-push' pressures generate unemployment rather than inflation.

The 'expectations-added' Phillips curve

Although monetarist economists have been highly critical of the trade union explanation of inflation, we have already noted that excess demand alone is an inadequate explanation of recent events in all the economically developed countries of the world.

However, the addition of a further variable, price expectations, to the excess demand theory, gives a more plausible explanation of recent developments. The expectations argument centres around the concept of a 'natural' or 'normal' rate of unemployment, which is that unemployment rate which will occur when labour markets are in equilibrium. Figure 19.1 shows a more sophisticated version of the Phillips curve, which was introduced in Chapter 14 (see Fig. 14.5). Starting at point A, policy-maker during the early 1960s would see this as representing the unpalatable but inevitable range of alternative combinations of inflation and unemployment available. He could choose to reduce unemployment, but only at the cost of higher inflation, and vice versa.

Having made this choice, he decides to manipulate aggregate demand by fiscal and monetary policy in such a way as to position the economy at point B on the Phillips curve depicted in Fig. 19.1. Note that the decision has been taken to hold the economy at a given rate of unemployment, and sustain the ensuing inflation rate, whereas the Phillips curve was based on the average of a series of observations of cyclical movements, and not a sustained, static position.

This is of crucial importance, because once inflation is stabilised at a given percentage rate (4%, for example, at point B), people will gradually realise that this is now permanent (rather than a temporary phase of a cycle, as had been the case in the past) and will adjust to it, specifically by building the inflation rate into their bargaining behaviour. If real incomes have tended to grow at say 3% per annum in the past, but inflation is now known to be 4%, then employees will automatically take the inflation rate into account and will demand a 7% higher money wage in order to obtain a 3% real wage increase.

The effect of this on the 'original' Phillips trade-off is dramatic. Previously the expansion of aggregate money demand resulted in some price increases, together with some increases in real output, as unemployment fell. But now that *all* prices in the economy are raised by the expected inflation rate, the initial increase in monetary demand will be absorbed entirely in price increases, so employment will move back to its original level. In Fig. 19.1 this is shown as a move from point B to point C. The policy-maker is now in the unfortunate position of having got the worst of both worlds – the higher inflation rate, which he had been prepared to accept in return for lower unemployment, but also the original unemployment rate, which returned once inflation had been fully discounted by expectations.

The response may be to try again to get the unemployment rate down, by the same method – increasing aggregate monetary demand. Starting from point C on Fig. 19.1, the initial impact of a further increase in demand would be to reduce unemployment, but further increase inflation. The economy would move initially to point D on Fig 19.1, in effect along a second, higher Phillips curve, parallel to the first but embodying inflationary expectations (of 4% in this case). But once the economy was held for any length of time at the inflation rate represented by point D, the events would repeat themselves. Wages would discount the new and higher rate of inflation, all prices would be marked-up at this rate as a starting-point, and the additional demand used to reduce employment would be soaked up in higher prices. Unemployment would drift back to the original level, and we would be at point E.

If the treatment were again repeated, the result would be the same – a movement up yet another Phillips curve associated with higher inflationary expectations, then an upward drift of unemployment once expectations of inflation had again risen. Our original

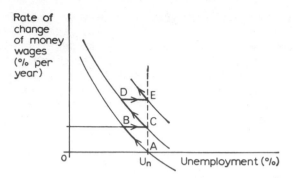

Fig. 19.1   The 'expectations-added' Phillips curve

Phillips curve has proved to be misleading. It only offers a temporary 'trade-off' between inflation and unemployment. Once inflationary expectations have been formed, unemployment drifts upwards again. In the long term, unemployment cannot be reduced substantially by manipulating aggregate demand. The only effect of attempting to do so is accelerating inflation.

The analysis depends on the proposition that in the long term there is some particular rate of unemployment which is compatible with long-term price stability. This occurs only when there is no general excess demand or excess supply for labour – i.e. when labour markets are in equilibrium. The unemployment rate at which labour markets are in equilibrium has been termed the *natural rate of unemployment*. In the analysis above, policy-makers have attempted to operate the economy with unemployment lower than the 'natural rate' and the result is accelerating inflation. As a first approximation, we could estimate the 'natural rate' of unemployment by taking it as the unemployment rate at which the original Phillips curve intersects the horizontal axis – the point U_n in Fig. 19.1. The original Phillips curve related to a period when fluctuations in prices did not show a systematic trend (rises were offset by falls, inflation rates were continually altering). In such circumstances, no trend of inflationary expectations is likely to have been established, and the 'natural rate' could be observed directly. However, there are a number of reasons for unemployment occurring, and these require more detailed examination.

The nature and causes of unemployment
Unemployment can be divided up into three major categories: *frictional*, *structural* and *demand deficient*. *Seasonal* unemployment

and *technological* unemployment are sometimes added as fourth and fifth categories. *Frictional* unemployment is the term used to describe the normal process of job changing that takes place in a dynamic economy, where tastes and technology change, and firms expand and contract as a result. Labour shifts from one job to another in response to these forces, and in the process of moving between jobs and searching for the best alternative available, is counted as unemployed. The longer people decide to take in looking for a job, the more choosy they are about the jobs they will take and the higher this level of frictional unemployment becomes. Essentially, frictional unemployment is voluntary in the sense that if they wanted to, people could find jobs immediately, but they choose to look for something which is exactly suitable.

Structural and *demand deficient* unemployment, on the other hand, are involuntary; there are simply no jobs available. Structural unemployment affects regionally based industries and occurs because of major shifts in demand or supply conditions which render entire industries obsolete. The steel industry in industrialised countries provides an excellent example. Apart from the general lack of demand due to recession, it is suffering a 'structural' shift in *demand* towards alternative materials such as plastics (as the car industry, for example, tries to reduce the weight of vehicles in order to improve fuel consumption). It also suffers a 'structural' change in *supply* conditions as developing countries become capable of producing their own steel (and sometimes exporting it) at prices competitive with the 'older' steel producers. This is likely to be a permanent change – steel is now a 'low technology' labour-intensive product, and countries with cheap labour should enjoy a comparative advantage (see Chapter 17).

These structural changes in demand and supply lead to large-scale regional unemployment in areas like Scotland, the Ruhr or Pennsylvania, which cannot quickly be eliminated by shifting labour into new jobs. Years may elapse before sufficient alternative employment is available. In some cases the decline is pervasive; regional economic 'multiplier' effects occur, with the reduction in demand spreading from the initially affected industry to all others in the area. 'Structural' unemployment is not removed by macroeconomic policy which applies to the economy as a whole, and requires specific policy measures to be applied regionally to offset fluctuations in employment that are too large to be absorbed by the normal market adaptation process.

Demand deficient unemployment has already been discussed in the context of the Keynesian model of Chapter 14. This is involuntary unemployment, which occurs, as its name implies, as a result of a deficiency of aggregate demand in the economy. The experience of the 1930s was clearly an example of massive aggregate demand deficiency. Macro-economic demand management policies of the type outlined in Chapter 14 are the primary means of resolving this problem and we referred to the use of such policies in our discussion of the Phillips curve.

Unemployment also occurs in industries where demand fluctuates sharply on a *seasonal* basis. Harvesting is the most obvious example – large amounts of labour are required for short periods, and at other times, it may be difficult to find continuous employment.

Technological unemployment is a term that is used to describe a loss of jobs in a particular industry due to the use of more productive 'high technology' capital equipment. Striclty speaking, 'technological' unemployment is an aspect of 'structural' unemployment as already discussed. Changes in the structure of supply lead to changes in the pattern of employment, which take time for adjustment. But in itself, the introduction of 'labour saving' capital equipment does not cause unemployment. Countries with high rates of investment and technological innovation, such as Japan and West Germany, have tended to have significantly lower unemployment than countries where new technology has been adopted slowly. As long as there is sufficient aggregate *demand* for an increase in national output, the fact that goods can be produced with less labour in one industry means only that more labour is available to produce other types of goods in other industries. To date there is no evidence that consumers in even the richest of economies have reached the point where they simply do not want more economic goods and services. It is reasonable to assume therefore that what is called 'technological' unemployment is in fact primarily the result of demand deficiency, with some structural and frictional elements included, as people find it difficult to switch from one industry to another.

The 'natural' rate of unemployment, being the long-run equilibrium rate, excludes by definition demand-deficient unemployment – and in principle excludes structural unemployment also. In practice, there are likely to be elements of structural unemployment present at any time, though they are not predictable. But it is the mistaken belief of policy-makers that the 'natural' rate includes some demand-deficient unemployment that is the root of the problem. Attempts to reduce it by increasing aggregate demand result in the generation of the inflationary pressures described.

The original Phillips curve data spans 1861–1957, and includes the period of the 1930s, in which large-scale demand deficient unemployment clearly existed, as did shifts in the patterns of demand and supply. These have resulted in the decline of important industries such as coal, textiles and shipbuilding (and the expansion of others such as air and motor travel or education), with major structural unemployment resulting in different regions.

In this respect, since the Phillips data includes this 'additional' unemployment which is independent of the long-term 'natural' rate, observations from 1861 to 1957 are likely to overstate the 'natural' unemployment rate. On the other hand, frictional unemployment will be affected by factors such as unemployment pay, which, by lowering the cost of unemployment, may increase the duration of the unemployment problems, and also by mobility of labour, retraining facilities, and such like. Changes in the structure and institutions of the economy over time mean that while the concept of the natural rate of unemployment can be pinned down in principle, deciding exactly what it is may be extremely difficult.

All industrialised countries in recent years have seen the unemployment rate increasing in a way that would have been almost beyond belief in the 1960s and early 1970s. It is likely that increases in frictional and structural unemployment have played some part in accounting for the increase, but there can be little doubt that a substantial part of recent unemployment has been due to demand deficiency. But governments have been unwilling to raise demand on the Keynesian principles outlined in Chapters 12 and 13 because they have been afraid that this will simply raise inflation, rather than real output, as our expectations-added Phillips curve suggested. The problems of inflation and unemployment can also be illustrated by examining its effects on aggregate demand and supply, which provides a useful and additional method of viewing the analysis of the Phillips curve.

Aggregate demand and supply

An alternative method of analysing the effects of government policy is to use *aggregate demand and supply analysis*. Aggregate demand and supply curves can be drawn which relate the demand for, and the supply of, real output to the price level, as in Figure 19.2.

An important word of warning is necessary here. The curves drawn here are deceptively similar to the demand and supply curves drawn in microeconomics for a single good, as in Chapters 3,

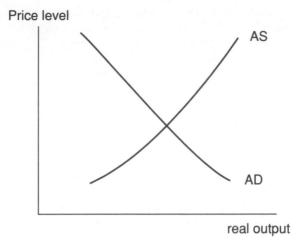

Fig. 19.2

5, and 6. But here we are looking at the economy as a whole, and the vertical axis of the graph shows the overall price level for the whole economy, not the price of one good in relation to other goods.

Aggregate demand
The diagram suggests that when there is an increase in the overall price level (i.e. when inflation takes place) the level of demand for real goods and services will fall, and vice versa – deflation would increase real demand for goods and services. This is more complicated to explain than the downward sloping demand curve of microeconomics.

There are *three* basic reasons why aggregate demand will fall when the price level rises. Initially the money supply is assumed to be fixed. The first effect is the interest rate effect. A higher price level will then raise the level of real interest rates, because the demand for money rises in relation to its supply. Higher real interest rates will reduce investment and aggregate demand. Real output will fall.

Secondly, there is a *wealth effect* when the price level rises. Anybody who is holding part of their wealth in the form of money, or savings accounts, will find that inflation has reduced the real value of these assets. Because people feel less wealthy, they will spend less. Alternatively, a fall in prices would raise the real value of money and monetary assets, and make their owners feel better off, and prepared to spend more. Changes in the price level therefore influence aggregate demand via these 'wealth' effects.

Finally, until and unless exchange rates adjust perfectly to trade imbalances, a higher price level will tend to cause a shift of demand away from domestic output and towards imports, as the domestic price level rises in relation to foreign prices. Again national income and output will fall as the price level rises, and vice versa. Exchange rates may adjust to the new situation and bring foreign price levels back into line, but not necessarily for some time.

Aggregate supply

The aggregate supply curve shows the effects of changing price levels on firms' willingness to supply output for the economy as a whole. Again we are not looking at the *microeconomic* effects of a higher relative price for one firm's output. The *macroeconomic* supply curve suggests that inflation brings about a rise in real output for the economy as a whole. But this is only true where a higher price level means higher profits for firms. This will only occur when prices rise faster than wages. An upward-sloping aggregate supply curve assumes that this happens – and that therefore real wages are reduced by inflation. We have already seen in our examination of the Phillips Curve that once an economy reaches full employment, and expectations adjust to inflation, this is no longer true. Money wages rise with inflation, and real wages do not change. It is therefore possible to draw a more sophisticated version of the aggregate supply curve, as in Figure 19.3 below.

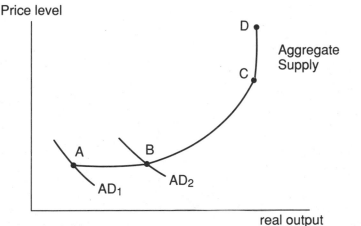

Fig. 19.3

Here the aggregate supply curve has three segments. The first between A and B, is a pure Keynesian situation, where the economy is well below full employment. High unemployment keeps wages depressed. Demand can increase without wages rising at all, so higher aggregate demand (AD₁ to AD₂) causes output to rise, without raising prices. This is the ideal situation for Keynesian demand management, most likely to occur in a depression such as the 1930s. Between B and C, increased aggregate demand causes both real output and the price level to rise. This would occur in the short-run, where wages adjust to changes in demand more slowly than prices – just as in our short-run Phillips Curves seen earlier. But between C and D, we are reaching the point of full employment, and real output cannot be increased by raising demand. Aggregate demand effects only the price level.

The aggregate demand curve can be shifted by changes in government policy. Fiscal expansion (tax cuts and increased government spending), or monetary expansion (increased money supply and lower interest rates) will raise the pressure of demand at any given price level. Reversing these policies shifts the aggregate demand curve to the left. An exchange rate depreciation shifts the aggregate demand curve to the right, because it increases demand for exports, and also for domestically produced goods rather than imports.

Inflation and unemployment again
Aggregate demand and supply analysis provides a useful method for analysing inflation. Demand-pull inflation occurs when there is an upward shift in aggregate demand that cannot be matched by an increase in aggregate supply. Cost-push inflation occurs when the aggregate supply curve is shifted upwards. The effects can be seen in Figure 19.4.

An initial rise in aggregate demand results in a move from the original equilibrium at point A to a new equilibrium at point B where the price level is higher, and real output increases. However this move may not be sustainable. If the original equilibrium at A represented a full employment level of output, higher demand will only have a temporary effect. For a while, until wages react, firms will find their profits rising due to higher demand. Profits rise because extra demand pulls up the price level, yet wages have not yet responded. Real wages have therefore fallen. Firms will attempt to raise output and employment, which in the short term they can do, by increased overtime working, and by hiring people whom

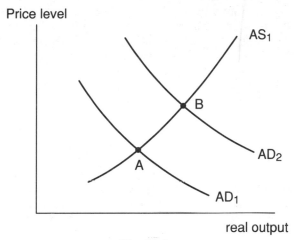

Fig. 19.4

they would not have considered without the reduction in real wages.

But the fall in real wages is temporary in this case. Workers will expect to be compensated for inflation and will push for higher wages. With demand high, and profits increasing, firms are unlikely to resist at first. The effect of an upward push on wages will be to shift the aggregate supply curve upwards, from AS_1 to AS_2 as in Figure 19.5.

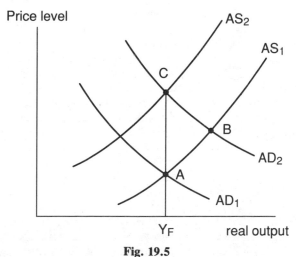

Fig. 19.5

The diagram shows the process completed by an upwards shift in the aggregate supply curve to give a new equilibrium at point C. Real output is back where we started, at Y_F – the long-run full employment level, or Friedman's natural rate of unemployment. But the price level has increased. So to summarise, if we start from a position of full employment, an increase in aggregate demand will lead to an initial boost to real output, as the price level rises. But as soon as wages respond to the higher price level, output falls back, eventually to its original level, because the aggregate supply curve shift matches the increase in aggregate demand. Changes in the price level have no long-run effect on real output.

We have used the technique of aggregate demand and supply analysis to examine the role of government policies towards inflation in exactly the same way as we used the Phillips curve analysis earlier. The movement from initial equilibrium at point A in Figure 19.5 corresponds exactly with point A in Figure 19.1 in the Phillips curve. Increased demand shifts us to point B on each of the two diagrams. The restoration of real wages shifts the aggregate supply curve up in Figure 19.5, causing a move to C where real output and employment fall back to their 'natural' note, as of point C on our Phillips curve of Figure 14.1. We are using two alternative methods of looking at the same process – first the Phillips curve, and then aggregate demand and supply.

One final point to note concerning the role of government policy. Raising aggregate demand fails to raise real output permanently in our analysis, because we assumed that the economy was at a full-employment equilibrium to start with. But if the economy gets 'stuck' in a period of recession, where there is a general problem of lack of demand, then by definition, raising aggregate demand will raise real output. The collapse of world trade in the 1930s certainly resulted in a loss of output which could have been reduced by an expansion of demand. In this case the economy started from a position of unused resources which could be put back to work without inflation. This is the position shown in the flat section of the aggregate supply curve in Figure 19.3. Much of the disagreement between economists on whether government demand management policies can increase real output can be seen as an argument over whether there is genuine excess capacity in the economy. If so, then as long as there are no deeply embedded expectations of inflation, the aggregate supply curve is almost flat, and increased demand generates increased real output with little inflation. On the other hand, if there is no excess capacity, and if there is recent experience of high inflation, then increased demand is likely to generate inflation with only very slight and temporary effects on real output.

Reducing inflationary expectations

The concept of the natural rate of unemployment, and the associated idea of the forming of inflationary expectations, provides an explanation of why inflation may accelerate and gather momentum, but equally importantly, it can also reconcile the apparent paradox that in recent years in Britain (and elsewhere) high inflation was associated with high unemployment; this is the opposite of what would have been predicted by the original Phillips relationship.

Fig. 19.6 illustrates what happens when policy which has brought about inflationary expectations is reversed, and aggregate demand is reduced in order to control inflation.

The economy reaches point E, by the process outlined above, and expectations are such that the unemployment–inflation tradeoff is depicted by a curve P_3P_3. At this point inflation is 15% and so are expectations, since we are now back at the natural rate on our diagram – in other words P_3P_3 is parallel to the 'original' Phillips curve, P_1P_1, but 15% above it.

In order to keep unemployment at point 'U_n' with prices and wages being raised at 15% a year (due to expectations), aggregate demand must be increased at 15% per year. If it is decided to reduce this rate of inflation, the initial result will be rising unemployment which puts downward pressure on both goods and labour prices. But with inflationary expectations at 15%, this results in a move down the curve P_3P_3 to F, at which point inflation remains high, and unemployment has risen. Should policy-makers be unwise enough to attempt to bring inflation immediately down to zero – or even to 5% which seemed to be regarded as politically acceptable at one time – the unemployment required would be massive. On the graph in Fig. 19.6, moving along P_3P_3 to the horizontal axis to find the unemployment necessary for zero inflation would take us to point 'X', where unemployment would clearly be very considerable.

The unemployment figure would be so high because we are now moving back along a short-run Phillips curve which temporarily embodies inflationary expectations of 15%. So if the rate of increase of aggregate demand is brought down to 10%, while prices are raised by 15%, 5% less goods are going to be sold and unemployment rises.

If aggregate demand is held to an annual increase of 10%,

expectations will eventually be revised downwards, in line with the fall in the rate of inflation. Thus we would move from point F to point G, once prices fall back in response to lower aggregate demand. A further reduction in the rate of increase of demand to 5% would result in a movement down the short-run curve associated with 10% expectations to point H, and subsequently to point I, as expectations are again adjusted to the lower rate of increase of demand. Finally, when aggregate demand is stabilised to a point where its rate of increase just matches the real growth rate of the economy, we move to point J, and ultimately with a sigh of relief to K – back at the natural rate of unemployment, but with prices once again stable.

The mechanics of this process, as depicted in Fig. 19.6, are in fact deceptively simple. It is easy enough to see that policy-makers may have been tempted to move *up* a series of Phillips curves generated by inflationary expectations, as in Fig. 19.1, but coming down again may be a much slower and more painful process. Moving up the curve, policy has had the effect of temporarily *reducing* unemployment below its long-term natural rate; coming down the curve must *increase* it temporarily to get expectations down. Two vital practical questions arise: firstly, how much unemployment is necessary to bring inflation down (i.e. what is the slope of each of our Phillips curves as we move back down them – the steeper the better for a downwards movement); and secondly, how long does it take before expectations are revised downwards at each stage – how long do we have to endure higher than 'natural' unemployment before dropping down to the next Phillips curve?

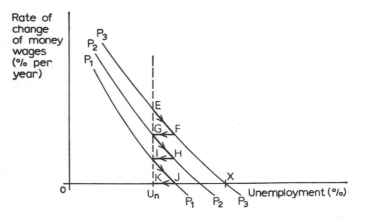

Fig. 19.6 The effect of reducing aggregate demand in times of inflation

The answer to both these questions is likely to depend on the sequence of past events and the social and institutional structure of the economy, as well as on the magnitudes of shifts in demand, and there is really no concrete evidence to answer either question. 'Optimists' believe that the adjustment, though painful and long drawn-out, is quite feasible, given the political will, while 'pessimists' believe that it would require such high and sustained unemployment to achieve stability that the social and political system would collapse, and that only an authoritarian regime could carry such a policy through. There is a good deal of scope for debate as to whether reductions in demand should be large, in the hope of foreshortening the adjustment process at the risk of large-scale unemployment for a short time, or should be gradual, to reduce the scale of unemployment, but spread it over a long time. Britain in the 1980s provided a graphic example of the huge cost in unemployment that had to be paid to reduce inflation when inflationary expectations only fall slowly.

One potentially very important way of reducing these unemployment costs is the use of some form of *incomes policy*. The major difficulty in restoring stability is removing inflationary expectations. An incomes policy should have just such an effect, if it is credible. It consists of government intervention in wage negotiations by advising, or sometimes decreeing, that increases in wages, or incomes in general, should conform to pre-determined guidelines. This will shift the Phillips curve of Fig. 19.6 downwards. In principle a credible and effective incomes policy that ordered a complete freeze on prices and wages introduced at point E on Fig. 19.6 would allow the removal of all excess demand immediately, and move straight to point K, by-passing all the intermediate stages. Unfortunately several difficulties arise. Price increases 'in the pipe-line' would still work through, even if everyone 'believed' the policy and stopped increasing wages and prices, which is highly unlikely. Where incomes policy is concerned, 'nothing succeeds like success', and conversely, when failure occurs, the policy loses credibility and becomes valueless.

Past experience of such policies has been poor, because originally it was naively believed that incomes policies could replace demand management. Consequently, in the 1970s for example, incomes policies were introduced without controlling aggregate demand. The result was that prices continued to rise, while some (but not all) incomes were restrained. People felt cheated, and immediately set about making up their losses by demanding even higher wage increases, which actually intensified inflationary pressures. So incomes policies must be used with demand management policies, and above all coordinated, so that account is taken of the lag structures involved (as discussed in Chapter 14). This first involves reducing aggregate demand, and then timing the impact of the incomes policy to coincide with the effects of measures to reduce demand – not a simple business. Although an effective incomes policy would certainly help to reduce the unemployment costs of an anti-inflationary policy, there is widespread scepticism as to whether a workable policy with lasting benefits can ever be implemented in practice.

We are left with two competing theories of inflation which both appear to fit recent experience; trade union, or, more generally, cost-push theories, and excess demand theories, taking into account inflationary expectations. In practice, it may be possible to reconcile these to some extent, since it may be hard to draw the line between 'militant' cost-push bargaining behaviour and 'defensive' bargaining which seeks only to implement price expectations. However, in Britain it would appear that the inflationary outburst since the late 1960s was probably initiated by union pressures – and in particular 'Real Wage Resistance'. This inflationary spiral was given an additional sharp twist by excess aggregate demand from 1971 onwards, after which inflationary expectations became firmly entrenched. The process of getting inflation down in the 1980s proved extremely painful, even when union pressures have largely disappeared, and accords almost exactly with the predictions of the 'expectations' Phillips curve approach. Nevertheless, the scale and duration of the unemployment came as a surprise to those who were optimistic that inflation could be reduced relatively quickly and easily. And it is clear that inflationary expectations are still deeply embedded, and can be revived easily by bouts of excess demand, as experience at the end of the 1980s showed.

The balance of payments and economic growth targets

The experience in Britain suggests that where attempts are made to actively 'manage' the economy in the *short term*, and in particular where policy-makers tend to err on the side of excess demand or an unduly optimistic full employment target, this has very adverse *long-term* effects on the balance of payments and economic growth. Excess demand generates inflation, which means that the price level becomes uncompetitive externally. This causes a deterioration in the balance of payments. Under the fixed exchange rate system operated up to the 1970s, governments which were reluctant to devalue were then forced to curtail expansion and deflate the economy in order to protect the balance of payments. This in turn would cause unemployment to rise, and once the balance of payments permitted, demand was again raised in order to reduce unemployment. At this point the cycle was precisely repeated again – the balance of payments deteriorated, the economy was deflated, unemployment rose as the balance of payments improved, and reflation took place again. This 'stop–go' cycle also resulted in a poor economic growth performance. Investment responds to increased demand with a time-lag. When the economy was expanded, the expansion was led by consumer and government expenditure. By the time producers were ready to start investment programmes to raise the supply of goods to meet the increased demand, policy was being reversed and investment plans were cancelled. The lack of productive investment meant that the next expansion, when it took place, had to rely even more heavily on imports to satisfy the increased demand, so that the balance of payments deteriorated more rapidly – and greater unemployment resulted from the more prolonged recession needed to restore external equilibrium. Thus in each successive 'crisis' the unemployment rate tended to increase, and the balance of payments to lurch into even greater deficit.

Active demand management policies have also been impeded by short-term electoral considerations. Because expansion and rising incomes are popular policies, governments facing re-election have been tempted to allow pre-election expansions that would have been quite inappropriate on economic grounds. Election time booms have tended to result in inflation and excess demand being allowed to persist, and the deflation which they make inevitable has to be greater as a result of the delay in implementing it.

In recent years there has been a strong reaction against the idea of actively managing the level of demand in the economy in order to stabilise all fluctuations. Britain's poor experience obviously lends weight to this view, and so too does the fact that in some of the most successful of the industrialised countries, notably Germany, government plays a much more passive role in short-term demand management. The timing and other technical problems in achieving successful intervention mean that it may be more effective to leave market mechanisms and the 'automatic' stabilisers referred to in Chapter 14 to cope with all but major fluctuations. Government's role is to ensure a steady and stable rate of growth of aggregate demand, and to give incentives to investment and innovation so that productive capacity can expand smoothly and continuously.

This is not to deny that in principle the optimum policy would be for governments to 'fine-tune' the economy by using taxes and their own expenditure to offset short-term fluctuations in demand. It is simply that the practical record of those countries that have attempted to do so (Britain and Italy in particular) has been very disappointing. Unfortunately, errors of economic management tend to be rather easy to recognise with hindsight, but extremely difficult to anticipate. This means that since the policy-maker can always see where he went wrong last time, he is unduly optimistic about avoiding similar mistakes in the future. Nevertheless, there seems to be a widespread view among economists that intervention should take place only in cases of large changes in demand such as occurred in the aftermath of oil price increases and North Sea Oil.

'Supply side' economics

The disillusionment with demand management policies is at least in part the cause of a renewal of interest in the 'supply side' of the economy. *'Supply side' economics* is a rather general term which is used to cover a number of different ideas. Its essence is the proposition that economic growth is determined by 'real' rather than monetary factors. In the long run, it is argued, the level of monetary *demand* in the economy does not affect the growth rate. The latter depends on factors such as the level of saving, and hence investment, the rate of population growth, the degree of labour mobility, the willingness of management and workers to adopt the most efficient technology available, and other related factors. All these variables have in common the fact that they affect the productive capacity, the supply potential, of the economy.

Above all, the supply-siders argue that properly functioning markets are the key to full employment and economic growth without inflation. In the long run, involuntary unemployment cannot persist if labour markets operate efficiently. If they do operate efficiently, unemployment results in a reduction in real wages which ensures that it becomes profitable for firms to hire more labour, thus eliminating the unemployment. The rate of unemployment that remains can then be described as the 'natural' rate of unemployment, as previously explained.

Supply-siders would therefore view the role of economic policy as ensuring that the 'natural rate', or vertical long-run Phillips curve, line U_n in Figs 19.1 and 19.6, should be kept as far to the left as possible. Policies to achieve this minimising of the natural rate would essentially be micro-economic, rather than macro. They concentrate on factors such as increasing job information in labour markets, so as to minimise frictional unemployment, and increasing the geographical mobility of labour by removing imperfections in the housing market. Supply-siders also argue that the 'natural rate' would be diminished by reducing the power of trade unions to use 'closed-shop' policies to exclude competition from non-union workers willing to take jobs at lower rates of pay.

However, although the term 'supply side economics' has been mainly associated with pro-market, *laissez-faire* economists, originally from the United States, the switch of emphasis from demand management towards the supply potential of the economy has been much more general, and has occurred on both the right and the left of the political spectrum. As we have seen, those on the right would implement 'supply side' policies by removing obstacles to the operation of markets, and generally reducing the direct role of government in the economy. On the left there is also a move towards concentration on the supply side, but this would be achieved by completely different policies. These would involve far more direct government intervention into the investment policies of specific industries, either by some form of central planning, or by increased direct government ownership of industry.

Despite the resurgence of interest in the supply side of the economy, it remains true that in practice the main focus of policy remains the level of aggregate demand. The bulk of government's economic policy-making resources are still concentrated on producing and assessing economic forecasts, and on estimating how to balance government expenditure and taxation instruments so as to achieve the rate of expansion of aggregate demand that the government chooses. It seems likely that in Britain at least, this will be the case for the foreseeable future, though with more attention now paid to the interaction between demand changes and supply responses.

Economic management in the developing countries

While governments in developing countries generally share with their colleagues in the industrialised nations the four aims of economic growth, full employment, price stability and external balance, the constraints they face are far more severe and limit their options very sharply. For example, in developing countries the problem of unemployment is essentially a 'structural' one in the sense that there is a structural imbalance in the economy because of a shortage of capital equipment in relation to the potential labour force. The excess supply of labour in relation to capital cannot be dealt with in the market by a fall in the relative price of labour. Labour is already receiving minimal subsistence wages in large sectors of the economy, yet substantial unemployment or underemployment still exists. Raising aggregate expenditure in the economy along Keynesian principles does nothing to increase labour employment, because real output is limited by the amount of capital available. Capital reaches 'full employment' at a point where vast numbers of people are still involuntarily unemployed. Further increases in aggregated expenditure only cause excess demand and inflation – unemployment is unaffected, since it is basically structural and not 'demand deficient'.

Thus in the developing countries the problem of short-run 'demand management' takes a back seat, and success is measured in terms of the ability to expand the long-run growth path of the economy. Living standards can only be raised by a combination of policies – on the one hand to raise the capital stock by investing as much as possible, and on the other hand to limit the growth of population which at present is only serving to swell the ranks of the unemployed and stretch national income even more thinly over more heads.

Growth policy in the developing countries

Policies to control population growth appear to be meeting with some limited success, but are strongly affected by social, religious and ethical considerations in each country which are beyond the scope of this volume. It is important to note that population growth in the past has been observed to decline as real *per capita* income grows. And some developing countries have had a measure of success in limiting the growth of population, simply by making reliable means of contraception widely available.

The problem of capital deficiency is an equally difficult one. Developing countries basically have three options:

1　To accumulate capital out of their current income
2　To rely on governmental aid from overseas
3　To rely on private investment from overseas.

The first option is very difficult to adopt since it means depressing consumption even below its present meagre levels in order to raise savings to invest in capital equipment. Countries which have marketable natural resources can exploit them for this purpose, but to those which are resource-poor, and as a result generally have the lowest *per capita* incomes anyway, domestic capital formation is practically impossible.

The second alternative is to rely on aid from the industrialised countries. The obvious difficulty is that the latter have in recent years been wrestling with their own domestic difficulties, and their generosity is somewhat limited. In addition they face a conflict of interest, in that aid policies which encourage industry in the developing countries produce competition for their own domestic industries and may result in internal structural unemployment. Governmental aid also takes the form of military support, which while it may or may not be politically desirable, does little to stimulate industrial development, and this is true also of food aid. So although specific inter-governmental aid projects to assist in industrialisation are extremely important, their scale must be substantially increased to make a real contribution to reducing the gap in incomes between 'rich' and 'poor' nations.

The third possibility is to attract overseas private investment. In recent years multi-national companies have moved away from concentration on raw material extraction towards the development of labour-intensive manufacturing facilities to take advantage of the lower real wage rates found in the developing countries. These activities are regarded with suspicion by some of the host countries because of the dependence created by large external capital injections into relatively small and undeveloped economies. But they do generate multiplier effects and raise demand for indigenous products, leading to rises in real income to the 'take-off' point at which domestic capital accumulation becomes feasible.

Multi-national companies try to ensure security for their investment by avoiding countries which are politically unstable (or politically 'undesirable', in some cases). Since political instability is often a consequence of discontent with miserably low living standards, countries in this position tend to remain in a vicious circle of low income, low investment and inability to control population growth.

Some countries have managed to obtain rapid changes of economic growth by each of the three methods outlined – China for example has adopted the first, the self-generation of capital, while countries such as South Korea and Taiwan have benefited from large-scale aid. Mexico has attracted direct investment from multi-national companies in manufacturing industry, while Nigeria and Venezuela are making use of oil revenues to accelerate industrialisation. But there remain many countries where *per capita* incomes are extremely low, huge unemployment exists, and population growth continues inexorably, and their problems simply cannot be solved without massive outside help.

Summary

Virtually all governments try to attain the goals of economic growth, price stability, full employment and external equilibrium. In industrialised countries attention in recent years has focused on inflation and full employment, with cost-push type theories emphasising the role of trade unions, in contrast with Keynesian and monetarist excess demand theories.

Trade unions may initiate inflation by militant bargaining. In a highly integrated economy their monopoly power over money wages is considerable. However employers have power over prices, so a spiral develops. This is very difficult to break, because anyone opting out unilaterally incurs relative losses. Hence the justification for incomes policy to stop the race. But trade union-induced (cost-push) inflation can only continue if aggregate demand is raised to accommodate it. If not, unemployment is generated. However, at least initially, governments may accommodate, since they have a full employment commitment. Once they stop doing so, inflation and unemployment will exist side by side for some time.

Excess demand theories can also explain simultaneous inflation and unemployment, once the effect of price expectations is allowed for. If governments try to keep their economies operating below their 'natural' rate of unemployment – or even at any stable inflation rate – inflation will be anticipated and prices raised accordingly. Unemployment will then rise as increased demand is absorbed in higher prices. Persistent attempts to keep unemployment below its 'natural' rate will generate even higher inflation. At some stage the policy will have to be reversed, but the lingering effect of inflationary expectations means that unemployment will have to be kept above its 'natural' rate for some time while inflation is brought down.

The two competing explanations overlap to some extent. It may be difficult to draw the line in practice between 'active' upward pressure on wage rates by unions, and 'passive' defensive reactions to inflation. Experience in Britain provides evidence of both factors operating.

Developing countries face a fundamentally different set of problems in that low incomes and overpopulation force them to concentrate on economic growth in order to achieve their other objectives. Capital can be generated internally, or come from external government aid, or from overseas private investment. While some countries have achieved quite rapid rises in growth based on these sources, others have been unable to escape the spiral of increasing population and falling living standards.

Questions

1   What do you consider to be the difficulties for the Government in trying to achieve its stabilisation objectives? (The Chartered Institute of Public Finance and Accountancy, Professional Examination 2)
2   Explain why the objective of full employment may be difficult for a government to achieve. (The Associated Examining Board, GCE, A-Level Economics)
3   'The Phillips curve suggested that high unemployment was associated with relatively low wage inflation.'
    (*a*)   Using a simple sketch, explain what is meant by this statement.
    (*b*)   What factors account for the high wage inflation and high unemployment currently prevailing in the British economy? (The Institute of Chartered Accountants in England and Wales, Foundation Examination, Economics)
4   Distinguish the different forms of unemployment and consider ways in which a government can try to tackle them. (The Institute of Cost and Management Accountants, Foundation Stage, Economics)
5   'It is obvious that even a Government with monetarist objectives must have some sort of incomes policy.' Do you agree? (Oxford and Cambridge Schools Examination Board, GCE, A-Level Economics)

Plan for Further Study

Introduction

This is a suggested programme for further reading. It is not intended as a definitive list, but is just a selection of some of the books which the authors and their students have found useful. It contains a mixture of texts. Some deal primarily with the theoretical foundations of the subject, while others concentrate on issues in applied economics, for example industrial organisation or government policy. Most of the books listed are at an intermediate level, assuming no more knowledge of economics than would have been gained from reading an introductory text of this kind.

To facilitate easy reference, they are grouped under the following headings:

1 Micro-economics
2 Macro-economics
3 Sources of economic statistics
4 Introductory mathematics and statistics for economists

The first two above correspond with Part One and Part Two of this book. The remaining sections cover additional material which the reader may wish to include in a study programme.

1 Micro-economics

Some good introductory texts explaining the theory of the operation of the market system are:

Begg, Dornbusch and Fischer, *Economics* – 3rd Edition, 1991

More Advanced Micro Text Books:

F. Glahe and D. Lee, *Microeconomics: Theory and Application* (second edition, 1989)

D. Laidler and S. Estrin, *Introduction to Microeconomics* (P. Allan 3rd edition, 1989)

Texts dealing with particular applications of microeconomics:

Industrial Economics:
D. Hay and D. Morris, *Industrial Economics: Theory and Evidence* (Oxford University Press, second edition, 1991)

Roger Clarke, *Industrial Economics* (Basil Blackwell, 1985)

The Public Sector:
C. Brown and P. Jackson, *Public Sector Economics* (fourth Edition, Blackwell, 1990)

P. Bennett and M. Cave, *Competition Policy* (Heinemann, 1991)

Brian Hurl, *Privatisation* (Heinemann, 1989)

M. Bishop and J. Ray *Does Privatisation Work?* (London Business School, 1985)

John Vickers and George Yarrow, *Privatisation: An Economic Analysis* (MIT, 1988)

John Kay and Mervyn King, *The British Tax System* (Oxford fifth edition, 1990)

Labour Economics
P. Fallon and D. Verry, *The Economics of Labour Markets* (Phillip Allen, 1988)

D. Hamermesh and A. Rees, *The Economics of Work and Pay* (4th edition)

Environmental Issues and Social Problems:
D. Pearce, A. Markandya, E. Barbier, *Blueprint for a Green Economy* (Earthscan 1990)

D. Helm and D. Pearce (ed.), 'Economy Policy Towards the Environment' *Oxford Review of Economic Policy* 1990

J. le Grand and R. Robinson, *The Economics of Social Problems* (Macmillan, 1984)

2 Macro-Economics (and other topics covered in Part Two of this text)

R. Levacic and Rebman, *Macroeconomics – An Introduction to Keynesian–Neo-classical Controversies* (Macmillan Second edition)

R. Dornbusch and Fischer, *Macroeconomics* (4th Edition McGraw Hill)

International Trade and Development:
D. Greenaway, *International Trade Policy* (Macmillan, 1983)
G. M. Meier, *International Economics: The Theory of Policy* (Oxford, 1980)
H. Myint, *Economic Theory and Underdeveloped Countries* (Oxford)
J. Williamson, *The Open Economy and the World Economy* (Harper and Row)
Malcolm Gillis *et al.*, *Economics of Development* (2nd edn, Norton, 1987)
M. P. Todaro, *Economic Development in the Third World* (4th edn, Longman , 1989)
A. P. Thirlwall, *Growth and Development* (4th edn, Macmillan, 1989)

Financial Institutions:
E. R. Rowley, *The Financial System Today* (Manchester UP)
J. Gilbody, *The UK Monetary & Financial System: An Introduction* (Routledge)
K. V. Peasnell and C. W. R. Ward, *British Financial Markets and Institutions* (Prentice Hall)

3   Sources of Economic Statistics

Every student should know what sources will provide facts about economic activity, instead of having to rely on second-hand figures quoted by politicians, the media and textbooks. Despite the formidable array of economic and social statistics produced by government and international agencies, one does not have to be an expert to find one's way through the maze.

Official Statistics:

United Kingdom:
Central Statistical Office, *Guide to Official Statistics* (HMSO, 1990)
Central Statistical Office, *United Kingdom National Accounts* (Annual)
Central Statistical Office, *The United Kingdom National Accounts: Sources & Methods* (3rd Edition)
Central Statistical Office, *Annual Abstract of Statistics*

Central Statistical Office, *Economic Trends*. Monthly
Central Statistical Office, *United Kingdom Balance of Payments* (Annual)

International:
United Nations:
Department of Economic & Social Affairs, Statistical Office: *Directory of International Statistics*, New York, United Nations
International Bank for Reconstruction and Development: *World Tables*. World Bank
Eurostat: *Basic Statistics of the Community* (28th Edition: European Communities)

Some Unofficial Sources:
The Economist: *One Hundred Years of Economic Statistics* (Economist Publication)
National Institute of Economic and Social Research: *National Institute Economic Review* (Quarterly)
The Financial Times: see also the *Guide to FT Statistics* which provides the answers to the questions often asked about the many statistics carried by the *Financial Times*, particularly the share prices on the back pages.

4 Introductory Mathematics and Statistics for Economists

For the non-mathematical, mathematics and statistics may seem very difficult, but there are many excellent texts now available, which assume only a very elementary knowledge as a starting-point. Among these we would suggest for mathematics:

A. J. Mabbett, *Work Out Mathematics for Economics* (Macmillan, 1986)
J. Black & J. Bradley, *Essential Mathematics for Economists* (Wiley)
G. C. Archibald and R. G. Lipsey, *An Introduction to the Mathematical Treatment of Economics* (Weidenfeld & Nicolson) (NB This is a more ambitious and difficult text)

Statistics:
D. Bowers, *Statistics for Economists* (Macmillan)
T. H. Wonnacott and R. J. Wonnacott, *Introductory Statistics for Business and Eocnomics* (Wiley, 4th edition 1990)
C. Johnson, *Measuring the Economy* (Pelican, 1988)

Index

Index

Absolute
  concentration, 174
  cost barriers, 142
  differences, 320
Accelerator principle, 268–71
Advances, 200
Advertising, 28, 48, 86, 102–4
  as a barrier to entry, 118, 128
Aggregate consumption, *see*
  Consumption
Aggregate demand
  components of, 254 ff
  excess, as cause of inflation,
    358, 368
  management of, 370–2, 374
Aggregate supply, 367–8
Agriculture
  and time lags, 162
  research and development, 164,
    see also Common Agricultural
    Policy
Allocation of resources
  as an ecconomic problem, 3–4
  in different economic systems,
    19–33 *passim*
  in the market, 46, 155
Allocative efficiency, 157, 160
Annual General Meeting, 58–60
Anti-trust legislation, 151
Assets, 299–300
  liquid and illiquid, 284–8
  real, 284

Autonomous expenditure, and
national income, 247–51
Average cost pricing, 143, *see also*
  Cost-plus pricing
Average costs of production, 70–7
  passim

Backward-bending supply curve,
  202
Balance of payments, 245, 337–42
  accounts, 339–40
  adjustment, 340–55 *passim*
  equilibrium, 217, 278, 340–1
  national income and, 245–51
    passim
Balanced budget multiplier,
  273
Bank
  accounts, 283, 308
  advances, 300–1
  balance sheet, 11, 299
  Charter Act, 287
  investments, 300–1
  money, 283, 303
  rate, 299, 311, 315
  reserves, 288–91, 293–302
    passim
Bank of England, 293–6, 299
Banking system
  creation of money, 288–92
  development of, 286–8

Barriers
  to entry, 110, 118, 141–2, 163
  to trade, 319, 322, 326–31
    passim
Barter, 231, 283
Base drift, 308
Black economy, 231–2
Bond prices, and interest rates,
    294–5, 305
Booms and slumps, 30, 242, 273
Bretton Woods, 346, 350
Budgetary policy, *see* Fiscal policy
Building Societies, 243–4, 286,
    300, 308, 313

Call money, 297–8
Capital
  account of the balance of
    payments, 338
  accumulation, 378
  consumption, 225–6
  deficiency, 377–8
  as a factor of production, 65–84
    passim, 191, 222, 225, 322
  fixed, 51
  human, 322
  intensive, production, 131
  returns on, 166, 176
  stock, 224, 265, 279
    adjustment principle, 270
  structure, of the firm, 51
  working, 51
Capitalism, 30, 122, 131
Capitalist countries, 102–4
Cartel, 140, 159, 160
Cash, 300
  squeeze on, 298–9
Central Bank, 11
  functions of, 293–7, *see also*
    Bank of England
Centrally planned economies, *see*
    Command economies
Central planning, 21–5 *passim*
  see also Command economies
Choice, consumer, 3, 19, 24, 86,
    88
  and advertising, 102–4

Circular flow of income, 213,
    222–55 *passim*
  disturbances to, 241–56
Classical economists, 30, 320
Clearing banks, 298–9
Club of Rome, 236
Coefficient of determination, 166
Collective
  agreements, 207
  bargaining, 205
Collusion, 140, 146–7, 152, 165
Collusive pricing, 140
Command economies, 19, 22–4,
    32
  with choice, 23–4
Commercial Banks, 299 ff
Commodity price boom, 326
Common Agricultural Policy,
    (CAP), 42, 332
Common Market, 8, *see also*
    European Community
Communist economies, 2
Companies Acts, 54
Comparative advantage, 320–6
Competition, 6, 107, 115, 156
  and efficiency, 164–5
  monopolistic, 126–8, 129
  non-price, 137 ff, 142, 152, 164
  perfect, 113, 117–18, 124, 128
Competitive market, 48, 109, 158
Complementary goods, 101, 102,
    105
Concentration, 131, 166–71
    passim, 172–3
  index, 131–2
  ratios, 141, 146, 151
Constant prices, GNP at, 229
Consumer
  behaviour, 86 ff
  choice, 26–8, 86, 88, 102–4
  demand
    aggregate, 93–104 *passim*
    individual, 88–93
  expenditure, 257–65
  goods, 64
  preferences, 27, 102, *see also*
    Tastes

sovereignty, 27, 104
Consumption
  expenditure, 258–66
  function, 259–63
  in national income flow, 213,
    242 ff
Contestable markets, 169–70
Convertibility, 287
Corporations, 49, 53, 104
Correlation, 7
Cost
  absolute, 320
  average, 70–4
  comparative, 320
  fixed, 78, 81
  marginal, 70–4, 115
  opportunity, 4, 16
    of holding money, 283, 306
    and international trade, 322
  real, 322
  transport, 322
  variable, 78, 81
Cost-benefit analysis, 161
Cost-plus pricing, 143
Cost-push theories of inflation, 358
Costs
  of growth, 2, 218, 230, 233–6
  long-run and short-run, 77–81
  of production, 69
Countervailing power, 148
Coupon and bond prices, 294
Credit
  control, 312–13
  creation, 288
Cross-elasticity of demand, 150
Cross-section analysis, 99
Currencies
  in European Monetary System, 353
  relative value of, 319
Currency
  controls, 325
  depreciation, 343–4, 346–7
  prices (exchange rate), 342
Current
  account (balance of payments),
    338
  prices, 228–9

Customs unions, 330
Cyclical fluctuations in demand,
  273–5
counter-cyclical policies, 272–6

Debentures, 54
Decision
  lags, 276
  theory, 47
Declining industries, 363–5
Deflation, 216, 374–5
Deflationary gap, 256–8, 263, 275
  elimination of, 271–2
Demand
  aggregate, 93–4, 258–72 *passim*
  curves, 88–94
    kinked, 137 ff
    shifts of, 90–2
  deficiency, 362
  derived, 26, 194, 205, 208
  elasticity of, 95–100
  excess, 357, 274
  for factors of production, 119 ff
  for imports and exports, 346
  for investment goods, 268–71
  for money, 305–6
  management, 374–6, 377
Depreciation
  capital, 61, 225–6
  currency, 343–4, 346–7
Depression
  and fiscal policy, 271, 317
  inter -war, 212, 240, 248
Derived demand, 26, 194, 205, 208
Devaluation, 344, 346, 349
Developing countries, 217–19,
  231–3
  economic management, 377–8
  economic union, 333
  growth policy, 378
  terms of trade, 323
Differentiated products, 126–8,
  142
Diminishing returns, law of, 68,
  195–7
Discount market, 296–8
  and call money, 299, 300

Disposable income, 259
Dis-saving, 248, 260, 262
Distribution of Income and
    Wealth, Royal Commission
    on, 192–210 *passim*
Diversification, 82–4, 141–2
Dividends, 51, 54, 60
Division of labour, 320
Double-coincidence of wants, 283
Double-counting, and national
    income, 223
Duesenberry's relative income
    hypothesis, 275

Earnings, 194
    transfer of, 203
East African Federation, 333
Econometrics, 5
Economic
    cycles, 273–5
    efficiency, 155–8
    forecasting, 6–7
    goods, 4
    growth *see* Growth, economic
    integration, 330–3
    objectives, 215, 221
        conflict of, 374, 377
    problems, 1–3
    rent, 203–4
    system, 19–33 *passim*
Economics
    definition of, 4–5
    measurement in, 5–6
    model-building, 10–15
    normative, 10, 16
    positive, 9, 16, 32
    techniques of studying, 5
Economies
    capitalist, 2, 104, 131
    command, 2, 19, 22–4 ff, 104
    dual, 232
    market, 24–7
    mixed, 19
    open, 217, 274
Economies
    of expansion, 82
    of scale, 74–7, 81

Economists
    classical, 30
    Keynesian, 240, 302, 356 ff
    monetarist, 302, 356 ff
Efficiency
    allocative, 156–7
    cost, 156–7
    economic, 155–8
    markets and, 155–69 *passim*
    prices and, 156 ff
Elasticity of demand
    balance of payments and, 346
    income, 97
    price, 95–100
Employment, full, 215–17, *see also*
    Unemployment
Engel's Law, 98
Entrepreneurship, 65, 191
Entry
    barriers to, 110, 118, 141–2,
        163, 167
Entry-limit pricing, 140
Equilibrium
    market, 38
    national income, 242, 246–9
European Communities (EC),
    331
European Economic Community
    (EEC), 331
European Monetary System
    (EMS), 353
Exchange rates, 342
    bi-lateral, 342
    determination of, 344–5
    effective, 343
Expansion, economies of, 82
Expectations
    and augmented Philips Curve,
        360–3
    and consumption, 263
    and demand for money, 305
Expenditure
    aggregate consumer, 261–5
    autonomous, 250
    final, 262, 268
    government, 246
    induced, 353

method of national income
accounting, 224–8
Exports
and developing countries, 324
and national income, 245
restrictions on, 325

Factor
cost, 225
endowments, 334
mobility, 163
Factors of production, 65, 191,
321
demand for, 194–7
payments to, 191–4, 221 ff
supply of, 197–204 ff
Fair Trading Office, 182
Family Expenditure Survey, 87
Flat money, 287
Finance, sources of, 50–3, 55
Financial institutions, 293–301
Fine-tuning, 375–6
Firms
barometric, 139
capital structure, 50–6, 61–2
diversified, 82–4
dominant, 139
growth of, 51–60 *passim*, 81–4,
151–2
objectives, 109–10, 145, 151–2,
194
Fiscal policy, 271–5 ff, 316
Fisher, Irving, 11, 13, 302
Fixed cost, 78, 81
Fixed exchange rates, 216, 344–50
passim, 374
Floating exchange rates, 216,
344–50 *passim*
Fluctuations
in demand, 255, 273–4, 278, 375
in exchange rate, 347
in money supply, 316–17
in price, 163
Foreign exchange market, 345,
347–9
Foreign trade, *see* International
trade

Forward exchange rate, 348–9
Free
goods, 4
market economy, 24–8
Trade, 329–30
Freedom of entry, 118
Frictional unemployment, 363
Friedman, Milton, 275, 304
Full employment, 215–17, 276,
359, 376
and the inflationary gap, 276
in developing countries, 377–8
and level of national income,
254–6, 317

Gains from trade, 320–1, 326
unequal distribution of, 330
Galbraith, J. K., 27, 131, 168
Game theory, 134–7
Gearing, 54
General Agreement on Tariffs and
Trade, (GATT), 328
*General Theory of Employment,
Interest and Money*, *see*
Keynes
Giffen goods, 92
Gilt-edged stocks, 294
Government
borrowing, 294–7, 309, 314–16,
358; *see also* Public Sector
Borrowing Requirement
control of the money supply,
309–15
determination of aggregate
demand, 271–6, 375
expenditure, 246, 271–6,
357
intervention in the market,
28–31, 214
stocks, 294
subsidies, 327
Gross Domestic Product
definition of, 86
in national income accounting,
225–6
Gross Fixed Capital Formation,
265–6

Growth, economic
  and the balance of payments,
    374–6
  as an objective, 1–3, 215,
    217–19, 278–80
  costs of, 233–4
  in developing countries, 378–80
  international comparisons of,
    229–32
  limits to, 236–7
  maximisation of, 236

Hecksher-Ohlin theory, 321–2
Hire Purchase restrictions, 263–316
Hicks, J., *Real Wage Resistance*,
  358
Hines, A. G., 358
Hot money, 340
Household consumption function,
  259–61
Hume, David, 303
Hyperinflation, 293, 315

Import
  penetration, 174
  restrictions, 97, 324–7
Imports
  and balance of payments, 346–8
  and cost-push inflation, 358
  and national income flow, 245
Income
  as a determinant of
    consumption, 259–65
  distribution of, 191–4, 208
  elasticity of demand, 97–100
  method of national income
    accounting, 223–8
Income effect of price changes,
  91–3
Income tax, 225, 271–6, *passim*
Incomes policy, 205, 369
Index numbers, GNP, 228–9
  concentration, 131–2
  terms of trade, 323–4
Indirect (expenditure) taxes, 100,
  274
  and national income, 227

Indivisibilities, of production,
  74–5
Industrial
  classifications, 108
  decline, 328
Industrial Reorganisation
  Corporation (IRC), 177
Industrial Revolution, 30, 53
Industry, 107
  supply curve, 121
Inelastic demand, 97, 105, 206
Infant industries, 31, 326, 329
Inferior goods, 91–2, 98
Inflation, 356–62
  and balance of payments, 374
  and export prices, 323–4
  and money supply, 306–8
  and unemployment, 276–7
Inflationary
  expectations, 360–2
  gap, 251–3, 272, 357
  spiral, 358, 374
Injections, into national income,
  222, 242 ff, 253
Innovation, 156, 173
Institutional investors, 58
Interest rates
  bond prices and, 295, 305, 310
  control of, 310–11, 313
  investment and, 263–5
International Monetary Fund
  (IMF), 232, 350
International trade, 319–35
Investment
  accelerator theory, 268–71, 276,
    277
  and business expectations,
    271–2
  capital account of the balance of
    payments in national income
    flow, 243–5
  marginal efficiency of
    investment theory, 266–8
  volatility of, 252, 262, 266, 274
Isoquants, 67–8

'J' curve effect, 346

Keynes, J. M. *General Theory of Employment, Interest and Money*, 214, 240, 272, 304
Keynesian macro-economic model, 240
and developing countries, 378
and growth, 279
and inflation, 356–7
and monetary policy, 304–8, 316–17
Kinked demand curve, 137–9, 141, 152

Labour
as a factor of production, 65, 191, 221
backward-bending supply curve of, 202
demand for, 190–7, *passim*
mobility of, 163
productivity of, 279
supply of, 201–4
Labour market, 198–201, 204–8
Laissez-faire, 158
Land
as a factor of production, 65 ff, 191, 221
economic rent, 203
supply, 201–4
Law of diminshing returns, 68–9, 195
Legal tender, 285
Lender of last resort, 293, 295–6
Limited liability, 53, 55, 62
Limits to the power of directors, 59
Liquid assets, 285, 300
Liquidity, 285
private sector, 308–9
Long run, definition of, 77
Luxuries, 98, 264–5

M_0, M_1, M_2, M_3, definitions of, 308
Machiavelli and the organisation of firms, 60–1
Macro-economic models, 15

Managed float of exchange rate, 344
Marginal
analysis, 73
and cost-plus pricing, 144–5
cost, 73–4, 80–1, 157–8, 160
of factors of production, 194–7
cost-pricing, 113 ff
and nationalised industries, 182–5
efficiency of investment, 266–8
physical product, 194–7
productivity theory, 200
propensity
to consume, 252–4, 260
to save, 254, 260 ff
to withdraw, 253–4
revenue, 111 ff, 143–5, 194 ff
utility, 89
value product, 195 ff
Market, 108
concentration, 131
efficiency, 155–69
equilibrium, 38–9
failure, 158
performance, 165–8
power, 108
structure, 34, 130, 165–9
weaknesses, 27–8, 159–65
Market economy, 24–7 ff, 104
and government intervention, 28–32, 40–4
policy, 173–90
Mark-up, and pricing, 144
Marshall-Lerner condition, 346
Marx, Karl, 30–2, 131
Mergers, 174 ff
Merit goods, 29
Micro-economics, definition of, 15
Minimum Lending Rate, 298, 311
Minimum wages, 205
Mixed economy, 28
Mobility of labour, 163
Model-building in economics, 10–15

Monetarist theories, 303–20,
   356–74
   international monetarists, 347
   practical monetarism, 310–12
Monetary
   base control, 311
   policy instruments, 314–17
   system
      institutions of, 293–301
      operation of, 309–14
Money, 282, 308–9
   at call and short notice, 296
   characteristics of, 284–5
   demand for, 305–6
   development of, 286–7
   functions of, 282–4
   markets, 35, 296
   quantity theory of, 303 ff
   velocity of circulation of,
      305–6
Money supply, 285–8
   control of, 293, 303, 309–16
      passim
   definition of, 308–9
   expansion of, 246, 288–92
   inflation and, 307, 356,
      359–62
Monopolies Commission, 104,
   174–82 *passim*
Monopolistic competition, 126–8,
   150
Monopoly, 109, 147–53
   bilateral, 199
   definition of, 121
   in factor markets, 197, 199
   government control of, 151,
      174–9 *passim*
   natural, 182
   price and output decisions,
      121–4
   price discrimination, 125–6
Monopsony, 197
Multi-national companies, 378
Multiplier, 251–6, 272–3
   balanced budged and, 273
   effects of direct foreign
      investment and, 378

National Debt, 294
   management of, 294–6
   money supply and, 309–10
National Enterprise Board (NEB),
   178
National income, 221
   accounts, 223–8
   circular flow of, 241–6
   equilibrium, 246–56 *passim*
   full employment level of, 254–6
   money supply and, 303–18
      passim
National Net Product (NNP),
   226
Nationalisation, 182–6 *passim*
Natural monopoly, 182
Near money, 285
Non-price competition, 137, 142,
   152, 164
Normal profit, 48, 69–70, 110 ff,
   128
   and monopolistic competition,
      127
   and oligopoly, 141

Oedipus effect, 8
Oligopoly, 109, 130–54, 170
Open
   economy, 217, 274
   market operations, 309–10
Opportunity cost, 4, 16, 283
   of holding money, 306
Organisation for Economic
   Cooperation and
   Development (OECD), 232
Output method of national income
   accounting, 223–8
Overhead costs, *see* Fixed costs
Overseas investment, 225, 378

Par value
   of bonds, 294
Paradox of thrift, 15, 243
Partnerships, 52–3
Pay-off matrix, game theory, 135
Per capita, measures of GNP, 229,
   232–3

Perfect competition, 48, 109,
    113–21, 123–4, 128
  characteristics of, 149
  comparison with other market
    structures, 147–50
  in factor markets, 194
Permanent income hypothesis,
    265, 275
Philips curve, 276, 360, 365–71
Planner's sovereignty, 22–3
Political economy, 5
Pollution, 2, 218, 233–5
  control of, 186–9
Population, 2
  control, 2
  growth, 218, 376–7
  income distribution, 3
Preference shares, 54
Price
  collusion, 40, 166
  controls, 40–4
  cutting, in oligopoly, 135–7
  deflator, 229
  determination
    in factor markets, 197–208
    in imperfect markets, 121–9,
      137–53
    in perfect markets, 40–1,
      107–21
  discrimination, 125
  elasticity of demand, 95–100
    and balance of payments,
      346
  expectations, 263, 360 ff
  fixers, 48, 133, 148–50, 159–60
  index, 6, 304
  leadership, 139–40, 143, 150
  mechanism, 26, 32, 41, 46,
    155–6
  rigidity, in oligopoly, 137–9
  stability, 162, 216–17, 276, 283,
    303–8, 356, 371–4
  takers, 48, 114, 148, 160
  wars, 136–7
Primary products, 217
  prices, 218
Private companies, 54–5

Private Sector Liquidity (PSL),
    308–9
Privatisation, 173, 182
Producer sovereignty, 104
Product
  differentiation, 128, 137, 142
  innovation, 156, 175
  range, 156
Production
  costs, 69–84
  factors, *see* Factors of
    production
  scale, 74–81
  techniques, 69–70
Productive potential, 215, 279
Profit maximisation, 48, 49,
    109–10, 115, 123
  and banks, 292–3, 313
  and demand for factors, 194–7
  and oligopoly, 145, 150–1
Profits
  excess, 118
  factor payment, 191–2
  normal, 118, *see also* Normal
    profit
  supernormal, 118–19, 123,
    127
  undistributed, 50, 59–60
Propensity to consume, and to
    save, 252
Property income from abroad,
    225
Protection, 324–8
Public
  expenditure, *see* Government
    expenditure
  goods, 28, 33, 158, 159
Public limited company (Plc), 55
Public Sector Borrowing
    Requirement (PSBR),
    314–15
Purchasing power parity, 344

Quantity theory of money, 303–4,
    357
Quotas, 324
  IMF, 350

Rate of interest, *see* Interest rates
Real
  purchasing power, 232
  wage resistance, 358
Recession, 272, 274, *see also*
    Depression
Redistribution of income
  by inflation, 216, 358
  by taxation, 217–18
  by transfer payments, 194
Relative income hypothesis, 275
Rent
  as factor payment, 191–2
  economic, 203
Research and Development, 169
Reserves, 288–91, 293, 295
  cash, 309–11
  gold and foreign exchange, 345
  ratio, 299
Residual error, in national income
    accounting, 225–6, 339
Resource
  allocation, *see* Allocation of
    resources
  misallocation, 218
Restrictive practices, 179–81
Restrictive Trade Practices Act,
    179
Retail Price index, 6, 304
Returns to scale, 74–7
Revenue, total average, and
    marginal, 110–13
Ricardo, D., 320–4
Risk capital, 51

Sales maximisation, 49, 110, 151
Savings
  function, 260
  and investment, 243
  and national income flow,
    242–5, 273
Scale of production, 74–81
Scarcity, 3–4, 19, 155–6, 215
Schumpeter, J. A., 16, 131, 165,
    175
Seasonal unemployment, 364
Secondary banks, 299–301

Seignorage, 293
Shareholders, 49, 53, 57–9
Shares, 51, 54–6, 60
Shifts in demand curves, 90–1,
    100–4, 123–4
Short run, definition of, 77–8
Smith, Adam, 30–2, 158, 320
Social costs, 160, 170, *see also*
    Costs of growth
Sole trader, 51, 54
Sovereignty
  of consumer, 27, 104
  of planner, 22–3
  of producer, 104
Special deposits, 312
Specialisation and exchange,
    206, 279–80, 320–35
    passim
Speculation, 204, 295
  in currency, 348–9
Speculative demand for money,
    306
Spot rate, 348
Stabilisation of aggregate demand,
    271 ff
Stabilisers, 274–5
Standard Industrial Classification,
    108
Standard of living, 3, 6, 31, 202,
    229
  comparisons of, 31, 232, 233
  in developing countries, 378,
    380
Stock appreciation, 225
Stock Exchange, 55–6, 60–1
Stop-go cycle, 375
Structural unemployment, 363–4
Subsidies, 29, 225, 325, 329
Subsistence
  economy, 241
  wages, 377–8
Substitutes, 91, 97, 101, 150
Substitution effect, 91–3
Supplementary deposits, 313
Supply
  and demand, 35–40
  curve of a factor, 201–3

curve of an industry, long-run,
  120
theory of, 47–63 *passim*
Supply side economics, 376–7

Take-over bids, 60
Tariffs, 97, 173, 324, 326–34
  passim
Tastes, 88, 89, 90, 102–3
Tax
  evasion, and national income,
    225
Taxation
  effects on demand, 100
  withdrawal from national
    income flow, 246–51, 271–6
    passim
Technological gap, and trade
  patterns, 322
Technology
  concentration of, 164–5
Technological unemployment,
  364
Terms of trade, 323 ff
Till money, 300
Time lags, 163, 243–4, 276
Time series, data collection, 99
Trade barriers, 324–8
Trade unions
  inflation and, 358–60
  labour market and, 204 ff
Transactions demand for money,
  305
Transfer
  earnings, 198
  payments, 193, 223
Treasury bills, 294, 296–8
Treaty of Rome, 331

Underemployment, 216
Undistributed profits, 50, 59–60
Unemployment
  benefit, 193, 274
  causes, 363

demand deficient, 363
in developing countries, 377–8
frictional, 363–4
import controls and, 346–7
inflation and, 276–8, 360–74
  passim
involuntary, 240–1, 363
natural rate of, 362, 365–7
structural, 363–4
technological, 364–5
Unit costs, 72–5
Unit of account, money as, 283
Unitary organisation of
  multi-product firms, 50
United states
  advertising in, 102
  anti-trust policy, 151
  long-run consumption function,
    264
  monetary policy, 306, 307–8
  organisation of firms, 50
  stock market collapse, 1929, 317
USSR, advertising in, 102
  and command economy, 31
Utility for consumers, 88–9, 103,
  105

Value-added, 223, 226
  tax (VAT), 227, 274
Value judgements, 6, 10, 16, 31–2,
  158
Variable cost, 78, 81
Velocity of circulation of money,
  304
  changes in, 305–6
Voluntary export agreements, 325

Wage
  differentials, 207
  increases and unemployment,
    276–7
Wealth, redistribution of, 3
Withdrawals from national
  income, 222, 242–57 *passim*